SOCIOLOGICAL
DILEMMAS
Toward a Dialectic Paradigm

SOCIOLOGICAL DILEMMAS

Toward a Dialectic Paradigm

PIOTR SZTOMPKA

Department of Sociology
Jagiellonian University
Krakow, Poland

ACADEMIC PRESS

A Subsidiary of Harcourt Brace Jovanovich, Publishers

New York   London   Toronto   Sydney   San Francisco

ACADEMIC PRESS, INC.
111 Fifth Avenue, New York, New York 10003

United Kingdom Edition published by
ACADEMIC PRESS, INC. (LONDON) LTD.
24/28 Oval Road, London NW1 7DX

Library of Congress Cataloging in Publication Data

Sztompka, Piotr.
    Sociological dilemmas.

    Bibliography: p.
    Includes indexes.
    1. Sociology. 2. Sociology--Philosophy.
3. Sociology--Methodology. 4. Sociology--Histori-
ography. 5. Knowledge, Sociology of. I. Title.
HM24.S953   301   79-51686
ISBN 0-12-681860-6

PRINTED IN THE UNITED STATES OF AMERICA

79 80 81 82   9 8 7 6 5 4 3 2 1

I dedicate this book to my students—
Polish and American

The clash of doctrines is not a disaster
but an opportunity.

—Alfred N. Whitehead

The task is to make us aware of Marxist method,
to throw light on it as an unendingly fertile
source of solutions to otherwise intractable dilemmas.

—Georg Lukacs

Contents

Preface

What are the shortcomings of sociological theory? The only way to answer this question is to study sociological theory analytically and critically. In conducting this type of study, I confronted several perennial dilemmas faced by sociological theorists since the beginning of scientific sociology. My attempt to overcome those dilemmas resulted in the clarification and reformulation of traditional assumptions. Then it occurred to me that the new dialectic "paradigm" produced as a synthesis of positivistic and subjectivistic approaches is, after all, not so new; it was already implicitly present in the theoretical works of Karl Marx. The further reading of Marx convinced me that there is still a lot to be learned from the author of *Capital,* especially if he is treated as a scientific theorist rather than a political prophet.

In this book I argue against the nihilistic rejection of sociological tradition, and for the creative reformulation of earlier theories; against opportunistic eclecticism, and for a clear theoretical commitment; against narrow empiricism, and for theoretically informed research; against closed, dogmatic "schools," and for the mutual cross-fertilization of theories. My case for dialectic sociology, and against both positivistic and subjectivistic sociology, is only as strong as these arguments. Only if they are found valid will the final message make sense. There is a way out of the theoretical crisis, and the way can be spotted by taking full stock of the sociological heritage, with due recognition given to Marx and Marxism.

ACKNOWLEDGMENTS

In the process of producing this book I have become seriously indebted to several persons. Listing my debts here is certainly not enough to repay them, but my creditors will perhaps find some consolation in the fact that I do remember.

To begin with, I am grateful to the large number of students who have attended my courses in the history of sociology, contemporary sociological theories, Marxian historical materialism, and philosophy of the social sciences, and by their critical, skeptical, and sometimes slightly aggressive attitude, made me strive hard for clarity of thought and exposition. Some of those students are Polish, since I usually teach at the Institute of Sociology of the Jagiellonian University in Krakow, Poland. But some are also American, since every summer since 1974 I have had the opportunity to teach at the Sociology Department of Columbia University. All of them have given some intangible contribution to the final intellectual result, and this explains why this book is dedicated to them.

I wish also to mention Robert K. Merton and Bernard Barber—two scholars who gave me invaluable encouragement in the struggle with concepts, ideas, and theories. I hesitate to call them my friends, because of the great reverence I feel for their scientific achievement and academic standing, but both of them are generous enough to treat me as a friend. This is a gift for which no gratitude is sufficient.

Finally, I have a great appreciation for the editorial staff of Academic Press—for their expert skills, friendly attitude, and most efficient arrangement of all practical matters, made more difficult than usual by the geographical distance separating the author from the publisher.

QUOTATION CREDITS

The author gratefully acknowledges permission to reprint excerpts from the following works.

Abel, T., *The Foundation of Sociological Theory*. New York: Random House, Inc., 1970. Copyright © 1970 by Random House, Inc.

Andreski, S., *Social Sciences as Sorcery.* New York: St. Martin's Press, Incorporated, 1972. Copyright © 1972 by St. Martin's Press, Incorporated.

Barton, A., Empirical methods and radical sociology: A liberal critique. In *Radical Sociology,* edited by J. David Colfax and Jack L. Roach. New York: Basic Books, Inc., 1971. © 1971 by Basic Books, Inc., Publishers.

Bierstedt, R., *Florian Znaniecki on Humanistic Sociology.* Chicago: The University of Chicago Press. Copyright © 1969 by The University of Chicago Press.

Bierstedt, R. *The Social Order.* New York: McGraw-Hill Book Company, 1963.

Birnbaum, N., The crisis in Marxist sociology. In *Radical Sociology,* edited by J. David Colfax and Jack L. Roach. New York: Basic Books, Inc., 1971. © 1971 by Basic Books, Inc., Publishers.

Blau, P., *Exchange and Power in Social Life.* New York: John Wiley & Sons, Inc., 1964. Copyright © 1964 by John Wiley & Sons, Inc.

Blumer, H., Sociological implications of the thought of George Herbert Mead. *American Journal of Sociology* 1, 1966. Copyright © 1966 by The University of Chicago Press.

Boulding, K., *The Impact of the Social Sciences.* New Brunswick, N.J.: Rutgers University Press, 1966. Copyright © 1966 by Rutgers, The State University.

Coser, L. A., *Masters of Sociological Thought.* New York: Harcourt Brace Jovanovich, Inc., 1971.

Dahrendorf, R., *Essays in the Theory of Society.* Stanford, Cal.: Stanford University Press, 1968.

DiRenzo, G. J. (Ed.), *Concepts, Theory, and Explanation in the Behavioral Sciences.* New York: Random House, Inc., 1966. Copyright © 1966 by Random House, Inc.

Durkheim, E., *The Rules of Sociological Method.* New York: Free Press, 1962. Copyright © 1962 by Free Press.

Eisenstadt, S. N. and M. Curelaru, *The Form of Sociology: Paradigms and Crises.* New York: John Wiley & Sons, Inc., 1976. Copyright © 1976 by John Wiley & Sons, Inc.

Fletcher, R., *The Making of Sociology,* Vols. 1 and 2. New York: Charles Scribner's Sons, 1971.

Homans, G. C., *The Nature of Social Science*. New York: Harcourt Brace Jovanovich, Inc., 1967.

Homans, G. C., *Social Behavior: Its Elementary Forms*. New York: Harcourt Brace Jovanovich, Inc., 1974.

Israel, J., The principle of methodological individualism in Marxian epistemology. In *Acta Sociologica,* Vol. 13. Oslo, Norway: Universitets for laget.

Kuhn, T. S., *The Structure of Scientific Revolutions,* 2nd ed. Chicago: The University of Chicago Press, 1970. Copyright © 1970 by The University of Chicago Press.

Martindale, D., *The Nature and Types of Sociological Theory*. Boston: Houghton Mifflin Company, 1960.

Merton, R. K., *Social Theory and Social Structure*. New York: Free Press, 1957. Copyright © 1957 by Free Press.

Merton, R. K., *The Sociology of Science*. Chicago: The University of Chicago Press, 1975. Copyright © 1975 by The University of Chicago Press.

Mills, J. S., *The Sociological Imagination*. New York: Oxford University Press, 1959.

Myrdal, G., *An American Dilemma: The Negro Problem and Modern Democracy*. New York: Harper & Row Publishers, Inc., 1964.

Myrdal, G., *Objectivity in Social Research*. New York: Pantheon Books, 1969. Copyright © 1969 by Pantheon Books, Division of Random House, Inc.

Parsons, T., *The Structure of Social Action*. New York: Free Press, 1968. Copyright © 1968 by Free Press.

Skidmore, W. L., *Sociology's Models of Man*. New York: Gordon and Breach Science Publishers, Inc., 1975.

Skidmore, W. L., *Theoretical Thinking in Sociology*. New York: Cambridge University Press, 1975. Copyright © 1975 by Cambridge University Press.

Sorokin, P., *Sociological Theories of Today*. New York: Harper & Row Publishers, Inc., 1966.

Staats, A. W., *Social Behaviorism*. Homewood, Ill.: The Dorsey Press, 1975.

Swingewood, A., *Marx and Modern Social Theory*. London: The Macmillan Press, Ltd., 1975. Copyright © 1975 by The Macmillan Press, Ltd. U.S. distribution controlled by Halstead Press, a Division of John Wiley & Sons, New York.

PART I

ON THE THEORETICAL
CRISIS OF SOCIOLOGY

CHAPTER 1

Critique of Sociology:
Traditions and Perspectives

CRITIQUE OF SOCIOLOGY:
TWO TRADITIONS

Judging by its level of critical self-consciousness, sociology is, indeed, the most developed discipline. Perhaps no other science has paid so much attention to its own deficiencies, no other science has spent so much of its creative potential for self-destructive purposes, and no other science has bred so many masochists who denounce their own jobs as "sorcery" (Andreski, 1972), "pseudo-science" (Kirk, 1961), or a bag of "fads and foibles" (Sorokin, 1956).

To be sure, some measure of criticism is simply indispensable for the development of science. As an eminent Polish sociologist has remarked, "Science, together with other domains of culture, is such a peculiar sort of reality, whose fate depends on the amount of thinking devoted to it [Ossowski, 1967, Vol. IV:1021.]" But there are various kinds of thinking, by no means equivalent in their potential impact on the course and the fate of science. Some thinking may be destructive, and some constructive; some may be fruitless, and some fruitful; some may lead to pessimism, and some to optimism. Whichever is the case depends to some extent on the abilities, skills, and attitudes of the thinker—but only to some extent. The decisive differentiating factor is to be sought elsewhere: It is the level (or dimension or aspect) at which the critical appraisal is focused. Whether one's sight is good or bad, whether one's glasses are black or pink, what one shall see is ultimately determined by the object at which one is looking.

Two foci of attention are possible if one is looking critically at the scientific enterprise. First, there is the surface level of problems, methods, results, and applications. All this can be grasped directly, by external observation of what is going on in the discipline—what are the questions most often posed, what are the research methods most often followed, what are the results most often yielded, and what are the uses most often made of those results. Such observations are usually boiled down into descriptive accounts known as "trend reports" (if relatively specific) or "appraisals of the state of the discipline" (if relatively general). Sociology abounds in both. Most often the reports or appraisals consist of the pessimistic diagnoses of this or that aspect of current achievements. Most often, the source of defects is located in the immaturity or backwardness of sociological research, and the proposed therapy amounts to mere symptomatic remedies, accompanied by the hope of a gradual coming-of-age of sociology as a science. I shall refer to this approach as "the poverty of sociology" trend in the criticism of our discipline.

Second, there is the deeper level of underlying assumptions: premises of the ontological, epistemological, and axiological type, as well as implications of the ideological and political type, which are presupposed by or consequent upon the practice of the discipline, whether the practitioners are conscious of them or not. This level can be apprehended only indirectly, by interpretation or reconstruction of what is assumed, or rather what logically must have been assumed if the research is to have any meaning. Such an interpretation or reconstruction of assumptions is usually translated into a methodological account spelling out what is known as "distinctive approaches," "general orientations," "methodological models," or (to use a more fashionable term) "theoretical paradigms." Their proliferation in sociology has prompted Merton's remark that, unluckily, "we have more approaches than arrivals [1957:9]." If the level of assumptions rather than of practice becomes the object of criticism, the conclusion is often as pessimistic as that of criticism directed at practice; sociology is said to remain in the preparadigmatic stage, to lack any adequate theoretical approach, and so on. But here the similarity ends, for the source of deficiencies is no longer located in the immaturity of the discipline but rather in the erroneous premises or the unacceptable implications. And the proposed therapy is no longer restricted to fragmentary improvements, but rather calls for the overthrow of existing paradigms, a total reorientation of research practice, and the introduction of a more adequate approach. I shall refer to criticism of this sort as "the crisis of sociology" trend.

It is easy to see that the analytical distinction posited above coincides to some extent with the chronological sequence of critical emphases in the history of our discipline. The tradition of "poverty of sociology" criticism is as old as scientific sociology itself. And it is by no means dead. Recent representative specimens would include Pitirim Sorokin's *Fads and Foibles in Modern Sociology and Related Sciences* (1956), or Stanislav Andreski's *Social Sciences as Sorcery* (1972). But it is not works of this sort that set the tenor of current disputes. Soon after the publication of Thomas Kuhn's immensely influential treatise on *The Structure of Scientific Revolutions* (1962, 2nd ed. 1970), the challenge to dominant, "mainstream" orientations and the search for a new paradigm began in sociology. "The crisis of sociology" trend began to prevail in the seventies owing especially to such important contributions as Alvin Gouldner's *The Coming Crisis of Western Sociology* (1971), Robert Friedrichs' *A Sociology of Sociology* (1970) and Shmuel Eisenstadt and M. Curelaru's *The Form of Sociology: Paradigms and Crises* (1976). The last touches the mood of the day, as in a remark such as this: "Sociology is in a period of great turmoil, in which basic premises and approaches are being re-examined and attempts at consolidation are being made. This has in turn reopened the fundamental problems of sociological analysis [Eisenstadt and Curelaru, 1976: 59]."

To be sure, radical criticism—not limited to the recording of failures but reaching to the roots of scientific enterprise, by revealing and rejecting the orthodox conceptual and theoretical framework—was not invented in this decade. A century ago, it was utilized quite successfully by, for example, Karl Marx in *Capital,* the subtitle of which is *The Critique of Political Economy.* But it is only recently that such an approach has found its conscientious implementation in sociology.

By now my own stance is, I think, obvious, but I shall state it explicitly: I believe that the "poverty of sociology" tradition is unproductive and fruitless. I share the opinion of Turner: "One of the simplest, but most fruitless, enterprises in sociology is to play a game called criticize-the-discipline [1974: 8]." Lamentations about the failings of our discipline usually lead nowhere. Blaming failures on immaturity is a most dubious procedure in view of the fact that sociology is at least 150 years old and that social thought has been developing for at least several millennia. The policy of leaving sociology to mature would require sociologists to wait another century or more before claiming scientific status for their enterprise. I, for one, am not that patient.

On the other hand, the "crisis of sociology" approach seems to me promising and fruitful. The suspicion that something may be wrong with the conceptual and theoretical core of the discipline is, at the very least, plausible. And the debate focusing on the essential, fundamental assumptions of sociology opens up an opportunity for a basic reorientation and progress. (Whether the opportunity is seized or not will be up to the sociologists themselves. I believe we can face the challenge it entails.)

Having declared my position, I hasten to warn that it would be misleading to push the distinction too far, and to put it in black-and-white terms. Adherence to the "poverty of sociology" position is not tantamount to damnation, as adherence to the "crisis of sociology" position is no guarantee of virtue. The appraisals of the state of sociology have certainly produced several revealing observations on the specific aspects of the sociological enterprise, and in general have raised the level of methodological self-consciousness among sociologists. It would be like throwing away the baby and the bathwater, and the bathroom as well, if one dismissed all that, while getting rid of the extreme, emotional, totalistic, and totally unproductive specimens of the tradition. And by the same token it must be recognized that the discussions focusing on approaches, orientations, or paradigms have produced a lot of muddled, biased, subjective, or ideologically loaded wishful thinking. It would be most inadvisable to accept such discussions and the position behind them uncritically. Therefore, to strike a balance and to sift the wheat from the chaff, a little more detailed review of both critical traditions seems necessary.

THE "POVERTY OF SOCIOLOGY" TRADITION

A scientific discipline is a complex and heterogenous entity. If it becomes a subject of meta-scientific appraisal, various aspects of it may be selected and referred to. First, there are the people who embody the discipline—those called scientists, who carry on research, write reports, articles, books, deliver lectures, prepare recommendations for politicians, and so on. Criticism may focus on them. For example, it is sometimes pointed out that their number is insufficient, their qualifications and skills inadequate, their productiveness meagre, their motivations too much infused with the need for recognition and too little with the quest for truth. This is a *personalistic* criticism of science. Second, there are the technical means necessary for scientific activities and there are other accompanying items: instruments to carry out experiments, money to hire interviewers, computers to count data, and all the things involved in publication. Criticism may focus here, emphasizing certain shortages, and sometimes justifying poor or scanty results by pointing to a lack of wherewithal. In this case the "poverty of sociology" thesis attaches a truly literal meaning to "poverty." Such an approach may be labelled as a *technocratic* criticism of science. Third, modern scientific research is pursued within a complex organizational or institutional framework—there are the universities, academies, research institutes, governmental or public agencies, and so on, and in some societies their relationships are carefully designed and planned. Criticism may focus here, pointing out the inefficiencies of administration, faulty management, irrationality of organizational designs. This may be called a *bureaucratic* criticism of science.

I have indicated these modes of criticism in order to objectify and hence detach myself from them in the ensuing discussion. Science, even modern science, is something more than personnel, equipment, and organization. Criticism of science must not be restricted to personalistic, technocratic, or bureaucratic points of view, for any such criticism touches only the periphery, or the marginal elements, of the scientific enterprise, and can never get to the heart of the matter. Granted, those peripheral matters may in some historical situations be most salient, but even then they are not to be mistaken for the core of science.

A fourth mode of criticism is, however, worthy of closer attention. Science is first of all what the scientists think—what ideas they conceive, what hypotheses they suggest, what research methods they utilize, what criteria of truth they apply to their conclusions. That there are thousands of people calling themselves or being called scientists means little. What really matters is the investigator's mental equipment. Likewise, there are millions of books classified as scientific—and likewise what matters is not the classification but the contents. There is today a proliferation of dazzling computers, and still what matters most is the quality of the data fed into them. A ton of money may be allotted for research, and what counts is how wisely it is spent. And if the management and planning behind a scientific venture are flawless, what still matters most is that they be conducive to achievement. Thus the intellectual substance of science may be the focus of criticism, and this criticism I shall call *analytic*. It will be the sole concern of this book.

So far the complexity of science as the subject of the meta-scientific appraisal has been only partly reduced to manageable dimensions. Focusing on the analytic dimension, one still faces a very intricate picture. And this is true even if the appraisal is restricted to the external aspects of science, to the surface level, leaving aside the deeper order of the assumptions, premises, and implications of actual scientific practice. Some systematic perspective must be introduced into the chaos to make sense of the multiple criticisms of the analytical sort directed by sociologists against sociology.

The heuristic device which seems most suitable for this purpose is the simplest model of science—the sequential. It represents scientific research as a process divisible into phases, with easily recognizable aspects. Thus, scientific research starts with specified *problems,* utilizes certain *methods* to solve the problems, and reaches certain *results* embodying the answers to the problems, which afterward yield *applications*. Scientific research is seen as a road from problems, via methods and results, to applications. Each of the analytic aspects so distinguished may become the object of criticism. And in fact one encounters numerous examples of criticism so directed in the "poverty of sociology" tradition. Let me systematize the main critical charges.

I. *The Choice of Problems Is Improper.* Many sociologists recognize the strategic importance of the selection of problems for the success of research. Merton remarks, almost paradoxically, that "it is often more difficult to find and to formulate a problem than to solve it [1957: ix]". Popper apparently shares this view: "As in all other sciences, we are, in the social sciences, either successful or unsuccessful, interesting or dull, fruitful or unfruitful, in exact proportion to the significance or interest of the problems we are concerned with [1976a: 88]." Therefore it is hardly surprising that this crucial aspect of science is often critically examined. Two typical charges are these:

A. Sociologists Do Not Pay Any Attention to Real Problems. "They have largely dispensed with that prime impulse of all science and scholarship, the concern with getting to the bottom of specific, concrete, and—if this word must be used—empirical problems. . . . Areas of investigation, 'fields of inquiry,' 'subjects,' and 'topics' chosen because nobody has studied them before, or for some other random reason, are not problems [Dahrendorf, 1968: 121]." There is—another author claims—"the absence of a firm sense of genuine problems [Mills, 1959: 33]."

B. Even If the Sociologists Do Pay Some Attention to Real Problems, They Select Them for Investigation by Means of Improper Criteria.

1. They choose easy problems and dismiss difficult ones: "Sociology has increasingly neglected a study of the fundamental problems, and has progressively wasted its creative energy in research on comparatively trivial, cognitively unimportant problems [Sorokin, 1966: 649]."

2. They choose problems that can be tackled by means of simple, or well-known, or easily available, or inexpensive, or fashionable techniques. The terms "technique-centrism," "means-centering" (Maslow, 1936), and "tool bias" (Mack, 1969: 54) capture well the sense—one is tempted to say the nonsense—of this procedure.

3. They choose problems that have no bearing on the main political or ideological issues of the day, and by the same token dissociate themselves from the real experiences, concerns, commitments and troubles of people. "Sociologists are basically engaged in the study of trivia, while all about them the truly significant problems of human society go

unexamined [Merton, 1973: 59]." Sociology becomes a strangely irrelevant science "having little or no concern with the pivotal events and
the historic acceleration characteristic of our immediate times [Mills,
1963: 12]," and notoriously neglecting such problems as "those dealing
with power-relations, class-struggle, with the potential claims of the
underdog, or with the autonomous creative potentials of individuals
[Eisenstadt, 1973: 3]." The implicit admonitions amount to something
like "Stop fiddling while Rome burns." This is by far the most pronounced criticism of problem selection to be heard these days.

But the choice of problems, if crucial, is yet only the initial phase of
sociological research. Thus, the next set of arguments deals with the deficiencies of methods adopted for problem solving.

II. *The Methods of Sociology Are Ineffective.* Here the textbooks of methodology provide innumerable illustrations of fallacies. Staying at the most general level, three types of arguments may be distinguished:
   A. The Methods—Techniques, Procedures—of Sociology Are Improp-
erly Executed. This argument has to do with the ignorance or at least the
insufficient skills of the researchers, and, concerned as it is with the
failings of individuals, does not merit any further comment. Except in
some research utopia, there will always exist unqualified or poorly qualified scientists. The next charge is more interesting.
   B. The Methods of Sociology Are Selected According to Improper
Criteria.
      1. They are poorly suited to the problems studied. This argument is
      due to the fact that some methods are invested with a sort of abso-
      lute, autonomous value, and are applied uncritically, and irrespective
      of the problem at hand. "We forget that techniques are tools, and see
      them as goals in themselves [DiRenzo, 1966: 249]." This abuse
      corresponds closely to the situation described earlier as a "tool bias".
      In fact it is the same situation, seen from the angle of method-
      selection, rather than problem-selection, and it entails equally un-
      welcome consequences.
      2. They are poorly suited to the intended goals of research. Every
      method is, by definition, instrumental for something. But any one
      may in fact be antiinstrumental, or at best totally ineffective for
      obtaining something else. For example if one is striving for theoreti-
      cal or explanatory results, quite different methods must be used
      from those for purely descriptive accounts.
   C. The Methods of Sociology Are Not Sufficiently Developed. Here the
charge takes either of two forms:

1. They are not developed at all. As somebody once said, the research armory of sociologists resembles a museum filled with curiosities, rather than a workshop full of tools. But more often the dissatisfaction with methods is expressed in a more moderate way.

2. They are developed in a disproportionate manner. There is a striking difference between the level of development achieved by the techniques of empirical data collection or elementary statistical data-processing and the strategies of theory construction, generalization, interpretation, theoretical systematization, and explanation. In other words, whereas we are relatively well equipped to deal with descriptive questions of the type "What is it like?", we are often powerless to answer theoretical questions of the type "Why is it so?". As Willer says: "Even if sociologists wished to construct testable theory today, there are no established guidelines for its construction [Willer, 1967:xvi]."

So much about methods. But according to the critically oriented observers, the poverty of sociology is revealed most openly when one looks at the results obtained by the discipline. Thus we come to the third group of charges.

III. *The Research Results of Sociology Are Inadequate.* It is obvious that what sociology, like any other science, ultimately produces is certain discoursive arguments, or claims. Therefore, if they are found inadequate, the fault may lie either in the nature of the smallest components of which the results are built (words), or in the higher-level substructures (sentences, propositions), or in the way those components and substructures are combined together (syntax). Accordingly, three types of charges are most often leveled against sociology:

A. The Language of Sociology Is Notoriously Imprecise. This defect is most attributed to the kinship of the terms utilized by sociology and the vocabulary of nonscientific speech, with the consequent diffusion of connotations from nontechnical language into the realm of the technical language of sociology. Some critics put it to the extreme and claim that:

1. There is no technical language of sociology, distinct from the vernacular. As a result, sociological terms "abound in ambiguity, vagueness, opacity, and contradiction [Lachenmeyer, 1971: 1]." But there are also other sins committed by sociologists, as far as their linguistic habits are concerned.

2. There is no consensus on the meaning of basic terms in the sociological community. Whole books have been devoted to the discussion of innumerable nuances in the usage of terms such as *group, community, nation, institution, culture, ideology, social action, social value,* and many others. The trouble is that in some cases sociologists ascribe disparate

meanings to the same terms, and in other cases they use the same terms to refer to diverse phenomena. Both situations produce terminological and conceptual chaos. As Sherif observes: "Even the basic definitional problems have not gone beyond the stage of controversy between more or less closed intellectual schools [Sherif, 1966: 208]."

But the language is only raw material for sociological research results. The real building blocks are sociological propositions. They are subjected to equally damaging criticism.

B. The Propositions of Sociology Are Unsatisfactory, and for Two Reasons: Logical (Formal) and Empirical (Substantive).

1. They are not full-fledged propositions at all. In other words, they pretend to be propositions, while in fact they are something else, or at most only weak or valueless propositions. This may occur when:

a. They are tautological, or devoid of any reference to empirical reality.

b. They are not testable: they presume to say something about empirical reality, but what they say cannot be checked.

c. They do not conduce to the formulation of laws: they are limited to empirical, descriptive generalizations summing up observed cases, and are devoid of any informational potential outside of the class of cases they address. As Manners and Kaplan assert: "Many social scientists would question whether their combined disciplines have produced any laws or theories deserving those designations [1968: 11]."

In all these cases, what is put forward for the status of sociological propositions is seen to lack the necessary qualifications. But even among those propositions that are logically acceptable, many will not withstand the substantive tests.

2. They are not confirmed as true. This may be the case when:

a. They are not sufficiently tested.

b. They are found false, or at least in need of qualification, in the process of testing.

Here, the argument goes, propositional status is accorded to claims that are either false or unverified. That sociology abounds in such propositions or, better, pseudo propositions does not require any further elaboration.

So far the criticism we have considered is directed at the terms and sentences formulated by sociologists. But terms and sentences serve to speak about something, to produce intelligible narrative structures. And the internal organization of such structures is the next target of criticism.

C. The Systematization of Sociological Propositions Is Insufficient. Two specific charges are often posited in this connection:

1. The sociological descriptions and theories are often the aggregates of disparate propositions, rather than logically interlinked systems. They resemble catalogues or inventories of findings, generalizations, or laws, and so "there is no form except that provided by typesetters and bookbinders [Mills, 1959: 55]." Or, as Homans puts it, "The intellectual work that would organize the findings remains largely undone [1967: 109]." Some leading spokesmen of the discipline seem to believe that it is precisely at this point that the main source of troubles can be located. To quote Homans again: "Our trouble has not been with making discoveries but with organizing them theoretically—showing how they follow under a variety of given conditions from a few general principles [1967: 105]." And looking from a little different perspective—an anthropological one—Kluckhohn perceives the same defect very clearly: "Anthropologists of all branches have been so preoccupied with field work that the profession has not organized and assimilated what is in fact 'known' [1957: 4]."

2. There is no satisfactory consolidation of sociological theory and empirical research. Whereas the previous charge focuses on the lack of systematic links between propositions within a homogeneous class—i.e., within the class of descriptive findings, within a class of generalizations, within the class of law-like statements—the present charge has to do with the relationship crossing the boundaries of such homogeneous classes, and particularly with the insufficient logical connection between theoretical propositions (laws) and empirical propositions (data). For Merton, "the consolidation of theory and research" is one of the basic goals for sociology (1957: 3,4). Homans claims that "there is no science [other than sociology, that is] in which the rich and varied findings bear so little relation to the theories in spite of endless pleas that they ought to be related [1967: 30]." And Cohen expresses a similar concern: "The relationship between theory and research in sociology is far from satisfactory [1968: 242]." There are two distinct ways in which this defect is seen to be manifested:

a. Empirical research is not informed by a theory, or to put it in more precise terms, empirical propositions subjected to testing are not systematically derived from theoretical hypotheses as their necessary, logical consequences, but are chosen at random, or at most in accordance with some extrascientific knowledge. "Not enough empirical enquiry is used to decide between the rival claims of different theories, at least to establish whether these claims are or are not incompatible with one another [Cohen, 1968: 242]." This is the case addressed by Mills (1959) under the suggestive label "abstracted empiricism."

b. Theory is not informed by empirical research, or to put it in more precise terms, theoretical hypotheses (laws) are neither heuristically suggested by empirical findings nor subjected to confirmation by reference to empirical findings. "Although sociologists have access to an increasing range of empirical findings this material has not been used to provide firm empirical content for even the most modest of recent theoretical analyses [Mulkay, 1971: 227]." This case is the converse of the one previously discussed. Mills (1959) addressed it under the label "grand theory."

In both cases theoretical thinking and empirical inquiry run their own separate courses. "The theorists are always about to get into contact with the data, but never do; and the empirical researchers, while waiting in vain for help from on high, do not create their own theories, because 'theory' is a special field pre-empted by others [Homans, 1967: 30]." Such a situation is most detrimental to the development of a scientific discipline. One has to agree with Blau: "Neither speculative theorizing uninformed by systematic research, nor empirical investigations that are not oriented to theoretical issues, can contribute much to a generalizing science like sociology, for the objective of such a science is to develop theories that can explain empirical observations, which requires that these theories be derived from systematic research and be testable in other research [1969: 128]."

So much about the results produced by sociology and their inherent defects. But some critics do not stop here; they claim that the most convincing case against sociology can be made by focusing on the uses—or rather, abuses and misuses—of the sociological results. And thus we arrive at the fourth set of charges.

IV. *The Utility of Research Results Obtained by Sociology Is Very Limited.* As I have emphasized before, the results produced by sociology—as by any other science—take the form of specific discursive structures. What is the possible use, instrumental function, or application of any discursive structure? Obviously, it may serve to answer certain questions, to provide some required information about a specific subject. There are several types of questions that can be asked, and several types of requisite information. And the ability of research results to answer such questions, to provide such information, may certainly be quite varying. Some research results of sociology may provide answers only to the simplest questions, of the type "What are those phenomena or processes like?" We shall say, then, that sociology is able to fulfill a descriptive function. Some research results may be able to answer more complex questions, of the type "Why are those phenomena or processes just like that?" Then we shall ascribe to sociology an explanatory function. Some research results may also provide answers to questions of another type: "What should those phenomena or processes be like?" Here, sociology performs a predictive function. And some research results may be able to answer such exciting questions as "What must be done to change the existing state of affairs?" In this case, sociology fulfills a practical function. Analytically speaking, the "poverty of sociology" may be revealed in its inability to perform any of those four functions. But in fact the critics of sociology usually do not concern themselves with the first one, admitting that sociology is, after all, able to provide more or less adequate information of the descriptive or factual sort. The real thrust of their arguments is to prove that such an achievement is insufficient and that sociology is to be judged severely as far as the other three functions are concerned.

A. Sociology Is Unable to Provide Adequate Explanations of Social Phenomena or Processes. This is the main weakness of sociology in the judgment of Homans: "The characteristic problems of social science, compared with other sciences, are problems of explanation. . . . The difficulties of social science lie in explanation rather than discovery [1967: 31, 79]." And a similar judgment is offered by a philosopher of the social sciences: "To provide a complete explanation is to say not only what happens, but also why it happens. . . . One of the major drawbacks of explanation in the behavioral sciences is that there has been too much mere description and not enough interpretation [DiRenzo, 1966: 232]."

B. Sociology Is Unable to Provide Dependable Predictions of Social Phenomena and Processes. At most it can formulate either unfounded prophecies or simple extrapolations of existing trends. The conditional, theoretically based predictions typical of mature sciences are missing. The opinion of Schrag can be quoted as typical of this line of criticism: "Sociology today may employ theories chiefly for heuristic purposes. Few of its theories have been formalized, and the capacity for successful prediction and control is limited [1967: 229]."

C. Sociology Is Unable to Provide Applicable Directives for Practical Action in the Social Realm. Sociological knowledge is unproductive of "know-how." Zetterberg complains that "the professional literature contains hundreds of sociological research papers in which the conclusion calls for further research, but only a handful in which the conclusion calls for practical actions [1962: 15–16]." And the recent appraisal of Collins is equally pessimistic: "Practical applications, for all the attention given [them], has made little real headway [1975: ix]." Thus, in respect of utility or practicability of results—whether explanatory, predictive, or practical—sociology is perceived as unsuccessful.

The foregoing review of 22 charges leveled against sociology by the critics of the discipline is probably incomplete. It was, however, intended to put forth the most common disappointments and dissatisfactions of the sociological community. But "common" does not mean "unanimous." As is to be expected, the discipline has bred its defenders, who attempt to counter the criticism. Two strategies of defense are usually employed, each treating a different aspect of the critical charges.

One aspect to be distinguised in every critical charge is the metascientific claim, describing the state of some selected fragment of sociological enterprise. For example, it is claimed that sociological language is close to the vernacular. Every such critical charge usually carries the axiological judgment evaluating this state of affairs as bad, improper, or detrimental to the professed goals of sociology. The closeness to the vernacular is conceived as a defect of the sociological language.

Accordingly, the counterarguments may reject either the metascientific claim itself or the attached axiological judgment. The first strategy deals with factual matters and the debate can have a conclusive solution. For example, if the critic claims that there are no testable propositions in sociology, it is enough to present some that are testable, or have been already tested, for the claim to lose its validity. But it is not so simple with axiological matters and therefore the second strategy that rejects the charge, by dismissing the attached evaluation, can never lead to a conclusive solution. For example, if the critic claims that sociological language is imprecise and ambiguous, the defender may say "And so what?"—arguing that without a language like this, the imprecise and ambiguous aspects of social reality could not be grasped. Here he simply adheres to an axiological system different from the one of the critic. In the defender's system, concreteness and closeness to reality rank higher than clarity and precision of expression. The debate degenerates into a battle of value preferences, and can be carried on indefinitely. This consideration may partly explain why the whole "poverty of sociology" tradition generates such heated and persistent controversies.

The main trouble with this tradition is its relative sterility as far as proposals for improvements are concerned. Certainly, a consciousness of the fallacies, weaknesses, and lacunae is significant in itself, but it does not guarantee the immediate remedy. The diagnosis of the "poverty of sociology," even if true, does not suggest how to enrich sociology. And this limitation is not due to a lack of imagination or of ingenuity on the part of the critics but rather to the character of the criticism itself. Its descriptive, external, superficial nature allows for only a most general admonition of the type expressed in such a statement as this: "Let us pick up more significant problems; let us be more careful with the choice of methods; let us strive for more thorough testing of theoretical propositions; let us put our results to more extensive uses." It is almost as if the criminologist, noticing the rising crime rates in the country, would cry out: "Let there be no more crimes!"—or, as if the physician detecting the rising temperature, would tell the patient: "Stop shivering and sweating, please!" In each case, the therapeutic worth of the advice would be just about the same. Effective therapy can be derived only from careful scrutiny of the fundamental, underlying, essential causes, and not from observation of symptoms alone. This is the reason why the criticism of sociology has recently started to be phrased in a different, and much more fruitful, way.

THE "CRISIS OF SOCIOLOGY" TRADITION

This relatively recent trend in the critique of sociology, which has become widespread, and perhaps even dominant, only in the 1970s, may be identified by its double focusing of attention. Whereas the previous forms of criticism within the "poverty of sociology" tradition were directed toward all the aspects of sociological enterprise—the problems, as well as the methods, results, and applications—the main concern of the "crisis of sociology" debate is the state of sociological theory. This is due to the almost universal recognition of theory as the most valuable ideal, or norm, of sociological research. Most sociologists would certainly subscribe to the view of Harre that "the ultimate ideal of any science is the formulation of a comprehensive and systematic theoretical structure, i.e., a set of highly interconnected, hierarchically ordered and logically closed propositions [1960: 30]." But the theoretical ideal has arisen only recently. It is enough to remind oneself that 25 years ago, the careful reappraisal of the state of our discipline carried out by Abel led to the conclusion that "the ascribed status of social theory must be rated as low in view of the prevailing tendency to regard discussion of social facts in general categories as an improper form of scientific reporting [1952: 159]." Luckily the glory of narrow empiricism, the joyful days of fact gathering, are already past, and the leading spokesmen for the discipline can now openly declare: "The conflict between theory and research in sociology, which has dominated the discipline for many years, is on the wane [Blau, 1969: 122]," or even more optimistically: "The old battles of theory versus empiricism may be considered to be over [Parsons, 1956a: 32]." This does not mean that all controversies are over—just the reverse: In theory they gain a most stimulating and rewarding object. The crisis of sociology begins to be seen as the crisis of sociological theory.

But the refocusing of critical attention does not end here. As was emphasized before, it leaves the surface of immediate content, and searches deeper for the hidden underlying premises. It is not what the theory says but rather what it assumes that becomes the main interest. The criticism aims at the roots of existing theories—philosophical, conceptual, or ideological presuppositions and implications rather than actual propositions. The widespread recognition of this infra-level of sociological theories and its crucial importance is manifested by the startling profusion of terms utilized by the sociologists to describe it. A casual review of current literature reveals more than 30 terms of this type: *frame of reference, conceptual framework, theoretical framework, analytical approach, analytical model, idealized model, analytical system, analytical theory, ideal system, scheme of interpretation, classification scheme, set of analytic categories, nonoperating definitions, orienting statements, definitional scheme, lines of conceptual abstraction, theoretical scheme, theoretical orientation, theoretical guideline, general sociological orientation, theoretical approach, methodological approach, conceptual model, theoretical model, theoretical perspective, meta-scientific perspective, conceptual picture, image of reality, cognitive set, cognitive map, paradigm, formal paradigm, philosophical–ideological–analytical paradigm.*

To quote Merton's apt wording again, "Approaches rather than arrivals" are increasingly subjected to scrutiny and criticism, due to the plausible belief that only the right approach can guarantee successful arrivals; whereas some cases of success achieved despite an obviously wrong approach must, at best, be considered as lucky accidents. And luck is certainly neither dependable nor an effective guideline for theoretical efforts. Thus the crisis of sociological theory begins to be seen mainly as the crisis of theoretical assumptions.

What is wrong with the theoretical assumptions accepted by "academic sociology," "conventional sociology," "mainstream sociology," "traditional sociology"? Several diagnoses are presented, but the leading theme seems to be the plurality and polarization of assumptions. It is by no means accidental that the book most often quoted by all the participants in the debate on the crisis of sociology is Thomas Kuhn's *The Structure of Scientific Revolution* (2nd ed., 1970). Here the leading historian of science admits:

> I was struck by the number and extent of the overt disagreements between social scientists about the nature of legitimate scientific problems and methods. Both history and acquaintance made me doubt that practitioners of the natural sciences possess firmer or more permanent an-

swers to such questions than their colleagues in social science. Yet, somehow, the practice of astronomy, physics, chemistry, or biology normally
fails to evoke the controversies over fundamentals that today often seem
endemic among, say, psychologists or sociologists. Attempting to discover
the source of that difference led me to recognize the role in scientific
research of what I have since called 'paradigms.' These I take to be universally recognized scientific achievements, that for a time being provide
model problems and solutions to a community of practitioners [Kuhn,
1970: viii].

No paradigm in Kuhn's sense of the word exists in sociology, and therefore
our discipline is still in the pre-paradigmatic stage of development—an
observation that has entered the catalogue of complaints addressed by
sociologists to sociology, and has gained the central position, overshadow-
ing other complaints.

There obviously existed a receptive climate for it in the 1970s; otherwise
its career is unexplainable, in view of the fact that similar charges were
formulated (and forgotten) much earlier. A century ago John S. Mill expressed a quite similar concern: "The laws of society are so far from having
attained a state of even partial recognition, that it is still a controversy
whether they are capable of becoming subjects of science in the strict sense
of the term; amongst those who are agreed on this point there reigns the
most irreconcilable diversity on almost every other [quoted in Frisby, 1976:
xliv]." And ever since, sociologists have tried somehow to cope with the
multiplicity and intricacy of mutual disagreements; or, to put it metaphorically, they have strived to find the way through "the jungle of sociological
controversy [Merton, 1973: 55]." For some the "jungle" was another sign
of the inchoate state of the discipline: "Diverse views on the same subject
are characteristic for the poorly developed sciences, and the level of ag-
greement on central matters may be taken as the single index of scientific
maturity [Geblewicz, 1967: 39]." For others it was a symptom of the irreducible specificity of social-scientific inquiry: "The history of almost continuous dispute suggests that controversy must characterize 'normal science'
in the social sciences [Frisby, 1976: xliii]."

Whatever the particular diagnosis, the plurality of standpoints in itself is
rarely regarded as something wrong, basically detrimental to the further
development of sociology. Just the reverse: The metaphor "the marketplace
of ideas" carries favorable connotations. It is only when the plurality is
accompanied by the strict separation or polarization of standpoints, with no
possible mutual openings, that critical concern arises. The concern most
often takes the form of an admonition against self-contained, dogmatic
schools of sociology. Stanislaw Ossowski was the leading exponent of such

criticism: "The most conducive conditions for the creation of schools immune to any integrative tendencies arise when the assumptions basic for the standpoint of the school are not formulated in the way enabling their verification, but rather are formulated for particular expressive or persuasive effects—for conveying attitudes, associations, emotions, and wishes. . . . Such controversies are insoluble [1962: 169, 173]." In different terms, the image of sociology as the battlefield of mutually exclusive schools is also drawn by Eisenstadt: "Sociology is here presented as consisting of completely closed, 'totalistic' paradigms which differ from one another not only in their analytical premises, but also in their philosophical, ideological, and political assumptions [1973: 6]." As a result there arises "the compartmentalization of 'schools,' each with its own paradigms and research programs and above all the tendency to develop ideological and metaphysical closure [Eisenstadt, 1976: 308]." The most dangerous trait of such divisions is their self-petrifying, and even self-amplifying, nature. "The consequent polarization leads each group of sociologists to respond largely to stereotyped versions of what is being done by the other. . . . They become self-confirming stereotypes as sociologists shut themselves off from the experiences that might modify them [Merton, 1973: 56]." The vicious cycle of reciprocal alienation and stereotyping is easily entered. When the marketplace of ideas is transformed into the battlefield of ideas, science usually retreats.

Both tendencies—the pluralism and the polarization of theoretical assumptions—seem to accompany the whole history of sociology. In this respect, the crisis of sociology is permanent. As Merton puts it, "It can be argued . . . that sociology has been in a condition of crisis throughout its history [1975: 21]." Why, then, the sudden eruption of the debate in the 1970s? Why the sudden sense of crisis so widely experienced by the sociological community? Birnbaum suggests two sets of circumstances that may be responsible for the more acute perception of a crisis. One is intrinsic, and has to do with the intellectual substance of theories accepted at a given time; the other is extrinsic, having to do with the possibility of applying those theories to the relevant phenomena and processes encountered, and experienced as important, in social life.

> A doctrinal or theoretical crisis in a system of thought occurs when either of two sets of abstract conditions obtains: (a) the possibilities of the internal development of the system exhaust themselves; the system's categories become incapable of transformation; the discussion generated by the system becomes scholastic, in the pejorative sense of the term, and (b) the realities apprehended by the system in its original form change, so much so that the categories are inapplicable to the new conditions [Birnbaum, 1971: 108].

And perhaps it may be added that the experience of a crisis is more acute if the level of expectations initially attached to the theories was high. All three circumstances seem to obtain in the 1970s with respect to the main theoretical orientations of the postwar period: structural functionalism and system theory, behavioristic exchange theory, and traditional, dogmatic Marxism. Each of them promised a lot, but delivered much less then what was promised, either achieving premature closure, or losing touch with the realities of social life and becoming utopian.

It would require a separate historical study to trace the main lines of criticism shattering those citadels of sociological orthodoxy. Unfortunately, the criticism was mainly destructive. It is a platitude that sociology is a field particularly receptive to all sorts of fashion, and this is also true of the critiques of sociology. It became fashionable, for example, to challenge and reject structural functionalism, or behaviorism, or dogmatic Marxism, but rarely did the critics attempt to save what was rational, valuable, or fruitful in these approaches. The results of such critiques can easily be guessed.

The acute sense of a crisis, the anomie in which the sociologists found themselves when without the guidance of any accepted theoretical paradigm, led to two typical responses. To draw a parallel with Merton's study of anomie, one may describe those characteristic patterns as retreatism and rebellion. In both cases sociologists dissociated themselves from the goal as well as the means of traditionally conceived scientific enterprise, the goal being the unified general theory, and the means systematic theory construction.

In the retreatist pattern, nothing new was suggested in place of traditional ways. Instead, a certain suspension of theoretical ambitions, at least temporarily, was recommended, and methodological and theoretical eclecticism was raised to a position of virtue. Coser, for example, gives the following advice: "Especially [in the case of] a young science such as ours in which there are still many pathways of which none can be proved at this moment to be the sole productive one, it is essential that there be a great deal of tolerance of contending directions in theory and research. Here I hold with Comrade Mao: 'Let a hundred flowers bloom' [1969: 132]." Stinchcombe, focusing on the strategies of theory construction asserts: "Constructing theories of social phenomena is done best by those who have a variety of theoretical strategies to try out. . . . Some things are to be explained one way, some another [1968: 4]." And focusing on research results Goode says: "I believe that the best sociology for the next fifty years will be made up of numerous nodules or theory fragments, each constituted by precise descriptions and predictions that apply to only limited areas of social behavior. [There will be] little islands of valid knowledge [Goode, 1975: 73]." In spite of the fact that all those remarks are carefully phrased, and furnished with several caveats, they carry similar dangers. The retreatist pattern can easily degenerate into an antimethodology of "Anything goes" or "Analyse as you please." In matters scientific, just as in any other, it is only a short step from permissive liberalism to destructive anarchism.

The opposite response to a crisis of sociology may be identified as the rebellious pattern. Here, in place of the traditional ways of science, new goals as well as new means are suggested. The only trouble is that one is no longer sure whether what is at stake is still science. Such doubts are continually born "as one surveys the present scene, noting the thrust of anti-scientific, antirational, and indeed antiempirical arguments parading under the spurious labels of either 'humanism' or 'radicalism' or both [Nisbet, 1974: vii]." Following this hint, one may point, on the one hand, to such much-publicized schools as "ethnomethodology," "the dramaturgical school," "phenomenological sociology," "ethogenetics," and so on, within the more general trend variously labelled "new humanism" or "revived subjectivism," and, on the other hand, to "radical sociology," "critical sociology," "action sociology," "reflexive sociology," or various brands of "neo-Marxism," within the other general trend, which may be labelled "new activism." It would be certainly ill-advised to dismiss those new developments out of hand. To be sure, they contain many valuable insights, together with a lot of unacceptable views. To sift and gather what is valuable would require a separate analytical and critical treatise. For the present discussion I wish only to stress that in my view none of those schools presents anything that could be a new paradigm for sociological theory. Their diversities are much more pronounced than their similarities, the last—"new activism"—being often restricted to the negativistic attitude toward "conventional sociology", or the "science establishment." Therefore, rather than bringing any unification, they contribute to the pluralistic and polarized picture of the sociological field. The promise of a Copernican revolution in social science, which all of them phrase in more or less explicit terms, remains unfulfilled.

By now, my standpoint is, I hope, clear: Both current responses to the crisis of sociology, which I labelled as "the retreatist" and "the rebellious" seem to me basically unsatisfactory. To put it cautiously, and without involving any final appraisal of their possible merits, they certainly do not overcome the crisis itself, as understood in this book. Perhaps it may even be said that they aggravate the crisis. The retreatist pattern with its eclectic strategy brings a passive reconciliation with the existing state of affairs, and puts off until some unspecified future any efforts aiming at improvement. The creative potential inherent in a crisis is thereby lost. And the rebellious pattern, with its multiplication of closed, exclusive, and often dogmatic schools, simply boils down to a new dimension to the theoretical chaos.

I concur with the view of Bottomore, who says: "I am reluctant to agree with those who argue, in the intellectual confusion of the present time, that each and every approach has some value in its own sphere and that we should simply accept their diverse results as parts of the vast unwieldy sum of sociological knowledge. Something more than this is needed. [1975: 171]." The response to the crisis of sociology that I shall attempt to adumbrate in this book could be labeled "innovative," in terms of the Mertonian scheme. I shall accept without any qualifications the traditional goal of science, that "ultimate and still very remote ideal of a unified, comprehensive theory [Merton, 1975: 52]." But I shall reject the commonly utilized means, or "approaches," and attempt to devise a more fruitful one. This shall not be some brand-new solution, one more proposal for a separate school, but rather a systematization and reconstruction of the components to be found within the sociological tradition, or, to be more precise, within one significant line of the sociological heritage. In this way, the full creative potential of a crisis will, I hope, be utilized, and the crisis itself surmounted.

THE THEORETICAL ASSUMPTIONS OF SOCIOLOGY

For this purpose one must take a closer look at the assumptions underlying the actual theoretical efforts. As was indicated before, the assumptions constitute the hidden depths of the sociological enterprise. They are rarely made explicit, and they are often unrecognized even by sociologists themselves. It is the job of a meta-scientific analyst to spot them, to explicate them, and to appraise their fruitfulness. But first, some order must be introduced into the world of theoretical assumptions; those considered crucial must be singled out, and their classification, or at least the working typology, construed. Otherwise, it is easy to get lost in their multitude and diversity.

Taking any sociological theory as a whole, as a systematic body of interlinked propositions, and not as a single, detached law-like statement, there will always be something the theory presupposes, and something the theory implies. This suggests the first rough classification of assumptions: presuppositions and implications. Presuppositions are to be understood as those claims that must have been accepted, by the force of logic or by the force of contingent facts, by anybody submitting, or subscribing to, a given theory. Implications are to be understood as those claims that follow by the force of logic, or by the force of contingent facts, from the suggested or accepted theory.

The substance of both presuppositions and implications varies from case to case. Usually, any theory will presuppose a certain view of the subject matter being explained (ontological presuppositions), and a certain view of the cognitive process that has led to its formulation (epistemological presuppositions). Also, it will often assume some specific characteristics of the discipline within which it is placed (methodological presuppositions). Any theory will also entail—or at least support, stimulate, or suggest—certain attitudes, beliefs, evaluations dealing with the social world (ideological implications), as well as some directives of practical action aimed at controlling and modifying the social reality (political implications).

This can be illustrated with the familiar example of a structural–functional theory. Since I have devoted a whole book—to which the reader is referred—to the systematic explication of assumptions typical of that theory (Sztompka, 1974), the treatment here, which serves purely illustrative purposes, is less detailed. In its orthodox form structural–functional theory claims that a society is a self-regulating system with a persistent tendency to preserve equilibrium, the tendency being due to the normative consensus among the members of society, safeguarded by the mechanisms of socialization and social control, efficiently eliminating deviations. Such an image of society presupposes—inter alia—some form of a holistic or organismic standpoint (ontological claim of collectivism), as well as some version of antireductionist research strategy (the methodological view of social laws as distinct from psychological propositions, and not derivable from the latter). At the same time the structural–functional theory entails, or at least supports, certain passivistic, apologetic attitudes justifying the status quo (the conservative ideological implication), as well as certain laissez-faire, anti-interventionist policies (political implications). The recent rejection of structural–functionalism was very often based on the critique of those and similar assumptions, linked, or sometimes only believed to be linked, with this particular theory.

Another dimension of order among theoretical assumptions is introduced by applying the next criterion. The criterion is based on the observation that assumptions of any given theory are not formulated at only one level of generality. Indeed, some of them are general, some are relatively specific, and some are quite concrete. Thus, the level of generality may be taken as a significant criterion differentiating among the theoretical assumptions. But what is meant by "generality" in this connection? Every assumption ascribes certain properties to certain objects. For example, ontological assumptions ascribe some properties to society; epistemological assumptions ascribe some properties to social cognition. Those properties constitute the scope of predication of a given assumption. The scope of predication is directly related to the denotation of the given property (the number and diversity of objects exemplifying the given property), and inversely related to its connotation (the informations provided on the characteristic features of the each and every one of those objects). Now, the generality of the assumption will be construed as synonymous with its scope of predication. The assumption will be conceived as more general in comparison with another assumption if its scope of predication is larger (if it covers more objects, but says less). And the assumption will be conceived as more concrete compared with another assumption, if its scope of predication is smaller (if it covers a smaller number of objects, but says more).

One example will illustrate these important distinctions. Compare three assumptions characteristic of the Marxian sociological theory: (a) Society is a totality of interrelated components, (b) Society bears internal contradictions, and (c) Society is characterized by economic exploitation. One may provide the following translation of those assumptions, without any loss of meaning: (a_1) Society has a structure, (b_1) Society has a conflictual structure, and (c_1) Society has an exploitative structure. Now it becomes obvious that assumption a is the most general, assumption b more specific, and assumption c the most concrete. To ascribe a structure to society is to say something about an extensive array of human collectivities, but the information provided is very limited: We are at a loss as to what sort of structure is at stake; and a lot of possibilities are still open—for example, the constitutive relationships may be consensual or conflictual. To ascribe conflictual structure to society is to say something about a somewhat narrower class of human collectivities—all societies with nonconflictual structures are excluded—but the information provided is more rich: we know what sort of relationships are characteristic of the structure, namely conflicts of all sorts, but in turn we are at a loss as to the particular basis of predominant conflicts. To ascribe an exploitative structure to society is to say something about the narrowest class of human collectivities—all societies with nonconflictual structure, and all societies with conflictual but nonexploitative structure, are left out—but the information provided is the richest: now we know something very concrete about society; not only do we know that there are some relationships and that the majority of them are conflictual, but we also know the basis of dominant conflicts—the economic exploitation of some people by other people. The price you pay for comprehensiveness is superficiality. The price you pay for depth is a narrowness.

The classification of theoretical assumptions introduced before was based on two criteria: the qualitative criterion allowing one to distinguish between presuppositions and implications, and the quantitative criterion allowing one to distinguish between assumptions of various orders of generality. Such a classification is helpful in delimiting the field of my analysis. Accordingly, I shall be concerned only with the theoretical presuppositions, and only with those of the most general type. When speaking about assumptions, therefore, I shall have in mind the most general presuppositions, accepted more or less explicitly by sociological theories. The rationale for this choice stems from the author's willingness to focus on those aspects of actual theories that determine their basic potentialities as well as limitations and that prejudge their real similarities as well as differences. I believe that it is precisely at the level of the most general theoretical presuppositions that such essential aspects of sociological theories are to be found. The corroboration of this belief will be presented in the course of the argument.

So far I have discussed theoretical assumptions in close reference to actual theories. The assumptions were conceived as derivations from the substantive propositions of a given theory, and each theory was seen as characterized by a distinct set of assumptions, different from those characteristic of any other given theory. Following that approach, one could identify certain clusters of assumptions systematized around current theories, or schools of a theory, or typical of a given author, or even specific to a given book. Thus, there would be some assumptions ascribed to structural–functionalism, some to exchange theory, some to Marxism. There would be some assumptions typical of Parsons, of Merton, of Homans, or of Blau. In some cases even that would not be enough and one would have to identify assumptions accepted by the young Marx as distinct from those of the mature Marx, early Parsons as opposed to recent Parsons, Merton of the period of the functionalistic paradigm and Merton of the recent structural-analysis period. This sort of approach is fruitful so long as one focuses on one particular theory or author or book and provides a critical reconstruction of the views expressed therein. But it is not adequate when the appraisal of the theoretical development of the discipline as a whole is intended, as is precisely the case with the "crisis of sociology" tradition. It is inadequate because the resulting systematization of assumptions is based on nonessential criteria. From the analytic point of view it is irrelevant who accepts certain assumptions—which school, which author, in which period of his life, in which book, and so on. It is only the content of the assumptions that counts. And in this respect, when the appraisal of content, and not the source, is in view, systematization of a historical sort is deficient in at least two respects: First, the clusters of assumptions are not mutually exclusive (there is always a certain degree of overlap), and, second, the clusters of assumptions are not internally consistent (there is often a certain degree of contradiction).

A radical change of perspective is needed. The assumptions must be abstracted from the concrete, actual theories in which they are rooted, dissociated from the works of particular authors, and critically discussed in and for themselves. Instead of searching for the assumptions in the actual theories, one must postulate the assumptions that can possibly, or potentially, be formulated, and then check by means of concrete illustrations whether or to what extent they are approximated by actual theories. Here the identification and systematization of assumptions is based on purely substantive, essential criteria; that is, on what they claim, and not on who is doing the claiming, and where and when. The mutual exclusiveness and internal consistency of the particular clusters of assumptions is now guaranteed by the analytic procedure. And the confrontation of the analytic possibilities with the reality of current theories puts their potentialities and limitations, as well as their real commonalities and diversities, in vivid relief. One may compare this strategy to the deductive procedure as opposed to the inductive one, or to the ideal-typical procedure as opposed to empirical typology. I shall deal with theoretical assumptions in this fashion. From now on, I shall provisionally turn from concrete theories and attempt to find out what may *possibly* be assumed by such theories, arranging those possible, or potential, assumptions in a systematic way. Only later will the time come for the excursion back (or "down") to the level of actual theoretical propositions. But by then we shall already be equipped with a powerful analytic tool.

There are two combined criteria that I propose to utilize in the analytic search for possible theoretical assumptions. The basic one is substantive; it refers to the type of most general questions that must be asked, and the most general problems that must be solved, whether in an explicit or in an implicit manner, by any theoretically oriented sociologist. The other criterion is formal; it refers to the principle according to which the separate assumptions can be combined. Here I apply the dualistic, or dichotomous, principle based on the common-sense intuition that every question can have at least two irreconcilable answers, or that with respect to every problem there are always at least two schools of thought. This method has a long ancestry. As Runciman observes, "The method of binary selection can be traced back to Plato's 'Sophist' [1973: 200]." I need not enter here into the old debate whether dualistic, or dichotomous, thinking is an inherent tendency of the human mind. It is enough to observe that this question also issues in two opposite answers. Such pairs of mutually exclusive, opposite assumptions, formulated in response to one and the same general question, will be referred to as the theoretical dilemmas of sociology.

THE THEORETICAL DILEMMAS
OF SOCIOLOGY

Six dilemmas will be identified and discussed. They are chosen because of the relatively greater intensity of debates surrounding them, in comparison with other possible dilemmas. But it must be borne in mind that my list of dilemmas is not exhaustive. An exhaustive list is a practical impossibility. I shall first introduce the selected dilemmas, and discuss them in detail in the chapters to come.

The first methodological problem encountered by any theoretically oriented sociologist deals with the relationship of his own domain of inquiry to other similar domains. This may be labeled as the problem of demarcation. In sociology, this problem gives rise to the persistent quest for a precise delimitation of the place and role of our discipline in the realm of sciences. In the debate on this issue two more specific questions arise: (*a*) What is the relationship of sociology to the natural sciences? and (*b*) What is the relationship of sociology to psychology?

Responding to question *a*, sociologists face the puzzle *science or humanities?* Seeing sociology as basically similar to the natural sciences, they accept the naturalistic assumption, but when seeing it as basically different from the natural sciences, they accept the antinaturalistic assumption.

Responding to question *b*, the sociologists face another dilemma: *science of man or science of society?* Seeing sociology as secondary and subservient with respect to psychology, they accept the reductionist assumption; and, conversely, defining it as an autonomous and independent discipline, they accept the antireductionistic assumption.

The second, epistemological problem of immediate relevance for any scientist attempting to produce a theory has to do with the nature of these ultimate theoretical results that are to be and can be obtained. In sociology, the dispute over the epistemological characteristics of a sociological theory tends to concentrate on two more specific questions: (*a*) What are the functions expected of a theory, what are its uses, what are the ultimate goals of theory construction? and (*b*) What is the structure of a theory, what types of propositions does it allow and what types does it forbid?

Responding to question *a*, the sociologists encounter the dilemma *knowledge or action?* Those who restrict the functions of a theory to the provision of adequate explanations, and consequently allow only categorical propositions, as opposed to normative ones, in the body of a sociological theory presuppose the cognitivistic assumption. On the other hand, those who consider a theory mainly in terms of its practical functions, and consequently require it to offer the normative, prescriptive advice for action, presuppose the activistic assumption.

Responding to question *b*, sociologists come upon the dilemma *detachment or bias?* Some refuse any place for valuations or value judgments in the research process and the resulting theories. They profess the totally objectivistic attitude, free from any valuations, as the only fruitful approach to sociological data. In this way they endorse the neutralistic assumption. On the other hand those who accept valuations as the necessary component of sociological research, and value judgments as the necessary ingredient in sociological theories, endorse the opposite, axiologistic assumption.

The third problem is perhaps the most significant of all. It deals with the fundamental ontological properties of the matter studied by sociology. The quest for the substance and scope of social facts generates two more specific issues: (*a*) What is the nature of man, the basic component of a society? and (*b*) What is the nature of social wholes—groups, collectivities, institutions, civilizations, and so on?

Responding to question *a*, the sociologists face the dilemma *man as object or man as subject?* Those who conceive of a human being as totally molded, determined, overpowered by external influences, societal or other, accept the passivistic assumption. Those who see a man as inner-directed, self-controlling, independent of external influences, at least to some degree, accept the autonomistic assumption.

Responding to question *b*, the sociologists face the dilemma *society as a whole or society as an aggregate?* Some consider a society simply as a sum of individuals—their activities, plus eventually the results of such activities. Thus they endorse the individualistic assumption. Others ascribe to society some sort of superindividual existence, positing specific properties and specific regularities that pertain exclusively to the social wholes. They thereby subscribe to the collectivistic assumption.

To recapitulate the major points of my argument: The classification of theoretical assumptions was carried out in view of the substantive issues of necessity encountered by any theoretically oriented social scientist, and it took into account the contradictory possibilities of solutions given to those issues in sociological theories. As a result I have selected six pairs of opposite assumptions, which I consider the most salient theoretical dilemmas of sociology:

1. Naturalism versus antinaturalism
2. Reductionism versus antireductionism
3. Cognitivism versus activism
4. Neutralism versus axiologism
5. Passivism versus autonomism
6. Collectivism versus individualism

Each of those dilemmas will be thoroughly scrutinized and discussed in the course of the book.

MODELS OF SOCIOLOGY

Each of the theoretical dilemmas can be studied separately, and each will be so studied in the chapters to come. But it must be emphasized at once that the solutions proposed to any of the dilemmas (the choices of assumptions within any of the dichotomies) are not independent of the solutions

proposed to other dilemmas (choices of assumptions within other dichotomies). There are definite, systematic links among assumptions; some of
them tend to cluster together, some tend to be mutually exclusive. This is
apparently recognized by Dahrendorf, who remarks, "There is an inner
connection between certain conceptions of the task of sociology, between
certain epistemological and logical–scientific positions and between certain
moral principles which also possess political relevance [1976: 129]."

Those links may be of two types. First, they may be of the strict logical
sort; one assumption analytically implies another or precludes another. In
this case the acceptance of a given assumption leads to the acceptance of
another one, or to the rejection of another one. To convey the intuition
inherent here, a common-sense illustration may be suggested: If John says
that he hates all sports, it would be logically inconsistent for him to say that
he loves swimming. Such a relationship obtains by definition between the
polar assumptions within each dichotomous pair. (If one accepts naturalism,
one has to reject antinaturalism; if one accepts reductionism one has to
reject antireductionism—at least as those positions are defined here.) But
such a relationship can also exist across particular dilemmas, and link specific assumptions (accepted as a solution to one dilemma) with another
assumption (accepted as a solution to another dilemma).

The second type of relationships between assumptions is of the more
loose, psychological sort. Here the acceptance or rejection of a given assumption on account of the other assumption's being accepted or rejected is
not logically necessary but psychologically most plausible. The answer given
to one of the questions does not imply the answer to another question, but
strongly suggests, stimulates, intimates, exhorts a direction in which such an
answer will be given. Again, a common-sense illustration may be helpful: If
John says that he is fond of the Preludes of Bach, it is not logically inconsistent but psychologically improbable that he loves Dean Martin.

Keeping in mind this important distinction, I shall abstract from it for a
moment. So far I have characterized the theoretical assumptions only in a
most superficial and sketchy way, and thus I am not equipped to detect, and
discriminate between, the specific types of relationships obtaining among
them. But staying at this superficial level I wish to venture some hypotheses
concerning their typical relationships.

The assumptions of the methodological sort seem to display systematic
interconnections. The comprehensive, coherent structures of mutually
linked general assumptions, providing specific solutions to the methodological dilemmas, will be referred to as *methodological models of sociology*. Only
two methodological dilemmas have been considered here. But they may be
treated as essential, or strategic, determining the character of the whole,
more complex model. The assumptions of naturalism and reductionism

seem central for the model that may be labeled *scientistic*. And the opposite assumptions of antinaturalism and antireductionism seem central to the model which may be labeled *humanistic*.

Again, the theoretical assumptions of the epistemological sort also appear to be systematically interconnected. The comprehensive, coherent structures of linked general assumptions, providing specific solutions to the epistemological dilemmas, will be referred to as *epistemological models of sociology*. Only two epistemological dilemmas have been considered here. But they may be treated as essential, or strategic, determining the character of the whole, more complex model. The assumptions of cognitivism and neutralism seem central to the model that may be labeled *objectivistic*. And the opposite assumptions of activism and axiologism seem central to the model that may be labeled *critical*.

Finally, the theoretical assumptions of the ontological sort do not make up a formless, random aggregate, but rather cluster together in specific, systematically interconnected structures. The comprehensive, consistent structures of linked general assumptions, providing specific solutions to the ontological dilemmas, will be referred to as *ontological models of sociology*. Only two ontological dilemmas have been considered here. But they may be treated as essential or strategic, determining the character of the whole, more complex model. The assumptions of passivism and collectivism seem central to the model that may be labeled *mechanistic*. And the opposite assumptions of autonomism and individualism seem central to the model which may be labeled *voluntaristic*.

As a result, the modified classification of assumptions may be presented, taking into account their typical clusterings, referred to as the *methodological, epistemological,* and *ontological models of sociology*.

   I. *Methodological Models*
      A. Scientistic, Including Naturalism and Reductionism, as Essential Components
      B. Humanistic, Including Antinaturalism and Antireductionism as Essential Components
   II. *Epistemological Models*
      A. Objectivistic, Including Cognitivism and Neutralism as Essential Components
      B. Critical, Including Activism and Axiologism as Essential Components
   III. *Ontological Models*
      A. Mechanistic, Including Passivism and Collectivism as Essential Components

B.   Voluntaristic, Including Autonomism and Individualism as Essential Components

It may be observed that the regular relationships may also obtain between the specific models of sociology. Usually, the accepted ontology is linked with the accepted epistemology, and this in turn with the accepted methodology. Such regular links will provide the foundation for the second-degree (or secondary) clustering of theoretical assumptions. And thus, two coherent, comprehensive clusters of this sort may finally be distinguished—two master models, or paradigms, of sociology. One includes the scientistic methodology, objectivistic epistemology, and mechanistic ontology. It will be labelled the *positivistic model of sociology*. The other includes the humanistic methodology, critical epistemology, and voluntaristic ontology. It will be labelled *the subjectivistic model of sociology*.

By the logic of my analytic argument those models of sociology are mutually contradictory and mutually exclusive. They represent the polar ideal-types of the prevailing modes of sociological inquiry.

Why the ideal-types? The model of sociology must be seen as the analytical construct, of a simplifying and idealizing nature; and that for two reasons: First, each of the assumptions is defined in extreme, pure form, and is rarely if ever encountered in reality (by "reality" is here meant the actual existing set of sociological theories). Even the most devoted naturalist is rarely so naturalistic as my assumption of naturalism would require; even the most devoted individualist is never so individualistic as my assumption of individualism would claim. People are seldom that extreme. And second, the combination of assumptions in a comprehensive and coherent system is also a sort of extreme, pure utopia, rarely if ever encountered in reality. People are seldom that consistent. As Brodbeck puts it, "The course of science is not always as smooth as the logical analyst would like [1969a: 286]."

Thus a model of sociology is here conceived as an ideal type, in the meaning given to that term by Weber (1949), or as a constructed type according to the meaning of Becker (1945), McKinney (1950) and others, or finally as a polar type according to the meaning of Winch (1947), except that in their usage an ideal type referred to the phenomena and processes of society, whereas in my usage it refers to the concepts, propositions, and assumptions of theoretical sociology. To put it otherwise: In their case it was a theoretical construct, and in my case it is a meta-theoretical construct. But whereas the subject-matter to which the ideal type is applied is different, the justification for its application, the functions it is expected to fulfill, are the same. To put it briefly, it is an instrument for better understanding. By comparing what is analytically possible with what actually exists, one is able to obtain a better comprehension of reality—in my case, the reality of theories, of theoretical schools, of theoretical disputes.

TOWARD A REAPPRAISAL OF SOCIOLOGY

The models of sociology—positivistic and subjectivistic—as defined in the previous chapter, seem to be approximated to a larger or smaller extent by the majority of existing sociological theories. If this is the case, then the current crisis of sociology, or the widespread feeling of dissatisfaction with sociological theories, can be seen as due to a pair of factors: First, to the inherent inadequacy of both models—the exhaustion of their heuristic potential and their inability to cope with the changing realities of social life— and second, to the polarization of the field between opposite models—the endless and fruitless disputes and controversies generated by their opposition. I assert that both factors are present at the heart of the crisis.

The ways out of the theoretical crisis that have been suggested in the current literature do not seem promising. As was already stressed, I do not sympathize either with the retreatist response of those who profess some form of eclecticism, combining opportunistically the assumptions taken from several antithetical models or with the rebellious response of those who push the humanistic, critical, and voluntaristic models to the extreme, arriving at some form of antiscientific obscurantism. I believe that the third response—the innovative one—is needed, which will start from the radical reappraisal of all the traditional assumptions, from the positivistic side, as well as from the subjectivistic side, and result in the construction of a new model, more fruitful for the study of society.

Several authors seem to endorse a similar program. Coleman says: "Indeed, there are points in the history of a discipline at which certain unexamined postulates are held up for inspection, certain assumptions looked at anew. The present time may be such a point in the history of sociology, at which the postulates and assumptions that govern sociological research and discourse must justify themselves or be replaced [1975: 78]." Giddens adds: "There is a widespread feeling among sociologists that contemporary social theory stands in need of a radical revision. Such a revision must begin from a reconsideration of the works of those writers who established the principal frames of reference of modern sociology [1971: vii]."[1] And Di-

---

[1]This and all subsequent quotes cited to Giddens, 1971, are reprinted from *Capitalism and Modern Social Theory* by A. Giddens by permission of Cambridge University Press. Copyright © 1971 by Cambridge University Press.

Renzo perceives the same situation not only in sociology, but in other social sciences as well:

> The contemporary stage in the behavioral sciences has an inevitably transitional character. Until rather recently, the philosophy of these sciences was discussed sparingly, and then only in very general terms. . . . Today many matters need to be subjected to reinterpretation in the light of advances which have been made not only in the areas of the philosophy and epistemology of science, but in each of the respective disciplines of the behavioral science as well [1966: x].

To put it briefly, the fundamental reappraisal and reinterpretation of sociology is called forth ever more vociferously. I intend to respond to this call, at least in some initial, tentative fashion.

The reappraisal and reinterpretation of sociology that is attempted in this book is guided by two basic beliefs, which must be disclosed at the outset. The first of them has already been discussed at length, but to reiterate it: What a theory implicitly assumes is often more essential than what it explicitly claims. The theoretical assumptions underlying a given theory, the models of sociology implemented in its concepts and propositions, are of crucial significance. They constitute the tap roots of theoretical activity. The way out of the theoretical crisis must start here, by grasping the roots directly. Therefore, the focus of my reappraisal and reinterpretation will rest on the meta-theoretical level of general assumptions, and not at the substantive level of theoretical formulations.

The second belief has to do with the continuity of sociological tradition. It is most unwise to reject this tradition in toto, and to start building sociology from scratch, because there is a lot to be learned from the masters, even though some masters are better teachers than others. The major debates focusing on the fundamentals of the sociological enterprise started as early as sociology itself. Merton is correct when he says that "the main lines of argument have a long and easily accessible history. Were that history carefully reviewed, the most recent announcements of crisis in sociology would be recognized as a continuation of theoretical issues long under debate [1975: 26]." In the course of these debates several matters have been cleared up, several points of agreement reached, several revealing observations made. One should not ignore all this. I share Abel's view that there is "the continuity of sociological enterprise" and that "not only [has] a proper foundation been laid but by now it is securely established [1970: 12]." Therefore, any attempt at reappraisal and reinterpretation must start from the careful scrutiny of sociological tradition. "The sociological tradition contains the best statements of the full promise of the social sciences as a whole, as well as some partial fulfillments of it [Mills, 1959: 24]." It is here, in this tradition, that the basic hunches and ideas pointing toward a new model of sociology shall be discovered.

Now that my own assumptions have been made clear, some more comment is needed on the concrete strategy that will be followed in the search for the new model of sociology. The strategy will consist of two stages; the first may be referred to as the analytic reconstruction, and the second as the dialectic critique.

The stage of analytic reconstruction is intended to identify the main assumptions of sociological theories, and render their meaning as definite and clear as possible. I fully concur with Stinchcombe that "for a social theorist ignorance is more excusable than vagueness" and that "social theorists should prefer to be wrong rather than misunderstood [1968: 6]." This clarifying effort is a prerequisite for any appraisal of criticism, because, almost by definition, theoretical assumptions are not openly stated but rather are accepted implicitly, and are well hidden under the surface level of actual theories. Several heuristic devices will be applied to spot the assumptions and explicate their meaning. Some of them are pointed out by Allen: "There are a number of ways by which broad conceptual frameworks can be identified. It is possible to see them through the initial assumptions which are made explicitly, through the analytical tools used, through the nature of the data awarded causal priority, by the conclusions which are reached [1975: 17]."

In the course of the reconstruction I shall attempt to stay in constant touch with the riches of sociological tradition. But I shall not be altogether bound to chronological order, and shall not attempt to cover all the components of this tradition. The ideas worked out by the social theorists in the history of sociology, and in contemporary sociology (if such a distinction is valid at all) will be considered as a common pool from which I shall draw heuristic inspiration and which I shall utilize for illustrating the reconstructed assumptions. I shall refer only to some selected authors, and to some selected schools. My approach to the masters of sociology is justified by the character of this book. It is analytical, not historical, and my interest rests solely with the content of ideas and their underlying assumptions, and not with the circumstances in which they originated or were disseminated. I want to be clear about what has been claimed, and not about when, where, why, and so on.

But this reconstructive stage is only preliminary and preparatory to the main concern: the dialectic critique of assumptions (the terms *dialectic overcoming, Aufhebung, positive critique* or similar ones could also be used). Having provided the explications of traditional assumptions and having ordered them in dichotomous pairs—theoretical dilemmas—I shall attempt in each case to formulate a third, alternative solution, which would save what is valuable (the rational core) of both extreme positions but at the same time reach a qualitatively new level of theoretical insight. This approach is in line with what Agassi believes to be the "intuitively felt program" of social scientists: "Many thinkers seem to have felt the need for a via media between the two traditional views, and even for a consistent synthesis between the reasonable elements in them [1973: 189]." I shall follow this program with respect to every single dilemma. The thesis embedded in one of the extreme assumptions will be combined with the antithesis embedded in the opposite extreme assumption, to produce a dialectic synthesis in the form of a third, alternative assumption. In this way each of the traditional dilemmas will be shown spurious and will be overcome. In the resultant solution the directive of continuity will be safeguarded by the incorporation of elements taken from both traditional assumptions, but at the same time the dilemma itself will be rejected, and the alternative assumption will be qualitatively distinct from both traditional ones.

This strategy itself may be called a dialectic one. It clearly resembles the approach Karl Marx used with respect to political economy, as well as to parts of philosophy and to the social sciences of his time. It is a result of the application of the general patterns of thinking characteristic of dialectics to the realm of scientific ideas. Those patterns of thinking are described by the leading Marxists in the following way: Lukacs suggests that "it is of the essence of dialectical method that concepts which are false in their abstract one-sidedness are later transcended [1971: xlvi]"; and Kolakowski offers a similar account: "Negation in the dialectical sense is not tantamount to the simple abolition of the existing system, but such an abolition which safeguards the valuable components of the abolished system, and moves it to the higher level [1976: 400]." It would be a question for a separate study whether the progress of social science follows this dialectical pattern in its historical reality. At any rate, the dialectical history of the social sciences could perhaps be written in those terms.

The dialectical model of sociology, just like the traditional models, is of course an ideal-type. But in this particular case a relatively close approximation to the model is to be found within the single theoretical tradition; namely, the Marxist tradition in sociology. As Bell observes fittingly, "Like all of us to this day, Marx was seeking to resolve a number of inherently irreconcilable dilemmas in the epistemology and sociology of the social sciences [1977, 189]." Following this lead I shall attempt to trace the dialectic solutions to several theoretical dilemmas of sociology in the works of Karl Marx. No attempt will be made to analyse the works of the Marxists— the followers of and commentators on Marx. The chief reason for precluding such an attempt is that one cannot understand Marxism without a thorough reading of Marx himself. As Ollman puts it, "What Marx said is the raw material to be used in explaining Marxism [1975: xv]."[2] I would say with him that "I wish to understand Marx with the aid of his voluminous writings, and not in spite of them [Ollman, 1975: 11]."

By now, the last of the predilections that inform my analysis has been made clear. I shall attempt to show that the most fruitful approach to sociological theory construction is the dialectic approach, particularly in its Marxian implementation. In my view the new paradigm for which contemporary sociology is waiting is, after all, not so new, and exists already. In its rudimentary form it was implicit in the works of Marx. Since that time it has been developed more or less consistently—albeit with several distortions, omissions, and additions by the Marxist sociologists—and it has been more or less consistently forgotten by all other schools of sociology. The crisis of sociology is due precisely to the neglect of this vital theoretical tradition, or, to put it more precisely, to the neglect of the scientific, paradigmatic aspects of Marxism, as distinguished from its ideological or political appeal.

Thus, this is a partisan book. It may be called, in a loose sense of the term, Marxist. But Marxism will be only its point of arrival, and not its point of departure. Marxian sociology will here be defended by arguments and not by decrees, and my partisanship will be seen to result from systematic analysis, and not from dogmatism. If I may venture a biographical aside, I am retracing here my own progress toward Marxism.

Marxism is usually discussed in terms of its ideological persuasiveness or political strength. And it is often forgotten that its ideological or political impact is not God-given, but due to its intellectual potential. There is much more to Marxism than some of the most outspoken Marxists have ever dreamt about. I shall focus exclusively on this primary, and strangely neglected, intellectual aspect. In the course of this analysis Marxism will be seen first as a scientific approach, rather than as a political program, and second as a theoretical and methodological orientation, rather than as a full-fledged, closed and final dogmatic system. I believe with Fåyerabend that "Marxism is not just an inventory of phrases, it is a philosophy and it demands from its practitioners a little more than a pure heart, strong lungs, and a good memory [1977: 373]." In the scientific, open, undogmatic Marxian orientation, the road out of the current theoretical crisis of sociology is to be discovered.

---

[2]This and all subsequent quotes cited to Ollman, 1975, are reprinted from *Alienation: Marx's Conception of Man in Capitalist Society* by B. Ollman by permission of Cambridge University Press. Copyright © 1975 by Cambridge University Press.

PART II

THE DILEMMAS OF DEMARCATION— METHODOLOGICAL

Sociology has been called a very young science of a very old subject. To be sure, some form of conscious reflection on the human condition is as old as humanity itself. Most probably, it has always taken precedence over reflections on natural phenomena. But it was not until the nineteenth century that several types of thought that often involved pre-scientific social thinking—common sense, theological thought, philosophical thought—gave way to the birth of the social sciences. Only since then has a knowledge of society begun to be obtained through the systematic means of scientific method, codified in the systematic form of scientific theories, and systematically applied to descriptive, explanatory, predictive, and practical functions. Since that time sociology has joined the family of sciences. This was a turning point, both for the fate of sociology and for the fate of society, the possibility of an adequate knowledge of and rational control over human affairs having been opened. One must agree with Martindale that "the single most dramatic intellectual event of the nineteenth and twentieth centuries has been the rise of the social sciences with their attempt to transplant techniques which proved so powerful in dealing with the physical world to the social world [1964: 488]."

As a new member of the family of sciences sociology had to fight for its identity and autonomy; it had to establish its specific status, and it had to distinguish itself from other sciences. But at the same time it wanted to speed up the process of maturation, to achieve full recognition on equal terms with other, more developed disciplines; and this required learning from its older siblings. Those tendencies were contradictory, and so they introduced a strain into the body of the new-born discipline, generating its first methodological dilemmas.

Those dilemmas centered on the problem of demarcation. The quest for intellectual legitimacy, and later institutional legitimacy, vis-à-vis other well-established disciplines of science, has become one of the focal preoccupations of sociology. As Merton observes, "Virtually every sociologist of any consequence throughout the nineteenth century and partly into the twentieth proposed his own answers to the socially induced question of the scope and nature of sociology and saw it as his task to evolve his own system of sociology [1973: 50]."

There were two borderlines that first of all had to be fixed for sociology to appear as separate and independent. The first divided sociology from the natural sciences. Sociology had to prove that it possessed a different subject matter or a different method, or both. But at the same time the natural sciences were already so successful in their domain that it was most tempting to imitate their ways of research and apply them to the social world. The dilemma science or humanities? *emerged, and a division of sociologists into two opposing camps was an immediate result. Some claimed that sociology is, or can be, or should be, as similar to the natural sciences as possible, in all respects except the content of its propositions. Thus they accepted the naturalistic assumption. Others claimed that the difference in the content of the propositions, due to the specific subject matter with which sociology deals, implies a basic divergence from the natural sciences in the realm of methods, and that therefore sociology is, or can be, or should be, completely distinct from the natural sciences. Thus they accepted the antinaturalistic assumption.*

The second borderline divided sociology from other disciplines of the social sciences. And here the most imminent danger and the most aggressive declaration of supremacy were coming from psychology. At first glance psychology was dealing with the same subject matter, human beings, and was at almost the same stage of development as sociology, and hence was equally concerned with its own identity and autonomy. "What is the real basis of demarcation between sociology and psychology?" This question troubled sociologists very much, indeed. But at the same time they felt that there must exist some close relationship between all the scientific disciplines concerned with man and his world. The dilemma science of individuals or science of society *emerged, and the next separation of sociologists eventuated. Some of them claimed that the uniqueness of sociology as a discipline is illusory, and that sociology is in a sense redundant, because all its terms can be translated without loss of meaning into the terms of psychology and all its propositions can be derived logically from the propositions of psychology. Thus, they accepted the reductionist assumption. Others claimed that sociology is completely distinct from psychology, dealing with a totally different subject or focusing on totally different aspects of human life, and therefore no possibility of definitional or propositional reduction exists. Thus, they accepted the antireductionistic assumption.*

The historians of science testify that the problem of demarcation is usually characteristic of the early stages in the development of the scientific disciplines. One can hardly imagine the contemporary physicist discussing the legitimacy of his field, or bothering to separate it precisely from say, chemistry. But this sort of concern is still very much with us in sociology. Either the field is still so immature or—what seems more plausible—the problem of demarcation is an unfortunate survival of the sociological tradition, which generates spurious and unfounded divisions among sociologists, contributing thereby to the crisis of sociology. I believe it is time to get rid of that problem and its accompanying dilemmas. But in order to do that effectively and justifiably, both dilemmas must be carefully examined and the procedure of their rejection made clear. Finally, more adequate solutions must be put forward. I propose to take up this complex task in this part of the book.

CHAPTER **2**

Science or Humanities:
Naturalism, Antinaturalism,
Integralism

THE NATURALISTIC TRADITION

The dispute between the naturalistic and antinaturalistic points of view started as early as scientific sociology itself, and is still going on. One can agree with Martindale that "it is not misleading to take these two methodological orientations . . . as the primary compass points of Western thought [1964: 453]." This could perhaps be a key for writing the whole history of sociology up to the present day. But leaving this job to the historian, I shall review the whole debate in brief, pointing only to the milestones.

The founding fathers of sociology—Auguste Comte, Herbert Spencer, John Stuart Mill, in Europe, and Lester Ward, in America—were all of the naturalistic persuasion. "They proposed to analyze historical, and ethnographic, materials by means of the methods of the physical sciences [Martindale, 1964: 467]." This could well be expected, because all of them were intent on insuring scientific status for a new discipline of sociology, and because the only known standards of scientific research, the only known indices of scientific status, were already firmly established by the natural sciences, providing the ready patterns to be imitated. As Eisenstadt and Curelaru describe this trend. "It was common for the initial generation of sociologists

41

to assert the scientific legitimacy of sociology by aping what they thought were the models of the established sciences; the mechanistic models of the physical sciences and the organismic models of the biological [1976: 99]."

Auguste Comte: A Call for Positive Science

Auguste Comte wished to transform social lore into positive science. The progressive emancipation of human thinking from theological and metaphysical notions had reached a stage when not only physics, chemistry, and biology, but also sociology could be established as positive science, studying social phenomena by positive methods of observation, experiment, comparison, and discovering social regularities—the constant relationships of coexistence or succession between phenomena. "In the final, positive stage," Comte says, "the mind has given over the vain search after absolute notions, the origin and destination of the universe, and the causes of phenomena, and applies itself to the study of their laws—that is, their invariable relations of succession and resemblance [1912: 2]." Sociology reaches the positive stage relatively late, owing to the complexity of its subject matter, but when it finally achieves scientific status it is able "to enjoy all the resources of the anterior sciences [Coser, 1971: 7]," by borrowing their methodological patterns.

To summarize Comte's position in the words of a contemporary French sociologist: "The combination of the law of three stages and the classification of the sciences eventually leads to Auguste Comte's basic formula: The method which has triumphed in mathematics, astronomy, physics, chemistry, and biology must eventually prevail in politics and culminate in the founding of a positive science of society which is called sociology [Aron, 1968, vol. I: 76-77]."

Herbert Spencer: Evolution as a Unifying Principle

Herbert Spencer attempted to incorporate sociology into a unified scheme of knowledge embracing all the sciences. "There can be no complete acceptance of sociology as a science so long as the belief in a social order not conforming to natural law survives [1894: 394]." Therefore, social facts must be conceived as completely natural. "Throughout this work there runs the assumption that the facts, simultaneous and successive, which societies present, have a genesis no less natural than the genesis of facts of all other classes [Spencer, 1894: 385]." The common unifying theoretical idea, describing the pattern of transformations typical of both natural and social reality is the "law of evolution." "The many facts contemplated unite in proving that social evolution forms a part of evolution at large [Spencer, 1893, vol. I: 584]." Because society is subject to the law of evolution, as are physical or biological phenomena, the science of society, applying methods similar to those of the natural sciences, is possible, even though it faces special difficulties.

Spencer's approach (in the words of a modern British sociologist) "was an illumination of the actual unity, connectedness, and coherence of all knowledge by the use of a conception which pointed to, and then analytically explored, the central process which lay at the very heart of, and characterized all the actualities and transformations of nature, human nature, and human society [Fletcher, 1971, vol. I: 255]."

John S. Mill: The Logical Unification of the Sciences

John Stuart Mill attempted to prove the unity of all the sciences, including sociology, on somewhat different grounds. In his view, there exists a common framework of method that can and should be applied in any scientific inquiries, notwithstanding differences in their subject matter. "The same process through which the laws of many simpler phenomena have by general acknowledgement been placed beyond dispute must be consciously and deliberately applied to those more difficult enquiries"—by which he meant "the study of mankind [1884, vol. VI: 546]." The social sciences have cognitive possibilities equal to those of any other science, even with respect to that ultimate test of scientific status, the predictive ability:

> Inasmuch, however, as many of these effects which it is of most importance to render amenable to human foresight and control are determined, like the tides, in an incomparably greater degree by general causes than by all partial causes taken together, depending in the main on those circumstances and qualities which are common to all mankind, or at least to large bodies of them, and only in a small degree on particular or peculiar idiosyncracies, it is evidently possible with regard to all such effects to make predictions which will almost always be verified, and general propositions which are almost always true [Mill, 1884, vol. VI: 554].

Mill devoted much attention to the justification of logical possibility of social-scientific studies, and to the countering of common-sense assertions of the basically imprecise, prognostically and practically useless character of social inquiry. In his view, there is no logical reason why the sciences of man should be considered as methodologically inferior to or different from the natural sciences.

Lester Ward: Science as the Universal
Way to Knowledge

Lester Ward, one of the central figures in the transplantation of sociology to America, was strongly influenced by Comte and Spencer. He shared their opposition to theological or metaphysical speculations, and advocated science as a most fruitful way to knowledge, and consequently to rational prediction and control. His ambition was to promote the extension of the scientific method from the realm of nature to the realm of society: "In the domain of physical forces and chemical substances man is able to exercise prevision in many ways to secure advantages and avert evils, but in most of the higher fields of vital, mental, moral, and social phenomena, these relations are either utterly ignored, or but dimly suspected, so that his knowledge of them avails him nothing. The great work before him, therefore, still is to study [Ward, 1902, vol. II: 21]." This can be done only by the application of the same methods proven fruitful in the natural sciences. This is because "man is an integral part of the universe, and in order to be correctly conceived and properly studied, he must be conceived and studied as an objective phenomenon presented by nature. Neither the animal and vegetable forms, nor the rock formations, nor the chemical elements, are more to be regarded as natural objects for scientific study than are individual men or human societies [Ward, 1902, vol. II: 3]."

As a modern American sociologist comments: "Lester Ward, who was a scientist in his own right as well as a careful reader of Comte and Spencer, agreed with them in the location of social science knowledge in a context of the physical sciences [Martindale, 1960: 75]."

The naturalistic trend is encountered not only in the formative years of sociology but also much later, when sociology had already established its intellectual and academic legitimacy. Two men of great stature who contributed to the continuation of this tradition are Emile Durkheim, in France, and Vilfredo Pareto, in Italy.

Emile Durkheim: The Codification of Positivism

Emile Durkheim declared that his "principal objective is to extend scientific rationalism to human behavior [1962: xxxiv]." To this end he provided the most extensive codification of methodological directives proper to sociology. There is no doubt that his rules of sociological method are informed by the patterns of the natural science—as can clearly be seen if one reads one of the master directives; for example, to treat social phenomena as things. Here Durkheim requires that a sociologist adopt the same approach toward data as the approach characteristic of the natural sciences: "Our principle demands that the sociologist put himself in the same state of mind as the physicist, chemist, or physiologist when he probes into a still unexplained region of the scientific domain [1962: xlv]." And in more specific rules of observation, explanation, and testing of social facts and regularities, a similar naturalistic orientation constantly reappears. I shall have much more to say about those rules in the further chapters, but now it suffices to sum up Durkheim's attitude: "Durkheim urged that, while there is a distinction between natural and social science, the methods of natural science are applicable to the social field [Martindale, 1960: 90]."

Vilfredo Pareto: Sociology as the Logico–Experimental Science

Vilfredo Pareto continued the attempts to make sociology more scientific by having it imitate the more developed natural disciplines. As he admitted: "Inspired by the example of the natural sciences, I determined to begin my 'Treatise,' the sole purpose of which . . . is to seek experimental reality, by the application to the social sciences of the methods which have proved themselves in physics, in chemistry, in astronomy, in biology and in other such sciences [quoted by Coser, 1971: 387]." He followed the patterns of the natural sciences in a double manner: First, he proposed to apply a logico–experimental method of inquiry to the field of social facts; and, second, he adopted by analogy certain notions from the physical sciences— like a system, equilibrium, and so on—and interpreted them for the sociological domain. Thus both formally (in how it proceeded in research) and substantively (in what it claimed), natural science was for Pareto a main source of inspiration.

Parsons gives an apt summary of this aspect of Pareto's contribution: "The interest in mathematics and physical science never left him, and both as a methodological model and as a substantive element of his thinking it must always be kept in mind in interpreting his work [1968, vol. I: 180]."

I have mentioned some outstanding representatives of the naturalistic orientation in the history of sociology. But the opposite orientation—the antinaturalistic—was equally significant, although it appeared almost fifty years later than the first proclamations of naturalism. Such a delayed appearance was by no means accidental. Sociology had to possess a very strong footing before it could break all ties with the natural sciences and still retain its identity. Martindale makes this point quite convincingly:

> Until such time as sociology was firmly established, the reaction to the physical-science bias of early sociology tended rather to take the form of a rejection of sociology altogether rather than of the establishment of a new

school of sociology. It was only after sociology became indubitably established and had made its way into the universities . . . that it became desirable formally to establish [a] . . . humanistic approach which still described itself as a sociological theory [1964: 478].

THE ANTINATURALISTIC TRADITION

For this reason it was only in the second half of the nineteenth century that the attempt to regain the social sciences for the humanities and to divorce them from the physical sciences was made. The attack on the strongholds of naturalism started in the German historiosophy of Wilhelm Dilthey and Heinrich Rickert, and was brought to the field of sociology by Max Weber. Thus, the whole antinaturalistic trend was initiated, which later expressed itself in the works of such authors as, for example, Alfred Vierkandt and Florian Znaniecki, each of whom started from different premises but arrived at a similar conclusion: one requiring the complete separation of the social sciences from the natural sciences. Before we directly consider sociology, a short comment on the philosophical roots of the antinaturalistic trend is necessary.

Wilhelm Dilthey based his case for separate cultural sciences on ontological grounds. He claimed that reality is essentially dualistic; it consists of facts and meanings. The world of facts may be called nature; the proper way to comprehend it is by experiment and causal explanation, and the sciences which deal with facts by means of causal explanations may be called the natural sciences. The world of meanings is culture; the proper way to comprehend it is by understanding and intuitive interpretation, and the sciences which deal with meanings by means of interpretation may be called the cultural sciences. Sociology, like history, belongs to the cultural sciences, and its subject matter, its goal, and its method are basically different from those of physics, chemistry, biology, or the other sciences of nature.

Heinrich Rickert followed a somewhat different tack, focusing directly on methodological divergences. In his view, the world can be approached in two ways. One consists of the search for regularities, causal laws; it is the way characteristic of science. The other consists of the search for concrete, unique configurations of events and values; it is the way characteristic of history. And Rickert located sociology closer to history, with its individualizing approach, than to science proper, with its generalizing method.

Max Weber: The Case for Humanistic Sociology

Max Weber combined both sorts of arguments, ontological and methodological, in his case for the separate status of sociology. "Sociology," he claimed, "is a science which attempts the interpretive understanding of social action in order thereby to arrive at a causal explanation of its course and effects [Weber, 1947: 88]." The proper subject matter of sociology–social actions—is totally different from the facts of nature, because its essential property is not external, observable behavior but rather a specific internal meaning in terms of which people orient themselves toward other people or toward the world at large. His definition of social action made it quite clear: "The action is social insofar as, by virtue of the subjective meaning attached to it by the acting individual (or individuals), it takes account of the behavior of others and is thereby oriented in its course [1947: 88]." *Action* is a comprehensive category, including at least two distinct types of components: First, there is the psychological context of action—intentions, motivations, purposes, reasons, calculations entertained by the actors. Second, there is the normative (or cultural) context of action—rules, norms, values, patterns prevailing in a given society and taken into account by acting people.

Neither of those crucial components of action can be reached by observation, experiment, or any other methods typical of the natural sciences. A totally distinct approach is necessary: the interpretative understanding, focused on the uncovering of the complete meaningful structure of human activities. "We do not 'understand'" (Weber says) "the behavior of cells, but can only observe the relevant functional relationships and generalize on the basis of these observations. This additional achievement of explanation by interpretative understanding, as distinguished from external observation, is, of course, attained only at a price—the more hypothetical and fragmentary character of its results. Nevertheless, subjective understanding is the specific characteristic of sociological knowledge [1947: 103]."

On both grounds—ontological and methodological—sociology must therefore be considered as a cultural science, fundamentally distinct from the natural-scientific disciplines. Abel provides an apt summary: "The essence of a sociocultural fact resides in the meaning and significance assigned to it by human beings. The relevence of values and motivational understanding to social facts limits the extent of abstraction and of elemental analysis employed by social scientists. [1970: 57–58]."

Alfred Vierkandt: The Beginnings of Phenomenological Sociology

An understanding of sociology, similar to Weber's is reached from different premises by Alfred Vierkandt, a forerunner of phenomenological sociology. He accepts the dualistic view of reality, in which natural events are opposed to intuitively grasped eidetic essences. For sociology it means that the external, objective manifestations of human actions, interactions, relations, and so on, must be distinguished from the internal, pure, universal, unchangeable, ahistorical forms, forces, or factors. The latter constitute the proper subject matter of sociology. To reach this innermost, essential layer of social reality, a special method—phenomenological—is necessary, quite incommensurate with standard observation or experimentation. Martindale describes it thus: "The phenomenological method consists in controlled examination of the process of awareness itself. . . . It represents a kind of 'immanent reflection' and concentration upon the inherent meaning of things as given. The phenomenological method attempts, through the analysis of experience, to uncover certain fundamental social dispositions . . . or essences" [1960: 269]."

Therefore, again for both ontological and methodological reasons sociology has nothing in common with the natural sciences.

Florian Znaniecki: The Humanistic Coefficient

Florian Znaniecki defends a new philosophical standpoint that he labels *culturalistic.* In one of his early works he declares: "It is time to substitute a new culturalistic philosophy for both idealism and naturalism [1969: 49]." This program is carried on in numerous later works. Its basic premise is again dualistic:

> Social theory and social practice have forgotten to take into account one essential difference between physical and social reality, which is that while the effect of a physical phenomenon depends exclusively on the objective nature of this phenomenon and can be calculated on the ground of the latter's empirical content, the effect of a social phenomenon depends in addition on the subjective standpoint taken by the individual or the group toward this phenomenon and can be calculated only if we know, not only the objective content of the assumed cause, but also the meaning it has at the given moment for the given conscious beings [Znaniecki, 1969: 84].

Physical reality is made up of things, social (or cultural) reality of values. "A value differs from a thing in that it possesses both a given content . . . and a meaning [1969: 140]."

The dualistic character of reality requires double methods for its study. "The essential and objectively significant side of cultural life remains forever inaccessible to naturalistic science [1969: 43]." For this reason, culturalistic science introduces a method involving a *humanistic coefficient,* which requires that any social phenomenon be studied "as it appears to the agent himself and to those who cooperate with him or counteract him . . . i.e., within the sphere of experience and activity of some particular people, individuals and collectivities [1969: 143, 137]."

Bierstedt summarizes Znaniecki's principal point thus: "Sociology is a social and not a natural science and . . . culture is a reality in its own ontological right [1969: 34]."

I have discussed some representative exponents of the naturalistic and antinaturalistic views in the history of sociology. The pervasiveness of the dispute in which some stand is taken by almost all masters of sociology adds plausibility to Martindale's assertion that "the most fundamental of all perspectives in western thought are those of humanism and science [1964: 487]," and to the similar opinion of Kmita and Nowak: "The issue of naturalistic and antinaturalistic character of the human sciences is without doubt basic for the methodology of that domain of knowledge [1968: 52]."

In my historical overview, I excluded one of the biggest names in sociology, Karl Marx. Did he take no stand on the crucial issue we've been considering? Of course he did, but his standpoint cannot be subsumed either under the naturalistic or the antinaturalistic label. To be sure, he has often been classified under such headings in textbooks. Some commentators have believed him to be a naturalist, and some (perhaps the minority) claimed that he was an antinaturalist in his basic persuasion. I think both groups are mistaken. Marx was, I believe, a representative exponent of the dialectical solution to the dispute, one who rejected both traditional solutions, and with them the whole dilemma of "science versus humanities." This dialectical standpoint will be labeled *integralism,* and discussed in detail later on.

NATURALISM AND ANTINATURALISM IN CONTEMPORARY SOCIOLOGY

Leaving historical considerations aside, I shall deal briefly with the present opposition between naturalism and antinaturalism. The matter is significant on at least two levels—the level of research, and the level of theory and interpretation.

The Opposite Trends of Empirical Research

If one takes a look at contemporary empirical studies in sociology, social psychology, political science, and so on, one shall find, on the one hand, highly formalized experimental or representative surveys that employ standardized techniques of observation and interpretation, and refined methods of statistical analysis and data processing. Here the results are presented in quantitative form. According to Warshay, this trend, positivist in its tone and tending toward the study of physical variables, develops and improves mathematical methods as the only valid mode of social research (1971: 26). But on the other hand, among the achievements of contemporary sociology or social anthropology there are numerous field and case studies that fail to meet the requirements of representativeness or standardization and rely on loose observation. Here the results are presented in qualitative or narrative form. The adherents of this trend, called by Warshay "the new humanism," reject the stringent scientific approach in favor of a looser methodology— participant observation, which, according to them, allows one to grasp the qualitative differences between social life and other kinds of phenomena (Warshay, 1971: 25).

In my view, the 1970s have clearly brought about a revival of the humanist orientation at the level of research practice. When empirically minded sociologists are no longer satisfied with their treasures of data, but try to arrive at general regularities, or to explain the mechanisms of phenomena and processes, then the study of human collectivities as they are in the actuality of all their aspects and forms turns out to be indispensable. But then, qualitative, nonstandardized methods of clinical observation and interviewing, case studies, etc., cannot be dismissed. And a similar tendency can also be noticed at the level of theoretical generalizations. But the more traditional, naturalistic trend is by no means eliminated. The strongholds of physicalism or behaviorism are still well defended.

The Physicalist and Behaviorist Tendencies

In the period immediately following World War II the physicalistic and behavioristic versions of naturalism reigned in sociology as the specific implementation of the more general philosophical tenets of neopositivism, and may be illustrated by the names of Lundberg, Dodd, Zipf, and Rashevsky, among others. Lundberg expresses the naturalistic bias typical of the whole group in the most straightforward manner: "My conclusion is that the best hope for the social sciences lies in following broadly in the paths of the other sciences [1947: 17]." The attempt was made to consider social reality in terms of observable physical phenomena, and consequently to apply the concepts as well as the methods utilized in physics, regarded as the most advanced of the natural sciences, to human activities and social processes. Society was discussed in terms of physical movements, gravitational pulls, energy transformations; it was supposed to consist mainly of fields, forces, atoms, particles, and attractions and repulsions; and the sociological method was seen as consisting of formalization, measurement, and quantification. It was a naturalism wrought to the extreme, the most unfruitful form of the "aping of what is widely mistaken for the method of science [Popper, as quoted in Frisby, 1976: xiii]." Since that time it has been subjected to devastating and convincing criticism (see, for example, Sorokin, 1966; Andreski, 1972; and Timasheff and Theodorson, 1976). But apparently no rational argument will prevail when emotions and attitudes are at stake. Anyway, those who love precision for precision's sake look for inspiration to the "true" sciences—that is, the natural sciences in their nineteenth century period—and proclaim the naturalistic creed over and over again. In the late 1960s Catton still declared that sociology would eventually become a science like physics or biology, because society does not possess any specificity as compared to the natural objects. In the 1970s, at one of the regional conferences of American sociologists, DeMaree supported another version of naturalism. He asserted that the basic empirical index of social phenomena is the overt behavior (physical movements) of human beings and that a social behavior is an act of physical motion of one individual that serves as a stimulus for the physical motions of others (1973). And at the annual ASA meeting, in 1974, Dodd proposed a refined version of his "Epicosm Theory," explaining its main tenets in the following way: "This cosmic theory, based on set theory, combinatoric formulas, and stochastic processes, is hypothesized to explain and predict the continual creating and operating of the whole cosmos including explicitly our material and mental World System within it [1974: 74]."

The Revival of Subjectivism

However, it is neither physicalism nor behaviorism which sets the tone of theoretical thinking in sociology and related disciplines. The most advertised and influential theoretical trends are located at the opposite, humanistic pole. The antinaturalistic tendency is in the ascendant. One important school that represents this tendency is deeply rooted in the historical tradition of Weber, Znaniecki, and MacIver and is presently most closely associated with the name of Parsons. This school holds to a theory of action. Society is here seen as the network, or system, of human actions, and a single action is interpreted in terms of a means/ends nexus, with such aspects as volitions, motivations, goals, definitions of situations in the focus of analytical attention. Scott identifies the antinaturalistic core of the Parsonian theory: "Two aspects of the action scheme are especially relevant here; its subjective reference to 'action from the point of view of the actor,' and its normative orientation, the claim that action always involves a reference to or consideration of some normative element [1969: 247]." Neither the subjective meaning that an action has for the actor, nor the normative context that provides the criteria for the choices, nor the "independent, determinate, selective factor" that allows for some measure of free will in any action can be grasped or comprehended by external observation of behavior, which is all that the natural-scientific approach can propose. The theory of action is certainly the most developed conceptually and theoretically among all contemporary antinaturalistic orientations (see, for example, Parsons, 1968; Parsons and Shils, 1962), but precisely for this reason it is apparently devoid of further developmental potentialities and is no longer at the center of theoretical controversies. Other trends are widely believed to be more promising. One can point to as many as five theoretical schools which clearly belong to the antinaturalistic current, and may be treated as the *signum temporis* of the 1970s.

The first of these is the school of symbolic interactionism, deriving from the pragmatist tradition, and in particular following the philosophical ideas of Mead, and the sociological considerations of Cooley, Thomas, and others. It is represented today by Blumer (1969), Rose (1962), and numerous social psychologists. The main theoretical idea of the school is an emphasis on the autonomous role of an active agent as the designer and performer of his own actions. Owing to his ability to use symbols, an individual can anticipate his own actions and shape them consciously and purposefully, depending on his goals and his actual situation as subjectively perceived and defined. The methodological consequence of such a view is the necessity of considering social phenomena and processes from the standpoint of an involved subject, and of providing an account of how the phenomena and processes are subjectively viewed by him. But since each subject has different perceptions and constructs his subjective world in different way, the social sciences have mainly descriptive tasks; the most that they can do is to reproduce, by means of empathy or in some other way the concrete and unique cases of human actions and interactions, as well as joint or group endeavors.

The second school, also clearly connected with the antinaturalistic premise, is the so-called dramaturgical school, represented mainly by Goffman (1963, 1967, 1969). The essence of social life is, for Goffman, its ceremonious and ritual character. People play roles; they strive to present themselves to others at their best; they manipulate the impressions made on others by their appearance and behavior. Life is a sort of theater, in which a script is written by tradition, accepted customs, and so on, and is performed time and again by countless actors. The task of the social sciences is to read the script, or the complex network of norms, patterns, and "rules of the game" that regulate and control human activities, even though some people are not conscious of their workings.

The third, and perhaps the most controversial, school is the so-called school of ethnomethodology, which is a sociological version of the philosophy of the common language. The founder of this new and avowedly revolutionary approach is Garfinkel (1967). Ethnomethodology studies the common, everyday life of people in its manifold manifestations. According to Garfinkel, there exists a sort of deep, hidden structure in social life, consisting of meanings, conventions, and rules, which an individual participating in interactions completely fails to realize. It is the task of sociology to reveal this structure by means of analysis of common conversations, disputes, quarrels, and so on, because the deep structure is reflected in the subtleties of interaction, particularly in conversations between actors. An empirically oriented sociologist uses participant observation, sympathetic introspection, and specific procedures of interpretation as his basic tools.

The fourth school is that of ethogenetics, represented by Harre and Secord (1972). These authors interpret social life as "conscious observation of norms and purposeful realization of plans" by acting individuals. They spot the most important specificity of human behavior in the ability to formulate a plan or assess a prospective action. Thereby a man can control his own activities; he is an active subject rather than a passive receiver of external stimuli. The task of social psychology, and presumably other social sciences, is to analyze actual "episodes"; that is, certain closed situations of a totalistic nature appearing in actuality, as opposed to artificial reactions in laboratories.

The fifth school is the phenomenological—a recent revival. It is associated with the names of Schutz (1967), Winch (1958), Berger and Luckmann (1967), and others. It approaches social reality as a construct of the people in a society. There is no other social reality than that experienced by common people in their everyday life. Of course, each community constructs its own reality, perceives the world in its own peculiar way, and bestows on it a meaning. It is possible to understand the social world only by adopting the perspective of the community that has built it up. Thus, the only proper method of sociology is something like the operation called *das Verstehen:* inner experience, empathy, insight into social processes or social phenomena.

This "new humanism," "revived subjectivism," "anthropomorphic model," on the level both of empirical studies and of theoretical interpretation, is treated by some authors as a Copernican revolution in the understanding of society, or (in fashionable terminology) as the "new paradigm" of the social sciences. In the interpretation of its adherents—or, perhaps better, its disciples—it is unrelentingly antinaturalistic. Since the controversy between naturalism and antinaturalism is perceived as a dilemma (social science is either identical to or completely different from the natural sciences), the followers of the new humanism persistently reject all patterns of natural knowledge. In consequence, they tend to reject not only what is peculiar to natural science but what is characteristic of science in general. The new paradigm of social science appears, in fact, basically antiscientific, and leads to the annihilation of social science and a return to prescientific social thought.

However, one can, I believe, recognize the significant peculiarities of man and society and also pursue an empirical science of them. But to do so, one must reject the false antitheses of naturalism and antinaturalism, and establish a valid perspective. The first step must be a closer look at both positions in the controversy, and the ways in which they are typically justified.

WHAT THE DISPUTE IS REALLY ABOUT: AN EXPLICATION

The controversy, as old and pervasive as it was, simply had to generate a great deal of confusion. At the most superficial level this can be perceived when one glances at the headings under which it has been carried on or discussed in the methodological literature. The most frequent labels are those used here: *naturalism* and *antinaturalism.* Sometimes, however, the standpoints are called *empiricism* and *humanism* (Nowak, 1970), *unification* and *separatism* (Rudner, 1966), *naturalism* and *phenomenology* (Goldstein, 1968), *objectivism* and *mentalism* (Brodbeck, 1962), *mechanicism* and *anthropomorphism* (Harre and Secord, 1972), or the *hard* and the *soft* standpoint (Warshay, 1971). But even forgetting the labels, it is not always clear what is really at stake, what is the real meaning of the controversy. I shall approach this issue from the negative side, and delimit those aspects relevant to the dispute from those that are not.

What the Dispute Is Not About

There are three ways in which the dispute can be interpreted. First, it may be seen as an ontological dispute over the fundamental properties of social reality. Here, the naturalistic position would be equal to some sort of ontological monism, whether materialistic or idealistic, and the antinaturalistic position would come down to some form of ontological dualism, or perhaps even ontological pluralism.

Second, the dispute can be seen in epistemological terms, as dealing with the relationship of the student of society to his subject matter. Here the naturalistic position would argue for the basic identity of the cognitive situation—cognitive opportunities and limitations—in all the branches of science, whereas the antinaturalistic position would ascribe an especially advantageous or else an especially inhibiting status to social studies.

Third, the dispute can be interpreted as a methodological one, concerning the delimitation of the scientific status of the social sciences in the family of scientific disciplines, or, more strictly speaking, the specification of the methodological characteristics of the social sciences. I shall construe the dilemma "science or humanities" and the respective controversy of naturalism and antinaturalism in this manner. I believe the real issue is methodological and the content of the assumptions adduced as the solutions to the dispute is always restricted to methodological matters. It is only in the arguments that are presented to justify a given assumption, whether naturalistic or antinaturalistic, that ontological or epistemological points are raised. But one should not confuse the substance of the claim with the ways in which it is justified; those are definitely separate questions. To sum up, I consider the dispute between naturalism and antinaturalism as dealing primarily with the specification of the methodological characteristics of the social sciences, and not with the ontological characteristics of social reality or with the epistemological characteristics of social cognition.

Such a methodological specification may be obtained by either of two strategies. One of them shall be called *direct*. It consists in reconstructing the methodological properties of the social sciences directly from research practice. The methodological identification of the social sciences attained by this strategy is autonomous, or inherent in them.

The other strategy may be called *indirect*. Here the reconstruction of the methodological properties of the social sciences is obtained through establishing their methodological identity with or, conversely, their basic differences from the natural sciences; accordingly, the methodological description of the latter is accepted as valid or rejected for the social sciences. The social sciences thereby gain their methodological identity by analogy with or by opposition to the natural-scientific discipline. Thus their identification is not autonomous but derived.

The whole great controversy between naturalism and antinaturalism is a simple effect of the application of the second strategy. One may wonder why it is that since the beginnings of social science the main current of its methodological effort has been towards comparing its own methods and achievements with those of the natural sciences. Whatever the causes of this penchant for comparison, it is a "fact often acknowledged but more often simply assumed by social scientists, that, because of their success in interpreting and explaining the events in nature, the exact natural sciences serve as the model for any and all sciences and therefore for the social sciences as well [Werkmeister, 1959: 483, see Gross, 1959]."

It should be noted that the use of the indirect, or comparative, strategy of reconstructing the methodological properties of the social sciences demands the answer to two related questions: (*a*) What is the relationship between the social and the natural sciences? and (*b*) what are the methodological properties of the natural sciences? If, answering the first question, one decides that the social and natural disciplines do not differ, then a methodological description of the natural sciences put forth in an answer to the second question will immediately provide us with a definite model. If, however, answering the first question one decides that the two big branches of science are incommensurate, then a methodological description of the natural sciences will provide us with no model, but rather a counter-model, implying the reconstruction of the properties of the social sciences by something like direct opposition to those of the natural sciences.

In principle, the answer to each of those two questions may become the issue of a separate argument. In fact, both questions are usually considered jointly in the literature; each time the models of the natural sciences are mentioned, there is presupposed some more or less clear underlying image of the natural sciences. This double reference of the actual positions in the controversy is pointedly reflected by the terms applied to them in contemporary methodology. When, for example, some position is labeled *positivistic naturalism* (Kmita and Nowak, 1968) the term indicates that a stand has been taken on two matters: The unity of the social and natural sciences and the validity of the positivistic model of the natural sciences have been proclaimed. When some other position is called *phenomenalist antinaturalism* (Nowak, 1974a: 102–105), it is thereby indicated that what has been accepted is, on the one hand, a separate status of the social sciences and, on the other hand, the phenomenalist model of the natural sciences.

It will be convenient to consider the two matters separately. I shall here discuss only the first problem; i.e., the purely comparative question of the relationship between the social and natural disciplines. Henceforth I shall treat the dispute between naturalism and antinaturalism as concerning only question *a*, which concerns the identity or discrepancy between the social and natural disciplines, irrespective of how the natural sciences, which are the point of reference for the comparison, are actually conceived, and therefore irrespective of the answer to question *b*. So I shall abstract from the multitude of problems stemming from the fact that "the opposition of the natural and the social sciences was predicated upon an almost complete misunderstanding of the methodological foundations and metaphysical implications of the natural sciences [Beck, 1968: 80]." To sum up, I consider the dispute between naturalism and antinaturalism as dealing primarily with the relative status of the social sciences with respect to the natural sciences, and not with the methodological characteristics of the natural sciences themselves.

Theses, Postulates, and Directives of the Opposite Positions

As was pointed out before, the focus of the dispute is the methodological characterization of the social sciences—the delimitation of a certain set of methodological characteristics peculiar to them. Now, it can readily be seen that the positions formulated in the controversy can differ either in the manner in which they arrive at ascribing some methodological characteristics to the social sciences or in the content of the characteristics ascribed. In this way one obtains two criteria to arrange systematically the possible positions in the controversy. I shall call one criterion the strength of a position, and the other its substance.

With respect to strength, the positions assumed in the controversy can be formulated in three ways:

1. "The social sciences *actually have* such and such methodological properties." The description offered is construed as reflecting the actual, present state of the social sciences. Any position formulated along these lines I shall call a *thesis.*

2. "The social sciences *can have* such and such methodological properties." The account offered is construed as pointing out a possibility, irrespective of its having been realized or not. I shall use the term *postulate* to refer to a position put forward along these lines.

3. "The social sciences *ought to have* such and such methodological properties." The description offered is construed as pointing out a desirable or even necessary methodological model. Such a position shall be called a *directive.*

We note that by accepting a definite directive we logically accept the postulate *If something ought to be, then it is possible that it could be.* However, by accepting a postulate only, we make no judgment either on how the things actually are or on how they ought to be; for neither facts nor obligations are necessitated by possibilities. Therefore, position 3 is the strongest one, position 2 is weaker, and position 1 is the weakest of the three.

With respect to the criterion of substance, the positions in the controversy can be formulated in three distinct ways. Any description of the social sciences can point to each of the three types of their methodological properties:

1. To those properties necessary and sufficient to treat a piece of knowledge as scientific. I shall call these the *criteria of scientific status.*

2. To those properties necessary and sufficient to treat a piece of scientific knowledge as empirical. I shall call these the *criteria of empirical status.*

3. To those properties necessary and sufficient to treat a piece of scientific and empirical knowledge as natural. I shall call these the *criteria of the natural-scientific character of knowledge.*

We note that by accepting a thesis, postulate, or directive of type 2, we logically presuppose a thesis, postulate, or directive of type 1; for the criteria of empirical status are contingent upon the criteria of scientific status. Similarly, by accepting a thesis, postulate, or directive of type 3, we logically presuppose theses, postulates, or directives of types 1 and 2; for the criteria of the natural-scientific character of knowledge are contingent upon the criteria of both empirical and scientific status of knowledge. However, an acceptance of a thesis, postulate, or directive of type 1 does not necessitate one of type 2 or types 2 and 3. Therefore, formulation 3 is the richest in its content, formulation 2 is poorer, and formulation 1 is the poorest.

The criteria of classification thus specified allow one to list 18 positions in the controversy over naturalism and antinaturalism: 6 theses, 6 postulates, and 6 directives. Each group of 6 positions reveals a continuum from the strongest naturalist position (ascribing to the social sciences most of the methodological properties identical with those of natural science) to the strongest antinaturalist one (refusing the social sciences the methodological properties typical of the natural sciences). I shall put forth these positions in the simplest formulations:

I. *Theses—Form: "What are the social sciences like?"*
   A. Theses of Naturalism
      1. The social sciences are empirical sciences of the natural type.
      2. The social sciences are empirical sciences.
      3. The social sciences are sciences.
   B. Theses of Antinaturalism
      1. The social sciences are empirical sciences, but not of the natural type.
      2. The social sciences are sciences, but not of the empirical type.
      3. The social sciences are not sciences.
II. *Postulates—Form: "What can the social sciences be like?"*
   A. Postulates of Naturalism
      1. The social sciences can be empirical sciences of the natural type.
      2. The social sciences can be empirical sciences.
      3. The social sciences can be sciences.
   B. Postulates of Antinaturalism
      1. The social sciences can be empirical sciences, but not of the natural type.
      2. The social sciences can be sciences but not of the empirical type.
      3. The social sicences cannot be sciences.
III. *Directives—Form: "What should the social sciences be like?"*
   A. Directives of Naturalism
      1. The social sciences should be pursued in the same manner as the natural sciences (the models of natural science ought to be applied).

   2. The social sciences should be pursued in the empirical manner
      (the models of empirical science should be applied).
   3. The social sciences should be pursued in the scientific manner
      (the models of science ought to be applied).
 B. Directives of Antinaturalism
   1. The social sciences should not be pursued in the same manner as
      the natural sciences (the models of natural science must not be
      applied).
   2. The social sciences should not be pursued in the empirical man-
      ner (the models of empirical science must not be applied).
   3. The social sciences should not be pursued in the scientific man-
      ner (the models of science must not be applied).

Thus, there are multiple formulations of the naturalistic and antinaturalistic positions. Their careful distinction is a prerequisite for any rational
appraisal of the dispute comprising them.

THE ARGUMENTS OF
THE CONTENDING PARTIES

How do the parties in the controversy defend their theses, postulates,
and directives? I shall begin with the arguments employed by the antinaturalists, because, as was shown before, they are presently the attacking
side, whereas the naturalists have been driven to defensive positions. But
before I present those arguments, some criteria of classification need to be
made explicit. Again, one criterion will refer to the strength of the argument, and another to its substance.

With respect to their strength, the arguments can be classified into two
groups:

1.   An argument can be descriptive, and then it answers the question
"Are the social sciences methodologically peculiar or not?" Such an argument provides the evidence or illustrations for a descriptive thesis, concerning the actual difference between the social and natural sciences. Its
strength is limited, because it can justify neither a directive nor a postulate.
It says something about what is, but nothing about what can be or what
should be.

2.   An argument may be explanatory, and then it answers the question
"Why are the social sciences methodologically peculiar in the manner
specified?" Such an answer allows one to determine whether the given
peculiarity is essential and necessary or accidental and unnecessary. Therefore, an explanatory argument is much stronger than a descriptive one; it

permits one to justify both a postulate and a directive. Indirectly, it also says something about reality, for to explain why a certain peculiarity actually takes place entails the assumption that it actually does so.

The arguments can also be classified into two groups by the criterion of substance, or by the type of circumstances brought out to illustrate or justify a given position:

1. Descriptive arguments refer to the imminent properties of science. Thus (*a*) some arguments concern the peculiarities of the method or research procedure actually used; (*b*) some arguments concern the results of research; (*c*) some concern the applications of the results; and (*d*) some concern the peculiarities of the historical development of science.

2. Explanatory arguments refer, of necessity, to quite different matters. In order to justify a postulate or directive, or to prove that the matters under consideration are essential and cannot be overcome, it is insufficient to identify them, and to indicate that they in fact occur. Their sources, lying somewhere outside the science itself, must be found out. Such sources or underlying roots of observed peculiarities are traced in two directions. Thus (*a*) some arguments concern the character of society as a specific object of the social science: They point out ontological peculiarities of the object of study. And (*b*) some arguments concern the peculiar relations between the object studied and the studying subject: They point out epistemological peculiarities of the subject–object relationship.

The Case for Antinaturalism

Having presented the classification of possible arguments, I shall apply it now, for the construction of a comprehensive list of arguments put forward by the proponents of antinaturalism.

I. *Descriptive Arguments—Form: "How are the actual troubles of the social sciences, or their peculiarities in respect of the natural sciences, expressed?"*
   A. Concerning Research Method
      1. Experimental research in the social science does not meet the requirement of isolation with respect to the variables. Even the laboratory experiments are always carried out in open settings, because of the personality variables that can never be eliminated—the particular genetic endowment of experimental subjects, and the whole particular world of individual experience brought by the subjects to the most rigorously isolated experimental situation.
      2. Experimental research in the social sciences does not meet the requirement of free manipulation of variables. The scope of experiments

on humans is limited, either because manipulating is impossible, or because it is forbidden, for moral, legal, or other reasons.

3. Empirical research (i.e., both experiments and observations of all sorts) in the social sciences does not meet the requirement of replication. When repeating a study we never deal with exactly the same object; the circumstances of the research are also changed, if only because of the influence of the research process on the studied object.

4. In social research we make use of introspection, which is a quasi-empirical procedure consisting of observation directed at one's own psychological experiences and their behavioral indicators, in order to arrive at conclusions about the psychological states of other people on the ground of behavioral indicators alone. This procedure is notoriously deceptive.

5. In social research we make use of empathy (i.e., the nonempirical procedure of putting oneself imaginatively in another person's place and looking at the world with another's eyes). It is by such means that we reach actors' hidden psychological states: their motivations, intentions, goals, dispositions, justifications, and so on.

6. We explain the social processes and phenomena in the peculiar manner called the method of understanding, or humanistic interpretation (i.e., by specifying the meaning of activities for the people involved in them). The notion of meaning covers subjective intentions as well as the objective structure of social-normative prescriptions (norms, values, taboos) according to which the individuals act and which they experience as external. In both cases we usually adduce the assumption of rationality, to the effect that people act to the best of their knowledge about a situation and in line with their patterns of preferences concerning the expected effects and costs of their actions.

7. Social phenomena and processes are explained in the peculiar manner called contextual interpretation or functional explanation; that is, by specifying their role and place in the broader social and cultural wholes to which they belong.

B. Concerning Research Results

1. In the social sciences there are no strictly general or universal laws, but at best historical generalizations. Social laws are always limited in their scope to a definite epoch, territory, or whatever.

2. In the social sciences there are no deterministic laws, but only probabilistic or statistical ones. Social laws never tell about unexceptional relationships between events or variables; they only define statistical probabilities of certain events as likely to happen in the wider class of events.

3. Social laws are themselves subject to change. What used to be a

social law in some previous epoch may not be a law today or in the future.

4. In social laws there are no extralogical constants—i.e., unchanging, quantitative coefficients, such as the gravitational constant, the speed of light, or the mass of a proton.

5. In the social sciences propositions are formulated in vague and ambiguous language, close to everyday speech; they are rarely formalized or quantified.

6. In propositions of the social sciences there occur certain syndromatic, or else contextual, variables; i.e., clusters of related variables closely correlated with each other, so much so that they cannot be defined independently of one another.

7. Evaluative terms are commonplace in the propositions of the social sciences.

8. Theories in the social sciences are never of the axiomatic or formalized sort.

C. Concerning Practical Applications

1. Predictions in the social sciences are reflexive, or self-altering; that is, their validity is modified by the very fact of their being formulated and made known. Sometimes a valid prediction, by virtue of being made known, brings about actions preventing its fulfillment, and thus the prediction is falsified or invalidated (a self-destroying prediction). At other times a fallacious prediction brings about actions effecting its fulfillment, so that the inherently invalid prediction is validated.

2. Social predictions are always uncertain. Even if we have at our disposal the relevant laws supporting the prediction, we never have full knowledge of the significant initial conditions.

3. Practical applications of social knowledge are extremely limited, owing to a lack of know-how or of the power necessary for enforcing specific social arrangements.

D. Concerning the Historical Development of Science

1. The development of the social sciences is marked by a lack of cumulative efforts. Social scientists do not deal with any systematic accumulation of achievements but rather with sudden random leaps and chance discoveries—returning to the same problems and questions repeatedly, and starting each time from the beginning, in disregard of earlier accomplishments.

2. The social sciences are marked by a particularly strong interdisciplinary disintegration, and there is a striking plurality of opposing schools within each social-scientific discipline.

These are the most important arguments by which an antinaturalist is apt to defend his opinion about the difference of status between social and natural science. However, the mere fact that those two branches of science are distinct implies different things and can lead to different conclusions. Sometimes these arguments are used to prove that the social sciences lag behind the natural sciences. (A lag can, of course, be overcome by further development.) Such an approach is antinaturalistic at the descriptive level, but at the same time naturalistic at the level of postulates and directives. In this view, it is possible to make the social sciences conform to the model of natural science, and moreover it is desirable to do so.

However, an antinaturalist may also believe these differences to be essential, fundamental, and ineradicable—the inherent peculiarities of the social sciences. Then, he will reject the possibility of their eventual approximation to the natural-scientific model, and thereby he will also deny the fruitfulness of maintaining such a model. But in such a case, an antinaturalist is obliged not only to justify his thesis but also to vindicate the antinaturalistic postulate and directive. For this purpose descriptive arguments alone will not suffice. An antinaturalist must resort to explanatory arguments. There are at least ten important arguments of this kind that can be presented.

II. *Explanatory Arguments—Form: "Where do the actual troubles or peculiarities of the social sciences come from?"*

A. Concerning the Essence of the Studied Objects (Ontological Arguments)

1. The argument referring to the unique character of social facts: Each social fact is unique in its full concrete form. This argument is supposed to explain the peculiarities of the social sciences referred to in the descriptive arguments IA3 and IC2.

2. The argument referring to the normative character of social facts. Each social fact has its normative aspect, related to the network of norms, values, and institutions functioning in society and taken into consideration by individuals in their social actions. This is relevant to the descriptive argument IA6.

3. The argument referring to the complexity of society: Human society is the most complex type of reality, both as to the number of its elements and as to their variety—relevant to IA1, IC2, and IC3.

4. The argument referring to the systemic character of society: Particular cultures, or historically existing human communities, are unique wholes in which the properties of elements depend on their place in the whole, and the properties of the whole cannot be reduced to the properties of elements—relevant to IA2, IA7, IB3, IB6.

5. The argument referring to the eternally changing character of society: A society is a process rather than an entity; it is permanently changing and fluid—relevant to IA3, IB1, IB3, and IB4.

6. The argument referring to the relative indeterminateness of social

processes: Such processes are, in a way, emanations of individual actions, and in individual actions the factor of choice, dynamic assessment, free will, and so on, is always present; therefore social processes are, at least in some measure, undetermined and free—relevant to IB2 and IC2.

7. The argument referring to the intentional character of social processes: A relationship between social facts is intentional rather than causal. Sequences of social events are the results of the rational actions of men, their conscious plans, and their strivings, as well as the network of norms and values taken into account when actions are undertaken—relevant to IA4, IA5, IA6, and IC2.

B. Concerning the Relationship between an Object and a Subject (Epistemological Arguments)

1. The argument about the cognitive limitation of a subject: A person is a product of society. His cognitive potentials are linked with the process of socialization, always taking place in a definite era, culture, society, group, and class. Therefore, one cannot altogether transcend one's socially and historically imposed limitations of perspective—relevant to IA7.

2. The argument about the quasi-reflexive relation of subject to an object. A person is an element of society. Studying it, in a way he is studying himself. Social knowledge is always in some measure the knowledge of oneself—relevant to IA2, IB7, IC1, and IC3.

According to the explanatory arguments, the most important of which have been listed here, the character of society and the character of social cognition preclude the possibility of making the social sciences similar to the natural sciences—and thus the postulates of naturalism must be rejected—and for this reason it is futile to search for methodological models in the domain of natural sciences: thus the directives of naturalism must be rejected, too. In view of those arguments the standpoint of naturalism seems to be questionable. However, the naturalists are not apt to forego their position.

The Case for Naturalism

The naturalists can logically defend their position against the arguments presented above in at least four ways. In fact, examples of all four defensive strategies can be found in literature of a naturalist position.

The first strategy consists of demonstrating the antinaturalistic description of the social sciences to be invalid. The essence of naturalist's retort is "It is not true that the social sciences are as the antinaturalist describes them."

Applying that strategy, a naturalist would declare, for example: "It is simply not true that in the social sciences there are no general laws." And he would point to some propositions of learning theory (see Homans, 1967). Or he would say: "It is not true that there are no axiomatic theories in sociology"—pointing to the theory of minority behavior (see Blalock, 1970). Or he would claim that there are in fact some dependable predictions in the social sciences; e.g., the demographic forecasts. Or he would reject the assertion that laws in social sciences change, and maintain it is not that laws change but that their initial conditions are met only in some situations, locations, or eras.

This strategy is weak. It can be applied only against the obviously fallacious antinaturalistic descriptions, and thus prevails against only a few of the antinaturalistic arguments.

The second strategy consists in admitting the soundness of the antinaturalistic descriptions of the social sciences, but at the same time denying their relevance to the thesis of incompatibility between the social and the natural sciences. A naturalist is apt to say, "It is true that the social sciences are such as the antinaturalist has described them, but similar shortcomings and difficulties are also characteristic for the natural sciences. Thus, there is a non sequitur in the logic of antinaturalism."

On that strategy, a naturalist would say, for example, "It is true that the opportunities for experimental manipulation are limited in the social sciences, but the same can be said of astronomy, geology, paleontology, and many other natural-scientific disciplines." Or he would claim, "It is true that we often resort to functional explanations in social inquiries, but the same holds for biology." Or "It is true that quantitative results are not easy to obtain in the social sciences, but the same is true of geology, or zoology." Or "It is true that the research process tends to modify the studied object, but the same happens in physical research, and according to Heisenberg's formula it cannot be otherwise." Or "It is true that some social predictions are uncertain, but, unfortunately, so are meteorological and seismological forecasts." Or "It is true that the social sciences develop by leaps, but this has been shown to be true of the development of the natural sciences."

This strategy of defense enjoys great popularity. Its remarkable efficiency seems to depend on two considerations: First, the differences emphasized by antinaturalists are mostly differences of degree rather than of kind. Second, though the antinaturalists erroneously assume that the natural sciences constitute a methodologically undifferentiated, unified whole yet within those sciences there are immense differences of method and approach between disciplines, and even between specialized subfields within a single discipline.

The third strategy consists in casting doubt on the validity of the antinaturalist's ontological and epistemological claims about the social sciences. The naturalist would say "It is not true that society is in its essence such as the antinaturalist describes it," or "It is not true that the cognitive position of the student of society is such as the antinaturalist believes it to be."

Applying that strategy, a naturalist says, for example "It is not true that society is particularly complex, for complexity is always a relative trait, depending on the point of view and cognitive interests of the investigator. In any study, we always take some factors into account and ignore others. Laboratory studies of small groups bring social research close to natural sciences with respect to the simplicity of the studied objects. On the contrary, when physics encompasses a host of variables, abandoning laboratory simplifications in order to account for actual conditions (e.g., in technology), it approaches the cognitive situation of sociology, or social anthropology, with respect to the complexity of the studied objects." (See Beck, 1968.) Some authors go even further and turn tables with the complexity argument by claiming that society is in effect less complex than the natural world, because under normal conditions one can always assume that individuals behave according to the principle of rationality, an assumption that simplifies the research situation enormously (see Popper, 1960: 140).

In a similar manner a naturalist rejects the argument about the unique character of social facts, pointing out that all facts, including natural ones, are unique in some aspects and not in others. There are no identical facts in an absolute sense; any two facts can be identical in some respects, but they must be different in others. In the process of scientific generalization we pay attention to some recurrent aspects in a certain class of facts, and dismiss their individuating differences. The sociological procedure of research is not different in this respect from physical, chemical, or biological procedures.

Also, the naturalist attempts to refute the argument concerning the indeterminism of social processes. He claims that while decisions, choices, and definitions of situations do in fact play a significant role in human conduct, such conduct is only apparently free. In fact it is determined by the combined effect of numerous circumstances, such as the experiences that have shaped the individual's perception of the world, his inborn personality dispositions, various external, situational influences on him, constraints on him, and so on. It is true that it is practically impossible to grasp all these factors, but this limitation has to do with our actual cognitive limitations, and not with any ontological properties of the human world.

In all the cases mentioned for illustration above, the naturalist's defense consists in proving that the ontological or epistemological differences between the social and natural sciences are only apparent ones, and that the illusion is born of the limitations of our knowledge. What is not familiar to us seems to be complex; we tend to see something as unique when we miss the recurrent aspects; and those phenomena are undetermined for which we fail to find a cause.

The fourth strategy consists in recognizing the soundness of the ontological and epistemological characterizations provided by the antinaturalists, but at the same time rejecting their relevance to the vindication of the antinaturalistic postulates or directives. The naturalist says, "It is true that the social reality, as well as the position of the student vis-à-vis the social reality, are as the antinaturalist describes them, but that by no means precludes the possibility of studying society by the same methods as those applied to the study of nature. The antinaturalist's logic is fallacious."

Applying that strategy, the naturalist would say, "It is true that there is always a subjective ingredient in social facts. But one may conceive of the research techniques that will make possible the intersubjective, testable, empirical cognition of psychological experiences, by means of observable physiological, behavioral, and other indicators. We should develop such techniques and improve them, rather than surrender the principle of intersubjective testability and resort to empathy, introspection, and other intuitive, untestable research-techniques." (See Nagel, 1961: 406–415.)

In a similar manner the naturalist refutes the argument about the normative character of social facts. "It is true," he says, "that human actions in a society are directed by the prevailing system of norms, values, and institutions. But rather than explain human actions by reference to them, one should ask why these particular values, norms, and institutions are operating and not some other ones. There is no reason to abandon the attempts to reconstruct genetically and explain causally the existence or prevalence of the given normative factors themselves."

Also, the naturalist attacks the argument about the systemic character of society. He admits that a society is a whole in which each of the elements must be considered as part of the system and not separately, but he points out that it is quite possible to elaborate sophisticated and precise techniques of investigation and study (see Jarvie, 1970). Moreover, contemporary statistics, as well as the use of computer simulation for the study of complex systems, already provide the tools adequate for an investigation of social reality.

In the foregoing cases the defensive strategy of the naturalists consists in proving that the ontological and epistemolgical peculiarities of the social sciences, even if they are taken for granted, may certainly be a source of troubles for social research, but not of insurmountable troubles; all of them can be overcome in the future, and so they are extrinsic rather than intrinsic. Such a line of defense is very efficient indeed, because an antinaturalist can only persist in his assertion that no methodological innovations are possible in the social sciences—which recalls the declaration attributed to a US patent officer in the nineteenth century: "There will be no new inventions, because everything has already been invented."

INTEGRALISM AS A DIALECTICAL SOLUTION

It might be expected that we should now consider the validity of the particular arguments and counterarguments, pass judgment on them, and thus contribute a new item to the extensive bibliography of works supporting one or the other position. Instead I should like to show that the controversy itself is based on a fundamental misunderstanding, and by disclosing it put an end to the dispute, redirecting the attention of methodologists and philosophers of social science towards the important controversial and unsolved problems.

Suppose that the whole dispute of "science versus humanities" and the accompanying controversy of naturalism and antinaturalism were to be rejected and some new solution to the problem of demarcation suggested. That would mean that the new solution would be in some sense opposed to both traditional assumptions, to naturalism as well as to antinaturalism. Moreover, to be opposed to both assumptions means to be opposed to all that they have in common. Thus a dialectical method of overcoming the traditional dilemma must proceed along the following lines: first, the common set of assumptions of a higher order shared by the naturalists and the antinaturalists alike must be reconstructed; second, those assumptions must be rejected and an opposite set of assumptions of a higher order shared by the naturalists and the antinaturalists alike must be reconstructed; second, those assumptions must be rejected and an opposite set of assumptions specified; and third, the solution to the dilemma—the integralist assumption—must be shown to follow from the new set of higher-order assumptions.

Common Meta-assumptions

But is there anything in common between the naturalistic and antinaturalistic standpoints? I believe there are at least four higher-order assumptions that both the naturalists and the antinaturalists simply take for granted. Only if those assumptions are accepted, can the whole dispute be meaningful. And correspondingly, if I want to prove the dispute to be meaningless, it is enough to reject those higher-order assumptions. To clarify this point by a common-sense illustration: If I am quareling with a policeman about whether he was justified in giving me a parking ticket, the whole dispute has a meaning only if both of us know and accept the same traffic code (the separate question has a pragmatic character—whether such a quarrel is practically advisable or not; and experience teaches that it is usually not).

The four higher-order assumptions taken for granted by both sides in the naturalism–antinaturalism controversy are as follows: First, it is assumed that the division of scientific disciplines into natural and social is logically sound; that is, that the respective classes are internally homogeneous, and exclusive of each other, or at least that there are pronounced similarities among the members of the same class, and pronounced divergences between the members of the opposite classes. To be specific, it is taken for granted that physics, chemistry, biology, and astronomy have more in common with each other than, say, biology and sociology; and similarly that sociology, psychology, anthropology, and economics have more in common than, say, economics and physics.

Second, it is assumed that the methods that should or should not be imitated are to be found only within the class of the natural sciences; the source of methodological patterns to be accepted or rejected is located exclusively in the natural-scientific disciplines, inasmuch as they are older, more developed, more mature, more exact. In an extreme formulation it is sometimes claimed that only one of the natural disciplines—physics—is the source of the best methodological patterns. To put it metaphorically, there is a magisterial effluence from the natural to the social sciences; physics is the teacher, whether certified or not, sociology the diligent pupil learning his methodological lessons, whether for good or for ill.

Third, it is assumed that the methods or techniques of research have some autonomous value in their own right; that is, that they can be judged as right or wrong irrespective of any applications to which they are put, or of the vindication they receive in the research practice. Thus it is ipso facto good (or bad) to resort to experiments, induction, or statistics, or to formalize theories. Methods acquire an inherent value, and are not to be judged by their instrumental utility.

Fourth, it is assumed that the methodological patterns of the natural sciences, which are the positive or the negative point of reference for both parties to the dispute, constitute a simple, homogeneous, undifferentiated set, which can either be accepted totally or rejected totally, and one cannot borrow freely from this set such selected patterns as seem helpful.

The Rejection of Common Meta-assumptions

All four higher-order assumptions are, I believe, totally and fundamentally mistaken, and must be replaced by their opposites. This is recognized to some extent by several contemporary philosophers of science, whose opinions shall appear in these pages.

The antithetical assumptions are as follows: First, it is observed that the division of scientific disciplines into the natural and the social is most open to dispute on logical grounds, for the respective classes are neither as homogenous nor mutually exclusive as is often supposed. In the class of the natural sciences one encounters such basically different members as astronomy and biology, physics and paleontology, geology and meteorology, and their differences cannot by any means be reduced to the divergences in their respective subject matters; they touch much more fundamental methodological characteristics. The same is true of the social sciences, where history versus psychology, sociology versus archeology, economics versus ethnography represent basically diverse methodological patterns. On the other hand, there exist important methodological similarities across traditional borders: Modern psychology has much in common with biology, ethnography with geography, and—as somebody has said, in jest— sociology with meteorology (as far as predictive possibilities are concerned) and with astronomy (as far as controlling opportunities are concerned). Therefore, to assume a dividing line drawn between the social and the natural sciences is invalid and misleading.

For this reason several authors have proposed applying different criteria of division to the family of science—criteria that would take into account essential methodological characteristics instead of superficial differences in subject matter. Three suggestions seem most instructive.

Helmer and Rescher have introduced the distinction between "exact" and "inexact" sciences. By exact sciences they mean those in which the reasoning process leading to an explanation and prediction of phenomena takes the form of a strict logico–mathematical derivation, connecting the hypotheses with the evidence (1969: 181); whereas in the inexact sciences reasoning is informal and vague, relying on intuitively grasped facts, and intuitively perceived connections between the facts and hypotheses. Obviously, some of the natural sciences and some of the social sciences will fall into each of these categories. For example, contrary to uncritical commonsense beliefs, "Some branches of the social sciences are in a better shape as regards the generality of their laws than various departments of physics, such as the theory of turbulence phenomena, high velocity aerodynamics, or the physics of extreme temperatures [1969: 185]." The authors conclude: "It is our contention that this distinction is far more important and fundamental from the standpoint of a correct view of the scientific method than is the case with superficially more pronounced distinctions based on the subject-matter diversities, especially that between the social and the physical sciences [Helmer and Rescher, 1969: 201]."

Brodbeck (1969: 372) has argued along similar lines for the distinction between "perfect" and "imperfect" sciences. Perfect sciences, of which celestial mechanics provides the best illustration, are those in which the theories are complete (i.e., they take into account all the relevant variables), closed (i.e., no variables outside the explained system affect the course of its functioning or transformation), and made up of process laws (i.e., laws allowing for the computation of the value of any variable at any moment from the known values of other variables). She says, "Perfect knowledge is the ideal, actualized only in certain branches of physical science. Elsewhere, as in biology, economics, sociology, psychology and the social sciences generally, knowledge is conspicuously 'imperfect' [1969: 375]." Here we do not know all the relevant variables, we must always insert a *ceteris paribus* qualifier with an eye to unknown external influences, and we never possess the process laws. Again, the distinction proposed by Brodbeck cuts across the traditional divisions of the social and natural sciences.

The third, a common-sense suggestion to the same effect is provided by Beck, to whom the crucial criterion of division is the complexity of the subject matter studied by the scientific disciplines. On this basis the sciences may be considered as either the sciences of the "complex" or the sciences of the "simple": "The common variable that I believe will account for both the unmistakable differences and the current rapproachments [sic] between the natural and the social sciences is complexity of the subject matter. It is my belief that the major differences between them are due to the greater complexity of the subject matter of the social sciences, and that differences of method and interpretation of results are due primarily to awareness of this difference [Beck, 1968: 81]." But marked differences in this respect exist also among the social-scientific disciplines, as well as among the natural-scientific ones. And therefore "The social sciences, when they deal with simple subject matters, are able to approach the natural science methods, and . . . the natural sciences, when they deal with complex subject matters, appropriate social science methods [Beck, 1968: 81]." Thus, the proposed classification of the disciplines is not in accordance with the traditional classification.

The last part of the quotation just given provides a bridge to the discussion of the second assumption, taken for granted in the dispute between naturalists and antinaturalists, and to its consequent rejection. It is observed that the borrowing of methodological patterns is not necessarily restricted by the traditional lines, where physics (or what is believed to be physics) influences the method of the social sciences; but rather that, as Piaget says, "The services are reciprocal. . . . Several of the techniques developed in the field of the sciences of man had a reverse influence on the biological and even physico-chemical disciplines [Piaget, 1970: 12]." It was already the case in the nineteenth century, when several ideas of the biological theory of evolution were inspired directly by demographic and economic studies. More recent examples, noted by Piaget, include the methods typical of information theory, which had a decisive impact on thermodynamics as well as genetics; learning theory, which influenced some branches of biology; and econometrical techniques and the theory of games, which were borrowed by thermodynamics and physiology. He concludes: "If there is a trend to 'naturalize' the sciences of man, there is also a trend to 'humanize' certain 'natural' techniques [Piaget, 1970: 40]."

Third, it is pointed out that the methods or techniques of research have only instrumental value and therefore must always be seen as relative to a specific subject matter, specific problem, or even specific research question. The means effective for one goal may be ineffective or even detrimental for another. Kantor calls it "a golden rule of science that the methods and procedures of investigation should be those best adapted to the data and problems [1953: 280]." The same point is made by Rose when, opposing the so-called technique-centric approach in favor of problem-centrism, he declares: "No technique developed to investigate one set of problems may be borrowed without modification and applied automatically without adjustment to another set of problems [1954: 255]." And McEwen develops this idea in greater detail: "Any given science can only be as precise and accurate as its subject matter will permit. . . . The mode of analysis must be adapted to the specific problem which the investigator aims at solving, and the verificative techniques must be pertinent both to the relevant data and to his stage of inquiry [1963: 117]." Therefore, no methods can be accepted in the social sciences solely on account of their successes in the natural sciences, and conversely no method can be rejected *a limine* simply because it obviously fails in some of the natural-scientific disciplines. The utility of methods must always be appraised with a specific subject matter, specific problem, and specific research question in view.

And thus we arrive at the fourth, and perhaps the most significant, of the higher-order assumptions, which must be rejected in order that the problem of naturalism versus antinaturalism may be solved. To return to the basic question: What does it mean to apply the models of natural science? Apparently, to imitate the methodological characteristics peculiar to the natural sciences. But which characteristics? All of them? or Some of them? In my opinion, the controversy of naturalism and antinaturalism ignores the observation that the methodological properties of the natural sciences do not constitute a homogeneous set. At least three quite separate classes, or levels, can be distinguished among them. Consequently one can distinguish at least three types of models of the natural sciences.

The first level is made up by those qualities (or, if one adopts the point of view of the social sciences, those methodological models) that determine the scientific character of natural-scientific inquiries. Their sum total makes up the methodological model of science. Here all those properties are included that are presupposed or implied by the basic goals of science, as opposed to other forms of cognition. Those goals are usually defined as explanation, prediction, and control of reality. Therefore, the most general principles of scientific method—the logic of scientific explanation, prediction, and control—will belong at this level of methodological patterns.

The second level comprises those properties that determine the empirical character of natural science. Together they make up the methodological model of empirical science. Here all those properties are included that are presupposed or implied by the orientation toward contingent data (phenomena, events, or processes), as opposed to the purely analytical procedures of formal science. Questions of intersubjectivity, verification and falsification, testing procedures, the criteria for acceptance of hypotheses belong at this level.

The third level is composed of those properties that determine the natural character of the natural sciences. Their sum total makes up the methodological model of empirical science of the natural type. Here all those properties are included that are presupposed or implied by the properties of the specific domain being studied or the specific aspects of that domain that are in the focus of attention, or even the specific research questions asked with respect to that domain. It is the level of research techniques.

And now, the justification for the imitation of natural-scientific patterns in the social sciences boils down to the question of the type of methodological patterns that are so imitated. Keeping in mind the distinctions just introduced, we can appreciate Gibson's witty observation that the use of physical models in sociology is as absurd as accelerating the British Lords in the cyclotron for the sake of studies of the parliamentary system (1960). Similarly, we should have no doubt how to view anyone who would study small groups of people with a microscope, or delinquency with a thermometer! We should have no doubt simply because these examples are so extreme, artificial, and grotesque. In fact a naturalist often seeks to do similar things. He attempts to apply to the social sciences the methodological patterns belonging to the third (the lowest) level—those which are specific for the natural sciences, or for their particular branches, or even for some specific research problems within a single natural-scientific discipline. His approach is then technique-centric (Maslow, 1936); forgetting about his object of studies and the problem at hand, he applies a technique proven useful in some other field, and when the technique proves useless, he is apt to change his subject matter or redefine his problem, rather than modify his method of research. Such an approach amounts to putting British Lords into a cyclotron.

But at other times a naturalist is apt to borrow methodological models from the other levels. When, for example, he proposes to apply the nomological–deductive scheme of explanation in sociology, he does so not because the scheme has proved its efficiency in physics but because logically it is the most conclusive one. Moreover, the reason why he considers physics a highly developed discipline is precisely that the nomological–deductive scheme of explanation is broadly applied there. In turn, when he postulates the use of mathematical formalizations in sociology, it is not because physics is highly formalized but because the language of mathematics is the most economical, precise, and heuristically fruitful one. Finally, when he postulates the use of experiment in sociology, it is not because physics is experimental but because experiment provides the most convincing justification for empirical propositions. In all these cases a naturalist tends to imitate those properties of the natural sciences that make them scientific and empirical. To put it another way, he applies the models of science, and the models of empirical science. Such an approach seems not only legitimate but highly desirable.

The distinction between legitimate and illegitimate imitations of the natural sciences, depending on the level from which the methodological patterns are borrowed, is apparently recognized by some philosophers of science. McEwen argues: "It is a basic premise of this epistemological synthesis that social-scientific analysis should not be forced into a natural-scientific mold. . . . It is to the appropriate demands of the epistemological pattern of reflective inquiry, rather than to the inappropriate demands of natural-scientific techniques, that we shall turn for assessing the achievements of social-scientific analysis [1963: 213]." And starting from quite different premises Schutz arrives at a similar conclusion:

> The social scientist can agree with the statement that the principal differences between the social and the natural sciences do not have to be looked for in a different logic governing each branch of knowledge. But this does not involve the admission that the social sciences have to abandon the particular devices they use for exploring social reality for the sake of an ideal unity of method which is founded on the entirely unwarranted assumption that only methods used by the natural sciences, and especially by physics, are scientific ones [1970b: 18].

The social sciences should thus seek the source of their methodological models not in the methods of natural science, but in the methods of science and of empirical inquiries.

Toward a Dialectical Alternative

The controversy between naturalism and antinaturalism can be interpreted in the terms just presented, and found to deal with two separate issues. The first issue is the applicability to the social sciences of the general patterns typical of empirical science. The standpoints taken here can be signified by the numerical subscript 1, and they will read thus:

Naturalism$_1$ = Social sciences apply (can apply, should apply) the methodological patterns of empirical science.

Antinaturalism$_1$ = Social sciences do not apply (cannot apply, must not apply) the methodological patterns of empirical science.

That the second alternative is not empty can easily be seen if one takes into account those tendencies, now quite publicized, that are overtly anti-intellectualistic and that reject, under the pretext of an opposition to "scientism," any scientific or empirical approach to social phenomena. One of the spokesmen of this trend may be quoted:

> The social sciences are not sciences at all; describing them by that name, purposefully misleading, is an expression of the same ideological process which actually constitutes their whole meaning and essence. . . . The only general sociological theories, structural functionalism and historical materialism, are in similar trouble when it comes to inspiring empirical research. This happens because neither of them is truly a scientific theory, but both are class-conditioned socio-political perspectives [Freiberg, 1973: 2, 6].

The second issue in the controversy is the applicability to the social sciences of the specific patterns typical of the empirical sciences of the natural type. The standpoints taken here can be signified by the numerical subscript 2, and they will read thus:

Naturalism$_2$ = Social sciences apply (can apply, should apply) the methodological patterns of natural-scientific disciplines. A good example is provided by the physicalistic or behavioristic trends discussed in the previous chapter.

Antinaturalism$_2$ = Social sciences do not apply (cannot apply, must not apply) the methodological patterns of natural-scientific disciplines. (Here, all the schools classified before under the heading *new humanism* would fit.)

Both aspects of the controversy are logically independent: There is no logical necessity for making a choice on the second issue by virtue of making one on the first, and vice versa. The combined positions are also consistent and noncontradictory. Therefore, both dichotomies can be cross-tabulated as shown in Figure 2.1.

The combination of *Naturalism*$_1$ with *Antinaturalism*$_2$ will be called *Integralism*. The term is intended to convey the idea that each scientific discipline is autonomous, or integral, with respect to its specific methods, techniques, or research-ways—but only within the limits set by the general principles of scientific logic and empirical inquiry. Of course, this standpoint may appear in weaker or stronger form as a thesis, a postulate, or a directive. In terms of the formulations distinguished in the traditional controversy between naturalism and antinaturalism, the integralist standpoint can be explicated by means of the following theses, postulates, and directives:

I. *Theses*
  A. The social sciences are empirical sciences.
  B. The social sciences are sciences.
  C. The social sciences are not sciences of the natural type.
II. Postulates
  A. The social sciences can be empirical.
  B. The social sciences can be scientific.
  C. The social sciences cannot be sciences of the natural type.
III. Directives
  A. One should apply the methodological models of the empirical sciences and reject the models of nonempirical or extraempirical cognition.
  B. One should apply the methodological models of science and reject nonscientific, extrascientific, or antiscientific ones.
  C. One must not apply the methodological models peculiar to the natural sciences but instead should develop the methodological models that are autonomous for the social sciences to promote specific methods of human research.

As can easily be observed, the integralist standpoint presupposes the rejection of all those higher-order assumptions associated with the traditional dilemma of naturalism and antinaturalism. First, integralism implies that a division of scientific disciplines into natural and social is relatively insignificant, because at the level of general methodological patterns all the scientific, empirical disciplines are unified whereas at the level of specific procedures, techniques, and so on, the more concrete differences of the subject-matter, the problems, or the research questions become crucial. Second, integralism implies that there are no predetermined directions in which the methodological cross-fertilization of scientific discipline may proceed, if only it is restricted to the legitimate level of general patterns. If it happens that some general methodological pattern (for example, the

The Aspect of Scientific Logic

		Naturalism$_1$	Antinaturalism$_1$
The Aspect of Research Patterns	Antinaturalism$_2$	Integralism	Antiscientism
	Naturalism$_2$	Scientism ("Aping")	

Figure 2.1

deductive-nomological pattern of explanation) is more fully worked out in a particular discipline belonging to the traditional natural sciences—in this case, physics—it can be and should be imitated by the social sciences. But it may also happen that some other general pattern will be more developed in a particular social-scientific discipline; then there is no reason against transplanting it to the natural sciences. Third, integralism is obviously problem-centric, considering each method, procedure, or technique in instrumental terms and relative to the concrete subject matter, problem, or research question. It does not attach any universally valid evaluation to any of the methods. Fourth, by definition, the integralist position takes into account the heterogeneous character of methodological patterns, especially with respect to their level of generality; it distinguishes the general principles of scientific logic from the specific rules of procedure.

Therefore, integralism is something more than a new solution within the framework of the old dilemma. It rejects and overcomes the dilemma itself, considering it as illusory and misleading, and replacing it with a qualitatively new, synthetic standpoint. It is a typical dialectic resolution of a dilemma: It combines continuation with negation; it preserves rational components of both extreme positions while raising the whole dispute to another dimension; and it establishes its own identity, remaining distinct from both the traditional standpoints.

INTEGRALISM IN THE MARXIAN SOCIOLOGICAL THEORY

I believe that a close approximation to the integralist standpoint is to be found in the works of Karl Marx, and it is precisely for this reason that he did not fit into my historical outline of the traditional dichotomy. To be sure, Marx was never directly concerned with the problem of demarcation, and his point of view must be reconstructed from the context of his writings. But there are some arguments that make an ascription to Marx of integralist assumptions plausible.

Those arguments are of two sorts, direct and indirect. The direct arguments demonstrate that Marx accepted, more or less explicitly, all of the higher-order assumptions typical of the integralist standpoint as well as the assumptions that constitute the standpoint itself. The indirect arguments demonstrate that only the integralist standpoint would be consistent with Marx's philosophical outlook, and in particular with his ontological and epistemological commitments.

Direct Proofs

Marx would, I believe, subscribe to each of the four meta-assumptions found to be presupposed by the integralist standpoint. First, Marx pays little attention to the natural-versus-social dichotomy of scientific disciplines. Interpreting his position on this issue, a commentator of today ascribes to him the view that "the trend towards drawing a distinct line of demarcation between the natural and social sciences in one or another field of scientific knowledge is a monstrous anachronism [Kedrov, 1968: 104]."

Second, Marx seems to perceive the possibility of mutual interchanges of methodological patterns between the scientific disciplines. As Kedrov puts it "In the general range of interrelated sciences the relations between the natural and social sciences rest on a mutual foundation; both have something to learn from each other and have spheres where they can help each other [1968: 103]."

Third, Marx assumes the problem-centric attitude. It is self-evident in numerous criticisms he directs against other scholars accusing them of the abusing and absolutizing specific methods. In regard to this, a well-known adage from *Capital* may be quoted: "Neither the microscope nor chemical tests are of any avail when studying economic forms [Marx, 1954: 19]."

Fourth, Marx seems to perceive the heterogeneity of methodological patterns, distinguishing the general principles of scientific logic (the method of dialectical materialism), and the specific procedures relative to the problem at hand. Kedrov interprets Marx's position as follows:

> The prerequisite for Marx's synthesis of sciences is that the dialectical method is of general importance and can be applied in any field of knowledge, at any stage of the study of an object. Naturally, depending on the specific character of the studied object, this method must be corre-

spondingly concretised, but its general foundation and general features
are preserved in all cases [1968: 80].

Thus in all four respects Marx rejects the traditional framework of assumptions typical of the controversy between naturalism and antinaturalism.

He also accepts both component assumptions making up the integralist
standpoint itself: the assumption of commonality at the level of general
methodological patterns (Naturalism$_1$), and diversity at the level of specific
methodological patterns (Antinaturalism$_2$). Swingewood describes his view
in 'this way: "The fact that the social sciences are characterized by human
subjectivity separates them from the natural sciences, but it does not follow
that this constitutes the sufficient grounds for rejecting the scientific
method which analyses society in terms of objective laws and tendencies
and defines society as a structured, dynamic whole [1975: 83]." And Kedrov may be quoted once again, emphasizing the same point:

> The community of the natural and social sciences, however, only lies in
> the fact that the processes studied by them are law-governed, determined
> and bear the character of dialectical changes and motions. At the same
> time, qualitatively the laws governing them are by no means identical;
> they are specific for each category of phenomena. Socio-historical laws
> differ from natural-historical laws. . . . We find the concrete unity in mul-
> tiformity, and not an abstract unity completely depriving sciences of their
> individuality [1968: 82, 104].

But what is the substance of those common, general methodological
patterns shared by the natural and the social sciences, and what is the
substance of those specific, distinguishing methodological rules ascribed
only to the social sciences? The complete answer to both questions would
require a critical reconsideration of the Marxian philosophy of science, such
as is outside the scope of this volume. Instead I shall refer briefly to the
reconstructions proposed by the Poznan school of Marxist philosophers—
Nowak, Topolski, Kmita, and others. Into the sphere of the "methodological characteristics of science, which in the view of Marx and Engels
are shared by the natural sciences at a par with the humanities," Nowak
(1974b: 109–142) incorporates the following main postulates:

1. A proposition may be qualified as scientific only if its truth value is
    decidable on the basis of experience.
2. Every observation and experiment is theoretically informed and re-
    vocable.

3. The laws of science are either factual or idealizational, and neither are totally reducible to the results of observations and experiments.
4. The factual laws are accepted on the basis of empirical verification, and idealizational laws on the basis of concretization.
5. Ultimate explanations refer to idealized laws.
6. Factual laws have realistic referents, idealizational laws refer to the essential factors.
7. The development of science is leading asymptotically toward a growing approximation with objective reality.

If this list may be treated as an adequate explication of Marx's views (and Nowak justifies each of the reconstructed postulates by reference to Marx's writings), then it will cover all that was described in my analysis as the general principles of scientific logic—the patterns of science plus the patterns of empirical science—i.e., the domain in which the mutual borrowing or imitation of methodological patterns is fully legitimate.

On the other hand the authors of the Poznan group describe several procedures or directives that in Marx's view, as they deduce it, were applicable only in the field of the social, or humanistic, sciences. For example they extensively discuss the so-called humanistic interpretation (Kmita, 1971), the genetic-functional explanation, the structuralist approach, the principle of rationality, the principle of class-oriented commitment, and so on. Those will fall into the class of specific methodological patterns that cannot be legitimately transferred to other domains.

Marx, I conclude, accepted, even if only implicitly, all the tenets of the standpoint defined as integralist.

Indirect Proofs

But to make the case stronger I shall also apply the second, indirect strategy. The point is to show that the integralist standpoint is fully consistent with the Marxian philosophical position, in its ontological as well as epistemological aspects.

Two basic tenets of Marxian ontology are summed up by Engels thus: "The real unity of the world results from its material nature [Marx, Engels, and Lenin, 1977: 94]"; and "Dialectics . . . is nothing but the general laws of motion and development of nature, human society, and thought [1977: 122]." The materialist monism that claims that the world is built solely of matter, accompanied by the dialectics which ascribes a specific pattern and mechanism of transformations to the world, constitutes the unique ontological perspective described as dialectical materialism. This perspective entails several methodological claims. One of them is precisely the unity of the scientific method insofar as it deals with that common material and dialectic properties of the world, whether natural or social—or, to put it in my terminology, the unity of the general principles of scientific logic. That the materialistic standpoint at the ontological level is commensurate with the scientific approach at the methodological level seems clearly to be implied by Marx. This is acknowledged by Spirkin, who reads Marx's view as saying that "Scientific knowledge of the world is the knowledge of matter; its structure, properties, and relationships [1968: 88]."

At the same time Marx perceived the basic diversity of forms in which matter is organized, and this necessitated the finding of specific methods appropriate for their scientific study. This point is well summarized by Kedrov: "A consistent materialist, Marx clearly saw that the link and unity between sciences were founded on the link and unity between phenomena of the material world. . . . From the unity of the world, dismembered [sic] into diverse spheres, stems the unity of sciences studying each of these spheres separately [1968: 79, 82]."

The same conclusion should be reached if one considers the Marxian epistemological standpoint. Marx is a consistent sensualist (in the epistemological sense of the word) and empiricist—though not of the mechanistic brand, for he allows for the active role of the subject in the process of cognition. "With me," he says, "the ideal is nothing else than the material world reflected by the human mind and translated into forms of thought [1954: 29]." This means that all knowledge must ultimately be rooted in experience, and it applies equally to natural and to social knowledge. Therefore, the scientific approach in all the branches of science must be based on empirical methods. The general rules of empirical methods join the general rules of the scientific method to form the common methodological patterns of both the natural and the social disciplines. At the same time the content and structure of experience is different in different domains of the empirical world, and therefore the specific empirical techniques adequate for grasping experience in all its multitudinous forms must be varied as necessary.

To sum up: That the world is material entails the common patterns of science; that all cognition is rooted in experience entails the common patterns of empirical science; that matter is differentially organized entails the specific procedures of science; and that the experience is substantively varied entails the specific procedures of empirical science.

Thus the integralist standpoint is shown to follow as the logical consequence of Marxian philosophical orientation—of his ontological as well as epistemological principles. The dialectical solution to the dilemma "science or humanities?" is fully congruent with the philosophy of dialectical materialism. Rejecting the spurious and misleading opposition of the naturalistic and antinaturalistic standpoints and replacing it with the integralist assumption, Marx was able to solve the problem of demarcation in an original and fruitful way. As Andreyeva puts it, "If the place of sociology in the system of sciences were determined according to the principle 'or—or', and if these alternatives were seen as logically delineated poles of the strategy of investigation, it would be impossible to work out the status of sociology as a scientific discipline and, at the same time, as a specific scientific discipline [1974: 15]."

CHAPTER 3

Science of Man or Science of Society: Reductionism, Antireductionism, Separatism

The second aspect of the quest for a clear demarcation of sociology as a scientific discipline was its status among other sciences of man. It was no longer a problem of external relationship between the social sciences and the natural sciences, but rather a problem of the location of the social-scientific field among the social or human disciplines. The main challenge to the aspirations of sociology was coming from psychology, already established and accepted. The relationship between these two disciplines has been marked from the beginning by ambivalence, and consequently by a perceptible strain. On the one hand, to guard the intellectual and the institutional legitimacy of sociology, it was necessary to distinguish it precisely from psychology. Staats has commented on this problem: "Each of the social sciences has a strong tradition of resistance to consideration of its subject-matter in terms of the principles of another science. . . . In the social sciences, in general, most of the antipathy toward consideration of the science's events in terms of another science area invokes psychological explanation [1975: 561, 563]." But there is another consideration. It has always been obvious that both sciences, dealing directly with man as their subject matter, must have something in common, and that there must exist some overlap and, possibly, concord. Fletcher has touched on this: "There was never any doubt that some relationship of the most intimate kind existed between psychology and sociology, and that it was necessary to work it out. Indeed, all the great theorists had something definite to say about it [1971, vol. II: 467]."

The ambiguity resulted in this dilemma: Was sociology a science of man or a science of society? This has troubled sociologists since the birth of the discipline. What follows are the main theoretical positions taken in the dispute, with some selected examples from the history of our discipline.

THE ANTIREDUCTIONISTIC TRADITION

Auguste Comte: Sociology as an Autonomous Discipline

Auguste Comte placed sociology at the top of the hierarchy of the sciences, over and above mathematics, astronomy, chemistry, physics, and biology. The hierarchy itself was based on double criteria—chronological and logical. Each of the disciplines reached the scientific, positive stage in time sequence, one after another; and sociology had to wait longest for scientific recognition. But this sequence was by no means accidental. There was a particular logic inherent in the development of scientific knowledge, based on increasing complexity of subject matter. Each of the sciences could be developed only on the intellectual ground provided by the sciences, preceding it, of less-complex phenomena; but at the same time each of the sciences was autonomous. Each dealt with a specific subject matter and had to utilize specific research methods. Therefore, no science could be reduced to any other science.

No science but sociology could explain two typical properties of society: its historical character, the cumulative tradition made up of institutions, skills, knowledge, beliefs, values, and so on; and its organic nature, the close systemic interrelationships of elements resulting in some measure of societal consensus. As Aron puts it: "The subject-matter of the social science [Comte] wanted to establish . . . was the history of the human race regarded as a whole [1968, vol. I: 78]."

To grasp these specific features of society, sociology had to apply particular methods, historical and comparative. A distinct subject matter and a distinct method were all that was necessary to provide it with autonomous, irreducible status. As Comte himself put it:

> Social phenomena, due to their significance as well as the difficulties in studying them deserve to be comprised by the separate category. . . . In all

social phenomena the impact of physiological laws on the individual is observed immediately, but there is also something peculiar which changes the results produced by physiological laws and is derived from the mutual interaction of individuals; this is most complex in the human race, because of the influence of every generation on the following generations. The proper research of social phenomena must therefore begin with the thorough cognition of laws referring to individual behavior. But on the other hand, it does not prove, contrary to the belief of some physiologists, that social physics [sociology] is simply a corollary of physiology [1966: 143, 151–152].

Herbert Spencer: Organic Analogy as Incomplete

Herbert Spencer argued for the separate status of sociology on grounds similar to Comte's. Society, though in some important respects analogous to an individual organism, is a superorganic entity, an organizational whole, by no means reducible to an organism. "A society as a whole, considered apart from its living units, presents phenomena of growth, structure and function, like those of growth, structure and function in an individual body [Spencer, 1894: 330]." Those specifically social structures must be studied in terms of the specifically social functions they fulfill, relative to the social organism as a whole (the regulative, sustaining and distributive functions), and the specifically social patterns of evolutionary development must be discovered at the level of society. To be sure, social knowledge is rooted to some extent in biological and psychological knowledge, but it is by no means reducible to them.

Emile Durkheim: Social Facts as
a Reality Sui Generis

The most radical case against the reduction of sociology to psychology was presented somewhat later by Emile Durkheim. He expressed his standpoint forcibly: "We refuse to explain the complex in terms of the simple. . . . Every time that a social phenomenon is directly explained by a psychological phenomenon, we may be sure that the explanation is wrong [Durkheim, 1962: 104]." Explanation must always be carried out at the same level at which the phenomena to be explained are located. Inasmuch as the level of social facts is distinct from the level of individual human facts—motivations, reasons, goals, and similar teleological phenomena—"it is in the nature of this collective individuality, not in that of the associated units, that we must seek the immediate and determining causes of the facts appearing therein." This directive was applied both to causal and to functional explanations: "The determining cause of the social fact should be sought among the social facts preceding it and not among the states of individual consciousness," and also, "The function of a social fact ought always to be sought in its relation to some social end. [Durkeim, 1962: 110]."

The implementation of such antireductionistic principles can nowhere be seen more clearly than in the Durkheim's classic study of suicide, where suicide rates considered as specific social characteristics were explained by reference to the disintegration of human communities and the anomic state of the social-normative system, rather than by reference to psychological predispositions or deviations at the level of the individual.

As Aron says: "Sociology as Durkheim conceives it is the study of essentially social facts and the explanation of these facts in a sociological manner [1968, vol. II: 68]." And Nisbet is even more explicit: "The real purpose of the 'Rules' is to demonstrate in every possible way the fallacy of reducing the social to the psychological [1974: 54]."

Max Weber: Social Action
Viewed Antipsychologically

The three representatives of antireductionism considered so far had one trait in common: Their substantive research was focused on specific social wholes, and not on individual actions. But if there exists a verifiable tendency for such a substantive focus to coincide with an antireductionistic assumption, yet this link is by no means necessary. It is quite conceivable to combine a concern with individuals and their actions with antireductionism. Of course, in this case the antireductionistic assumption cannot be justified on ontological grounds; that is, by the postulation of some superindividual entities or social substances. Other arguments are called for. A singular example of the rejection of superindividual entities combined with the antireductionistic position is provided in the works of Max Weber.

In his view psychological knowledge is only, and at most, supplementary to sociological knowledge, and can never supplant it. "Through social-psychological research, with the knowledge of individual institutions as a point of departure, we will learn increasingly how to understand institutions in a psychological way. We will not, however, deduce the institutions from psychological laws or explain them by elementary psychological phenomena [Weber, 1949: 88–89]." The knowledge of internal, psychological processes does not suffice to provide an interpretative understanding of human action; i.e., to discover its fundamental, underlying meaning. Weber maintains explicitly:

It is erroneous to regard any kind of "psychology" as the ultimate foundation of the sociological interpretation of action. . . . The use of the results of psychology is something quite different from the investigation of human behavior in terms of its subjective meaning. Hence, sociology has no closer logical relationship on a general analytical level to this type of psychology than to any other science. . . . The rational deliberation of an actor as to whether the results of a given proposed course of action will or will not promote certain specific interests, and the corresponding decision, do not become one bit more understandable by taking "psychological" considerations into account. But it is precisely on the basis of such rational assumptions that most of the laws of sociology, including those of economics, are built up [1947: 108-109].

What is perceived here is a significant distinction between (a) the interpretation of a man and his actions from the external perspective of his relationships to the world, including other people (according to notions of rationality, the meaning of an action, and so on), and (b) the interpretation from the internal perspective of his mental, emotional, or psychological processes. Perspective a is proper to sociology, perspective b to psychology. Both perspectives are necessary and complementary, but never reducible to each other. As Fletcher reads Weber's position: "What is certain is that he agreed with all insisting that sociological explanation could not be reduced to psychological terms and any kind of compounding of them [1971, vol. II: 401]."

Florian Znaniecki: Individuals in the Network of Cultural Values

Another example of a scholar who combined an individualistic focus on social action with an explicitly antireductionistic standpoint is Florian Znaniecki. To him, both the sociological and the psychological perspective are necessary but mutually independent, and reduction is untenable.

> By conceiving society as a synthesis of psychological individuals we preclude the possibility of a rational solution of all particular problems which can be solved only with the help of common social schemes acting in and through individuals and yet existing independently of each of them. By conceiving the individual as [a] synthesis of social schemes, we preclude the possibility of the solution of all those problems in which the continuity of personal life or the uniformity of experiences in all conscious individuals independent of the social groups to which they belong are the necessary presuppositions [Znaniecki, 1919: 285–286].

Bierstedt gives a good summary of Znaniecki's position:

> He opposed any effort to deduce propositions about actions from psychology, whether the psychology was of the Freudian, behavioristic or any other variety, and insisted that social actions had to be investigated and studied independently, as independent empirical data, without any relationship to psychological theory . . . He would have rejected out of hand the reductionist tendency [1969: 26].

Franklin Giddings: Psychology as a Corollary of Sociology

A new dimension of the dispute was introduced by the founders of American sociology, and I shall refer briefly to one of them in this connection. Franklin Giddings advanced the point of view of Durkheim. Durkheim had claimed that sociology is not an adjunct of psychology, and Giddings extended this view to the point of holding that, in a sense, psychology is an adjunct of sociology. It is not only the case that sociology cannot be reduced to psychology, but that adequate psychology itself must always be informed by a sociological perspective. No understanding of human life is possible without the sociological point of view, and this includes the understanding of human psychological processes. A purely individual-centered, asocial psychology is simply impossible.

The arguments Giddings advanced evoke the social nature of individuals and the associational nature of society. When individuals are grouped together—and they are always together because an isolated individual is an abstraction, never met in reality—the level of associational facts emerges, which influences to a great extent individual minds:

> There is a group of facts of great interest to the sociologist and to the man of affairs for which the name "social mind" can with entire propriety and with great convenience, be used. . . . When, then, two or more individuals at the same moment are receiving like sensations, perceiving the same relations, experiencing the same kinds of emotion, thinking the same thoughts . . ., a state of facts exists in the population which evidently must be classed among facts of mind, and yet must be distinguished from the mental activity of an individual. . . . Certain mental products result from such combined mental action which could not result from the thinking of an individual who had no communication with fellow-beings [1898: 119–121].

Before Giddings, the antireductionistic claims had been limited to promoting the establishment of sociology as an autonomous discipline; with him the claim amounted to considering sociology not only as autonomous but as a fundamental discipline among the social sciences.

THE REDUCTIONISTIC TRADITION

When we turn to a review of reductionistic standpoints, a certain historical regularity may again be observed. They begin to appear later than the antireductionistic positions, and the possible reason may be that sociology had to become an established intellectual force before some sociologists could perversely argue that it could, at least potentially, be eliminated in favor of psychology. Something must firmly exist before it can be proved superfluous or redundant.

John S. Mill: Psychology as the Basic Social Science

John Stuart Mill considered psychology the fundamental science of man. Psychological laws are basic in the sense that all the regularities referring to societal facts can be derived from them. "If the phenomena of human thought, feeling and action are subject to fixed laws, the phenomena of society cannot but conform to fixed laws, the consequence of the preceding [1884: 572]."

The secondary, derivative character of social laws was argued on ontological grounds. Mill rejects the independent existence, and consequently the independent causal effectiveness, of any entities—institutions, groups, collectivities, societies, and so on—over and above the acting individuals.

> The laws of the phenomena of society are and can be nothing but the laws of the actions and passions of human beings united together in the social state. Men, however, in a state of society, are still men. Their actions and passions are obedient to the laws of individual human nature. Men are not, when brought together, converted into another kind of substance with different properties as hydrogen and oxygen are different from water.... Human beings in society have no properties other than those which are derived from and may be resolved into the laws of the nature of individual man [Mill, 1884: 573]

Mill describes in detail the logic of the reductive procedure, and here a very significant idea appears for the first time, the notion of *axiomata media,* or the "middle principles" necessary for the derivation of the sociological laws from the psychological ones. These are empirical generalizations providing a link between some sociological concepts and some psychological concepts (describing, for example, how changes in economic organization influence human motivation, or vice versa). Such principles must be included as premises in a valid derivation. If and only if such middle principles are provided will the sociological laws describing the influence of, say, economy on the forms of the family, be resolvable into the laws of human motivation. Mill proposed a separate scientific discipline that could formulate and test middle principles and gave it the name *social ethology*.

To summarize Mill's views in the words of Fletcher: "His fundamental persuasion was that all social phenomena are rooted in the nature of human individuals; that all phenomena of society are, when properly considered, phenomena of human psychology" [1971, vol. I: 207]."

Gabriel Tarde: The Social Outcomes of Psychological Tendencies

Gabriel Tarde is sometimes considered "the most consistent and extreme representative of psychologism in sociology [Szczepański, 1969: 247]." He centered his attention on the processes of invention and imitation, as the basic constituents of social life. Both processes occur at the level of individuals, and they are born of two universal tendencies of human nature: spontaneous inventiveness and blind suggestiveness.

The origin of all events in a society is located in new ideas and inventions conceived by individuals. Then, owing to imitations, the inventions spread out from the center, where they had appeared, to the periphery, where they are borrowed. As there are many simultaneous inventions, the consequent processes of opposition, or conflict, and eventual adaptation appear. The ultimate component of all those processes is, nevertheless, the interplay of individual minds, of human beliefs and desires.

As Timasheff tersely puts it: "All social phenomena can be reduced, ultimately, to the relation between two persons, one of whom exerts mental influence on the other [1967: 105]."

William McDougall: Instincts as Crucial Factors of Social Life

William McDougall searched for the explanation of social processes in the fundamental traits of human nature. In his view, there is a set of genetically acquired, hereditary tendencies to act in a specific way, which he labeled *instincts*. Instincts are common to human kind, and they provide the springs of all human activities. In the course of their actualization, instincts become associated with specific sentiments. Some forms of rational control of instinctive tendencies appear as well, and finally a self is established in the individual.

While the lower forms of social conduct are the direct issue of the prompting of instinct . . ., the higher forms of social conduct, which alone are usually regarded as moral, involve the voluntary control and regulation of the instinctive impulses. Now, volition or voluntary control proceeds from the idea of the self and from the sentiment, or organized system of emotions and impulses centered about that idea [1948: 151].

But at the core of all social forms reside human instincts, and the sociological explanation cannot be considered as adequate and final until it refers to those fundamental factors.

Vilfredo Pareto: Residues as the Roots of Human Activities

The reductionistic point of view was pushed further along similar lines by Vilfredo Pareto. For him, all social and cultural forms are only the expression of universal, enduring psychological forces. Therefore all the differentiations observed among societies and cultures, as well as all social transformations, may be explained by the differential distribution of those psychological forces in the human populations—by the variety of possible forms in which the psychological forces attain equilibrium. Constant psychological dispositions or sentiments are displayed in the recurrent features of those human activities that Pareto labels *residues,* and that are counterpoised to the variable rationalizations or justifications that people supply for their activities, called in Pareto's language *derivations.* An analysis of residues reveals the real motive forces of human conduct, and in the distribution of residues the explanation of social equilibrium, as well as of the cycles of societal change, is to be sought.

As in the chapter on naturalism, the omission of Karl Marx from the preceding review may be noticed. Marx's position does not conform to either a reductionistic or an antireductionistic category. The dialectic solution he developed entailed the rejection of both traditional standpoints, and consequently it overcame the dilemma itself, as misleading and spurious. The dialectic alternative to reductionism and antireductionism will be labeled *separatism,* and discussed in detail later on.

REDUCTIONISM AND ANTIREDUCTIONISM IN CONTEMPORARY SOCIOLOGY

The continuation of the dispute in contemporary sociology should be noted. As with other problems, the problem just considered was not solved once and for all by the masters of sociology, and so all its aspects have been vigorously disputed in our own day. Hovard has remarked that "recent developments in science have witnessed both reductive and counterreductive movements in the theory and practice of many disciplines [1971: 97]." In sociology it may be observed both at the level of research practice and at the level of theoretical generalization.

The Differing Trends of Empirical Research

To avoid misunderstandings, it must be emphasized that neither the particular techniques utilized in empirical research nor the particular substantive foci of the research presuppose the way in which the results will be conceptualized or theoretically systematized. Therefore, a choice of technique or of subject matter does not directly entail either the reductionistic or the antireductionistic approach. But even though in theory there is no necessary, logical link, in fact some techniques and some substantive foci appear more conducive to reductionistic than to antireductionistic interpretations. In an extensive study of contemporary American sociologists, Javetz has discovered some significant correlations between the research techniques they most often chose and the theoretical orientations they profess. For example, she found that among behavioristically oriented sociologists, the most favored techniques are the survey with a self-administered questionaire, sociometric tests, and laboratory experimentation (Javetz, 1972: 134). She believes that "sociometric methods..., experimentation and projective methods appeal probably only to those sociologists who are interested mostly in psychological factors [Javetz, 1972: 127]."

Similar factual trends may certainly be detected with respect to the preferred, strategic field of empirical inquiry. In particular, those who focus on small groups, or microsociological phenomena, are more often than not reductionistically oriented, and those who study the comprehensive historical processes, or macrosociological phenomena, tend toward antireductionistic interpretations. This regularity is noticed by Sorokin:

> Such an approach leads atomistic–singularistic [in my term, reductionistic] investigators to concentrate their research on concrete, perceptional, largely "microsociological" phenomena, because only concrete things can be perceived as single or separate variables and because many vast unified wholes are discreet and do not have perceptional concreteness [1966: 41].

Therefore, at the risk of some oversimplification, one may say that the bulk of experimental microsociological research is indicative of reductionistic tendencies, whereas the bulk of macrosociological survey research is a mark of the antireductionistic orientation. Both orientations coexist in contemporary sociology, and neither tendency can be said to prevail. Rather, one observes fluctuations in their popularity, due more to fashion than to principle.

A much more unambiguous picture appears at the theoretical level. Here, some contemporary orientations are openly reductionistic, others antireductionistic. Some selected illustrations follow.

The Psychological Reductionism of George C. Homans

The strongest reductionistic assumptions can be discovered in those sociological theories informed, at least to some extent, by psychological behaviorism. The logic of behaviorism is inherently reductionistic. Philosophers of science are unanimous on this count. Hempel, for example, observes: "Behaviorism ... in all its different forms has a basically reductionist orientation. [1966: 108]." And Luria apparently shares this view: "Behaviorism accepted as its foremost goal the resolving—or reducing—of most complex structures into their elementary components [1975: 82]."

In contemporary sociology, the most influential champion of behavioristically informed psychological reductionism is undoubtedly George C. Homans. He conceives of sociology, together with other social sciences, as devoid of separate intellectual identity, and ultimately reducible to psychology.

> Durkheim provided sociology with a theory it could feel was really its own. If I am right, sociology must give up this kind of identity. But it need not feel too badly; it will have companions in misery, if misery it be. All the other social sciences will have to give up their identities at the same time; the general propositions of all the social sciences are the same, and all are psychological [Homans, 1968: 6]

And in a different connection Homans has said: "Sociology is a corollary of psychology at least in the sense that social phenomena require general psychological propositions for their explanation [Homans, 1967: 60]."

In order to understand this declaration correctly, two matters require comment: First, what Homans means by "psychology" or "psychological propositions", and second, what he means by "general propositions of sociology." Of the first matter Homans has remarked: "They are propositions about the behavior of individual human beings, rather than propositions about groups of societies as such; and the behavior of men, as men, is generally considered the province of psychology [1967: 40]." This is a

rather unusual delimitation of psychology as a discipline—at once too re-
strictive, because psychology is certainly interested in a lot more than behavior, and too liberal, because psychology does not say all there is to say
about human beings and men as men are certainly studied by other disciplines, from different points of view. As for the second matter, Homans
considers the generality of a proposition as relative to a theory, understood
as a hierarchical system of statements ordered by explanatory (deductive)
relations. General propositions for a given discipline are those that close the
proposed explanatory system at the top. In sociology, such propositions
refer to groups, collectivities, and other superindividual entities. But in
Homans' view those propositions must be treated as intermediate or pro-
visional, because they themselves require further explanation. If the explanatory procedure is pushed to the limit, it will always appear that the most
general explanatory propositions from which the sociological ones can be
derived are not sociological but psychological, in the sense mentioned before.

Two sorts of arguments are provided by Homans to justify the reductionistic assumption—philosophical and factual. First, he takes a particular
ontological standpoint, holding that "the basic units of social behavior are
the actions of individuals and . . . that the actions are a function of their
payoffs [Homans, 1973: 550]." This is coupled with the claim that "the
characteristics of social groups and societies are the resultants, no doubt the
complicated resultants but still the resultants, of the interaction between
individuals over time—and they are no more than that [1974: 12]." And the
conclusion is obvious: If all there is in a society is reducible to social behavior, and "if the ultimate units of social behavior are men and their
actions, then the general propositions used to explain social behavior must
be propositions about men and their actions; that is, they must be what I
have called psychological propositions [1967: 62]." The second type of
argument is not philosophical but factual. Homans attempts to show that all
sorts of theories put forward by sociologists in the attempt to account for
social phenomena—whether structural, functional, or historical theories—
are inadequate.

> Of the types of explanation used in the more "social" of the social scien-
> ces . . ., the structural type is not an explanation, and the functional type is
> not contingent. There remain the historical and the psychological types.
> But the historical type turns out to be in fact psychological. By elimina-
> tion, then, it looks so far as if the only type of explanation that stood a
> chance in social sciences were the psychological [Homans, 1970: 319]."[1]

[1]This and all subsequent quotes cited to Homans, 1970, are reprinted from *Explanation in
the Behavioral Sciences* edited by R. Borger and F. Cioffi by permission of Cambridge University
Press. Copyright © 1970 by Cambridge University Press.

Homans' statement of the reductionistic position is the most developed of all, and it has had a very strong impact on sociological theory. But its period of prominence seems already over. The field is dominated by antireductionistic thinking. It may be illustrated by two quite divergent theoretical orientations. One of them is the structural-functional theory represented by Talcott Parsons, Robert Merton, Neil Smelser, Marion Levy, and many others (see Sztompka, 1974). The second is the revised version of exchange theory developed mainly by Peter Blau.

Structural-Functionalism: Society as an Irreducible System

As a contemporary commentator observes: "The theoretical approach of the functionalists in sociology has been that sociology should be independent of psychology, and it should concern concepts of societies, institutions, and social groups of various kinds [Staats, 1975: 563]." In functional terms, societies, institutions, and groups are viewed as specific wholes, or systems, irreducible to their parts (i.e., to individuals or single actions or the single results of single actions). Gouldner is most emphatic on this point: "The notion of a system is an intellectual fundament of functional theory in sociology [1959: 241]." Social wholes have specific, superindividual properties, and they display specific, superindividual regularities. An important category of such properties is composed of functional needs, requirements, imperatives, or prerequisites; and an important category of regularities comprises the ways in which those needs are satisfied by the elements. Generally, such regularities are conceived as the self-regulating principles that safeguard the fulfillment of functional needs, within a certain range of tolerable systemic disturbances.

Of course, there are several varieties of systemic-functional models, but generally speaking, any reductionistic explanation in which the social whole and the respective regularities are explained by reference to constituents and their behavior must obviously be rejected, and a functional explanation, in which every component is referred to the whole and characterized by its place in the wider systemic context, must be accepted. Thus, sociology is shown to possess its own, distinct domain of study, and to be able to attain laws and theories in its own right.

The Exchange Theory of Peter Blau: The Focus on the Social Organization

A similar antireductionistic conclusion is also reached by another influential orientation in contemporary sociology—the exchange theory, represented most fully by Peter Blau. What is particularly striking is that the point of departure taken by Blau in constructing his exchange theory was definitely different from that of the functionalist or systemic approach, and much closer to Homans' type of psychologism. "The problem is to derive the social processes that govern the complex structures of communities and societies from the simpler processes that pervade the daily intercourse among individuals and their interpersonal relations [Blau, 1964: 2]." Also: "The basic social processes that govern associations among men have their roots in primitive psychological processes [1964: 19]." But premises similar to Homans' led to a conclusion antithetical to his: "New social forces emerge in the increasingly complex social structures that develop in societies, and these dynamic forces are quite removed from the ultimate psychological base of all social life. Although complex social systems have their foundation in simpler ones, they have their own dynamics with emergent properties [1964: 20]." In a polemical context this thesis is formulated still more explicitly: "A basic assumption I make is that the behavior of organized aggregates follows its own principles, and the discovery of these explanatory principles does not require the detailed knowledge of the principles that govern the behavior of sub-units [Blau, 1970: 338]."[2]

Emergent properties appear already in the phenomena of interpersonal social exchange, and they are multiplied on higher levels of complexity, up to the level of social organizations, institutions, and global society. The focus on social structure—the study of those emergent sociological properties and sociological laws at various levels of complexity—is the proper domain of sociology, distinguishing it from psychological research.

> The raw material of psychology and sociology, as well as the other social sciences is the same. Their empirical data ultimately refer to patterns of human behavior. But this raw material is differently conceptualized.... The variables that enter into strictly sociological explanations characterize collectivities, not individual human beings ... The objective of sociology is to explain how collectivities of men become socially organized, and the underlying psychological processes must be taken as given in developing a system of theoretical propositions for this purpose [1970: 337–338].

This is a clear and convincing statement of the modern antireductionistic position. It seems to be gaining wide acceptance in contemporary sociology.

I have reviewed, citing typical examples, the positions taken in the dispute between reductionism and antireductionism, both in earlier periods of sociology and in the present. All the significant aspects of the dilemma

[2]This and all subsequent quotes cited to Blau, 1970, are reprinted from *Explanation in the Behavioral Sciences,* edited by R. Borger and F. Cioffi by permission of Cambridge University Press. Copyright © 1970 by Cambridge University Press.

science of man or science of society? were touched on in the discussion. It remains for me to analyze, explicate, and systematize them thoroughly in order to prepare for the eventual rejection of the dilemma itself.

WHAT THE DISPUTE IS REALLY ABOUT: AN EXPLICATION

As might be expected, the controversy over reductionism and antireductionism has generated a great deal of confusion. Thus, at the outset, I must clarify some of the pervasive misunderstandings. The discussion will begin by considering what the dispute is not about.

What the Dispute Is Not About

First of all, it is not about ontology, but rather about methodology. It is not the nature of social reality that is at stake, but rather the relationship between the scientific disciplines studying social reality. The question is not "What is really real—individuals or social wholes?" but rather "What is the status of sociology with respect to psychology?" The dispute discussed here is logically independent of the controversy over individualism and collectivism (which will be analyzed in Chapter 7). To be sure, ontological considerations enter into the dispute at various points, but they serve only to justify this or that standpoint, and are not immanent, substantive components of the standpoint itself. One must always be as clear as possible about the difference between what a given standpoint claims and how its claim is justified or substantiated—two quite distinct matters.

Second, the dispute is not about the status of psychology as such, but only about its status relative to sociology. It is a gross misunderstanding to categorize sociologists as reductionists or antireductionists on the basis of their proclaimed interest or lack of interest in psychological questions. The fact that a given sociologist discusses human behavior, learning, motivations, attitudes, and so on, and refers to those matters in his theories does not of itself make him a psychological reductionist. Similarly, the fact that some other sociologist does not mention psychological factors in his theories does not of itself make him an antireductionist, but at most attests to some limitations of his perspective. It is only when the former claims that sociology is actually, or at least potentially, redundant, because all there is in sociology can be expressed in psychological terms, and when the latter claims that sociology is valid, because its content is distinct from that of psychology, that they begin to qualify as a reductionist and an antireductionist, respectively.

The antireductionists are often involved in psychological considerations, but they treat them as complementary or supplementary, and not as being of overriding importance to sociological problems. Neither Durkheim nor Parsons doubted the need for a psychological perspective, and both contributed to psychology. Conversely, the reductionists do not reject all sociological considerations, but they regard them as derivative of psychology. Both Mill and Homans had much to say about society, and not only about individuals. To be a reductionist in sociology it is not enough to be interested in psychological matters; it is also necessary to assume that there is a specific relationship between psychology and sociology—the derivability of the latter from the former. And to be an antireductionist in sociology it is not necessary to dismiss psychology; it is enough to reject the validity of subsuming sociology under psychology.

Third, the dispute is not about verification, but rather about conceptualization and explanation. The issue does not concern the way in which sociological propositions are empirically tested, but rather the way in which they are theoretically conceptualized and explained. To be sure, sociological propositions often involve unobservables—theoretical terms having no direct empirical reference and needing to be operationalized by means of observable indicators before any verification is possible. As Mandelbaum puts it: "It is always necessary to translate such terms as 'ideologies' or 'banks,' or a 'monogamous marriage system' into the language of individual thought and action, for unless we do so we have no means of verifying any statements which we may make concerning these societal facts [1969a: 637]." And it is also true that those theoretical terms often refer to social wholes, and their empirical indicators to individuals and their activities: Armies, nations, ideologies are not directly observable, whereas soldiers, citizens, politicians are. They may be interviewed, questioned, and involved in laboratory experiments, and their behavior, attitudes, beliefs revealed. But it is only on the basis of some extreme verificationist theory of meaning (for example, extreme operationalism) that a sense of any statement is treated as equal to the results of testing operations, and theoretical statements are dissolved into the observational protocols.

This theory of meaning is certainly not accepted by any of the participants in the dispute about reductionism, and it is also almost completely rejected in the practice as well as the philosophy of contemporary science. There seems to be general agreement that if in the process of operationalization we attain statements equal in truth value to a theoretical hypothesis, yet those statements are by no means equivalent in meaning to such a hypothesis. Danto makes this point very clearly: "It may very well be that only through verifying by observation certain sentences about individuals, shall we ever be able to confirm a sentence about social systems. But this does not mean that sentences about social individuals are really to be understood as about that, the observation of which will confirm them [1973: 320]." Even though we can test any statement about an army only by studying soldiers, the meaning of the statements about the army is different from the meaning of the statements about the soldiers. And even if we could test a statement about class ideologies only by asking the members of a class what they really think, the meaning of the theoretical and observational propositions would not be the same. It is a mistake to confuse an indicator with what it is supposed to indicate. And therefore, it is also a mistake to consider the empirical verification of sociological propositions by reference to individual behavior, beliefs, attitudes, and so on, as tantamount to psychological reductionism. Otherwise, all empirically oriented sociologists would be doomed to inevitable reductionism, and the only way to save sociology as a distinct discipline would be through the rejection of any empirical research. Such a perspective is neither plausible nor promising.

In fact, all the participants in the dispute—reductionists and antireductionists alike—see sociology as an empirical discipline, and the question of verification is not the dividing issue. Rather, the problem of reduction is referred to the manner in which sociological propositions are formulated and logically systematized; that is, the possible links of the concepts and laws of sociology to the concepts and laws of psychology. The core of the matter is grasped by Blau:

> A distinctive problem of the social sciences is that the ultimate empirical. referent of its concepts is an aspect of human life, which means in my opinion inevitably, patterns of behavior of individuals, whereas the conceptual unit of analysis is not the individual but the social organization— the economic system, the political institution, the class structure, the organization of factories or of government agencies, or the social structure in small groups [1969: 120].

The problem of reduction is whether the conceptual level of analysis typical of sociology is ultimate and autonomous (i.e., it cannot be derived from any other conceptual level) or tentative and secondary (i.e., it can be reduced to some other level, in this case to the conceptual level characteristic of psychology).

Fourth, the dispute is not about the substantive focus of research, but rather about the methodological orientation toward the subject matter, whatever its particular properties. In particular, it is not logically coextensive with the distinction between microsociology and macrosociology. I have pointed out before that there is an empirical, contingent tendency observed in contemporary sociology for the reductionists to be mainly concerned with microsociological research, and for the antireductionists to be mainly concerned with macrosociological research. But such links are by no means necessary, and it would be a gross oversimplification to consider every student of small groups a reductionist and every student of large ones an antireductionist. The problem is not where we are conducting our studies, but what we are studying—how we conceptualize and explain our subject matter. For example, no other science is more reductionistically oriented than economics, dealing by definition with macrostructures. Yet Robert Bales, one of the chief representatives of microsociological research, while focusing his studies on small groups and their behavior in laboratory settings, interprets the group in systemic, structural-functional terms, postulating some superindividual imperatives for its operation, and looking at individuals not from the vantage point of their subjective, psychological experiences, but rather from the objective perspective of their contribution to the fulfillment of the postulated imperatives. Macrosociological studies can well be conducted in a reductionistic fashion, and microsociological studies can apply an antireductionistic approach. One must be on guard against mixing up their quite distinct characteristics.

The Concept of Reduction

Now that some major misunderstandings surrounding the controversy over reductionism and antireductionism have, I hope, been cleared up, I shall approach the matter from the positive side, and attempt to explicate the meaning of both methdological positions. Since the crucial notion is that of reduction, we must start from it.

Nagel, in a classic formulation, defines reduction as "the explanation of a theory or a set of experimental laws established in one area of inquiry, by a theory usually though not invariably formulated for some other domain [1961: 338]." In our discussion, reduction refers to the explanation of theories or sets of experimental laws established in sociology by theories established in psychology. As Addis puts it: "Sociological theory is reduced to psychological theory, if having defined the sociolological variable in terms of the psychological variables, the laws of sociology are deduced or deducible from the laws of psychology [1969: 325]." The methodological standpoint accepting this sort of explanation shall be called reductionism, and the methodological standpoint rejecting this sort of explanation shall be called antireductionism. This is not the only terminology to be encountered. Some authors speak about the opposition of "methodological individualism" and "methodological holism" (or else, "methodological collectivism," or even "methodological socialism"). Others counterpoise "psychologism" and "sociologism." I am choosing the terms *reductionism* and *antireductionism* as most neutral, and single-dimensional; for I need a term that refers solely to this selected methodological dilemma, which I have singled out for discussion in this chapter. The term *methodological individualism* has a more comprehensive meaning, and often covers ontological matters, which I wish to discuss separately; whereas the term *psychologism* carries some pejorative connotations and seems to prejudge the limited value of that approach. I would rather avoid any judgements of this sort before the substantive discussion.

The following are typical characterizations of the reductionistic and antireductionistic positions, chosen more or less at random from the enormous literature. Brown defines reductionism as "the methodological thesis that all law-like explanations of group behavior can and should be . . . superseded, in the long run, by explanations referring to the law-like behavior of individual members [1970: 301]." Watkins considers a rule of "methodological individualism" as asserting that "There may be unfinished or halfway explanations of large-scale social phenomena (say, inflation) in terms of other large-scale social phenomena (say, full employment); but we shall not have arrived at rock-bottom explanations of such large-scale phenomena until we have deduced an account of them from statements about the dispositions, beliefs, resources, and inter-relations of individuals [1957: 271]." Goldstein sees the "principle of M.I." as "a doctrine in the philosophical foundations of social science which demands that all of the concepts used in social science theory be exhaustively analyzable in terms of the interests, activities, volitions, and so forth of individual human beings [1969: 612]." Lukes conceives of it as a theory which "entails that all predicates which range over social phenomena are definable in terms of predicates which range only over individual phenomena, and that all statements about social phenomena are translatable without loss of meaning into statements that are wholly about individuals [1968: 121]." And Agassi defines *psychologism* as "the suggestion that we should not be satisfied with any explanation of social phenomena unless this explanation is the assertion about human nature and material circumstances [1973: 198]." Antireductionism, then, can be defined by the tenor of each of these statements.

It can easily be seen that there is a complete consensus as to the basic meaning of reduction and reductionism that centers on the notion of explanation. But agreement on the general definition of reduction does not preclude disparity in respect of concrete types of reductive procedure. It is important to specify what type of reduction is at issue in the dispute between reductionist and antireductionist standpoints, insofar as the dispute is carried on in sociology. As we shall see, it is a particular type that is commonly assumed here.

First, sociologists are concerned with heterogenous, or interdisciplinary, reductions, and not with the homogeneous, or intradisciplinary, ones. The establishment of an explanatory systematization of theories or propositions within a single domain, by deductive subsumption of less general under more general (or more universal, or more inclusive) ones, is the strategy widely accepted as the most effective means of theoretical development in any scientific discipline. Nobody doubts the multiple benefits of such systematization, and this is certainly not at issue between reductionists and antireductionists. In fact it is perhaps misleading to speak of this sort of homogeneous reductions at all, and it would be advisable to restrict the application of the term only to heterogeneous reductions, in line with the suggestion of Brodbeck: "Deduction is also reduction only when the deduced laws are in a different area from those that serve as premises [1969a: 287]." This type of reduction is certainly problematic, and it is with reductions of this type that sociologists have troubled themselves since the days of Comte. Hovard is right in saying:

> It has been with "heterogeneous" reduction that serious logical, theoretical and practical dilemmas have emerged. This form of reduction is performed on theories which are concerned with previously delineated subjects, supposedly composed of dissimilar traits and material, and therefore often possessing significantly differentiated theories and bodies of evidence [1971: 86].

The definition given before fits precisely the situation of sociology as counterpoised with psychology.

Second, sociologists are concerned with interdisciplinary reduction, and not with intertheoretical reduction. They quarrel about the feasibility of dissolving sociology in psychology, both considered in equally totalistic terms, and they rarely discuss the possibility of deriving of some selected sociological theory from some selected psychological theory. But what could it possibly mean that one discipline is to be reduced to another? Apparently it means that all the theories formulated in the former are to be derived from some of the theories formulated in the latter. Conceding the possibility of oversimplification, it may yet be said that every theory is built up of two basic components: concepts and laws. Therefore, to derive one theory from another would mean to define one theory's concepts by means of the concepts typical for the other, and to explain its laws by reference to the laws of the other. And accordingly, to derive sociology from psychology would mean to define all sociological concepts by means of some psychological concepts, and to explain all the sociological laws by reference to some of the psychological laws. Both types of reduction, definitional and explanatory, are obviously relevant to the controversy between reductionists and antireductionists in sociology.

But one point requires additional comment. It has to do with the meaning of psychology, conceived as the reducing discipline. It is self-evident that the feasibility of reduction depends to a large extent on the scope of the discipline to which the other one is to be reduced. And it is perhaps not accidental that the adherents of reductionism define the scope of psychology in a very comprehensive manner, whereas the adherents of antireductionism tend to view psychology as a much more restricted field. Reductionists often refer to psychology as the science of human individuals, the science of human nature, or the science of men as men. A very wide class of problems is thus ascribed to psychology, definitely wider than the class psychologists actually choose to deal with. On the other hand, antireductionists see psychology as the science of human mind, human personality, or human mental processes. Here the class of psychological problems is exceedingly narrow; in particular it excludes the study of human behavior or human action, the processes of socialization or education, the formation of attitudes and motivations in a social milieu, and so on. It is therefore narrower than the actual interests of psychologists. One cannot refrain from the suspicion that the image of psychology is tailored to the standpoint taken on the issue of reductionism, and that therefore we here encounter a classic example of begging the question.

Third, sociologists are concerned with reduction to components (elementary concepts and laws) and not with reduction to qualitatively distinct phenomena or processes (substantively different concepts and laws). Both sociology and psychology are seen as dealing with basically the same subject matter—sociology, however, with more complex aspects (social wholes), and psychology with more elementary aspects (individuals). As Brodbeck puts it: "Social concepts are macroscopic relative to psychological ones [1973: 109]," and accordingly social laws are macroscopic relative to psychological laws. The derivation of concepts and laws dealing with complex social phenomena from concepts and laws dealing with elementary psychological phenomena is logically possible if the composition laws are discovered and confirmed that "state what happens when several elementary situations are combined in specific ways. . . . The composition laws supply the empirical premises from which the deduction is made. Given the composition laws, the reduction of sociology to psychology is a purely logical matter [Brodbeck, 1969a: 299]." The dispute between reductionists and antireductionists revolves around the question whether such composition laws are given or not. In any case, the reduction of sociology to psychology is seen as basically different from, say, the reduction of chemistry to physics, or of psychology to physiology, where qualitatively distinct phenomena or processes, irrespective of their relative complexity, are interrelated, one might say horizontally and not vertically, by means of specific empirical connecting laws, cross-sectional laws, or bridging principles.

Now, if the reduction of sociology to psychology is treated as the reduction of complexes to their components, the crucial question is how those complexes and those components are defined. Three distinctions must be introduced here. First, to put it in metaphorical terms, the components of society may be conceived either at the atomistic level or at the molecular level. For example, the atomistic approach would focus on individuals, the molecular approach on groups, as the elementary components of a society. Second, the components of a society may be conceived in concrete or in abstract terms. For example, the concrete approach would focus on persons, the abstract approach on social roles, social positions, social actions. And third, the society as a whole as well as its component parts may be conceived in diachronic or in synchronic terms. For example, the synchronic approach would focus on societies and societal members, the diachronic approach on historical processes or singular events that make up the historical processes. The cross-combination of these possible approaches results in eight distinct types of reduction to components. One warning must be proffered: Speaking about the reduction of complexes to components I have always in mind the reduction of concepts and laws dealing with complexes to concepts and laws dealing with components. Reduction as construed here is a linguistic matter—a relation between statements, propositions, and so on—and not an ontological matter (the relation between actual objects). In the tradition of the dispute between reductionism and antireductionism, the main preoccupation has been with the atomistic–synchronic–concrete and the atomistic–synchronic–abstract type of reduction. But I believe that all other types, despite their neglect in actual controversies, are relevant to the dilemma, and must be included in its general explication.

The analysis just carried out justifies the conclusion that the meaning of reduction encountered in sociological discussions is quite specific, and limited in comparison with the general issue of theoretical reduction. In the context of sociological discussions, the dispute focuses only on heterogeneous, interdisciplinary, definitional, and explanatory reduction to components, conceived mainly in atomistic and synchronic terms. Reductionists accept this type of reduction between sociology and psychology; antireductionists reject it.

Varieties of Reductionism and Antireductionism: Theses, Postulates, Directives

Both methodological standpoints can be formulated in various ways, and consequently there are several varieties of reductionistic and antireductionistic positions. Two differentiating criteria seem most significant; the first refers to the scope of the claim, the second to its strength.

As for the aspect of scope, if sociological propositions are to be reduced to propositions about the components of a society, then the crucial issue is what properties of the components are allowed in the ultimate, reducing psychological propositions. Two possible candidates for the inclusion in ultimate elementary propositions are (*a*) autonomous properties, describing a component in itself, irrespective of any external links to other components, and (*b*) relational properties, characterizing the relationships of the given component to other components (its "place" or "position" among them). An example of an autonomous property of an individual is his age; an example of a relational property, his prestige. Or again, if we say of somebody that he is intelligent, we apply autonomous characterization, and ascribe an autonomous property; but if we say that he is a leader, a relational characterization is made, and a relational property is ascribed.

Now, it is not the same, on the one hand, to say that sociological propositions are reducible to propositions mentioning autonomous properties of individuals and, on the other, to say that sociological propositions are reducible to propositions mentioning relational properties of individuals. Remembering the warning formulated earlier, we may say that in the first case society is reduced to individuals, in the second case to individuals plus their interactions or social relations. Conversely, it is not the same to reject the possibility of reduction to components without relationships, and to reject the possibility of reduction to components with relationships. In the first case society is seen as something more than a plurality of individuals (it is easy to accept this view); in the second case, as something more than individuals and the network of their relationships (it is not easy to imagine what this "something more" could possibly be).

These distinctions are not mere hair-splitting: To quote two formulations of the principle of methodological individualism (that is, the reductionistic standpoint) as they are encountered in the literature, Homans (emphasizing autonomous properties) says, "Methodological individualism holds that sociological propositions, propositions about the characteristics of social groups or aggregates, can in principle be derived from, or reduced to, propositions about the behavior of individuals [1970: 325]." On the other hand Morgenbesser interprets methodological individualism as "a view perhaps best described as maintaining that all statements about social groups and collectivities are reducible to statements about human beings and, of course, their interrelations [1967: 160]." The prominent "of course" implies that relational properties are to remain at the center of attention. It is only with respect to reductionist positions of the second type (accepting reducibility to components-plus-relationships), and to antireductionistic positions of the second type (rejecting reducibility to components-plus-relationships), that a so-called "problem of emergence" can be meaningfully posed. The position according to which there is nothing more to society than individuals and their social relations may properly be called *anti-*

emergentist, and the position according to which there is something more to society than individuals and their relationships may be called *emergentist.* Thus *emergentism* is here defined as extreme antireductionism, and *anti-emergentism* as moderate reductionism. The two remaining positions are neutral with respect to the problem of emergence, understood in this way. Thus the criterion of scope has led us to the explication of four distinct formulations of methodological standpoints in the dispute over reductionism and antireductionism.

Another criterion may be introduced at this point. It consists in the strength of methodological positions. Three situations are possible: First, the standpoints may be phrased as factual statements describing the existing relations between two scientific diciplines—"Sociology is or is not actually reduced to psychology." Any position formulated along these lines shall be called a *thesis.* Second, the standpoints may define some specific relation between two disciplines as the principal, potential possibility or impossibility—"Sociology is reducible or irreducible to psychology." I shall use the term *postulate* to refer to a position put forth along these lines. Third, the standpoint may prescribe some specific relation between two disciplines as proper or prohibit it as improper—"Sociology should or must not be reduced to psychology." The standpoint phrased in this manner will be considered a *directive.*

The criterion of scope, combined with the criterion of strength, allows one to distinguish 12 possible standpoints in the dispute. As listed here they sum up the explication.

I. *Theses* ("What is the actual relationship of sociology to psychology?")
   A. Theses of Reductionism
      1. Sociology is reduced to propositions about individuals (extreme psychologism).
      2. Sociology is reduced to propositions about individuals and about relations between individuals (antiemergentism).
   B. Theses of Antireductionism
      1. Sociology is not reduced to propositions about individuals.
      2. Sociology is not reduced to propositions about individuals, or to propositions about relations between individuals (emergentism).
II. *Postulates* ("What relationship can obtain between psychology and sociology?")
   A. Postulates of Reductionism
      1. Sociology may be reduced to propositions about individuals.
      2. Sociology may be reduced to propositions about individuals and about relations between individuals.

    B. Postulates of Antireductionism
       1. Sociology cannot be reduced to propositions about individuals.
       2. Sociology cannot be reduced to propositions about individuals, or to propositions about relations between individuals.
III. *Directives* ("What relationship should obtain between sociology and psychology?")
    A. Directives of Reductionism
       1. Sociology should be replaced with individual psychology.
       2. Sociology should be replaced with social psychology (understood as the science of human behavior and interactions).
    B. Directives of Antireductionism
       1. Sociology must not be replaced with individual psychology; it is concerned with something more than individual psychology.
       2. Sociology must not be replaced even by social psychology; it is concerned with something more than individual and social psychology together (emergentism).

This enumeration brings our explication of the dilemma to a close. But before I can attempt to overcome the dilemma, and to show the alternative solution to the problem of demarcation, it is proper to review the most representative arguments put forth by reductionists and antireductionists in defense of their positions.

THE ARGUMENTS OF THE CONTENDING PARTIES: AN OVERVIEW

Obviously, the types of arguments and counterarguments utilized by both parties to the dispute depend on the strength of the claim that is defended, or challenged. The theses of reductionism or antireductionism can be argued on factual grounds, by reference to the actual practice of the respective disciplines. The postulates of reductionism or antireductionism can be argued on principled grounds, by reference to the possible relationship of sociology and psychology rooted in their respective characteristics. And the directives of reductionism or antireductionism can be argued on normative grounds, by reference to some ideal relationship between both disciplines, which is supposed to serve best the proclaimed goals of science. Thus the arguments in the dispute can be classified into factual, principled, and normative. I shall give a brief review of the most typical arguments in this order, counterpoising the arguments of the reductionists with those of the antireductionists.

I. *Factual Arguments: What Is the Case?* Arguments of this type attempt to answer the question "Is sociology actually separate from psychology, or is it not?" Let me review the contentions.

  A. The Arguments of the Reductionists

    1. All concepts and propositions of sociology are in fact reduced to the concepts and propositions of psychology. Sociology does not exist as a separate science in the substantive sense; that is, as a separate body of thought. At most it exists only nominally, inasmuch as some men dealing with selected aspects of a human being choose to call themselves sociologists and some university departments, research institutions, and so on, are sociological in name. This is an extreme argument that nobody seriously entertains, but I include it here as a hypothetical standpoint of some dogmatic reductionists. And in fact, antireductionists sometimes seem to believe that this is precisely what reductionists claim.

    2. The weaker argument of this sort says that some sociological subdisciplines, or some sociological theories, or some selected concepts and propositions of sociology, are in fact reduced to the concepts and propositions of psychology. At least a part of what is called sociology is viewed as redundant, and sociological only in name.

    3. The last argument of the factual type claims that of all the propositions that have been submitted up to now as general sociological laws, there is none that could not be reduced to propositions about individuals and their behavior, if one only tried hard enough so to reduce it. The potential possibility of formulating a sociological law sui generis definitely irreducible to psychological laws is not excluded, but treated as most improbable.

  B. The Counterarguments of the Antinaturalists. To counter the factual arguments of the reductionists two strategies may be utilized by antireductionists: Either they may show the facts posited by the reductionists to be untrue, or accepting the facts they may challenge their relevance to the core issue being disputed. Both strategies are encountered in the literature, and can be illustrated by the following counterarguments.

    1. The reduction of all the concepts and propositions of sociology to those of psychology is certainly not yet accomplished. Sociology exists as a separate body of thought, a specific intellectual entity, and not merely a nominal one. Only somebody completely unacquainted with the realities of contemporary social sciences could claim otherwise.

    2. The so-called reductions carried out in sociology do not meet the logical criteria of validity, and must be dismissed on this ground. "All attempted reductions fail or are incomplete [Gellner, 1969: 256]."

3. Even if some successful reductions of single propositions or particular theories have in fact been carried out, it still does not establish the reductionist case, because the real issue at stake is the total redundancy of sociology and its complete reduction to psychology.

4. At least some of the sociological, general laws proposed in contemporary theories can be shown to resist any attempts at psychological reduction, and thus a general reductionistic claim can effectively be refuted. For example Blain claims to counter the Homans' reductionism "by presenting a sociological proposition that is general, that cannot be deduced from psychological propositions, that explains, and that cannot be restated without residue as a set of psychological propositions [1971: 6]." His instance of such a proposition is the "high correlation between the degree of literacy in a society and its degree of industrialization [Blain, 1971: 7]." Another example of the same strategy is to be found in Blau, who suggests as a test case the proposition of organization theory that connects the level of structural differentiation with the type of coordinating mechanisms, and argues that it is fundamentally irreducible to any psychological statements (Blau, 1970: 335).

II. *Principal Arguments: What Can Be the Case?* The question is posed now in a different manner: "Is the reduction of sociology to psychology ultimately, fundamentally possible?" And the arguments adduced to justify each of the positions differ accordingly.

A. The Arguments of the Reductionists. Now, the arguments must substantiate the potential possibilities and not the actual facts. And for this reason they must refer to some more fundamental properties of the relation between sociology and psychology. Such fundamental arguments may be of two types: Either they may stipulate some specific logical relationship between the concepts and propositions of the respective disciplines, or they may refer to the domains of reality studied by both and expose the ontological affinities of those domains. Let me illustrate both strategies of argumentation.

1. Sociology and psychology meet all the logical criteria necessary for the eventual reduction of the former to the latter. So there is no logical reason why the ultimate reduction should be precluded.

2. In society, all that really exists is individuals, their activities, and the products of the activities. Therefore, all sociological laws must ultimately deal with individuals—which makes them by definition psychological laws.

B. The Counterarguments of the Antireductionists. To counter the principal arguments, antireductionists must show either that both the logical and the ontological circumstances mentioned by reductionists do not obtain, or that even if they do obtain they are not relevant to the dispute.

1. The reduction of sociology to psychology may be at most distributive (partial), never collective (complete). The logic of derivation allows a single sociological concept or sociological law to be reduced only at the price of some other concepts and laws remaining unreduced. The elimination of all sociological assumptions is logically impossible. "When any given institution is 'reduced' to the aims of individuals, this is effected only at the cost of introducing some other whole; which in turn can be reduced but only at a similar price. Thus, the social whole, the Government, can be replaced by an individual, Mr. Gladstone, when 'the Government decided' is replaced by 'Mr. Gladstone signed an order.'"... But this can be done only because Mr. Gladstone acted in his institutional capacity as a Prime Minister.... Whatever whole is 'reduced,' some whole is always left unreduced [Wisdom, 1970: 274–275]."[3]

2. The social wholes are superindividual and exist in their own right as a reality sui generis. Such wholes must be the subject of distinct concepts and distinct laws; namely, sociological concepts and sociological laws.

3. Even if it is granted that only individuals and their actions exist, it does not follow that all laws must refer only to individuals. Between the individuals and their individual actions there exist complex relationships, and the specific type of laws, so-called composition laws describing those interrelations and their outcomes, are sociological and further irreducible. "Planets may be conglomerations of atoms but no one would deny reality to planets. Likewise, crowds may be groups of individuals, but there are also crowds. Universities exist just as much as professors, students, and administrators, although the university is not a separable fourth thing but a name for relations among the other three [Brodbeck, 1973: 106]."

III. *Normative Arguments: What Should Be the Case?* The question is now phrased in the strongest terms: "Is the reduction of sociology to psychology desirable and prescribed, or not?"

A. The Arguments of the Reductionists. This is a different order of argumentation. It leaves factual ground and introduces axiological elements. Even if reduction is in fact achieved, it does not preclude the

---

[3]This and all subsequent quotes cited to Wisdom, 1970, are reprinted from *Explanation in the Behavioral Sciences,* edited by R. Borger and F. Cioffi by permission of Cambridge University Press. Copyright © 1970 by Cambridge University Press.

question whether it is desirable or not. Even if reduction is possible, still
it is not established whether one should strive for it or not. Normative
arguments require some comparative standard, or ideal, to answer questions of this sort. The reductionists have such an ideal of science in mind,
and defend reduction as instrumental for the attainment of this ideal.

1. Science should be unified. It is only by reduction that unification of
the sciences dealing with man can be achieved, and their disintegration
and specialization, with the accompanying lack of systematic accumulation, overcome.

2. Science should be parsimonious; that is, it should contain the smallest possible number of concepts and laws with which the greatest scope
of actual experience can be grasped. Reduction guarantees maximum
parsimony of scientific structures, limiting the effective number of
concepts and laws to those from which all others can be derived.

3. Scientific theories should have the form of explanatory structures
closed at the top with the most general laws, which themselves cannot
be explained further, and which explain all other laws. Only psychological propositions dealing with men and their "elementary social behavior" can serve as the most general explanatory principles in
sociological theories.

4. Scientific theories should be universal; that is, their most general
laws should be immutable with respect to time. Only propositions
about human nature (dispositions, intentions, motivations, the
mechanisms of acquiring experience, learning) can be treated as universal in the sciences of man.

5. Scientific theories should be verifiable; that is, they should possess a
definite empirical content; and the only observable constituents of
society are human individuals and their actions, including the products
of their activities. Science must guard against hypostases, reified entities of an unobservable, metaphysical sort; otherwise it will lose its
verifiable, empirical status.

6. Science should be practical; that is, it should deal with manageable
phenomena, which are amenable to manipulation, at lest potentially.
Only then can it offer practical directives for conscious and purposeful
control. The only phenomena in human society that can be managed
and manipulated are human activities. To be practical, the social sciences must deal primarily with them.

B. The Counterarguments of the Antireductionists. To counter arguments of this sort two ways are open: First, it is possible to reject the
proposed ideal of science, or some of its components. Second, it is possible to accept the proposed ideal but at the same time show that the
suggested means to realize it are either not necessary, or detrimental to

that goal. Consequently, the antireductionists challenge either the reductionists' ideal of science or the instrumental indispensability of reduction in achieving that ideal. The arguments are formulated in the following fashion.

1. Scientific disciplines should first of all be autonomous. They must possess their own subject matter, method, and goals, distinct from those of any other scientific discipline.

2. The criterion of parsimony and economy requires precisely the rejection of reductionistic attempts. Reduction results in the multiplication of atomistic statements, and the enormous complexity of their logical relationships. It is much more practical to formulate laws about social wholes, even if such laws be taken only as a shorthand convenience. "Elusive as such macroscopic explanations can be, they are infinitely simpler to both formulate and test than explanations in terms of the multitude of individuals [Brodbeck, 1973: 110]." "If there be, as in principle there probably are, composition rules from which the behavior of groups may be predicated, these are most likely of such compexity and difficulty that it may well be the better part of wisdom for social scientists to look for whatever imperfect connections may exist among group variables [Brodbeck, 1969a: 303]."

3. The view of a theory as an explanatory system is not the only possible reconstruction of a theoretical goal. If theory is understood in some different way, the search for the most-general propositions will not be a prerequisite of adequate theory.

4. To aim at universality of propositions in the social sciences is a basically misguided effort. All propositions in the sciences of man are historical, relative to time and place. There is no immutable, universal human nature, and therefore it cannot be discovered even with the help of psychological knowledge.

5. Observability is a variable quality. It is neither restricted to individuals, nor possible for all their characteristics. Some social wholes are directly observable (small groups, crowds), whereas some individual properties are not (motivations, intentions). Reduction is therefore no guarantee of increased empirical content and increased verifiability of propositions. As Lukes comments: "Many features of social phenomena are observable (e.g., the procedure of a court) while many features of individuals are not (e.g., intentions). Both individual and social phenomena have observable and non-observable features [1968: 122]."

6. Practical directives dealing solely with individuals and their actions will be most impractical: They do not take into account interaction effects, mass effects, combination effects—that is, the unintended and unpredicted consequences of the interplay of multiple individuals in

social settings. And this may restrict any practical effectiveness of sociological knowledge, or even render this knowledge totally useless. "Psychological laws may have mass effects, making the behavior of institutions or crowds different from that of individuals [Brodbeck, 1973: 107]." Reduction may in effect be detrimental to the practical value of research results.

I have enumerated several typical arguments and counterarguments encountered in the dispute between reductionism and antireductionism in sociology. Rather than judge the validity of each and draw up a balance sheet of merits and limitations, I shall attempt to show that the dispute itself can be done away with, and a new, more adequate and fruitful solution can be found.

SEPARATISM AS A DIALECTIC SOLUTION

The dialectic rejection of the dilemma *science of man or science of society?* will be carried out by the same strategy as in the case of the earlier dilemma, *science or humanities?* To recapitulate the main ideas of this strategy: If a new solution to the dilemma is to be found, it must be opposed to both traditional assumptions, reductionist as well as antireductionist. And to be opposed to both assumptions means to be opposed to all that they have in common, to all the beliefs that are included in their common area of agreement. Thus the dialectic method of overcoming the traditional dilemma must proceed along the following lines: First, the common set of assumptions of a higher order (or meta-assumptions) shared by reductionists and antireductionists alike must be reconstructed; second, those common meta-assumptions must be rejected and the opposite set of meta-assumptions specified; and third, the distinct alternative solution to the dilemma must be shown to follow from the new set of higher order meta-assumptions.

Common Meta-assumptions

But is there really anything in common between the reductionistic and antireductionistic standpoints? I believe there are several higher-order meta-assumptions that both the reductionists and the antireductionists simply take for granted. Only if those assumptions are accepted can the whole dispute be meaningful. And correspondingly, if I want to prove that the dispute is meaningless, it is enough to reject those higher-order assumptions, to show them as untenable.

The five meta-assumptions taken for granted by both sides to the reductionism–antireductionism controversy are the following: First, it is assumed that the initial distinction between sociology and psychology is logically adequate; that is, that the content of the concepts and propositions formulated within the borders of each discipline is internally more homogeneous, and externally more heterogeneous, with respect to the propositions formulated within the borders of another discipline. To put it simply, it is assumed that the concepts and propositions called psychological have more in common with each other than with the propositions and concepts called sociological, and vice versa. Both disciplines are treated as internally fully developed, possessing separate and identifiable bodies of concepts and laws. Only on such an assumption may the issue of their reduction arise. The antireductionists will wish to keep each discipline separate; the reductionists will opt for merger. But there clearly must be something to reduce before any talk about reduction can make sense. And only such things as are initially distinct may eventually be reduced to each other.

Second, it is assumed that there is a single, unique, predetermined direction of reduction, that this operation can be executed only one-way—from the secondary to the primary discipline. And psychology is always treated as primary with respect to sociology, with the justification that it treats elementary components, and sociology complex wholes. Reductionists accept the reduction of sociology to psychology; antireductionists reject it, but both sides take for granted that it is only reduction of this sort that is problematic. Brodbeck records the dominant point of view: "In reduction, the premises are generally microscopic, as physiology is microscopic relative to psychology which, in turn, is microscopic relative to sociology [1969a: 287]."

Third, it is assumed that reduction is an either–or matter. Only a complete reduction in which sociology is simply dissolved in psychology and eliminated as an independent scientific discipline is treated as the real point at issue between reductionists and antireductionists. It is a program of "sociology without sociology [Hummell and Opp, 1968: 205]."

Fourth, it is assumed that reduction is a matter of principle and not of contingent fact. Both sides take it for granted that there must exist some fundamental, unique relationship between sociology and psychology that is invariable with respect to the specific, substantive, or problematic domains of both disciplines. Reductionists define this relationship as one-sided dependency, antireductionists as mutual independence; but both agree that such an invariable relationship exists.

Fifth, it is assumed that reduction of concepts and reduction of laws always go hand in hand, in some parallel or interconnected way. In other words, it is commonly believed that there exists a one-to-one correspondence and a necessary complementarity between the definition of sociological concepts in terms of psychological ones and the derivation of sociological laws from psychological ones. Definitional reduction and explanatory reduction are treated as indivisible aspects of a single procedure.

The Rejection of Common Meta-assumptions

All five higher-order meta-assumptions are, I believe, mistaken, and must be replaced by their opposites. This is recognized to some extent by contemporary authors, whose opinions shall presently be cited.

First, it may be observed that sociology and psychology are in fact far from being so separate as is commonly assumed, and that from the inception of both disciplines, there has always existed much overlap. Psychologists, dealing in principle with individuals, have not been able to abstract from the societal environment, nor sociologists, dealing in principle with social wholes, from individual motivations, purposes, beliefs, and attitudes. Professional psychologists have contributed much to sociology, and professional sociologists to psychology. We note, for example, the impact of behaviorism or psychoanalysis, or learning theory on sociology, and the contributions of Mead, Parsons, and other sociologists to psychology. Besides, very often there is a much closer, substantive affinity between some theories formulated in those separate disciplines than between some formulated within either one. For example, there is a lot more in common between the theories of developmental or educational psychology and the theories of socialization or social control formulated by the sociologists, than, say, between theories of educational psychology and theories in the psychology of perception or between socialization theory and the theory of revolution. Any attempt at clear-cut delimitation of both disciplines must fail, and produce mutually overlapping and internally heterogeneous classes. As Fletcher observes: "Already . . . in the 'conspectus' accomplished by the end of the nineteenth century, this 'psychological dimension' of society was recognized and stated with great clarity as a necessary part of a satisfactory sociology [1971, vol. II: 468]." At the same time all authors "saw the psychological experiences of individual men as coming to be what they were within the context of changing cultural, historical systems of ideas, values, and institutions [Fletcher, 1971, vol. II: 470]," and saw their study as the prerequisite of a satisfactory psychology. And it is all the more true of later thinkers in both disciplines, at least as far as their actual practice, and not programatic creeds, are concerned. The dogmatic separation of sociology and psychology must be treated as an anachronism.

Second, it may be observed that there is no inherent necessity for reduction to proceed only in one direction, from sociology to psychology. There is no reason to conceive the science of elementary components as primary and the science of complexes or wholes as secondary. It is often the case that the behavior of elements is completely incomprehensible without reference to their wider context, and then, in a sense, the elementary microproperties or laws may be seen as derived from or reduced to the properties and laws of a complex macrotheory. Human behavior, beliefs, motivations, attitudes can often be understood or explained only by reference to the position of an individual within a certain group, community, social class, nation, and so on, and here sociological theories dealing with social wholes of this sort acquire a primary, explaining character. As Cohen puts it, "Many of the characteristics of the elements are inconceivable apart from their participation in the whole [1968: 12]."

The traditional emphasis on reduction to elementary propositions was directly entailed by narrow empiricism. As Hovard observes:

> Empiricists are adherents to the view of reduction with the macro-theory secondary, and the micro-theory as primary. Both psychologism and physicalism represent extreme, yet inevitable consequences of such a logical and pragmatic confusion. Both fail to recognize that what is basic or "real" in various fields of inquiry is a historical function of the language, theory and methods employed [1971: 88].

He points out this possibility: "Composition-laws concerning the organization of a particular phenomenon . . . focused on a macroscopic domain, might be able to explain the laws operating at a lower level and studied by a separate, 'microscopic' discipline" [Hovard, 1971: 88]." A similar possibility is acknowledged by Luria, who distinguishes a "downward-oriented" reduction to the components from an "upward-oriented" reduction to the wholes (1975: 83). Staats makes the same point: "The general point is that in a real hierarchical theory there is intimate interaction between adjacent theory levels. This interaction involves influence in both directions, not a dominance or preeminence of one over the other [1975: 567]." If those distinctions are taken into account, four varieties of the standpoints relevant to the dispute may be singled out. First, the position accepting "downward" reduction—psychological reductionism. Second, the position rejecting the "downward" reduction—sociological antireductionism. Third, the position accepting "upward" reduction—sociological reductionism. Fourth, the position rejecting "upward" reduction—psychological antireductionism. Traditionally the dispute was assumed to deal only with two possibilities—psychological reductionism and sociological antireductionism. Now it is obvious that two additional standpoints are equally possible, one called "sociological reductionism" and another "psychological antireductionism." Reduction is seen as a multidirectional and not a unidirectional procedure.

Third, it may be doubted whether the reduction of sociology to psychology must really be treated as tantamount to the total elimination of the former. Instead, a more moderate claim to partial mutual reduction and partial independence may be put forth, according to which some theories of sociology may be reduced to some theories of psychology, or vice versa, whereas some other theories would remain basically sociological and irreducible to psychology, and some basically psychological and irreducible to sociology. The idea of a differential readiness for reduction in various sub-disciplines or problem areas of the social sciences is expressed by Staats: "While certain parts of sociology or anthropology may be concerned with a conception of man, with principles of human behavior, with a behavioral philosophy of science, with research methods on aspects of human behavior, and so on, there are other areas where these matters are not of immediate concern [1975: 579]."

Fourth, it may equally be doubted whether there exists any inherent, necessary, essential relationship of dependence or independence between both disciplines. Instead, it may be suggested that both disciplines can be treated as dependent or independent in view of a concrete problem studied and the concrete approach taken by the student. Then, the interdisciplinary relationship is seen as a matter of contingent fact or methodological fruitfulness, and not as a matter of principle. Such a standpoint seems to be taken by Brodbeck:

> If we knew everything . . . we should be able to say whether or not there was a deductive relationship between our physics, our psychology and our sociology. It would depend upon the facts. But our philosophers, reductionists and antireductionists alike, make assertions about what must be the case, not about what merely happens, as a matter of fact, to be the case. . . . In some instances, laws are closer at hand if the scientist sticks to the macroscopic level of the complex concept. In other instances, the microscopic or psychological approach might be more fruitful, in still others a combination of these approaches [1973: 93, 110].

A similar, liberal approach is a component of the view Wisdom advances under the label *transindividualism*:

> Both individuals and the independent power of groups are factors in explaining a social phenomenon; in some cases one factor will be the greater influence, in other cases the other. . . . Transindividualism allows equal weight in principle, or any proportion of weights, to individuals or the societal facts, in governing the course of individual life in a group or society [1970: 295].

One more example of the same insight may be found in the so-called "method of coduction" proposed by Kurtz:

> Coduction refers to mutually reinforcing accounts of how and why an event occurs. To coduce is not to reduce to one explanatory principle, law, or theory, but rather to sets of correlative principles. There are many factors that will explain the given event, and many levels of interpretation.... Coduction does not deny that we may be able to find comprehensive theories in a basic science, nor even that connecting theories on higher levels might be attainable, but it does not prejudge either directive on a priori grounds [1965: 67, 77].

The fifth and last point is perhaps most significant of all. Definitional reduction of concepts and explanatory reduction of laws may be interpreted as separate and at least partly independent procedures. Their substance and their logic are seen as basically distinct. Israel expresses the relevant divergences:

> Reductionism can refer to two completely different problems: (*a*) definition in individual terms, (*b*) laws of sociology deduced from the laws of psychology. The first concerns the description of social events. It answers the question what social events are and what their identifying characteristics are. The second type of reductionism concerns the explanation of social events. It answers the question why the described events occur and tries to formulate generalizations and laws [1972: 149].

It is not the same to render the meaning of sociological terms by definitional reference to psychological (individualistically oriented) terms and to explain the contingent laws discovered in sociology by contingent laws established in psychology. The possibility of definitional reduction does not necessitate or preclude the possibility of explanatory reduction; for to carry out the latter one must also possess composition laws describing the mass effects of individual phenomena, and the existence of such laws, as well as the knowledge of them, is a matter of empirical fact, not definitional convention. Brodbeck makes this point: "The denial of descriptive emergence does not entail the denial of explanatory emergence.... It is logically possible that, irrespective of definitional reduction, we may have perfect knowledge of society, in the sense of having a process theory whose laws contain only macroscopic or group variables [1969a: 302]."

Toward a Dialectical Alternative

If Brodbeck's view is accepted, then it becomes obvious that in the dispute between reductionism and antireductionism two distinct and independently variable aspects are intermixed. One may be called the aspect of meaning; it refers to the question whether sociological concepts ultimately denote individuals (their activities, the products of their activities), or rather some entities of superindividual nature. The second may be called the aspect of explanation; it refers to the question whether sociological laws can be deduced from psychological laws. Distinct answers are possible to both questions. The positions obtained as answers to the first question may be marked by the numerical subscript "1", and they will read as follows:

Reductionism$_1$ = the meaning of all sociological terms (their denotation) can be rendered by reference to the terms signifying individuals, their activities, the products of their activities. (Sociological concepts and propositions are about individuals.)

Antireductionism$_1$ = sociological terms refer to superindividual entities (as their denotation), and therefore their meaning cannot be rendered with the help of exclusively individualistic terms.

The positions obtained as answers to the second question may be marked by the numerical subscript 2, and they will read as follows:

Reductionism$_2$ = sociological laws are derivable from psychological laws by means of the available composition laws.

Antireductionism$_2$ = sociological laws are not derivable from psychological laws, because the necessary composition laws are unavailable.

As was already emphasized, both aspects of the controversy are logically independent; there is no logical necessity for taking a particular decision on the second issue, by virtue of taking some decision on the first, and vice versa. The combined positions may be formulated by means of cross-tabulation, without the risk of logical inconsistency (see Figure 3.1).

The combination of Reductionism$_1$ and Antireductionism$_2$ produces a specific standpoint, which will be called *Separatism*. The term is adopted to convey the idea that despite the fact that both sociology and psychology ultimately refer to the same subject matter: men, their activities, the products of their activities, and hence the sociological concepts have a common denotation with the psychological ones; both disciplines are basically separate and distinct in the content of their propositions. Gellner has expressed the main idea of this standpoint cogently: "Perhaps, in the end, there is agreement to this extent: (human) history *is* about chaps—and nothing else. But perhaps this should be written: History is *about* chaps. It does not follow that its explanations are always in terms of chaps. Societies are what people do, but social scientists are not biographers *en grande serie* [1969: 268]."

The Aspect of Meaning

	Reductionism₁	Antireductionism₁
Antireductionism₂	Separatism	Isolationism
Reductionism₂	Destructionism	

The Aspect of Explanation

Figure 3.1

But where does the distinctiveness of laws reside, if not in the distinctiveness of the ultimate subject matter? Here the crucial idea of the whole separatist standpoint is to be spotted. The laws of psychology deal with individuals and their actions from an internal perspective. They describe the internal mechanism of individual functioning and the internal structure of individual human actions. The laws of sociology deal with masses of individuals and the plurality of individual actions. Individuals and their actions are not perceived as isolated, but rather as closely interrelated. There is a certain network of those interrelations, a particular structure external to acting individuals, even though ultimately produced by their actions. Those interrelations of individuals and interrelations of actions (interactions) are described by sociological laws. To be sure, interrelations obtain between human beings, and therefore the laws of interrelations refer to human beings and nothing else; but they say something else, and something more than can be said of the individuals participating in the interrelations. They describe the composition effects or mass effects, or "systemic-organization effects" (Hovard, 1971: 89) of the multiple, combined activities of the pluralities of people. This external, interpersonal perspective of sociology cannot be translated without residue into the internal, intrapersonal perspective of psychology. As Blau comments: "There is nothing wrong with studying individual behavior, of course, but it is not the same as studying the characteristics of social structures [1969: 127]."

The standpoint of separatism may appear in a weaker or a stronger form, as a thesis, a postulate, or a directive. Returning to the formulations of the standpoints in the traditional controversy between reductionism and antireductionism, one may grasp the crucial ideas of separatism by means of the set of following assumptions:

I. *Theses*

A₂. Sociology is reduced to propositions about individuals and about relations between individuals (antiemergenism).

B₁. Sociology is not reduced to propositions about individuals per se.

II. *Postulates*

A₂. Sociology may be reduced to propositions about individuals and relations between individuals.

B₁. Sociology cannot be reduced to the propositions about individuals per se.

III. *Directives*

A₂. Sociology should be integrated with social psychology (understood as the science of human interactions).

B₁. Sociology must not be replaced with individual psychology.

As can easily be shown the separatist position presupposes the rejection of all those meta-assumptions associated with the traditional dilemma of reductionism and antireductionism. First, an organic link between sociological and psychological perspectives is acknowledged, but with due regard given to their differences. Neither the view merging them both together, nor the view isolating them and claiming complete autonomy for each, is acceptable any longer. Second, reduction is allowed to proceed in any direction, either from sociology to psychology or the other way round, both downward and upward, as the concrete problem may require. Third, partial mutual reductions of selected theories, or even of single propositions, do not destroy the identity and specificity of sociology and psychology. Both have different foci, different perspectives; sociology focuses on the external interrelations of human phenomena, psychology on the internal mechanisms of their operation. Fourth, reduction is seen as a pragmatically useful procedure, and not as a mandated principle. It is adopted or dismissed on the basis of purely instrumental considerations and expected fruitfulness for theory construction, depending on the concrete subject matter and specific problem being studied. Fifth, owing to the logic of its construction, the separatist standpoint takes into account the difference between definitional reduction and explanatory reduction, and acknowledges the possibility of independent variation of those procedures.

Therefore separatism must be treated as something more than a new solution within the framework of the old dilemma. It rejects and overcomes the dilemma itself, considering it as illusory and misleading, and replacing it with a qualitatively new, synthetic standpoint. It is a typical dialectic resolution of a dilemma, inasmuch as it combines continuation with negation, rescuing some rational components of both extreme positions, and rejecting the one-sided absolutization of either. It uplifts the whole debate into another dimension, providing a solution qualitatively different from either of the traditional standpoints, and it avoids the intellectual chaos they necessitate.

SEPARATISM IN MARXIAN
SOCIOLOGICAL THEORY

I believe that a close approximation to the separatist standpoint is to be found in the works of Karl Marx, and it is precisely for this reason that he did not fit into my historical outline written in terms of the traditional dichotomy. Of course, Marx was not a philosopher of science and he did not concern himself directly with the problem of reduction. It would be hopeless to search for any statements dealing with this matter in his works. Therefore, the most one can do is "to find an interpretation which fits the spirit of the man's work, and to realize at the same time that it is probably futile to expect to find any interpretation which can account for everything the man said [Addis, 1969: 319]." It seems to me that separatism "fits the spirit" of Marx's work much better than any of the traditional standpoints, and to justify this claim I propose two sorts of arguments. The direct arguments consist of the suggestion that Marx accepted implicitly all of the meta-assumptions presupposed by the separatist standpoint, and was opposed to the meta-assumptions presupposed by both traditional standpoints, and also that he accepted implicitly all the constitutive assumptions of the separatist standpoint itself. The indirect arguments consist of the proof that only the separatist standpoint is consistent with Marx's more general philosophical outlook, and in particular with his ontological and epistemological commitments.

Direct Proofs

We shall begin with the direct strategy, and examine the higher-order assumptions typical of the separatist standpoint once again. First, it seems that Marx was never particularly concerned with the classification of the sciences into neat pigeonholes; he did not bother himself with the drawing of clear-cut borders between the scientific disciplines. His approach was definitely interdisciplinary. He was predominantly problem-oriented, wished to solve the questions that appeared to him as significant for ethical, practical, or political reasons, and never hesitated to venture into all possible realms of knowledge in search of an adequate answer. He did not want to construct a separate science of society, which was an ambition of many nineteenth-century masters, but rather wanted to discover the laws of motion operating in the social world, drawing from whatever source was available. The ambition to safeguard autonomy and to defend independence of any scientific discipline was alien to his thought, and consequently he did not treat sociology or psychology—or, for that matter, economics or anthropology, etc.—as separate bodies of concepts and propositions, but rather all of them as a common pool of knowledge about man and society.

Second, Marx saw every object, human individuals as well as human societies, as implicated in a complex totality of interrelations. Every object is at once a component in the wider network of relationships and itself a network of more elementary relationships. Luria interprets the Marxian position in such a way: "The object of scientific research is not an isolated thing, but a thing in all its connections and relations; the deeper we know those connections and relations, the richer is our concept of the thing (event, process, etc.) [1975: 86]." Nikitin clarifies this idea in more precise terminology:

> The essence of an object is determined by its double-sided structural organization. In fact, the structural organization of an object is not limited to its internal structure, but rather is a unity of its internal and external structure. Every object is not only structurally organized inside, but is also an element in some larger, external structure—superstructure. . . . The essence of an object is determined not only by its internal structure, but equally by its place in the external structure. Therefore, the structural explanation consists not only in the discovery of the internal structure of an object, i.e., in the explanation of a whole in terms of its parts (components) but also in the establishment of the place and role of an object in the external structure, i.e. in the explanation of the parts (components) in terms of the whole. . . . All complex systems require such two-sided structural explanation [1975: 112, 115].

A quite similar interpretation of Marx's view of society is given by Ollman:

> Marx's subject-matter is not simply society, but society conceived of "relationally." Capital, labor, value, commodity, etc., are all grasped as relations, containing in themselves, as integral elements of what they are, those parts with which we tend to see them externally tied. . . . In Marx's view, such relations are internal to each factor . . ., so that when an important one alters, the factor itself alters; it becomes something else. Its appearance and/or function has changed [1975: 15].

Thus, certain properties of society must be seen in terms of its internal structure; they must be derived from the properties of individuals and their relationships. In other words, they must be reduced "downward." But at the same time, certain properties of individuals must be seen in terms of the external structure in which the individuals are involved; they must be derived from the properties of the social whole. In other words, they must be reduced "upwards." Knowledge of society is in part reducible to knowledge of individuals, and knowledge of individuals to knowledge of society. The mutuality of partial reduction between sociology and psychology seems to be clearly stipulated in the Marxian approach.

Third, for Marx partial, mutual reduction does not imply the elimination of the disciplines involved. Sociology does not disappear because some of its concepts and laws may be put in individualistic terms, just as psychology does not when some of its concepts and laws are derived from knowledge of social wholes. Reduction has much more in common with a sort of peaceful coexistence between disciplines than with their mutual annihilation. Neither the concepts nor the laws of each are eliminated in the process of reduction. Topolski's comment is relevant here:

> When Marx shows quite explicitly that, for example, a capitalist class is a sum of single capitalists, i.e. when he accepts the possibility of reduction of the terms referring to wholes to the elementary terms, it does not mean that he neglects the difference between a holistic term and a sum of individual terms. Eventual reducibility does not eliminate the terms referring to the whole.... Aside from the single capitalists making up a capitalist class, the class as a whole is considered too.... When Marx speaks of single capitalists, he invokes the knowledge about the whole class. [And the same is true not only of concepts but also of laws:] It is often the practice of Marx to analyze the law referring to the wholes, by means of the more elementary laws dealing with parts of those wholes, but it does not imply the elimination of the laws of the wholes. The laws referring to the wholes (e.g. laws of the whole capitalist economy) remain as something separate [Topolski, 1970: 52–53].

Fourth, the problem-centered orientation of Marx seems to determine his approach to reduction as a matter of instrumental convenience, relative to a subject matter and concrete problem at hand, and not as a domineering principle . It may be shown that in his own theoretical considerations, sometimes he resorts to reduction and sometimes he does not, guiding himself solely by the expected fruitfulness of the procedure.

Fifth, in his theoretical practice, though certainly not in explicit methodological proclamations, Marx seems to acknowledge the difference between the definitional reduction of concepts and the explanatory reduction of laws, as Topolski's remarks clearly implied.

Thus, with various degree of plausibility all five higher-order assumptions that I found to be associated with the separatist standpoint seem to be consistent with Marx's approach. The same may be said of both constitutive components of the standpoint itself, the assumptions of Reductionism$_1$ and Antireductionism$_2$. The ultimate definitional reducibility of holistic concepts (i.e., the possibility of rendering their meaning by reference to the ultimate objects they denote—human individuals and their activities) is clearly implied by a famous statement of Marx's (even though the statement itself is couched in ontological rather than in methodological language): "History does nothing; it does not possess immense riches; it does not fight battles. It is men, real, living men who do all this, who possess things and fight battles. It is not 'history' which uses man as a means of achieving—as if it were an individual person—its own ends. History is nothing but the activity of men in pursuit of their ends [1960, vol. II: 114]." Hence, when one speaks of society or history, one in fact always refers to individual people and their activities. It is this aspect of the Marxian standpoint that Israel has in mind when he ascribes to Marx "the nonreified version of methodological individualism [1972: 150]." But on the other hand, the irreducibility of holistic laws is due to the fact that individuals do not act in isolation, but rather within an intricate network of social relationships. As Israel puts it in his interpretation of the Marxian standpoint:

> Only at the lowest level of sub-systems may the influence of each individual be visible. This does not imply that the total system and its subsystems are not "run by men," but only that the functioning of the total system is so complicated that the effects of individual acts, carried out alone or in cooperation with others, in one's own name or as a representative of a large organization, often can no longer be understood as such and conceptualized accordingly [1972: 148].

The same idea is put into more general, philosophical terms by Luria: "The inclusion of the object to the ever more complex system of connections and relations may lead to the appearance in the object of the qualitatively new structures which could not have been born outside of such a relational system. . . . New internal structures must often be considered as a result of those new external connections in which an element is implicated [1975: 86]." Hence, the internal structure of individual personality or individual action cannot be understood if we treat an individual as an isolated being, outside the whole external structure of interindividual relationships. To say everything there is to be said about society and about history we must possess concepts and laws that refer to such a structure, aside from concepts and laws referring to individuals. In other words, we must possess structural (holistic) concepts and laws together with individualistic ones. It is this aspect of Marxian ideas that Swingewood has in mind when he says: "The stress is on society as a definite structure within which human intentions and actions occur. In essence, therefore, Marx's approach is the opposite of methodological individualism [1975: 37]."

The direct arguments seem to confirm that Marx accepted, more or less implicitly, all the tenets of a standpoint definable as separatist. What follows further supports the idea that the separatist standpoint is fully consistent with the Marxian philosophical position, in its ontological as well as its epistemological aspects.

Indirect Proofs

The materialistic outlook of Marx, dialectical materialism, is basically different from mechanistic materialism. Whereas the latter attempts to rediscover the simple, unique form in which matter of whatever type is organized, the former assumes the multiplicity of levels on which matter and its dynamic motion appear. The idea of the qualitative differentiation of matter, depending on the various forms of its organization, lies at the core of Marxian ontology. As a contemporary Marxist philosopher puts it:

> The dialectical materialism . . . rejects the possibility of constricting matter to some single, simplest form or forms. . . . The crucial point of dialectical materialism is the claim that each form of a matter, be it a planetary system, atom, particle, man or whatever else, has its own qualitative specificity. Therefore matter cannot be seen as a simple set of constitutive elements, with the properties equal to the properties of elements. The qualitative specificity of any object is safeguarded by the particular form of interlinks, existing among its components [Spirkin, 1968: 91, 92].

The same point is made by Eilstein:

> The most general materialistic and dialectical characteristics of the universe as a whole are put together in the notion of the unity and multiformity of the material world. The matter is characterized by the qualitative variety of its components, multidimensionality, structurality, and the relationships of mutual determination between objects of different levels, between any complex structure and its elements. . . . One aspect of this qualitative variety of objects and structures is grasped by the Marxian thesis of the so-called "forms of motion" which expresses the specificity of complex structures. . . . On the other hand, the objects which participate in the given, higher forms of motion, are specific only in certain respects; are only partially different from the objects characterized by the lower forms of motion. In some sense, the higher form of motion is "comprised" by the lower [1961: 163, 169, 170].

Such a view of reality has its immediate implications in the domain of methodology. The first methodological implication is the prescription "to take into account the specific properties appearing at each level of the organization of matter [Spirkin, 1968: 92]." Consequently "physics is not reducible to mechanics, chemistry to physics, biology to the totality of mechanical, physical and chemical aspects; and sociology to any other form of material organization [Spirkin, 1968: 92]." Or to put the same in the words of Luria: "Each discipline must focus its attention on the precise analysis of those concrete levels on which a given phenomenon appears [1975: 85]." Such a directive is clearly in line with this aspect of the separatist position which was labelled Antireductionism$_2$. But at the same time the second methodological implication is "not to forget about some common characteristics of all levels as well as the connections, mutual interrelations of the different levels. . . . Simple forms of organization are always included in the more complex forms [Spirkin, 1968: 92]." This directive is tantamount to the aspect of separatism which was labelled as Reductionism$_2$. The plausible conclusion seems to be that separatism is the only solution of the reductionist dilemma which is fully congruent with the foundamentals of Marxian ontology.

A similar conclusion is also entailed by a consideration of the basic tenets of Marxian epistemology. In the first of the *Theses about Feuerbach* Marx and Engels say: "The chief defect of all hitherto existing materialism . . . is that the thing, reality, sensuousness, is conceived only in the form of the object, or of contemplation, but not as human sensuous activity, practice, not subjectively" [1968: 28]." And in the eleventh thesis he makes another famous point: "The philosophers have only interpreted the world, in various ways; the point, however, is to change it [1968: 30]." In the Marxian model of the cognitive process we find therefore "at least two dialectical processes functioning in the manner of feed-back mechanisms. One is the basic process of acquiring knowledge, containing the reciprocal relationship of influence between subject and object. The other is the dialectical relation between the process of formulation of theories and of practical action [Israel, 1972: 146]." If this interpretation of Marxian epistemology is valid, then both constitutive assumptions of the separatist standpoint, Reductionism$_1$ and Antireductionism$_2$, are most congruent with such a view of a human cognitive process. Israel draws this conclusion explicitly:

> The acceptance of the basic Marxian epistemological position . . . requires the acceptance of the nonreified version of methodological individualism [Reductionism$_1$] in combination with a nonreductionist approach at the explanatory level [Antireductionism$_2$]. The position of methodological

individualism accounts for the notion of the active, creative human being.
It stresses the role of the subject. The non-reductionist approach tries to
explain human action in terms of the total social situation. . . . The acceptance of a non-reductionist position alone may make it possible for
sociologists to interpret the world in different ways. Accepting in addition
the position of methodological individualism may create a chance to
change it [1972: 150].

Thus, the separatist standpoint is shown to be fully in line with the spirit
of Marxian philosophical orientation, of his ontological as well as epistemological commitments. The dialectic solution of the dilemma *science of
society or science of individuals?* was shown to be congruent with the philosophy of dialectical materialism.

Rejecting the spurious opposition of the reductionistic and antireductionistic standpoints, and replacing it with the alternative assumptions of
separatism, Marx was able to solve the problem of demarcation in an original and fruitful way. One asset of this solution is emphasized by Popper,
who is reported by Morgenbesser to believe that: "Marx's greatest contribution to the social sciences was his reasoned establishment of the thesis of the
autonomy of sociology [Morgenbesser 1967: 171]." But this is only one
side of the coin. The other side is stressed by Morgenbesser: "Marx, as
many of his recent commentators have emphasized, did not think that a
theory of man is completely dependent upon or consists of sociological
premises [1969: 172]." Sociology, for Marx, appears as a distinct scientific
discipline, but not as a queen of the sciences of man, rather as an important
partner, on equal terms with all other disciplines, in the family of the social
sciences. It has its own significant contribution to make, but it also depends
to a large extent on the contributions made by psychology, or other disciplines dealing with an individual human being.

PART III

THE DILEMMAS OF
SOCIAL COGNITION—
EPISTEMOLOGICAL

Alongside the attempt to delimit its scope with respect to other sciences, whether natural or social, sociology from its very inception as a separate scientific discipline has experienced another problem—how to dissociate itself as precisely as possible from the prescientific traditions of social thought. The new science of society had to fight for emancipation on double fronts. It had to confirm its status as a specific social science vis-à-vis the natural sciences, as well as the science of man; and it had to confirm its status as a social science, vis-à-vis several prescientific or extrascientific varieties of social thought. The first problem generated the methodological dilemmas of demarcation, discussed at length in the preceding part of the book. The second problem generated a new set of epistemological dilemmas, which shall now be our concern.

The fundamental question underlying this new set of dilemmas was how to distinguish scientific knowledge of society from other types of social knowledge, and in particular from common-sense social lore, as well as from the philosophical doctrines dealing with social (or political or ethical) matters. It was evident that the distinguishing criterion was not to be found in the content or subject matter of sociological theories: As a rule they dealt with the same questions as both common sense and philosophy; they inquired about the nature of man, the essence of society, the course of human history, and the role of the individual in society and in history. Those questions were eternal, they had been suggested by the social experiences common to all men since the birth of human kind, and they had preceded by several millennia any scientific sociological considerations. Thus it was not in what it was saying that sociology could search for its distinctiveness, but rather how it was saying it. It was not in the questions themselves but in the shape and form of the answers that the specific, scientific character of sociology was to be discovered.

What were the essential properties of those brands of knowledge that competed with sociology in the search for truth about society? One particular aspect of the manifold characteristics of prescientific or extra scientific social knowledge was picked up and made the focus of attention. It was pointed out that most often those forms of social thought had both practical and evaluative orientation; they were prescribing some means for social reforms, and they were critically appraising the existing institutions, suggesting openly some goals to be achieved. As a result, in social lore as well as social philosophy two sorts of statements could always be encountered: directives of practical action (whether in the form of common-sense proverbs or political programs), and value judgments (whether in the form of moral precepts or images of the ideal society).

Therefore, to dissociate a real, positive science of society from social lore and social philosophy seemed to require the elimination of those practical and evaluative aspirations and any prescriptive or evaluative statements from sociological theories. The image of sociology as free of any practical functions and any normative content seemed necessary for its emancipation.

But at the same time, the conditions in which sociology was born pressed in exactly the opposite direction. In Europe, the fundamental transformations of societies after the industrial revolution, the acceleration of social change, the breakdown of traditional institutions, the appearance of new social, political, economic, and moral forms necessitated the involvement of social scientists in large-scale social reforms. In America, the multiplication of so-called social problems, pathologically pervasive throughout various spheres of life owing to the heterogeneity and vitality of the young society called for small scale efforts at piecemeal improvements, and sociologists could not help getting involved in them. Mills observes: "In contrast to their European forebears, American sociologists have tended strongly to take up one empirical detail, one problem of milieu at a time. . . . It is advisable to proceed to reform this little piece and see what happens, before we reform that little piece too [1959: 85]." In both cases, to be accepted sociology simply had to prove the practical relevance, not only the truthfulness, of its propositions.

Thus, the ambivalence of the situation in which the fathers of the new discipline had found themselves strained its foundations. As a result two theoretical dilemmas appeared, which have proved to be bothersome up to now.

The first dilemma centered on the question of the goals, or functions, that a sociological theory should primarily serve, and correspondingly on the development of a theory necessary for the effective achievement of those goals. It may be called the dilemma knowledge or action? *Some sociologists emphasized the cognitive goals of science, and relegated any practical considerations to the extra-scientific domain. The goal of social science, they said, was to know the truth; whereas practical action, relevant to needs or interests, is the responsibility of public men and the like. To be sure, the majority of sociologists believed in the ultimate usefulness of sociological knowledge for men of affairs, but it was not their immediate concern, and the relationship between sociological theory and social practice was conceived as external to the discipline per se. Science was seen as an instrument or a tool to be used by anybody for his own purposes, whatever they may be. As a consequence, sociological theory was allowed to contain only veritative or categorical statements describing the social world, and any normative statements, prescribing practical action, were excluded from the scientific domain. The criterion of truth, as opposed to the criterion of utility or practical relevance, was proposed as the only touchstone for sociological results. This standpoint, stressing the cognitive goals of social science, and consequently requiring a purely cognitive content for sociological theories, shall be here referred to as* cognitivism.

But cognitivism was not accepted as the only possible solution to the dilemma. Another group of sociologists emphasized the practical goals of science, and treated practical considerations as the animating principle of sociological theories. The goal of social science, they said, is to change society, and the adequacy of theory is to be measured solely by the pragmatic effectiveness of its directives. Obviously, sociological theory was now conceived as normative and prescriptive, rather than veritative and descriptive. The criterion of practical relevance was seen as the basic touchstone of sociological theories. This standpoint, stressing the practical as opposed to the cognitive goals of social science, shall be referred to as activism.

The second dilemma centered on the question of the approach or method through which an adequate theory could be attained, and correspondingly on the development of a theory resulting from the application of that approach. It may be called the dilemma detachment or bias? *Some sociologists opted for a completely objectivistic approach to social data, purely fact oriented and free from any valuations. Consequently they rejected the possibility of any value judgments to be included in the body of a social theory. Valuations were conceived as extrascientific activities, and value judgments as extrascientific propositions. This standpoint, emphasizing the neutrality of science with respect to values and focusing exclusively on facts, shall be referred to as* neutralism.

The opposite solution to the dilemma allowed valuations as valid scientific activities and value judgments as the substantive components of sociological theories. The separation of facts and values was rejected. Such a standpoint, stressing the axiological content of science shall be referred to as axiologism.

Now it is becoming clear that the dilemmas knowledge or action? *and* detachment or bias? *deal ultimtely with the issue of the form that a proper sociological theory should take. In the first case, the debate concerns the inclusion or the exclusion of practical directives, whatever their substance, in a theory, and the arguments are based on the assumed functions of a theory, the goal it is supposed to serve. In the second case, the debate concerns the inclusion or the exclusion of value judgments, whatever their substance, in the body of a theory, and the arguments are based on the assumed origin of a theory, the course that any social research is supposed to follow.*

I shall attempt to show that both epistemological dilemmas are spurious and misleading, and that they should be rejected. In their place I shall propose alternative solutions to the valid and significant problems that generated them. To this end, a careful reappraisal of each dilemma is necessary.

CHAPTER 4

Knowledge or Action: Cognitivism, Activism, Constructivism

THE COGNITIVISTIC TRADITION

As in the case of all other theoretical dilemmas, the history of sociology provides ample illustrations of both the cognitivistic and the activistic standpoint. But whereas in the previous case one could spot a nearly equal number of sociological theorists subscribing to each of the polar solutions, in the dispute now to be analyzed there seems to exist much more unanimity among the masters, and the majority of them apparently lean toward only one of the possible points of view. The compromise between an attempt to be as scientific as possible and the attempt to participate in the creation of a new social order was achieved within the framework of a cognitivistic position. The prevailing view may be characterized thus: The goal of sociology is to find out the truth about society, and, if the truth is discovered, then it may serve social reform. Such an external relationship between knowledge and practice seemed typical of the natural sciences, which, once they achieved reliable results, usually applied them as the basis for all sorts of technology. The search for truth and the applications of results were seen as dissociated in at least three respects: (*a*) chronologically, for research was conceived as preceding application; (*b*) analytically, for both were seen as different types of activities; and (c) personally, for usually the two activities were treated as fields for different persons—scholars and technicians, respectively. It was to be expected that the founders of sociology would attempt to adapt the methodological pattern of the natural sciences to their new discipline. Naturalistic orientation and cognitivistic orientation supplemented each other within the wide positivistic model of sociology that became predominant in the early days of theorizing.

Auguste Comte: *"Savoir pour Prevoir, pour Prevenir"*

The standard formulation of the cognitivistic assumption, which has been reiterated innumerable times by later authors, was provided by Auguste Comte. The positive science of society that has gained ascendency over theological and metaphysical social thought adopts as one of its fundamental guidelines the following rule: Knowledge for the sake of prediction; prediction for the sake of prevention and action. The precondition for any rational policy is the knowledge of laws that operate in a society as well as in history—the constant patterns of coexistence or succession existing among social phenomena, the regularities of social statics and social dynamics. A knowledge of such laws is a precondition for prediction. "Every real connection, whether statical or dynamical, discovered between any two phenomena enables us both to explain them and to foresee them, each by the means of the other.... The true positive spirit consists above all in seeing for the sake of foreseeing; in studying what is, in order to infer what will be, in accordance with the general dogma that natural laws are invariable [1896: 20]." The knowledge of laws is also a precondition of action. "For it is only by knowing the laws of phenomena, and thus beeing able to foresee them, that we can ... set them to modify one another for our advantage. Whenever we effect anything great, it is through the knowledge of natural laws [1896:20–21]." The discovery of the natural laws of social statics and social dynamics is the proper goal of the positive science of society known as sociology.

One may summarize Comte's views in the words of a contemporary French sociologist: "The conclusion Comte drew from the analysis of the society in which he lived is that the basic condition of social reform is intellectual reform. It is not by the accidents of a revolution nor by violence that a society in crisis will be reorganized, but through a synthesis of the sciences and by the creation of positive politics [Aron, 1968, vol.I: 75]."

The same focus on social knowledge as separate from, even though providing the basis for, social action, and the same limitation of the goals of social science to the discovery of social facts and their regular interconnections, can be encountered in the works of Herbert Spencer, John S. Mill,

Emile Durkheim, Vilfredo Pareto, and many others. Our overview of their thinking on the matters now under consideration will touch those new points that they added to the prototypical formulation of cognitivism given by Comte.

Emile Durkheim: Rationally Justified Practice

Emile Durkheim wished to focus sociological study on the domain of social facts, and the explanation of their causes as well as functions by means of social laws. Objective, intellectually (not practically) oriented research is the proper goal of social science, and the results of such research can easily be translated, by equally intellectual procedures, into directives for practical action. From objective explanations by means of laws, there is a direct, logical road to prescriptions for rational change.

> It can be shown that behavior of the past, when analyzed, can be reduced to relationships of cause and effect. These relationships can then be transformed, by an equally logical operation, into rules of action for the future. What critics have called our "positivism" is only one certain aspect of this rationalism. . . . Correctly understood, facts are as basic in science as in practical life [1962: xxiv,xl].

Giddens gives the following summary of Durkheim's position on this issue: "Durkheim often stresses in his writings that scientific activity is worthless if it does not in some way lead to practical results. Nevertheless, it is of the essence of science that its procedures and objectives be detached from immediately practical requirements; only by the maintenance of a disinterested attitude can scientific enquiry attain its maximal effectiveness [1971: 201]."

Vilfredo Pareto: Truth versus Utility

Another significant idea was added to the cognitivistic doctrine by Vilfredo Pareto. So far, all the thinkers seemed to share the belief that there is a sort of one-to-one correspondence between scientific adequacy and practical effectiveness: What is true is useful and only that which is true can conceivably be useful. Pareto adds some reservations concerning the second part of this claim. An analysis of mythologies, ideologies, doctrines and other nonlogical "theories" widely accepted in human societies brings him to the conclusion that false beliefs can have quite a strong practical impact.

> We realized that from the logico-experimental viewpoint they were absolutely lacking in precision and devoid of any strict accord with the facts.

On the other hand, we could not deny their great importance in history and in determining the social equilibrium. This realization gave strength to an idea which had already come to mind and which will acquire greater and greater importance as the inquiry develops, namely, that there is a clear distinction between the experimental "truth" of certain theories and their social "utility"—these being two things which are not only quite different from one another but may be, and often are, in direct contradiction [Pareto, 1966: 215–216].

A comment of Parsons on this aspect of Pareto's sociology is relevant here:

The standard of truth which he continually employs is that of logicoexperimental science. An untrue doctrine is, then, one which departs from this standard. But in this sense the view that only true doctrines should be useful would mean that society should be "based upon reason." This, however, as has been shown, Pareto considered impossible. . . . Hence society, so long as the value element plays a part, will always be characterized by the currency of untrue, i.e. nonscientific doctrines. These doctrines moreover, partly manifest, partly constitute, elements essential to the maintenance of the social equilibrium [1968, vol.I: 275–276].

Max Weber: Diagnosis Primary to Action

So far it appears as if the acceptance of the cognitivistic assumption always went together with the naturalistic orientation. In fact, all the authors mentioned above combined those two assumptions in their works. But it is not a necessary, logical link—as will be seen when we consider two leading representatives of the antinaturalistic tradition who adopted the standpoint of cognitivism.

Weber, the first of the two, saw the goal of sociology to be a thorough description and explanation of social actions, social relationships, etc., by a method relying on ideal types and interpretative understanding. "Sociology is a science which attempts the interpretive understanding of social action in order thereby to arrive at a causal explanation of its cause and effects [1947: 88]." The establishment of practical directives for action was seen as lying outside the domain of science: "It can never be the task of an empirical science to provide binding norms and ideals from which directives for immediate practical activity can be derived [Weber, 1949: 52]." Weber believed with Comte that in order to act practically, one must obtain a valid diagnosis of an actual state of affairs and discover underlying causal mechanisms.

As McRae describes his approach, "Weber was primarily a scholar. He was a learned man, a theorist, seeking to diagnose rather than engage in prophetic judgment." His goal was to obtain "understanding as completely and clinically as possible [1974: 68]."

Florian Znaniecki: Against Narrow Practicality

A second antinaturalistic thinker who seems to accept the assumption of cognitivism is Florian Znaniecki. He adds several important dimensions to the dispute, and for this reason his views require a somewhat extended review.

There is a certain duality in Znaniecki's position. On the one hand, the criterion of practicality is introduced explicitly as the ultimate test for validating sociological knowledge:

> A realistic science begins to base its claims not on the abstract philosophical justification of its presuppositions, but on the practical applicability of its results. . . . Sooner or later science must pay her debts. . . . This demand of ultimate practical applicability is as important for science itself as for practice; it is a test, not only of the practical, but of the theoretical value of the science [Znaniecki, 1969: 38, 66].

But at the same time Znaniecki forcibly rejects the "fallacy of the practical sociology" in which "an immediate reference to practical aims, and the standards of the desirable and undesirable are the grounds upon which theoretical problems are approached." And he asserts: "Only a scientific investigation which is quite free from any dependence on practice, can become practically useful in its applications [1969: 58]." Such an investigation must be carried out only with cognitive ends in view, and its cognitive integrity is the best guarantee of its practical usefulness:

> We must have an empirical and exact social science ready for eventual application. And such a science can be constituted only if we treat it as an end in itself, not as a means to something else, and if we give it time and opportunity to develop along all the lines of investigation possible, even if we do not see what may be the eventual applications of one or another of its results [1969: 65].

If pure sociology must be restricted to cognitive goals, yet there is a need for applied sociology, or social technology, which will link theoretical results and practical action.

> The laws of science are abstract, while the practical situations are concrete, and it requires a special intellectual activity to find what are the practical questions which a given law may help to solve, or what are the scientific laws which may be used to solve a given practical question. . . .

> The special task of the social technician is to prepare, with the help of both science and practical observation, thorough schemes and plans of action for all the various types of situations which may be found in a given line of social activity, and leave to the practitioner the subordination of the given concrete situation to its proper type [1969: 108–111].

Thus despite Znaniecki's heavy emphasis on the utility of science, he construes the relationship of theory and practice as the external relationship of two distinct spheres of activity, with both sociological theory and social technology serving as neutral instruments to be applied as the needs arise by those whose province is action.

All the representatives of cognitivism just discussed shared a common perspective: Adequate knowledge was seen as the basis for practical action, and the goals of sociology were restricted to providing such knowledge— practical action was beyond the pale. The findings of sociology were to be relevant to action as all truths are ultimately useful; namely, as guidelines for appraising an actual situation, its likely development, and the possibilities for acting on it. But whether such guidelines would be followed, by whom, and for what reasons were questions lying outside sociology's proper domain.

THE ACTIVISTIC TRADITION

The opposite orientation, activism, defines the province of sociology in much more comprehensive terms. The primary goal of a sociologist is to change social situations, social relationships, social institutions, social organization—the whole society. His primary responsibility is to provide clear blueprints of a good society, to condemn a bad society, to provide practical directives for transforming the latter into the former, and moreover to participate directly in the process of transformation. This requires knowledge, but knowledge is for practical action. Therefore, who uses sociological knowledge, and for what purposes, is a question most relevant both from a sociological and an extrasociological perspective.

In the activistic tradition, the relationship of theory and practice is again construed in an external way, but, one might say, with a different "vector," in a different direction. Whereas in cognitivism a theory is seen as entailing practice, in activism practice is seen as requiring theory. In the former, the focus is on theory and the basic preoccupation is knowledge; in the latter, the focus is on practice and the basic preoccupation is change.

It is not easy to find examples of unalloyed activism in the history of sociology. The intellectual fecundity of cognitivism, so plausible to common sense and so much in accord with the experiences of the natural sciences, ensured its ascendancy. But the activist impulse may be discovered both in large-scale theoretical systems and in small-scale descriptive and practice-oriented sociological research.

Henri de Saint-Simon: Utopian Socialism

Henri de Saint-Simon, considered one of the founders of what is called "utopian socialism," perceived European society after the industrial revolutions as ridden with crisis and chaos. He wished to contribute to its reorganization by promoting a new form of "organic order." The way out of a social crisis, he felt, is primarily through "change, improvement of ideas, and popular creeds," and the establishment of a new political system. The reorganization of society depends on science, which is, along with industry, the mainspring of progress. A golden age of society shall be reached if the scientists combine their efforts with industrialists in a union of the two leading social powers. Among the sciences, a special role was ascribed to the sciences of man, whose representatives were best qualified to solve political problems by the same methods and means as were utilized in their scientific activities. Social reform is nothing else but the conscious application and realization of ideas. A social order cannot be constructed if a clear philosophical notion of the good society is not present beforehand. Thus the goal of social scientists is both the creation of a blueprint for a future society and a realization of its substance (see Szczepanski, 1969: 25–48).

In his own scientific activity, Saint-Simon remained faithful to this methodological creed. As Martindale comments, "He was one of the first writers on a new style of social reform [1960: 60]." And Strasser adds, "For the first time, Saint-Simon designed his sociology on the radical assumption that social progress could be organized by man himself [1976: 5]."

Ferdinand Tönnies: Pessimistic Social Criticism

Another and much later author who must be mentioned in respect of activist tradition is Ferdinand Tönnies. Even though he accepted to some extent the cognitivistic standpoint, in his interpretation it became basically qualified by two observations that brought it close to conformity with activism.

The first observation dealt with the course of historical development. Whereas earlier nineteenth-century authors were predominantly optimistic in their view of the developing modern industrial order, Tönnies saw a *Gesselschaft* type of society as a step backward as against the traditional *Gemeinschaft*-type. In his view, according to Fletcher, "The qualities of life, mind, morality, and behavior brought about by the hyperrational calculation (and market-manipulation) of the special contractual relationships of mercantile trade and industrial capitalism, were very much an impoverishment, diminution and worsening of the living qualities of whole men fulfilling their clear tasks in traditional communities [1971, vol.II: 40]." Therefore, a new society, just being born, should become an object of thorough and critical scrutiny by social scientists, who must not refrain from voicing their doubts and warnings in forthright value judgments.

The second observation, related to the first, dealt with the role of science in a new society. Whereas earlier thinkers were almost unanimous in their view of science as inherently progressive—an instrument and precondition of a new better social order—Tönnies introduced a pessimistic and skeptical note. Science in itself is, according to him, no guarantee of progress, and that for two reasons: First, because its employment is not inevitably right and proper; it may be used both for and against emancipation and self-realization. Only if coupled with sound ethics and kept subservient to ethically prescribed ends can science become a tool of progress. Second, because science itself is potentially an element of the dehumanizing, *Gesselschaft* tendency, and if not informed by humane values, expressed in social, moral, or political philosophy, it may contribute to the further disruption of the traditional *Gemeinschaft* order.

Richard LePlay, Charles Booth, and Sociography

Another brand of activism of which a concern with specific social problems and narrow practicality of approach are typical may be traced back to the nineteenth-century "sociographers" Richard LePlay and Charles Booth. They believed that "the method which most surely leads to social reforms is the observation of social facts [LePlay, as quoted in Szczepanski 1969: 94]." LePlay wished to derive the directives for the prevention of social revolution and for a conservative social policy from minute, precise, descriptive studies of families, conceived as the microcosm of society. Booth, moved by reformist and philantropic impulses, undertook a monumental study of the *Life and Labour of the People of London*—17 volumes of descriptive accounts. Statistical and factual data on the living conditions of all classes, strata, professional communities, and so on, would, he believed, inspire directives for legislative action directed against poverty and other forms of social pathology.

Elton Mayo, Robert Park, Samuel Stouffer, and Gunnar Myrdal: Practice-Oriented Research

More recent examples of sociological studies directly subordinated to specific practical goals may be found (*a*) in the work of Elton Mayo and his collaborators, attempting to discover ways by which the efficiency of workers can be raised; (*b*) in the ecological studies of Robert Park and the Chicago School on the distribution of crime and delinquency in big cities, regarded as a base for preventive actions; (*c*) in Samuel Stouffer's research on the American soldier, undertaken with the hope of improving cohesiveness and morale in the U.S. Army; and (*d*) Gunnar Myrdal's *American Dilemma,* conceived as a thorough diagnosis of racial prejudice and intended to support antisegregationist legislation.

In these, as in innumerable instances of similar, perhaps less famous, projects, the focus is on directives for practical, step-by-step reforms; and any cognitive results, whether conceptual or theoretical, are treated as by-products, sometimes to be neglected and sometimes to be developed in full much later, usually by other authors, as so-called "continuities." This is the case with Merton, who has developed some of the theoretical insights of Stouffer's studies (see Merton, 1957); with Homans, who has systematized and amplified the results of Mayo (see Homans, 1950); and with the "ecological school", which has drawn inspiration from the studies of Park.

The name of Karl Marx is once again missing: Marx (as a later portion of this chapter will demonstrate) was closer than any of his fellow-students of society to the dialectical position that represents the most viable alternative to cognitivism and activism as delineated in the preceding discussion. But before treating Marx, we shall consider the pervasiveness of the traditional solutions in contemporary sociology.

COGNITIVISM AND ACTIVISM IN CONTEMPORARY SOCIOLOGY

If, as I have indicated, the dominant theoretical orientations in the history of sociology seem to come close to the cognitivistic extreme, yet one may observe the reverse trend, toward all forms of activism in contemporary sociology. To be sure, the cognitivistic positions are still well defended, but the balance seems to be more and more favorable to the activists. We shall start with some typical statements of cognitivism encountered in sociological theory.

George Lundberg: Sociological Technique

George Lundberg presents a case for the complete divorce of science and politics, suggesting the placement of sociological knowledge "beyond the reach of political upheavals [1961: 16]." Sociology should be a neutral technical instrument for the implementation of goals determined outside itself. "The services of real social scientists would be as indispensable to Fascists as to Communists and Democrats. . . . Physical scientists are indispensable to any political regime. Social scientists might well work toward a corresponding status [Lundberg, 1961: 17]." The closer sociology comes to attaining a purely technical ideal of the natural sciences, the better will it be able to legitimate its claims to knowledge and the more mature it will become:

> Social scientists, unfortunately, have failed as yet to convince any considerable number of persons that they are engaged in a pursuit of knowledge of a kind which is demonstrably true, regardless of the private preferences, hopes and likes of the scientist himself. . . . Physical scientists are, as a class, less likely to be disturbed than social scientists when a political upheaval comes along, because the work of the former is recognized as of equal consequence under any regime. Social science should strive for a similar position [1961: 16].

The purely cognitive tasks for the social scientists are outlined in accordance with his implied directive. Sociologists are to provide only diagnostic and prognostic accounts of social reality, and at most the technical directives for effective action, which can be followed by anybody, for whatever purposes:

> Social scientists as scientists had better confine themselves to three tasks: First and foremost, they should devote themselves to developing reliable knowledge of what alternatives of action exist under given conditions and the probable consequences of each. Secondly, social scientists should, as a legitimate part of their technology as well as for its practical uses, be able to gauge reliably what the masses of men want under given circumstances. Finally they should, in the applied aspects of their science, develop the administrative or engineering techniques of satisfying most efficiently and economically these wants, regardless of what they may be at any given time, regardless of how they may change from time to time, and regardless of the scientist's own preferences [1961: 17–18].

Hans Zetterberg: Theoretical Consultations

Hans Zetterberg advocates a program of applied social theory. There is a clear though unacknowledged continuity between his position and the position that posits an ideal pattern of relationship between social science and social policy—the latter worked out 13 years earlier by Robert Merton. "Basic theory embraces key concepts (variables and constants), postulates, theorems and laws. Applied science consists simply in ascertaining (*a*) the variables relevant to the problem at hand, (*b*) the values of the variables, (*c*) in accordance with previous knowledge, setting forth the uniform relationships between these variables [Merton, 1949: 181]."

Zetterberg shares the view that what is ultimately necessary in order to arrive at any rational directives for action is a systematic theory of society. His main attack is aimed against the narrow descriptive approach to practical problems epitomized in the slogan "Let us do some research about it." As he points out:

> Such descriptive knowledge is, of course, essential. One ought to know the facts before one leaps into action. However, even the most orderly and systematic collection of descriptive facts and trends does not give any specific advice on what action to take. At best it may indicate that some action is necessary, but it does not tell which one. To know what action is going to be effective, we need more than reliable, descriptive facts. We need reliable laws which say that if this and this is done, such and such an outcome is likely [1962: 34].

Sociology possesses a large number of such laws: "There is a body of seasoned sociological knowledge, summarized as principles of theoretical sociology [Zetterberg, 1962: 22]." Therefore, in order to be useful, a sociologist should simply rearrange and codify them in a manner more relevant to practical problems, and then provide theoretically based scholarly consultations to practitioners. And if such laws are missing, he should strive to establish them, before any attempt at practical application is made. "Applied sociology should proceed from the client's problem to something very abstract—theoretical problems and theoretical solutions— and then back to the client's problems with a practical solution [Zetterberg, 1962: 9–10]." Such a practical solution is presented as a set of multiple alternative possibilities, arising in view of the facts of the case, and in view of general sociological laws.

But the scientist does not make final choices; he is detached from any values or ultimate goals, which the active agent must decide for himself.

> A consultation can only help a client to a scholarly understanding of his situation and it can give him useful ideas for solutions. But a consultation is not meant to remove the necessity for making decisions, nor the agony and anguish in making them. . . . A scientist can aid a decision maker by providing the stuff out of which decisions are made—knowledge. . . . But he is not particularly competent to make the decision itself [1962: 178, 185].

This is a clear statement of the cognitivistic assumption, even though the whole discussion is geared toward the problem of practical applications. The crux of the matter is the traditional, external definition of the relationship between knowledge and practical action. Knowledge is still treated as a separate fund out of which anybody can draw, and those who draw from it are distinct from those who contribute to it.

George C. Homans: Explanatory Sociology

A particularly forceful and influential statement of the cognitivistic position is presented by George C. Homans. In his view, the origins of the major inadequacies of current sociology can be traced to a neglect of explanatory tasks. Therefore, the preeminent focus of sociological research should be theoretical explanation. "It is not in its findings, which are now numerous and well attested, that social science gets into trouble, but in its explanations. . . . The characteristic problems of social science, compared with other sciences, are problems of explanation [1967: 28, 31]." To overcome such problems, sociologists should take standards of explanation more seriously and resist the tendency to limit their research to the level of descriptive generalizations. "The objectives of sociology are those of any science: the discovery of empirical relationships in the data, and the explanation of those relationships [1969: 80]." "Though stating and testing relationships between properties of nature is what makes a science, it is certainly not the only thing that a science tries to do. Indeed we judge not the existence but the success of a science by its capacity to explain [Homans, 1967: 22]." By implication, any questions of practical applicability are secondary, and chronologically later than explanatory objectives—and, of course, practical objectives are beyond the proper scope of sociology.

Lewis Coser and Philip Hauser:
Recent Spokesmen for Cognitivism

Some of the recent statements of the cognitivistic position are couched in polemical terms and directed explicitly against the prevailing activistic one. In the "Letter to a Young Sociologist" (1969) Lewis Coser attacks two fallacies which he associates with activism; narrow practicality and narrow empiricism: "I would contend that exclusive concern with these issues [of immediate practical relevance] and neglect of problems that have no direct impact on the affairs of the hour could be most unproductive. The stress on the need for relevance . . . has always appeared to me extremely shortsighted. It is, moreover, controverted by the whole history of science [1969: 132]." The basic preoccupation of a social scientist should be a disinterested search for truth. Practical usefulness results of its own from such an intellectual endeavor: "It is this search for truth that puts us at the service of the common weal [1969: 132]." To be valuable and consequently useful, research cannot be restricted to diagnostic, narrow empirical endeavors: "Any research in a particular setting that does not provide us clues for generalizations beyond that setting is not likely to be very fruitful. This, by the way, accounts for the scientific sterility of much so-called applied sociology, even where it seems 'relevant' [1969: 132–133]."

Philip Hauser formulates a similar case for a detached, intellectually oriented social science, on the basis of Weber's distinction between a sociologist qua sociologist and a sociologist in his extrascientific roles (for example, that of a citizen, an activist, or an administrator). "It is the mission of the sociologist qua scientist to add to sociological knowledge. He should not yield to the temptation to turn activist at the expense of his functions as a scientist. ... Sociology as a craft would do well to avoid direct participation of any kind in the general political arena in the interest of maximizing its contribution to the finding of knowledge [1971: 438–439]. Any practical activities are secondary with respect to cognitive tasks, and fall beyond the professional role of a sociologist. "It is possible for the individual sociologist to play many roles in addition to his role as scientist—that of husband, father, musician, religious believer and, also, that of citizen or social engineer [1971: 428]." Hauser's is as extreme a statement of cognitivism as one can find. And this seems a proper moment to leave the illustrations of cognitivistic standpoints and turn to the opposite camp in the dispute, namely, the main representatives of the activistic approach.

Robert Lynd: Knowledge for What?

Coser is right when he considers Rober Lynd and C. Wright Mills as the forerunners of the contemporary activistic trend (see Coser, 1969: 132). It was Lynd who in a seminal little book first posed the searching question "Knowledge for What?" (1939). In his view the role of a sociologist is not merely

> to stand by, describe, and generalize, like a seismologist watching a volcano. There is no other agency in our culture whose role it is to ask long-range and, if need be, abruptly irreverent questions of our democratic institutions; and to follow these questions with research and the systematic charting of the way ahead. The responsibility is to keep everlastingly challenging the present with the question: "But what is it that we human beings want, and what things would have to be done, in what ways in what sequence in order to change the present as to achieve it?" [Lynd, 1939: 250].

This is a totally different view of the sociologist's calling, his rights, and his competence—different from all of the traditional formulations of the cognitivist position.

C. Wright Mills: Knowledge for Whom

In his far-reaching critique of mainstream American sociology in the 1950s, C. Wright Mills attacks the cognitivistic assumption: "My conception stands opposed to social science as a set of bureaucratic techniques which inhibit social inquiry by methodological pretensions, which congest such work by obscurantist conceptions and which trivialize it by concern with minor problems unconnected with publicly relevant issues" [1959: 20]." To divorce sociology from real life is illusory, because "whether he wants it or not, or whether he is aware of it or not, anyone who spends his life studying society and publishing the results is acting morally and usually politically as well [1959: 79]."

That a moral and political involvement is necessary is due to the fact that sociologists can produce two sorts of knowledge; they can provide technical information for the "ruling elite," which can be used for manipulative purposes, and they can furnish their subjects, men in society, with a particular quality of mind, labeled the *sociological imagination*. This is described as a socially oriented self-awareness of those who are able to see their individual fate in a historical and structural context, as a link in the chain of the historical process and as an element of a complex and differentiated social whole. At the same time, *sociological imagination* is also a sort of individually oriented social awareness, which enables one to interpret historical processes and social wholes in terms of their impact on individual human beings.

> The sociological imagination enables its possessor to understand the larger historical scene in terms of its meaning for the inner life and the external career of a variety of individuals.... The first fruit of this imagination ... is the idea that the individual can understand his own experience and gauge his own fate only by locating himself within his period, that he can know his own chances in life only be becoming aware of those of all individuals in his circumstances.... By the fact of his living he contributes, however minutely, to the shaping of his society and to the course of its history; even as he is made by society and by its historical push and shove [Mills, 1959: 5–6].

The creation of a sociological imagination is the paramount objective of sociology. It is a felt need of the people. The creation of a sociological imagination is at the same time an intellectual and a political act, inasmuch as it transforms society—the consciousness and the consequent activities of its members. "By such means the personal uneasiness of individuals is focused upon explicit troubles, and the indifference of publics is transformed into involvement with public issues [Mills, 1959: 5]."

To use Strasser's apt distinction, Mills places sociology at the service of "a social–emancipatory interest," as opposed to the traditional "social–technological interest." (Cf. Strasser, 1976: 9.) And he rejects the "elitist" model of sociology, whereby social knowledge is addressed to those who possess prerogatives of manipulation, arguing in behalf of a "populist" model, whereby sociology is addressed directly to ordinary men and women.

Alvin Gouldner: Clinical Sociology and Reflexive Sociology

Gouldner is a proponent for a particular type of activistic sociology. Two of his significant contributions to the debate must be mentioned. The first was his effort to delineate two submodels of applied sociology, which he called the *clinical* and the *engineering* (Gouldner, 1956: 169–181). The term *clinical* model is intended to suggest a similarity to the procedures utilized by psychiatrists, who do not rest content with the introspective reports and self-appraisals provided by a patient (or, to put it another way, with a patient's definition of his problem), but rather treat them as aids to reaching their own diagnoses. In sociology, the clinically oriented applied scientist does not take the problems defined by his clients at face value, but probes deeper, uncovering aspects not perceived and not experienced consciously by them. Also, he is not restricted to the goals set by his clients, and even contrary to their beliefs guides himself, in behalf of their well-being, by the light of his own more comprehensive and deeper appraisal. Warshay describes this sort of approach, as quite widely accepted nowadays: "The issues-oriented new humanists posit a more total orientation in questioning both goals and means of society, rather than leaving these to the politician, businessman, clergy, or foundation dispenser [1971: 26]." Producing recommendations and aiding in their implementation, the clinical sociologist takes a responsibility for effecting specific changes. He is not a detached hired expert moving within the strict limits of a contract; he takes up the initiative and becomes himself an agent of change.

There is a clear continuity from the case for clinical sociology to the defense of the so-called "reflexive sociology"—the second of Gouldner's contributions to the present issue. Here Gouldner attacks the traditional detached, aloof attitude that a sociologist is apt to take with respect to the subjects of his research. Such an attitude is a consequence of a dualistic point of view, opposing scientists to the people being studied. He says, "We would increasingly recognize the depth of our kinship with those whom we study. They would no longer be viewable as alien others or as mere objects for our superior technique and insight [1971: 490]." The traditional engineering approach to society, modeled on the natural sciences, must be overcome and replaced by the different conception.

> Such a view of social science premised that a man might be known, used, and controlled like any other thing; it "thingafied" man. . . . The opposite conception of social science held that its ultimate goal was not neutral "information" about social reality, but rather such knowledge as was relevant to men's own changing interests, hopes, and values and as would enhance men's awareness of their place in the social world rather than simply facilitating their control over it [Gouldner, 1971: 492].

Similarly, the traditional separation of a sociologist qua sociologist, and sociologist qua citizen is untenable. "A Reflexive Sociology embodies a critique of the conventional conception of segregated scholarly roles and has a vision of an alternative [1971: 495]." This alternative is spelled out thus: "Reflexive Sociology believes that sociologists are really only mortal; that they inevitably change others and are changed by them, in planned and unanticipated ways during their efforts to know them; and that knowing and changing are distinguishable but not separable processes [1971: 497]." Therefore, a sociologist must be seen as "both knower and as agent of change [1971: 497]"; his cognitive activity is never to be detached from his active intervention in the world of his studies, the social world. Sociology seeks to transform the world, and not only to understand it.

Current Radical Sociology

The critique of a cognitivist, detached "mainstream" sociology guided solely by the search for abstract truth is prominently on display within the so-called "radical" school. Since it is still too new to have bred its own historians, I can comment only on some selected contributions.

Certainly, there is a whole spectrum of radicalism. In its fight for relevance the school easily falls into a trap of militant antiintellectualism. This extreme may be illustrated by this remark of Freiberg's:

> Social sciences are not sciences, but are purposively misnomered as part of the same ideological process which is in fact their essence, their project, and their meaning . . . In technological society, ideology not only passes for science, i.e. sociology, but science has now become state ideology. . . . Sociology is most condemnable among the pseudo-sciences, the most used in a direct and indirect manipulative fashion by the science-preaching ruling classes" [Freiberg, 1973: 2, 10].

But more often, radical sociologists formulate more moderate and more justified claims, which do not lend to the total rejection of the social sciences, but rather to the inclusion of organizational and political activism (or, more generally, the dimension of social practice) within the domain of sociology, and the creation of a closer link between sociologists and the subjects of their research. As Colfax and Roach put it: "The politically radical sociologist commits himself to organizational tasks and activism. . . . The immediate and primary task of the radical sociologist is to continue to raise public and professional consciousness through radical research and practice, as well as to engage in radical organizing on and off the campus [1971: 15, 18]." Similarly, Szymanski characterizes radical sociology by its commitment to three values: scientific curiosity, questioning scepticism, and human self-realization: "Since we produce knowledge, we must control its uses. We must insure that our theories and research contribute only to the development of understanding and to the realization of human potentialities, and that they in no way contribute to the maintenance of the oppresive system or are used for the purposes of control and manipulation [1971: 100]." This requires specific activities:

> The radical sociologist must serve as a constant social critic. . . . Moreover, the radical sociologist must contribute to the development of a strategy by which a society in which man's potential would be realized could be brought into being. . . . Finally the role of the radical sociologist must be to relate people's personal troubles and day-to-day concerns to the dynamics of social structures, thus translating them into political issues. [By engaging in such multiple activities radical sociologists avoid] a schizophrenic dissociation of their academic and political activities [1971: 105–106].

They also avoid reification of people, treating them not as subjects of manipulation but as equal partners in the common fight for human emancipation.

To refer to Strasser's apt formulation again, the radical sociologists may be treated as a brand of "social emancipists who are primarily concerned with the materialization of theory, not with its confirmation [1976: 11]." In this sense, they occupy the opposite pole with regard to traditional cognitivists.

The foregoing has outlined some typical standpoints taken in the dispute of cognitivism and activism both in earlier and in more recent sociology. The main dimensions of the dilemma *knowledge or action?* are already becoming apparent, but they require some additional explication and systematization before an alternative solution is presented.

WHAT THE DISPUTE IS REALLY ABOUT:
AN EXPLICATION

One way to dispel the most pervasive misunderstandings surrounding the dilemma *knowledge or action?* is by considering the question in its form: "What is the dispute certainly not about?"

What the Dispute Is Not About

First of all, the dispute is not about the extrascientific involvement of a scientist in practical affairs. Both cognitivists and activists will certainly agree that any sociologist plays multiple social roles, besides that of scientist. He is always a member of several groups: To name but a few, he is a member of an academic community, a professional association, perhaps a political organization, and a club, and he is a citizen. In all those roles he participates in various activities that have consequences, and maybe ideological or political implications. There are two schools of thought concerning the effects of such extrascientific involvements on the pursuit of scientific activities. Some defend the ascetic idea of limiting participation of this sort, which may prevent full immersion in scientific research. As Hauser has remarked:

> It is becoming imperative for the advancement of sociology as a science for sociologists to say "no"—both in response to invitations to attend the round of endless meetings and conferences and to the invitations to social action which impair research productivity.... I suggest that all sociologists under fifty-five hold to a minimum their committee, conference, consulting and social action assignments [1971: 436].

Other sociologists believe that participation in all sorts of extrascientific activities encourages and stimulates the scientific productivity, for it provides them with personal experiences, strong motivation, and in general raises their level of total behavioral mobilization.

Perhaps the matter boils down to the personality and temperament of the individual scholar, and no one precept can be given. Anyway, it is certainly not the point at issue between cognitivists and activists. What they really quarrel about is the practical involvement of a scientist qua scientist; that is, in his scientific role. Should he or should he not guide himself by practical considerations in his research or theorizing? Should he or should he not incorporate practical directives or advice in his scientific results? Should he or should he not participate in putting into practice his findings? Such are the real dividing issues.

Second, the dispute is not about the ultimate practical motivations at the root of both individual scientific activities and the whole enterprise of science. It is acknowledged by cognitivists and activists alike that most often scientists are moved by the desire to help solve real-life problems, and that since at least the Middle Ages this sort of motivation has informed the ethos of science in its civic aspect. No sociologist, whether cognitivist or activist, would despise the prospect of his results being implemented, and both cognitivists and activists view with suspicion such purely academic exercises as can never be of use. The real difference between them is rather that an activist wants to implement sociological results himself and only for the causes he approves of, while resisting their implementation for other causes; whereas the cognitivist considers implementation to be someone else's business and pledges disinterest in respect of the concrete causes served by sociological results.

Third, the dispute does not concern the historical origins of sociology as a science. There is consensus that sociology developed in response to pressing practical needs—in Europe, the demand for total social reconstruction; in America, the necessity of healing many social ailments. The dividing issue is strategy: What is most conducive to meeting those needs. For cognitivists, it is the policy of truth, for activists the policy of participation.

Fourth, the dispute is not focused on the characteristics of social practice but rather on the properties of social knowledge. Cognitivists and activists alike would certainly agree on some basic prerequisites for effective practical action; for example, both would require it to be rational—that is, backed up by adequate knowledge of circumstances as well as general regularities, and guided by some unambiguous calculus of preferences. What is really at issue between them is rather the status of social science, its proper, distinguishing qualities. They do not doubt that the practical activity should be scientifically informed, rather than a haphazard, hit-or-miss affair. What they do quarrel about is whether the scientific activity should be immediately practical, or even totally immersed in practice, or rather completely detached, purified of any practical ingredients.

Fifth, the dispute is not focused on the characteristics of applied sociology, conceived as the subdiscipline concerned with the translation of research results into practical directives. The possibility of such a translation is acknowledged by both parties to the dispute, cognitivists as much as activists. Contrary to a dominant presupposition, the proponents of applied sociology do not by the same token become activists. Of course, they may become activists, but as a matter of fact, most often they may be classified as cognitivists par excellence. For them, the prime consideration is usually to effect as adequate a translation as possible, and to produce extensive inventories of practical (or "sociotechnical") directives suitable for any conceivable purpose. On the other hand, activists never profess a disinterested attitude as to the ultimate uses of scientific results. For them the main concern will be to subordinate scientific results to a specific cause, and produce only such directives as may be instrumental for this cause and detrimental for opposing causes.

Thus, to opt for applied sociology does not determine one's standing in the dispute. And the reason is that the dividing line between the activists and the cognitivists lies somewhere else. The real issue is whether in theoretical or "pure" science one should primarily, or even exclusively, search for truth, or rather orient one's efforts to practical applications and strive to effect such applications oneself for the sake of the values one cherishes, and prevent applications for the sake of values one condemns.

Sixth, the dispute is not focused on the way sociological research is conducted, but rather on the characteristics of results that it attains. To be sure, sometimes the controversies are formulated in a way that suggests the opposite. For example, some stress the requirement that research be controlled by practical considerations, and the belief that practice inspire research. They devote less attention to the question what scientific knowledge itself must be like in order to be practically useful. However, it is this meaning of the postulate that seems to be logically the essential one. Indeed, what we actually put to practical uses is not research but knowledge. No sooner can we define the desirable character or direction of research than we define the desireable qualities of what is the objective of research; that is, of scientific knowledge. A similar opinion has been expressed by Kotarbinski:

> A dilemma arises, what must go first: science as research activities, or science as a pattern of propositions, written or spoken? The authorities are more apt to support the activities rather than sets of theorems, and thus science as an activity gains the upper hand over science conceived as the contents of learned books, but such priority concerns the sequence of actual considerations only, and not the rational sequence of enterprise. From the latter standpoint, what comes to the fore is an insight into the realm of doctrines, theories, hypotheses and their patterns, since the variety of forms of research activities, and even more so the variety of their needs, can only be fully understood by reference to their intended or actual achievements [1970: 86].

Mutatis mutandis; these words apply to our present analysis, too.

In view of the preceding discussion, I shall interpret the dispute between cognitivists and activists as dealing primarily with the quality of legitimate sociological results, the types of components such results should include, and the types of structures in which those components should be organized, as well as the types of functions sociological results are expected to serve.

The Focus of the Dispute: The Notion of a Theory

We may now leave consideration of selected misunderstandings and pose the question in its positive form: What is the dispute really about? There is general agreement on the ultimate theoretical goals of sociology. Robson has noted that "pronouncements about theory in sociology at the present time tend to be of the same order; we are all for it [1968: 368]." Sociological theory is most often viewed as the final, legitimate, prescribed result of sociological inquiry. I believe that the real core of the dispute between the cognitivists and actionists is precisely the image of sociological theory that is proposed as the guiding standard for sociology as science. All other differences that may exist are secondary to and derivative of this main concern. The cognitivists and activists conceive of sociological theory in basically divergent ways. Owing to the central place of theory in the edifice of sociology, their images of sociology itself must differ profoundly.

The notion of theory is notoriously elusive. As Homans observes: "No 'big' word is more often used in social science than the word *theory*. Yet how seldom do we ask our students—or, more significantly, ourselves—what a theory is [1967: 22]." To grasp the essential difference between cognitivistic and activistic images of sociological theory, a sketch of some of the most important meanings that attach to the term *theory* in our discipline is necessary.

There are two approaches that are used in the attempt to answer the question "What is a theory?" First, those who employ the direct approach define the structural features (i.e., the specific properties of elementary propositions or the specific properties of their systematization) that distinguish a theory from other products of sociological research. As a result they arrive at some structural definition of a theory. Second, those who employ the indirect approach define at the outset the functional features (i.e., the specific expected applications, contributions, or uses) that distinguish a theory from other products of sociological research, and only later derive its structural properties as the necessary prerequisites of expected functions. As a result they arrive at some functional definition of a theory (see Sztompka, 1973).

Some of the definitions, whether structural or functional, seem typical of the cognitivistic standpoint, and some of the activistic one. The core meaning of both standpoints may be rendered by considering those typical definitions associated with each of them.

The Cognitivistic Notion of Theory

What follows is an analytic systematization of those definitions that seem characteristic of the cognitivistic standpoint.

I. *Structural Definitions* (Scheme: "A theory consists of particular types of propositions organized in a particular fashion")

    A. By Reference to the Nature of Component Propositions (Scheme: "A theory is a set of cognitively oriented, categorical, factual propositions"):

        1. The theory is a set of propositions stating an interdependence between phenomena or variables—as opposed to a descriptive statement of isolated facts (Example: Stinchcombe, 1968: 15).

        2. A theory is a set of conditional propositions—as opposed to an existential statement of facts (Example: Zetterberg, 1962: 34).

        3. A theory is a set of law-like propositions—as opposed to historical or empirical generalizations (Example: Malewski, 1961: 46).

        4. A theory is a set of highly general propositions—as opposed to "ordinary" propositions of low generality (Example: Easton, 1953: 4–5, 65).

        5. A theory is a set of propositions employing theoretical terms or unobservables—as opposed to statements of observational facts (Example: Kemeny, 1959: 122).

    B. By Reference to the Nature of Systematization Linking Together the Theoretical Propositions (Scheme: "A theory is a set of propositions organized in a particular systematic fashion"):

        1. A theory is a semantically (substantively) organized set of propositions connected by the identity of a substantive domain or of a common problem or of a common conceptual framework (Example: Bunge, 1967, vol.I: 391).

        2. A theory is a syntactically (formally) organized set of propositions connected by logical, deductive relationships (Example: Gibson, 1960: 113).

II. *Functional Definitions* (Scheme: "A theory as intended to fulfill a particular cognitive function, and therefore it must possess a particular internal structure")

    A. By Reference to Autonomous Functions Fulfilled by a Theory within the Domain of Scientific Activities:

        1. A theory is a means of systematic and economical accumulation of knowledge—it is a warehouse of scientific informations.

        2. A theory is a tool for suggesting important research problems and hypotheses—it serves needed heuristic functions (Example: Parsons, 1964: 213, 219–220).

B. By Reference to Instrumental Functions, Fulfilled by a Theory within the Extrascientific Domain:
   1. A theory provides a prediction of future states of affairs.
   2. A theory provides an explanation of phenomena and regularities (Example: Homans, 1967: 106).

Because of the logical symmetry of scientific explanation and scientific prediction the two definitions quoted above amount to the same thing. A theory is understood here as any scientific result that fulfills an explanatory function. The structure of that particular result—that is, the types of characteristic component propositions and the form of their interrelations—is to be considered a necessary prerequisite for fulfilling the explanatory function (see Sztompka, 1974: 6–23; Sztompka, 1976a: 12–14).

The Activistic Notion of Theory

The representatives of the activistic standpoint rarely devote any attention to meta-theoretical questions, and therefore it is difficult, maybe impossible, to detect overt definitions of theory in their writings. But the definitions they seem to accept implicitly are relatively easy to identify. The following is an analytic systematization of typical definitions assumed by activists. The order followed is the same as before.

I. *Structural Definitions* (Scheme: "A theory consists of particular types of propositions organized in a particular fashion")
   A. By Reference to the Nature of Component Propositions (Scheme: "A theory is a set of practice-oriented or normative propositions"):
      1. A theory is a set of critical judgments referring to an existing state of affairs, an establishment, etc. (critical theory).
      2. A theory is a set of images describing preferred states of affairs, social ideals, etc. (images of the future, or better future).
      3. A theory is a set of norms (prescriptions) specifying the means considered proper, just, or right for achieving specified goals (programs for action, directives for moving from an existing to a preferred state of affairs).
   B. By Reference to the Nature of the Systematization Linking Together the Theoretical Propositions (Scheme: "A theory is a practically systematized set of propositions"):
      1. A theory is a semantically (substantively) organized set of propositions related to a common objective (e.g., a theory of attitude change), or referring to a common type of means (e.g., a theory

of propaganda), or implementing common higher-order values (e.g., democratic doctrine).

2. A theory is a syntactically (formally) organized set of propositions connected by relations of preference (e.g., the relative balance of means, ends costs, etc.), or relations of pragmatic coherence (e.g., the instrumental relationship between single propositions describing a sequence of prescribed activities, or the coherent, empirically consistent image of a possible better society).

II. *Functional Definitions* (Scheme: "A theory is intended to fulfill a particular practical function, and therefore it must possess a particular internal structure")

1. A theory should provide an image of the preferred and attainable future.

2. A theory should allow for effective control of a specified phenomena or processes.

3. A theory should provide the means for a global reconstruction of a society in accordance with a preferred image.

4. A theory should provide the means of obtaining a generalized and prolonged ability to control phenomena or processes (should help to obtain power).

After completing the foregoing review of definitions, one can define a cognitivistic standpoint as assuming the image of sociological theory described by any of the definitions included in the first set, and an activistic standpoint as assuming the image of sociological theory described by any of the definitions included in the second set. Cognitivists, therefore, ascribe to a sociological theory some cognitive functions or see it as constructed of categorical propositions, or both; whereas activists ascribe to a sociological theory some practical functions or see it as constructed of normative propositions, or both.

Varieties of Cognitivism and Activism: Theses, Postulates, Directives

But surely the concrete formulations of both standpoints may differ in various respects, two of which seem most significant: One shall be called the scope of the given position, and the other its strength. The first criterion refers to what a given position claims, the second to how the claim is phrased.

As to the first criterion, the crucial difference seems to obtain between those claims that ascribe to a theory a single, exclusive function and a single, exclusive type of component and those claims that characterize a theory in terms of mixed functions and allow mixed types of components to be included in the body of a theory. In the first case a position, whether cognitivistic or activistic, may be said to be of homogeneous scope, in the second case of heterogeneous scope.

As for the second criterion, it is already well known to the reader. Namely, the given position may be formulated either as a factual thesis, describing the actual character of existing sociological theory, or it may be formulated as a postulate referring to the possible shape or possible uses that a theory potentially has, or it may be formulated as a directive requiring a theory to be constructed in a specific way and to fulfill a specific function.

The two criteria combined together allow me to present the following systematization of cognitivistic and activistic standpoints.

  I. *Theses ("What is the actual nature of sociological theory?")*
     A. Theses of Cognitivism
        1. Sociological theory serves only cognitive functions and contains categorical propositions.
        2. Sociological theory serves cognitive and practical functions and contains both categorical and normative propositions.
     B. Theses of Activism
        1. Sociological theory is not restricted to cognitive functions and categorical propositions.
        2. Sociological theory serves only practical functions and contains only normative propositions.
 II. *Postulates ("What is the possible—potentially achievable—character of sociological theory?")*
     A. Postulates of Cognitivism
        1. Sociological theory may be formulated in such a way that it will serve only cognitive functions and contain only categorical propositions.
        2. Sociological theory may be formulated in such a way that it will serve both cognitive and practical functions and contain both categorical and normative propositions.
     B. Postulates of Activism
        1. Sociological theory need not be restricted to cognitive functions and categorical propositions.
        2. Sociological theory may be formulted in such a way that it will serve only practical functions and contain only normative propositions.
III. *Directives ("What is the proper, required character of a sociological theory?")*
     A. Directives of Cognitivism
        1. Sociological theory should be subservient exclusively to cognitive functions, and must contain only categorical propositions.

  2. Sociological theory should serve both cognitive and practical
     functions and should contain both categorical and normative
     propositions.
 B. Directives of Activism
  1. Sociological theory must not be restricted to cognitive functions
     and categorical propositions.
  2. Sociological theory should be subservient exclusively to practi-
     cal functions, and must contain only normative propositions.

The following is a brief review of the typical arguments put forward by
cognitivists and activists in defense of their positions.

THE ARGUMENTS OF THE CONTENDING
PARTIES: AN OVERVIEW

The types of arguments used by both cognitivists and activists to defend
their positions is related to the strength of their claims. To defend a thesis of
cognitivism or activism it is enough to cite some factual considerations
drawn from the history of science or from the actual practice of science. To
defend a postulate, one must refer to principles of an epistemological or an
ontological sort. And to defend a directive, normative considerations must
be adduced rooted in specific axiological preferences. The dispute between
cognitivism and activism most often revolves around the last type of argument; it is usually a dispute about value commitments, and not about facts
or principles. Probably it is the reason for the inconclusiveness of the controversy and the difficulty of reaching a compromise. In the following review, I shall present the arguments of the activists first, then those of the
cognitivists.

Factual Arguments: What Is the Case?

I. *The Arguments of the Activists*
 A. It Is Illusory That Social Knowledge Is a Neutral Instrument. In fact it
is utilized for the oppression and manipulation of human beings, against
their vital interests. Several examples are cited: human-relations school,
market research, military research, "Project Camelot." As Szymanski
puts it: "The uses of survey methods lie rather in the provision of practical knowledge for the purpose of intelligence, manipulation and control
[1971: 96]."
 B. It is Illusory That Social Knowledge Is at the Service of the Whole
Society. In fact it is utilized by the political or economic elites for the

maintenance of the existing social order, providing scientific legitimacy or justification for the establishment. Therefore "corporate sociology" is seen as basically conservative. To quote Szymanski again: "The functions of sociology for the dominant institutional structure are basically two-fold: It fulfills the system's need for legitimation and for practical knowledge [1971: 94]." Examples of research on propaganda, indoctrination, manipulating political attitudes are cited in this connection.

C. All Significant Results in the History of Sociology Have Been Born of Practical Considerations, as a Response to Pressing Social Issues. The selection of research problems or foci of theoretical studies on the basis of practical issues guaranteed the relevance of results (as opposed to trivia), and provided the immediate test of their validity (as opposed to abstract, unverifiable academicism).

D. All Significant Results in the History of Sociology Have Been Born of Compassion for the Underprivileged, the Oppressed, the Exploited, the Victimized—in Short, the Underdogs.

II. *The Counterarguments of the Cognitivists.* To reject factual arguments one can either provide the different facts, or he can accept the facts themselves but prove them to be irrelevant for the case. Both strategies are employed by the cognitivists.

A. Social Knowledge Is Equally often Applied for the Promotion of Humane Values, for the Improvement and Amelioration of the Human Condition. As Barton observes: "To be sure there is a lot of market research and research on how to manipulate the workers, done by university graduates working for industry or by university research organizations. But there is a large body of research which does not fit into this category, including most of the major academic studies [1971: 461]." Here, such examples as Myrdal's *The American Dilemma,* Adorno's *The Authoritarian Personality,* Lipset, Coleman, and Trow's *Union Democracy* are mentioned.

B. Social Knowledge Is Not Necessarily Subservient to Power Elites Promoting Their Vested Interests. To quote Barton again: "The research techniques and theories are not in themselves conservative or procapitalist. It all depends on whether the knowledge is made available to narrow interest groups only . . . or to everyone in the system; and whether the workers, consumers, black people, or colonial populations are organized to make use of such knowledge [1971: 462]." The examples of powerful social movements, social reforms, or social revolutions basing their strategies on scientific knowledge prove that social science can be equally conducive to counter establishment causes.

C. Sociological Research and Theory Are Not Always Inspired by Immediate Practical Interest or Immediate Needs. Usually, there is a time-lag between a moment of discovery and its application; and the results apparently impractical at a certain time prove to be of practical value later. As Coser puts it: "No one who undertakes scientific work at the present moment can be sure of the ultimate impact and 'relevance' of his work. . . . And the great majority of those men who in their day, worked on the 'relevant issues' remain of interest, at best, to specialized historians of ideas [1969: 132]." The narrow practical approach would limit the field of inquiry and prove suicidal in the long run. And a narrow empirical focus would restrict the results to descriptive diagnoses, preventing the formulation of abstract laws, which are logically necessary for the derivation of any practical recommendations.

D. Scientists, Owing to Their Broad Intellectual Perspective, Are Usually More Responsive Morally and More Often Raise Their Voices Against Various Forms of Injustice Than Nonscientists. But this is extrascientific activity, irrelevant to the correctness of their scientific research and the validity of the theories they formulate.

Principal Arguments: What Can Be the Case?

I. *The Arguments of the Activists.* Here, the activists must refer to more fundamental characteristics of social reality or the cognitive situation of social scientists vis-a-vis social reality. In effect, several ontological and epistemological points are raised.

A. Social Scientists Live in a Society and Satisfy Their Needs Through It. They cannot split themselves in half, and their practical orientation and practical interest in the social world must be reflected both in research and in the resulting theories. As McClung Lee puts it: "We are all also creatures of our time, place, sex, class and ethnic group [1976: 2]."

B. The Social World Is to a Large Extent a Human Creation, the Result of Human Activities. The attitude of the creator toward his products is never purely cognitive; it is always loaded with practical interests. The social scientist, being to some extent a producer of society, cannot avoid a practical orientation toward his subject.

C. Social Knowledge May Have a Direct, Immediate Impact on Society, and in This Respect It Is Unique in Comparison with Any Other Type of Knowledge. In the natural sciences the relation of knowledge and action is mediated by technology (the practical directives of "know-how"); in the social sciences knowledge itself (of a "know-that" type) may acquire practical potency as soon as it is perceived by people and included in the motivations for their activities. Friedrichs makes this point cogently:

> Of critical import to the social and behavioral sciences alone is the fact that the very discovery of an order in the realm of the social must inevita-

bly, by the very grammar that adheres to social or behavioral research, act to some degree as a new and unique element in the stream of empirical events that make up human interaction. . . . The simple knowledge of a given empirical sequence is a cognitive factor interactive with the cognitive, affective, and evaluational factors that are part of the societal matrix from which the uniformities were originally precipitated. Such awareness is fed back into the matrix by the researcher, the colleagues who seek to substantiate it, and all to whom it is communicated as a new and unique anticipatory factor, which will, to greater or lesser degree in the shorter or longer run, short-circuit one's capacity to verify it or its particular magnitude in the future. . . . All social research is in principle action research [1972: 266–267].

Others are also conscious of this peculiarity of the social sciences. Burns points out that "theories in action become a material force. . . . Once they enter into collective knowledge and 'consciousness,' they affect beliefs, orientations and actions and, therefore, become 'real, that is social facts [1976: 6]." And Bell and Mau put it thus: "What people believe about the way the world works can contribute to making it work that way [1970: 220]." This is the presumed basis for the phenomenon discussed in philosophy and sociology under the name *Oedipus effect* (Popper), *self-destroying and self-fulfilling prophecies* (Merton), *reflexive predictions* (Buck), and which is succinctly defined by Lasswell as a situation in which "a prediction, by becoming itself a factor in the definition of the situation, guarantees or prevents the emergence of anticipated results [in Eulau, 1958: 240]."

D. Social Research Itself Has a Significant Impact on the Course of Social Events and Social Processes. The intervention of a scientist in the course of social affairs, whether in the conducting of experiments, interviews, or even external observations, introduces some change in the beliefs, motivations, dispositions, emotions, attitudes of his subjects, transforms their relationships, the organization of their groups, the axionormative systems they accept, and so on. Therefore, whether he wants it or not, a sociologist is acting practically simply by conducting a sociological research.

II. *The Counterarguments of the Cognitivists.* Again, the strategy of defense against such arguments may consist in showing either that the principle, fundamental characteristics mentioned by activists do not obtain, or that they are not relevant to the issue in question.

A. The Individual Plays Many Roles in His Life, Both Consecutively and Simultaneously. Two strategies are available to prevent possible conflicts between their respective demands. One is to isolate and insulate each role from the others. The other is to eliminate some of those roles most apt to produce conflicts. Both strategies may be utilized by a social scientist. On the one hand, he may isolate his scientific activity from practical or political involvements, abstainig from any prescriptive or normative statements in his capacity of scientist. As Coser advises sociologists, "Let us then, by all means, be active citizens, social critics, historical actors. But let us not demand that all those activities be carried out in our roles of sociologists [1969: 137]." On the other hand, the social scientist may also get rid of those practical and political involvements altogether, devoting himelf exclusively to scholarship. In fact, since energy and time are limited, it may be advisable to give undivided loyalty to science; Extrascientific commitments impair scientific production. This ivory-tower ideology is defined by Hauser: "It is the mission of the sociologist qua scientist to add to sociological knowledge. He should not yield to the temptation to turn activist at the expense of his functions as a scientist [1971: 438]."

B. It Is True That Ultimately Society Is a Product of Human Activities. But it becomes dissociated from the ultimate producer, acquires objective properties, and can be studied as any other object, with a detached, disinterested attitude.

C. The Phenomenon of Self-fulfilling and Self-defeating Prophecies Is a Concomitant of Such Ignorance as May Be Dispelled. There is no reason why systematic, scientific knowledge cannot be obtained on the effect of social knowledge on social reality; specifically, describing how subjects would react to sociological information. If such knowledge (only temporarily not at hand) were taken into consideration in the process of formulating predictions, the specter of self-confirmation or self-falsification would disappear.

D. The Acknowledged Effect of Research on Studied Subjects Indicates the Imperfection of Current Research Procedures. This impact can and certainly will be eliminated with the improvement of objective techniques of social inquiry.

Normative Arguments: What Should Be the Case?

I. *The Arguments of the Activists.* To substantiate the directives of activism, one must resort to axiological or normative arguments. At this level the opposition between activists and cognitivists appears to involve opposing value preferences, and is particularly difficult to resolve. There is a specific axiological syndrome, which shall be called *a sociocentric ethos,* that underlies the standpoint of activism. It is composed of five components:

A. Sociology Should Guide Itself by Emancipatory Interests. Its primary goal should be to contribute to the full self-realization of human potentiality. And its primary preoccupation should be with the implementation

of social knowledge for this purpose. As Strasser puts it: "Social emancipists are primarily concerned with the materialization of theory, not
with its confirmation [1976: 11]."

B. Sociology Should Guide Itself by Means of a Populist Orientation.
The primary reference group for the sociologist in the process of research
and theory construction should be the people, and particularly the underprivileged, exploited, oppressed or victimized groups. And the ultimate
addressee of sociological knowledge should be the masses of people.

C. Sociology Should Guide Itself by Maintaining a Critical Attitude. It
should promote skepticism, criticism of the status quo, nonconformity,
and active dispositions to transform society.

D. Sociology Should Guide Itself by the Ambition to Provide Enlighten-
ment. It should implement its findings by education and promulgation.
It should treat people as partners who must be convinced of a given policy before they adopt it freely, and hence as subjects able to learn, understand, accept, and realize directives of action. Dahrendorf aptly describes
this approach as "the notion that through the theory, and through the
enunciation of the theory, one can immediately stir people and arouse
them to action [1976: 128]."

E. Sociology Should Appraise Its Problems and Its Results by the Criterion of Practical Relevance, as the Fundamental Indicator of Scientific
Adequacy. Relevance should be taken as the ultimate guideline for the
social scientist.

II. *The Counterarguments of the Cognitivists.* The cognitivists seem to reject
all those value preferences and to accept the opposite axiological syndrome,
which shall be called the *science-centric ethos.* To be sure, sometimes they do
not state their values explicitly, but then quite plausible interpretation is
provided by their opponents, and in such cases I shall refer to the values
that the activists ascribe to the cognitivists. The science-centric syndrome
consists of five components.

A. Sociology Should Guide Itself by Technological Interest. Its ultimate
goal should be to contribute to the enrichment of human control over
other people, social institutions, social organizations. And its primary
preoccupation should be with the confirmation of theoretical propositions able to provide a logical and sound basis for practical directives.
"The major objective of science is not primarily to control and predict,
but to understand. Effective control is a reward of understanding, and
accuracy in prediction is a check on understanding [Krech, Crutchfield,
and Ballachey, 1962: 2]."

B. Sociology Should Guide Itself by the Elitist Orientation. The primary
reference group for sociologists in the process of research and theory
construction should be the scientific community, and particularly fellow

social scientists. And the ultimate addressee of sociological knowledge should be the administrative or political bodies with legitimate preroga- tives for shaping policy. As Horowitz describes this approach: "Social scientists to the extent that they become involved with policy-making agencies, become committed to an elitist ideology. They come to accept as basic the idea that men who really change things are on the top. Thus, the closer to the top one can get direct access, the more likely will in- tended changes be brought about [1967: 353]."

C. Sociology Should Guide Itself by a Neutral, Detached Attitude. It should describe, explain, point to alternative possibilities of future devel- opments, and alternative courses of possible action, but abstain from eval- uative judgments, the choosing of alternatives, and intervention in the course of social affairs.

D. Sociology Should Guide Itself by the Ambition of Providing Instru- ments for Effective Manipulation. It should open possibilities of inducing changes in the functioning of human collectivities and in social processes. It should treat human populations as objects, and make them follow spe- cified ways of action and pursue specified goals, even without their accep- tance or against their will.

E. Sociology Should Appraise Its Problems and Its Results in Terms of Theoretical Fruitfulness and Empirical Validity as the Fundamental Indi- cators of Scientific Adequacy. Truth should be the ultimate guideline for the sociologist, just as for any other scientist.

CONSTRUCTIVISM AS
A DIALECTICAL SOLUTION

The dialectical rejection of the dilemma *knowledge or action?* will be car- ried out by the same strategy as was used for the earlier dilemmas. To reiterate the main elements of this strategy: If a new solution to the di- lemma is to be found, it must be opposed to both traditional assumptions, cognitivism as well as activism. To be opposed to both assumptions means to be opposed to all, including beliefs, that they have in common. Thus, a dialectical method of overcoming the traditional dilemmas must proceed along the following lines: First, the common set of assumptions of a higher order shared by cognitivists and activists alike must be reconstructed; sec- ond, those assumptions must be rejected and an antithetical set of assump- tions specified; and third, the solution to the dilemma—the constructivist assumption—must be shown to follow from the new set of higher-order assumptions.

Common Meta-assumptions

But is there really anything in common between the seemingly an-
tithethical standpoints of cognitivism and activism? It seems to me that
there are at least five higher-order assumptions that both the cognitivists
and the activists simply take for granted. Only if those assumptions are
accepted can the whole dispute be meaningful. And correspondingly, if I
want to prove the dispute meaningless, it is enough to reject those higher-
order assumptions.

The five taken for granted refer to the characteristics of the object of
social cognition, to the characteristics of the cognitive process itself, and to
the characteristics of the results achieved by the cognitive process.

First, both the cognitivists and the activists typically share the belief that
the social world exists objectively in the same way as the natural world; that
is, independent of and external to those who approach it with a cognitive or
practical interest. The social world is given; it exists "out there," whether it
is studied or not, discovered or not, understood or not, or controlled or not.
The cognitivists will demand that this existing social world be described and
explained, in accordance with the primary goal of social science. The activists will demand that this existing social world first of all be controlled and
transformed. Both seem to believe that society is quite like any natural object: for example, like the organism that can be studied for the sake of
understanding its objective laws, or healed, but that obviously exists independent of the activities of the physiologists or physicians.

Second, both seem to believe that social reality is "objective" or "given"
in another meaning of these terms; namely, that it represents some constant, static, unchanging qualitites or states of affairs. The cognitivists wish
to discover these qualities and to describe and explain these states of affairs;
the activists wish to change them, to push them forward from their existing
inert position. Again, both treat society as if it were a natural object, such as
a piece of iron ore that can be analyzed for its composition or made into
steel, but whose existence is independent of any activities of a geologist or a
metallurgical engineer.

The third assumption is corollary of the previous two. It says that society
must be approached from the outside, or, as Durkheim would have put it, as
a thing, resting somewhere "out there" and waiting to be discovered, described, and explained, or else waiting to be modifed and transformed. Thus
the cognitivists profess an external contemplative attitude, the activists an
external manipulative attitude, toward society: The common ground is externality of approach.

The fourth assumption introduces the dichotomy of cognitive and ex-
tracognitive human activities. It seems to be commonly believed by both

the cognitivists and the activists that description and explanation of social reality constitutes a separate category of human activity, distinct from practical action. Only if one believes in such a strict distinction can the claim for the primacy of cognition over action or the claim for the primacy of action over cognition make sense. A relation of primacy can obtain only between distinct and separate objects.

The fifth assumption is a corollary of the fourth at the level of the linguistic structures in which the results of cognitive or practical interest in the social world are expressed. It is a belief in the dichotomy of facts and directives, categorical and normative statements, *sein (is)* and *sollen (ought)*. The basis of the dichotomy is the supposedly clear distinction of the functions or uses that statements of a specific type may have, or, to put it more precisely, the belief in a one-to-one correspondence between the structure of propositions *about* society and their function *for* a society. Thus, it is believed that categorical propositions of a descriptive or explanatory nature have a cognitive function only, providing information about the actual qualities or regularities of the social world. And, correspondingly, it is believed that normative propositions have a practical function only, providing directives for the effective transformation of the social world. Even though propositions of the first type are usually considered as the intellectual premises for the derivation of propositions of the second type, that the two types are separate and distinct is held to be self-evident.

The Rejection of Common Meta-assumptions

Now, let us attempt to reject all the assumptions listed above, and replace them with their opposites. Since some suggestions in this direction can be found in recent sociological literature, I shall draw on it as needed.

First, there are compelling theoretical trends in sociology that reject the image of the social world as objectively, externally given and perceive it rather as created or constructed by men. One could adduce a whole spectrum of standpoints typical of the humanistic orientation in sociology, from those who, like Weber or Znaniecki or the symbolic interactionists, believe in the particular importance of the meaning dimension attached to the objective substratum of human activities by acting individuals to those who, like Winch, Schutz, or the social phenomenologists, focus exclusive attention on the domain of meanings, values, and symbols, neglecting any consideration of the objective, material substratum of the social world. Similar emphasis may also be discovered in some branches of sociological research; for example, the sociology of culture or the sociology of art. In this perspective society is no longer viewed as existing independent of human activities, as a natural object, but rather as a complex product of human activities, of conscious and purposeful orientation toward the world, which can be understood only if the qualities and regularities infused by the creator are taken into consideration. To clarify by analogy, it is impossible to grasp the essential qualities of, say, an apartment house by studying the composition of bricks: The crucial dimension would comprise the architectural structure, the purpose for which the house was built, the actual uses it has, etc. The same is true of society, where the crucial dimension would comprise the structure of social relationships, the motivations, intentions, and dispositions people reveal in their activities, the functions of those activities both for individuals and for the society as a whole, etc. All this would not exist were it not for individuals and their activities: Society is in an important sense man-made.

Second, more and more often society is viewed not as a static object with permanent, fixed qualities, but rather as a fluid process of constantly changing characteristics, or, to put it another way, not as a "being," but rather as "becoming." Process orientation is singled out by contemporary commentators as a significant trend in the history of sociology and several scholars are mentioned as its representatives (see Boskoff, 1971: 1–12).

The image of society as a man-made process has important implications for the epistemology of social research as well as the strategy of social engineering. Consequently, the third assumption, that of the external approach—both at the level of cognition and at the level of control—must be rejected. Man, whether studying society or attempting to change it, is at the same time a member of society. His relationship to the object is not external but internal. As Popper has observed: "Nowhere is the fact that the scientist and his object belong to the same world of greater moment than in the social sciences. . . . We are faced, in the social sciences, with a full and complicated interaction between observer and observed, between subject and object [1960: 14]." In the epistemological dimension, social knowledge appears to be a form of self-knowledge. The student of society does not stand in a detached, external position vis-a-vis his subject matter; rather he is studying something that is in part his own creation and which undergoes changes dependent in part on his own activities. Each student of society is thereby a student of himself. And it becomes still more obvious if we leave the individualistic, distributive perspective and interpret the process of social cognition in collective terms. The collective knowledge of society acquired at a certain moment in the history of science by a community of scholars, and more or less widespread among the people, must be considered as the internal experience of a society by itself—union of the subject and the object of cognition. As McRae puts it: "Sociology is a major form of human self-consciousness, a kind of imperfect looking glass in which we may see reflected back the visage of society [1974: 7]." Consequently, there is no radical distinction between the activity of professional students of society and the experiences of the ordinary people who participate in social life. Rather, they make up the poles of the same spectrum. Sociology, in this view, is nothing but sophisticated and refined common sense.

The same is true if we consider the characteristic properties of social engineering, the practical intervention of men in social affairs. It is not a manipulation of a detached object. Rather, it is the modification of a process by conscious and purposeful participation. From the individualistic, distributive perspective, each member of a society contributes something to the social process; from the collectivistic perspective, the activities of the masses of men are the only factors responsible for the social process; in fact, they *are* the social process. In the words of Swingewood: "Man intervenes directly in the historical process but only as a part of that process [1975: 29]." Obviously, the levels of participation vary: The actual impact of society's members on society may be anywhere on a wide range of forms—from the most self-conscious effort at political planning and control to the habitual doings of everyday life. But there is no unbridgeable gap dividing the activities of a social engineer and an ordinary person who has never heard of sociology. All of them take part in the construction of their social world.

It follows that another dichotomy must also be rejected; namely, that between the cognitive activites and the practical activities of people. The dissociation between them suggested by the fourth assumption is found misleading and spurious. If society is seen as a constructed process and one's relationship to society as conscious, real participation in that process, then self-consciousness must be seen as the outcome of participation, and participation as the embodying of the actually attained level of self-consciousness. The interplay of cognition and practice makes up the "unending spiral of the creation of society [Bell and Mau, 1970: 226]." Social cognition is seen as a precondition of effective practice and an important codeterminant of its course. "The actual future is to some extent a consequence of the images of the future that are present within a society [Bell and Mau, 1970: 230]." On the other hand, social practice is seen as both the stimulus and the test of the cognitive representations of society. "Human action entails problem-solving activities and manifests a pattern of development or an 'unfolding' as theory or theoretical paradigms interact with practice [Baumgartner *et al.*, 1975: 5]." Or to quote Bell and Mau again: "As the actual future emerges, an opportunity occurs to assess the adequacy of beliefs about the past, the present, and social causation, and desirability of goals and their relevance to basic values. Thus old images of the future and beliefs may be revised [1970: 225]."

This unity of two inseparable aspects of basically the same process has been commented on by Strasser: "The processes of cognition are inseparable from the creation of society and cannot therefore function only as means of maintenance and reproduction of social life, but serve equally to establish the very definitions of this life. [1976: 10]." The same point is made by Burns: "We are concerned with the processes whereby humans try to develop more adequate theoretical accounts of the world and to create 'technologies,' not the least of which are social devices, through which theory can be carried out in social action [1976: 8]."

So far our concern has focused on the ontological characteristics of the social world and the consequent intimate relationship of human cognitive and practical activites. But I have defined the dilemma *knowledge or action?* as revolving around the characteristics of social theory. The passage to the linguistic dimension, crucial for my argument, will be effected by the rejection of the fifth assumption shared by cognitivists and activists alike. This is the assumption of a basic dichotomy between facts and directives, or between categorical and normative statements in terms of their supposedly distinct functions, cognitive and practical, respectively. That such a dichotomy is untenable will be seen if we consider two situations, typical of the social sciences and related to their basic peculiarities. First, it has been observed by several that the relationship between factual, categorical knowledge of society (of the descriptive, explanatory, or prognostic sort) and the practice of social transformations is not always of the same type as in the natural sciences. Whereas in the natural sciences the relationship is normally mediated by the formulation of the directives of action (know-how) derived from basic knowledge, and the translation of basic knowledge into directives is a quite complex endeavor, requiring special scientific sub-disciplines of the so-called practical, technical or applied sciences, in the social sciences this is not always the case. Very often descriptive or explanatory knowledge, by virtue of being in a significant respect self-knowledge or consciousness of society as including oneself, may become immediately influential for social practice— for the conduct of human affairs, from the simplest everyday acts to the most complex political decisions. This immediate relevance of social knowledge to social practice was often discussed as the mechanism of so-called self-fulfilling and self-destroying prophecies, where the sheer fact of a prediction's becoming known among those whose behavior it concerns can validate the initially invalid prediction, and invalidate the initially valid one. A relatively recent formulation of this peculiarity is given by Friedrichs:

> Of critical import to the social and behavioral sciences alone is the fact that the very discovery of an order in the realm of the social must inevitably, by the very grammar that adheres to social or behavioral research, act

to some degree as a new and unique element in the stream of empirical events that make up human interaction. . . . Such social knowledge stands as a new and unique factor entering into the social matrix that includes both the researcher and his subjects, transforming it in some measure from the matrix that might have been if the order had not been revealed [1972: 266].

Thus the purely factual statements of the social sciences may be seen as serving practical functions. What Polak remarks about history may be generalized to include all the social-scientific disciplines: "The writing of history merges imperceptibly into the responsible act of creating history. . . . The formulation, as well as the act of describing the image of the future, may influence the future itself [1961, vol.I: 57]." Bell and Mau emphasize the same point with respect to sociology: "In recent years, sociological 'truths' have come . . . to influence the way people see themselves and their societies and, thus, have been consequential for the behavior that emerges from such conceptions [1970: 208]." And therefore "sociologists can help to change the world through their reinterpretation of it [Bell and Mau, 1970: 239]." Therefore, categorical, factual statements in the social sciences may play a double role—to provide the information about society, and also influence the transformations of society.

    The same may be said of directives, or normative statements. They certainly provide guidelines for social practice. But at the same time—although this is rarely noticed—they furnish some information about society. For example, if they are rational and realistic, they certainly tell us what goal states are obtainable in a society (what qualities the society may possibly take), and what activities can be undertaken in a society to obtain those goals, if only a sufficient number of people are willing to pursue them. Thus normative statements, too, play a double role in the social sciences, cognitive as well as practical. There is a fundamental reason for such a dualism: Both the factual and the normative statements reflect at the linguistic level the mixed cognitive and practical experiences of society. Both of them have their origin in social experiences and both are tested by reference to such experiences.

    From such considerations, eliminating the rigid separation of facts and directives, there is only a short logical step to the notion of a sociological theory as comprising both factual and normative propositions as its valid core. Such a notion is advocated by Easton:

    It is deceptive to counterpose value to causal theory; in practice each is involved in the other. The distinction between these two classes of propositions is logical only. [And therefore] a political theory consists of four major kinds of propositions: factual, moral, applied, and theoretical. Strictly speaking, we ought to say that these are several logical aspects of propositions, since no statement can ever refer exclusively to facts, values, or theories. Each aspect of a proposition is usually involved with one or more of the others [1953: 52, 310].

A similar complex view of the structure of sociological theory is proposed by Strasser, who develops hints given by Galtung:

What is suggested here is a concept of sociology as a science based on three ... types of sentences. A sentence constitutes the basic unit of knowledge about reality. Sentences may take the form of data-sentences—that is, verbal reports about facts or their composite products, empirical generalizations; there are also theory-sentences, so called hypotheses arrived at by deductive reasoning inside open sets of propositions; finally value-sentences, usually referred to as axioms, dichotomize the scope of reality under study in points accepted and points rejected [1976: 12].

Whereas the data-sentences reflect some aspects of the observed, actual world, the theory-sentences deal with the "foreseen world," and the value-sentences (normative or directive propositions) refer to the "preferred world" (see Strasser, 1976: 17). Finally, it may be of interest to note that allowance for the normative ingredients in sociological theory has recently been made by the founder of mathematical sociology, and one of the most sophisticated research workers in contemporary social sciences: James Coleman. He states his methodological creed thus:

I do not expect all sociologists to agree that normative social theory is possible. I can only reiterate, that it appears to me as a sociologist eminently possible and to me as a person eminently desireable.... It is desirable, because it constitutes an intellectually satisfactory way of bringing our values as persons and our theoretical activities as sociologists closer together [1975: 93].

The discussion so far has shown that assumptions of the higher order accepted by both cognitivists and activists are by no means self-evident, and can quite plausibly be rejected. In fact, they have been found deserving of rejection by several representatives of contemporary social science. Therefore, the cognitivist and activist standpoints do not provide the only possibilities; a third solution—the dialectic—is possible.

Toward a Dialectical Alternative

The whole dispute of cognitivism and activism has been construed here as referring mainly to the nature of sociological theory. Now, it may be noted that the implicit question has at least two distinct and independent aspects. One is the aspect of content (the substantive aspect), referring to what a proper theory should say. Another is the aspect of use (the functional aspect), referring to the needs that a proper theory should serve.

Taking into account the substantive aspect, one may specify the following opposing standpoints, signified by the numerical subscript "1":

Cognitivism$_1$ = A theory must say something about the world, provide some information on the qualities and regularities obtaining in the world.

Activism$_1$ = A theory must say something about prescribed, proper conduct instrumental for reaching specified goals, whether it is rooted in objective knowledge or not.

Taking into account the functional aspect, one may specify the second pair of opposing standpoints, signified by the numerical subscript "2":

Cognitivism$_2$ = A theory must satisfy the need for intellectual illumination or comprehension, understanding of the world, orientation to the world.

Activism$_2$ = A theory must have immediate impact on the world, contributing directly to its changes.

As both aspects are mutually independent, one may without the risk of contradiction combine together both dichotomies. The cross-tabulation of possible theorietical standpoints shown in Figure 4.1 will result.

The Aspect of Substance

	Cognitivism$_1$	Activism$_1$
Activism$_2$	Constructivism	Ideologism
Cognitivism$_2$	Contemplativism	

The Aspect of Function

Figure 4.1

The combination of Cognitivism$_1$ with Activism$_2$ generates a specific standpoint, which will be called Constructivism. The constructivist standpoint has two theoretical foes. The first is Activism$_1$, which considers a sociological theory as a purely ideological expression, devoid of any empirical, objective validity. As against the Activism$_1$, the standpoint of constructivism requires any theory to have some informational content. But according to the constructivist standpoint such informational content can be included not only in factual, categorical statements but also in normative directives, as both types of propositions reflect the social world, more or less adequately. The second foe of constructivism is Cognitivism$_2$, which considers a sociological theory as an instrument for satisfying purely intellectual needs, without any immediate practical relevance. As against Cognitivism$_2$ constructivism requires any theory to have some immediate practical function. But according to the constructivist standpoint, such a function can be effected not only by normative directives, but also by factual, categorical statements, since both types of propositions influence the conduct of people in society and produce social transformations.

The unity of cognition and practice, or knowledge and action, is recognized by the constructivist standpoint in two ways: first, by granting that normative propositions are at a par with categorical propositions as the proper components of a sociological theory; and second, by ascribing to both types of propositions—categorical and normative—double functions: cognitive and practical. Thus, a double nexus of knowledge and action is proclaimed: one of the external type, owing to the coexistence of knowledge-oriented (categorical) and action-oriented (normative) propositions in every sociological theory; the other of the internal type owing to the duality of uses that each kind of proposition has in society. The term *constructivism*, adopted here to signify such a standpoint, is intended to convey the idea that a sociological theory reflects the social world, which is constantly being constructed and reconstructed by people, and also participates in the construction of the social world, by providing knowledge of its qualities and regularities together with directives for changing it.

The standpoint of constructivism may appear in a weaker or a stronger form—as a thesis, a postulate, or a directive. In terms of the formulations distinguished earlier, the constructivist standpoint can be represented and explained by the following set of theses, postulates, and directives:

I. *Theses*
   A. Sociological Theory Serves Cognitive and Practical Functions and Contains Both Categorical and Normative Propositions (Descriptive Anti-ideologism).

B. Sociological Theory Is Not Restricted to Cognitive Functions and Categorical Propositions (Descriptive Anti-intellectualism).

II. *Postulates*

A. Sociological Theory May Be Formulated in Such a Way That It Serves Both Cognitive and Practical Functions, and Contains Both Categorical and Normative Propositions.

B. Sociological Theory Need Not Be Restricted to Cognitive Functions and Categorical Propositions.

III. *Directives*

A. Sociological Theory Should Serve Both Cognitive and Practical Functions and Should Contain Both Categorical and Normative Propositions.

B. Sociological Theory Must Not Be Restricted to Cognitive Functions and Categorical Propositions.

Constructivism must be considered as something more than a new solution within the framework of the old dilemma; for it rejects and overcomes the dilemmas itself, treating it as illusory and misleading and replacing it with a qualitatively new, synthetic standpoint. It is a typical dialectic resolution of a dilemma, inasmuch as it combines continuation with negation, rescuing some rational components of both extreme positions and rejecting their one-sided absolutization. It lifts the whole debate into another dimension, providing a solution which is qualitatively different from each of the traditional standpoints and avoiding their intellectual fallacies.

CONSTRUCTIVISM IN MARXIAN SOCIOLOGICAL THEORY

I believe that the most developed and consistent formulation of the constructivist solution to the dispute we've been considering is to be encountered in the works of Karl Marx, and in the Marxist tradition of sociological theorizing. Again, it must be stressed that Marx was never directly concerned with explicit methodological questions, and it would be futile to search in his writings for any specific pronouncements on the nature of sociological theory, its content or functions. Thus, one must undertake a reconstruction to reveal the components of the constructivist standpoint implicit in the content of Marxian theory.

Two strategies of reconstruction will be followed. First, I shall attempt to show that all the higher-order assumptions presupposed by the constructivist position can be plausibly ascribed to Marx on the basis of his own statements and the consensus among his adherents and commentators. Second, I shall attempt to show that a sociological theory of his has a form prescribed by the constructivist position, and therefore may be considered as the actual, concrete implementation of a more general approach assumed by Marx to be proper for any theory construction in the social sciences.

The Assumptions of Constructivism as Acknowledged by Marx

The first higher-order assumption of constructivism referred to the object of social studies and stated that it is constructed by men. Marx and Engels say: "The chief defect of all hitherto existing materialism—that of Feuerbach included—is that the thing, reality, sensuousness, is conceived only in the form of the object, or of contemplation, but not as human sensuous activity, practice, not subjectively. . . . Hence [Feuerbach] does not grasp the significance of 'revolutionary,' of 'practical-critical' activity [1968: 28]." The practical activity of men is the real matter of which society and history is made. As Swingewood puts it: "Society and history are characterized by certain laws, but it is man who ultimately makes the world through his praxis. . . . Marx's social theory is characterized by the precept that society is made, not given. . . . History has meaning only insofar as men made it [1975: 7, 13, 214]." As a result of praxis the external world is transformed from the "world in itself" to the "world for us," the outcome of human creation (see Jaroszewski, 1974: 96, 344). In effect, "the subject is confronting no longer a 'raw objectivity' but rather the objectivity transformed by the activities of the subjects [Jaroszewski, 1974: 313]." The world of man is man-made: "Labor has created man, and also the whole human world [Jaroszewski, 1974: 96]." There is no society outside the historical praxis of people— praxis including "besides the productive activity, also the manifold forms of social activity changing the interpersonal relationships, the political struggles and in particular the revolutionary class-struggles [Jaroszewski, 1974: 110]."

The second assumption of constructivism characterized the object of social studies as a constantly changing process rather than a stasis—as "becoming" rather than "being." Interpreting the Marxian method, Lukacs formulates this assumption in the following way:

> Praxis has its objective and structural preconditions and complement in the view that reality is a "complex of processes." . . . This reality is not, it becomes. . . . Man must be able to comprehend the present as a becoming. He can do this by seeing in it the tendencies out of whose dialectical opposition he can make the future. Only when he does this will the present be a process of becoming that belongs to him. Only he who is

willing and whose mission it is to create the future can see the present in
its concrete truth [1971: 202–204]."

The same point is clearly perceived by Jaroszewski in his discussion of
Marxian epistemology; "The object of cognition consists (for Marx) in constantly humanized nature, and constantly transformed interpersonal relationships. . . . The subjects of cognitive efforts are people embedded in
dynamic, changing relationships [1974: 351]."

The third assumption dealt with the specificity of the relationship between the subject and object of social cognition and social engineering, due
to the constructed and dynamic character of the social reality. In the Marxist
tradition the idea of the intimate union, or at least of the reciprocal links,
between a subject and an object, seems to be openly acknowledged. As
Swingewood argues convincingly: "Since society is made, then knowledge
of it cannot be regarded simply as a reflection or imitation of objective
realities. . . . Social theory must embody within its own concepts the making, not completion, of social structure—social theory must grasp its human
and historical nature [1975: 13]." The process of social cognition is described and interpreted by Marxists as the process of acquiring self-
consciousness by the social subjects in the course of their practical activities.
Kolakowski describes the Marxian position thus:

> Understanding the world is not supposed to consist in its "external" ap-
> praisal, its moral evaluation or scientific explanation; rather it is conceived
> as a self-understanding of society, thus an act in which an object is
> changed by a subject, by a sheer activity of understanding, which is possi-
> ble only when the subject and object coincide, when the difference be-
> tween an educator and the educated disappears, when thought itself be-
> comes a revolutionary act, self-consciousness of the human condition
> [1976: 146].

Jaroszewski makes the same point: "The production of knowledge of the
world is, according to Marx, closely connected with the practical mastering
of that world. . . . The history of humanity is, in some respects, tantamount
to the history of developing human self-consciousness [1974: 98]." A similar observation is found in Birnbaum, who stresses "Marxism's denial of a
total separation between subject and object in the process of historical
knowledge. The knower is immersed in the substance he seeks to elucidate
[1971: 127]." And the process of social influence or control is similarly
interpreted, in terms of participation rather than external manipulation:
"Man changes both himself and the social world. . . . Social theory must
grasp this union of subject and object at both the epistemological as well as
the practical level [Swingewood, 1975: 76]."

The fourth assumption claims the basic unity of the practical and cognitive activities within the field of human praxis. We learn the properties and

regularities of the social world as we change it, and we base our endeavors to change the world on knowledge of its properties and regularities. Both processes go hand in hand, and cannot be considered in dissociation. Such a view is ascribed to Marx by a contemporary commentator:

> Marx asserts that the process of acquiring knowledge is an active, constructive process.... There exists a dialectic relationship between the cognitive structure and the practical process (creating objects by transforming nature and creating the social conditions within which the basic process of production occurs). The cognitive, constructive process is the basis for praxis and praxis in turn functions as means of verification for the cognitive, theoretical process [Israel, 1972: 145].

Almost the same interpretation of Marxian epistemology is provided by Jaroszewski: "Marx described cognition as active cognition, closely interlinked with material practice.... He considered historical human practice (first of all, material production) as the essential source and ultimate goal of all cognition, and also as the criterion of truthfulness of our images of the surrounding world [1974: 90, 324]." To quote Marx himself: "In practice man must prove the truth, that is the reality and power, the this-sidedness of his thinking. The dispute over the reality or non-reality of thinking which is isolated from practice is a purely scholastic question [Marx and Engels, 1968: 28]."

The fifth assumption posits a complex relationship between the structural characteristics of the propositions included in social theory and their functional significance for a society, and on this basis rejects the strict opposition of categorical and normative statements. The famous Marxian statement that ideas can become a material force if they move the masses may be read as implying the immediate, direct impact of social knowledge on social reality. As Swingewood puts it, for Marx "social theory... becomes itself part of the struggle to change the world [1975: 29]." Or in the words of Giddens: "In Marx's conception, the theories of the social thinker themselves form a part of the dialectic in terms of which social life both 'changes men' and is 'changed by men' [1971: 207]." And at the same time, the normative ideas, directives, programs, and images of the future society included in social theory are also a specific reflection of human historical praxis—they serve a cognitive function providing information about that praxis, and the historically circumscribed stage it has reached, on par with purely descriptive and explanatory propositions. And comment by a well-known Polish philosopher, Jaroszewski, sums up this point very clearly:

> In the perspective of Karl Marx's philosophy, the philosophy which self-consciously does not restrict itself to "explanation of the world," but purports to change it—philosophy which bases this intention to transform the world on the scientific scrutiny of its objective qualities and laws—

the axiological and directive propositions are never detached from the ontological, facutal propositions, and vice versa. . . . The tendency of Marxian scientific socialism was to overcome the opposition typical of utopian socialism as well as the earlier dominant philosophy, namely the nondialectic opposition of existence and prescription, description and value, science and ideology [1974: 168–169].

So much for the first line of argumentation. I hope to have shown that Marx had rejected those assumptions that characterize traditional stand-points, whether cognitivistic or activistic, and accepted—more or less expli-citly—the alternative, original assumptions of the constructivist position. But there is also a second line of argument that can corroborate the ascrip-tion of the constructivist assumption to Marx. This is based on an analysis of actual Marxian theories, and particularly the form they have. The key to understanding the Marxian methodology of theory construction is here be-lieved to lie in the actual theoretical results that Marx produced, and a form he furnished them with. It seems a safe supposition that an author will usu-ally follow his own theoretical and methodological creed in his own theore-tical practice, and therefore in the results achieved by means of a given method (with the help of particular assumptions) the characteristics of the method (the nature of those assumptions) will clearly be reflected.

Marxian Theory as an Illustration of Constructivism

The students of Marxian theoretical contributions to sociology are cer-tainly agreed on one point—the internal complexity of their form. As Meyer expresses the prevailing sentiment, "Marxism is not merely social science; it is something more [1969: 45]." The duality of categorical (fac-tual) and normative (prescriptive) dimensions is perceived in at least three ways: (a) as the duality of propositions in the Marxian system, namely, some of them obviously describe and explain, whereas some of them condemn and call for practical measures to be taken; (b) as the duality of focus in the Marxian intellectual biography, the young Marx is supposed to be mainly concerned with reform, the mature Marx with analysis of the laws of motion of human society; and (c) as the duality of impact that Marxism has, being on the one hand the political doctrine of revolution and the ideological rationale of the communist movement, and on the other hand the source of theoretical insights and hypotheses on the functioning of human societies and their historical development.

Those commentators who subscribed more or less consciously to the traditional positivistic dichotomy of facts and directives were led to believe that there is an internal contradiction in Marxism, and that at all three levels.

They claimed that there are two distinct sides to his theoretical system, normative as opposed to scientific; that there are two distinct periods in his intellectual biography, humanistic and critical as opposed to analytic and theoretical; and that there are two distinct spheres of his impact, ideological or political as opposed to academic.

Such beliefs gave birth to the doctrine of "two Marxisms"—scientific Marxism as opposed to critical Marxism—expounded most forcefully by Gouldner:

> Among the most ingrained theoretical contradictions of Marxism is its ambivalence with respect to science. As an intellectual system, Marxism vacillates concerning its most fundamental "paradigm." . . . At times Marxism looks to science, indeed to positive science, as its paradigm. . . . There are however other times when he clearly thinks himself something different, when he regards himself as a "critic" and his work as a "critique." . . . There are . . . two tendencies in Marxism: one toward critique, which I shall call the "Critical Marxism," and another toward science which has called itself "Scientific Marxism" [1972: 2–3, 6].

Gouldner is correct in his perception of two dimensions in Marxism, but he is wrong in opposing them to each other and considering them as contradictory. In fact, they constitute a unity, and Marxian approach to theory cannot be grasped without their simultaneous consideration. This unity in complexity, rendered by the Marxian notion of a historical human praxis, is pointed out by several commentators as the crucial distinctive element of Marxian sociological theory. As Giddens observes: "Marx conceived his works to furnish a platform for the accomplishment of a definite Praxis, and not simply as academic studies of society [1971: 185]." And Jaroszewski makes the same point: "The Marxian philosophy of praxis combines theoretical considerations with practical commitment and practical participation in the class struggles [1974: 169]."

The unified duality of the Marxian theoretical system can be perceived at three distinct levels: first, at the level of theoretical concepts. It is typical of Marx to frame and utilize concepts that have at the same time categorical and normative meaning: They describe certain phenomena or properties, but at the same time convey critical, evaluative, or prescriptive judgments. Consider such concepts as alienation, exploitation, profit, surplus value, pauperization, fetishism and many others: They are clear examples of that which some contemporary Marxist philosophers call by the name *substantive valuations,* as opposed to *pure valuations.*

> Within the class of normative statements we distinguish some which possess a dual meaning and some which have a singular meaning The first

may be called substantive valuational statements, the second pure valuational statements. The substantive valuational statement has axiological
meaning . . . and also—being a statement—normal informational meaning
[Nowak, 1974a: 108].

The second level at which the categorical–normative duality of Marxian
theory may be discovered is the level of theoretical propositions. As
Birnbaum observes: "Marxism . . . claims to represent a total system, not
alone a description of society but a prescription for human action within it
[1971: 109]". Similarly, Wiatr sees the "uniqueness of the Marxist social
theory" in "the way in which it is able to unite three basic components:
values, explanation, and directives for action." And he continues: "Marxist
social theory is at the same time both normative and explanatory. . . . Social
theory . . . should be considered as a system of mutually interrelated values,
explanations, and directives for action. Its objective, to use Marx's famous
words, is not only to explain the world but to change it as well [1973b: 1,
3–4]." For example:

> When Marx talks of the iron laws of capitalist development he does so
> only in terms of a social theory whose function is to unmask the ways in
> which capitalism works so that consciously planned change can take place;
> it is not a blueprint for preordained, pregiven ends, but to show how the
> negative element, the proletariat, through its praxis can transform
> capitalism into socialism [Swingewood, 1975: 30].

In this as well as in many other cases of Marxian propositions

> Theory here is understood as a way of both predicting and creating the
> future. . . . The main task of Marxist theory is not to formulate these
> abstract predictions of the future but to shape the future by advocating
> directives, which are based on accepted basic values, explanations of rela-
> tionships between social phenomena and knowledge of anticipated de-
> velopments which have to be avoided and/or altered. . . . Marxist social
> theory manifests its original structure as value–explanation–action theory.
> It is this structure of Marxism that makes it basically different from all
> schools of "academic" social science [Wiatr, 1973b: 4, 7].

The third level at which the duality of the Marxian system manifests itself
is the level of subtheories, or partial theoretical structures of which the
system may be seen as composed. Some subtheories may be more directly
focused on the formulation of practical, normative directives, some others
on an explanatory account of reality. Wiatr believes that in terms of such
distinct foci one may distinguish within a Marxist sociological theory three
distinct subtheories—first, the "normative model," presenting the image of

the preferred and possible society; second the "explanatory theory," supplying the systematic set of hypotheses and law referring to the actual functioning and development of society; and third the "theory of socialist development," providing the directives how to get from "here" to "there," how to transform the actual into the possible. Such "constructivist theory" is "a particular proposal for building a socialist society, based on the assumed normative model of such a society, on knowledge about the functions of societies so far appearing in history, and on knowledge concerning the efficient means of social action [Wiatr, 1971: 57–59.]"

Thus, the unity of categorical and normative components is encountered at all three levels of the Marxian theoretical system. But this unity of the external sort is still strengthened by the fact that, as I observed earlier, in terms of Marxian epistemology there is an internal duality of functions played in a society by both categorical and normative propositions—categorical propositions having immediate practical impact on human conduct, and normative propositions conveying the cognitive informations about the possible social world. The unity of cognition and practice, knowledge and action, appears as multidimensional, closed and complete.

The arguments presented above, both indirect (concerning the higher-order assumptions) and direct (concerning the proper content of the constructivist standpoint), seem to corroborate the interpretation according to which Marx rejected both cognitivistic and activistic positions, and accepted a dialectical alternative described here as constructivism. Instead of a summary, some additional, more synthetic appraisals of contemporary commentators will be quoted. They point out the crucial role of constructivist assumptions in the Marxian paradigm of the social sciences. Giddens makes it very clear: "Only by the union of theory and practice, by the conjunction of theoretical understanding and practical political activity, can social change be effected. This means integrating the study of the emergent transformations potential in history with a program of practical action which can actualize these changes [1971: 20]." As if continuing this point Birnbaum remarks:

> Movement, reflective movement, between these two aspects of Marxism seems to me to constitute one of the most valuable possibilities of Marxism as a system; it allows a qualitatively different test of thought than that provided for in the model of social discourse fashioned after the natural sciences. It also recognizes antinomies and discontinuities in the human situation; it denies both the total independence of thought and the notion that thought somehow reflects realities outside it [1971: 112].

And Jaroszewski points out that: "The Marxists raise this particular link of practice, or creative activity with cognition, to the rank of the attitude, philosophical orientation, and cognitive strategy which explains the sources, goals, foundations, as well as the conditions of effectiveness and the criteria adequate with respect to the human knowledge about the world [1974: 103]." Rejecting the misleading opposition of the cognitivistic and activistic standpoints, and replacing them with the constructivist assumption, Marx was able to solve the problem of social cognition in an original and fruitful fashion.

> In the theory of cognition the category of praxis allowed one to overcome the antinomy of the contemplative character of all earlier mechanistic materialism and the activistic character of several trends typical of the "postcritical," subjective, and idealistic gnoseology. . . . The old contemplative materialism, considering human cognition as the passive reflection of objects and phenomena in the surrounding natural world, is replaced with an activist materialism, which treats social cognition as the component of the historical and social process of conquering nature, creating the human environment, and improving interpersonal relationships [Jaroszewski, 1974: 90, 126].

CHAPTER 5

Detachment or Bias: Neutralism, Axiologism, Commitment

The problem of valuations is certainly as old as science itself. Perhaps it is even as old as any conscious human reflection on the surrounding world, because men have always been moved by two sorts of questions: They have wanted to understand the world and have phrased descriptive or explanatory questions ("What is the world like?" and "Why is it so?"), but they have also wanted to appraise the world and have formulated evaluative or normative questions ("Is it good or bad?" and "What should it be?"). And the relationship of the categorical answers, establishing facts, and the evaluative answers, upholding values, has never been completely clear.

The duality of questions and the resulting dichotomy of facts and values has been inherited by that most systematic and orderly type of human reflection: science. The problem of the place and role of evaluational activities in the research process, and the corresponding problem of the place and role of value judgments in research results, have been posed in all the branches of science (see Bronowski, 1965). But nowhere have they caused so many disputes and controversies as in social science. Edel is certainly correct that "when the intellectual history of contemporary social science comes to be written, one of its major themes will be the relation of social science to values [1965: 218]." A similar appraisal is given by Mills: "Work

183

in social science has always been acompanied by problems of valuations [1959: 76]." And discussing recent trends Martindale remarks: "The place of values in sociological theory is being moved to central concern in the councils of sociological theory [1974: viii]."

There are fundamental reasons for the particular significance of the problem of valuations in the social sciences, as opposed to the natural sciences. Also, there are reasons for the particular significance of the problem of valuations in contemporary social science, as opposed to social science in earlier periods.

The first of them is *ontological*—it has to do with the peculiarities of the subject matter studied by the social sciences. Their subject matter is man and his world. And this has at least two implications: First, as Ossowski has emphasized, "In the humanities, the scientist is constantly concerned with the same reality, for the good of which the results of his studies are to be utilized; namely, with man [1967, vol.IV: 108]." In the natural sciences the subject matter is usually much more indirectly related to human interests. Hence, in the social sciences the valuational components are more apt to enter the research process or its results.

The second reason is that social reality is essentially infused with values. Human activities are usually moved by or oriented toward values, and the products of human activities always possess some valuational meaning. As an eminent Polish historian observes:

> All culture is intimately linked with valuations. To measure paintings in square meters, or sculptures in kilograms, may be instructive for a moving company, but not for the student of culture. The study of values by means of nonevaluational methods may sometimes produce some secondary results, but it will never get to the heart of the matter [Kula, 1958: 146].

The presence of valuational components in the subject matter of science must have some bearing on the methods used and results achieved. For example, is there any way to distinguish a murder from an execution, deviant behavior from innovative behavior, alienation from self-fulfillment, except through the application of a valuational perspective?

Another reason is *epistemological*—it has to do with the peculiar relationship between the student of social reality and his subject matter. It is a peculiar internal relation: The student is himself a component of the reality being studied; social cognition is always in some respect self-cognition—a sophisticated form of self-consciousness. Since social reality is of necessity studied from the inside, a completely detached, external approach seems inherently impossible.

Shils calls attention to this epistemological situation: "In purely cognitive respects, sociology could be a science like any other science, and it might well become such. Sociology is not, however, a purely cognitive undertaking. It is also a moral relationship between the human beings studied and the student of the human beings. . . . This is true not only of the procedure of sociological inquiry, but of the results of inquiry as well [1965: 1413]." Dahrendorf makes a similar observation: "More than other scholars, the sociologist, himself inseparably a part of the subject matter of his research, is in danger of confusing his professional statements with his personal value judgments [1968: 13]." Boulding refers to the social sciences as a branch of the moral sciences, and justifies his opinion thus:

> An essential part of the sociosphere and one of the major determinants of its dynamic course is man's knowledge of it—that is, of himself and of his society. . . . Man himself and his knowledge is a part of the system which he studies. . . . It is essential to the understanding of the relations between the social sciences and the social system to realize that the social sciences are themselves part of the social system and are produced by it [1966: 4, 15, 102].

The final reason for the particular salience of the problem of valuations in the social sciences may be labeled *axiological*. It refers to the nature of valuational standards that are applied to the appraisal of human activities and the products of those activities. Consequently, it also refers to the nature of the valuational standards applied to the appraisal of social research and social knowledge. Those standards seem to be much more ambiguous and relative than the standards of the natural, or technical, sciences. An eminent Polish sociologist perceives this difficulty quite clearly:

> In other sciences which provide the means for the control of phenomena . . . those standards are sometimes quite simple, and at least within certain limits quite unambiguous. This is, for example, true of medicine, where life, health and organic efficiency are taken as fundamental values. . . . But in technically oriented sociology, in social engineering, the fundamental value systems cannot be formulated in a simple and unambiguous fashion. . . . Those value systems have an ideological character and are coordinated with concrete organized groups, whose interests can be conflicting [Hochfeld, 1963: 128–129].

This observation is extended by Ossowski: "The way in which the social utility of humanistic research is perceived is very strongly influenced by the ideological creed of the scientist; some will see benefit precisely where others recognize social damage; some intend to serve the interest of this or that group; others profess more universal goals [1967: 108]." And almost the same idea occurs to Gibson: "In social practice—in this respect unlike medicine—there is no agreement on ends. 'We,' in the sense of men in general, have no common purpose on the achievement of which we may ask for a social scientist's advice. And the powers-that-be are not likely to accept advice on ends they do not share. [1960: 208]." In other words, a well-built bridge is useful for a worker as well as for a banker, whereas a good government is usually beneficial to one and detrimental to another. A science that helps to build bridges serves an unambiguous, positive social role. But a science that helps to organize efficient government may serve a positive function from the perspective of the rulers and at the same time quite a negative function from the perspective of the ruled. Thus, in social research values cannot be simply taken for granted; they must be carefully and critically analyzed and their social roots in the interests of particular groups discovered and revealed.

Aside from the fundamental reasons explaining the particular significance of the value problem in the social sciences, there are some historical circumstances that explain why the concern with values has recently become so prominent. Our era has been called "the age of the social sciences." This may be read as expressive of the considerable progress of the social-scientific disciplines in terms of their theoretical sophistication or the wealth of factual data, but even more so as the acknowledgment of the growing effect of social-scientific findings on social life. To quote Boulding again: "As we move towards more secure and exact knowledge of the social system, the process of change is likely to accelerate. The rate of social invention is likely to increase, and in a relatively short time we may see profound transformations in social institutions and behavior, as a result of accumulating knowledge about the system itself [1966: 7]." The possibilities of practical manipulation of social variables are certainly constantly expanding, and at the same time the scope of human populations subjected to manipulation is widening. And when any science becomes increasingly relevant to human fate, it is apt to inspire moral or evaluational problems. As Gouldner puts it: "Far as we are from the sociological atomic bomb, we already live in a world of the systematic brainwashing of prisoners of war and of housewives with their advertising-exacerbated compulsions; and the social science technology of tomorrow can hardly fail to be more powerful than today's [1969: 617]."

Those are the main reasons for the particular significance of the value problem in the contemporary social sciences. The significance is attested by numerous labels under which the dispute is presently carried on. In this chapter I shall use the terms *neutralism* and *axiologism* to signify the opposing standpoints; but there are several other terms in common use; for example, *descriptivism* and *prescriptivism, objectivism* and *subjectivism, scientism* and *ideologism, segregationism* and *unificationism, detached approach* and *biased approach, categorical conceptions of science* and *normative conceptions of science.*

NEUTRALISM AND AXIOLOGISM IN THE SOCIOLOGICAL TRADITION

Whereas the problem of valuations has accompanied the social sciences since their birth, its self-conscious recognition is a relatively recent phenomenon. All the great masters of sociology have had to deal with this problem in some way, either by excluding value judgments from the body of their theories (e.g., John S. Mill) or conversely by allowing them on par with categorical propositions (e.g., Leonard Hobhouse). But only some of them have discussed the issue in an explicit and critical way.

Herbert Spencer: Biases and Ways to Overcome Them

Herbert Spencer is one of the first sociologists to devote considerable attention to the analytic study of methodological or meta-theoretical questions. He was particularly concerned with the defense of the scientific status of sociology. One of his books, perhaps among his less known ones, is entitled *The Study of Sociology* (1894), and deals exclusively with the methodological difficulties that a young science of society encounters as well as the means to defend against them. At least half the book touches the issues immediately relevant to the present discussion; namely, the problem of subjective or emotional difficulties leading to biases in sociological theories. As Spencer puts it:

> Stated in full, the truth is that no propositions, save those which are absolutely indifferent to us, immediately and remotely, can be contemplated without likings and repugnances affecting the opinions we form about them. . . . The associated ideas constituting a judgment are much affected in their relation to one another by the co-existing emotion [1894: 147–148].

The impact of emotions on judgments of facts appears, as a rule, in the realm of common sense, but also in those branches of science directly relevant to human interests. The social sciences epitomize such a relevance and such a danger.

> When the reader has admitted, as he must if he is candid with himself, that his opinion on any political act or proposal is commonly formed in advance of direct evidence, and that he rarely takes the trouble to inquire whether direct evidence justifies it; he will see how great are those difficulties in the way of sociological science, which arise from the various emotions excited by the matters it deals with [Spencer, 1894: 150].

Spencer discusses at great length several instances of biases, which he groups under the headings "educational bias," "the bias of patriotism," "the class-bias," "the political bias," and "the theological bias." All these biases are traced to the peculiar position of a social inquirer vis-a-vis his subject-matter.

> In this case, though in no other case, the facts to be observed and generalized by the student, are exhibited by an aggregate of which he forms a part. In his capacity of inquirer, he should have no inclination towards one or other conclusion respecting the phenomena to be generalized; but in his capacity of citizen, helped to live by the life of his society, sharing in its activities, breathing its atmosphere of thought and sentiment, he is partially coerced into such views as favour harmonious cooperation with his fellow-citizens [1894: 387].

Biases constitute a major obstacle to the social sciences, because for dealing scientifically with social phenomena a certain "equilibrium of feeling" is required: "To see how things stand, apart from personal and national interests, is essential before there can be reached those balanced judgments respecting the course of human affairs in general, which constitute sociology [1894: 204]."

Therefore biases must be overcome—but how? Spencer's proposed remedy is to train social scientists in rigorous discipline of thought, by schooling them in various fields of the natural sciences: "A fit habit of thought, then, is all important in the study of sociology; and a fit habit of thought can be acquired only by the study of the Sciences at large [1894: 316]." Those particularly important for a sociologist include the "abstract sciences" of logic and mathematics, as well as the "concrete sciences" of mechanics, physics, chemistry, and most of all "the science of life," biology.

Already in the work of Spencer, the problem of valuations acquired one of its most typical formulations. It was defined in psychological terms, as the result of human emotional tendencies. The biases born by such tendencies were appraised as detrimental to the scientific status of sociology, and the directive to eliminate them was formulated. The suggested remedy was also conceived in psychological terms, as the necessity for a particular mental or intellectual discipline. The exemplars of such a discipline were sought in the realm of the natural sciences.

Emile Durkheim: Studying Social Facts as Things

The last point, which is a tenet of the positivistic creed, reappears in a slightly modified form in the work of Durkheim, who was expressly concerned with methodological problems, in *Rules of the Sociological Method:* "Our principle . . . demands that the sociologist put himself in the same state of mind as the physicist, chemist or physiologist when he probes into a still unexplored region of the scientific domain [1962: xlv]." And the principle itself, taken from the natural sciences and found equally relevant to the science of society, was a famous prescription to study social facts as things: "Social phenomena are things and ought to be treated as things [1962: 27]."

In spite of its simple and brief formulation, this methodological rule is quite complex, and seems to involve at least six more specific prescriptions, three of which are relevant to our present concerns. The six components of Durkheim's doctrine are as follows.

First, the rule requires that all presuppositions, assumptions, common sense beliefs, and biases should be eliminated before the scientific investigation starts. The sociologist "must emancipate himself from the fallacious ideas that dominate the mind of the layman; he must throw off, once and for all, the yoke of these empirical categories, which from long continued habit have become tyrannical [Durkheim, 1962: 32]." "When he penetrates the social world he must be aware that he is penetrating the unknown; he must feel himself in the presence of facts whose laws are as unsuspected as were those of life before the area of biology—he must be prepared for discoveries which will surprise and disturb him [1962: xlv]." Here Durkheim directs his attack against the impact of common-sense or everyday knowledge on the scientific domain. Such impact, which is particularly profound in the social sciences, owing to the necessary and immediate experience of social reality by the members of society, significantly impairs their objectivity.

Second, the rule requires that all emotional attitudes toward the subject matter be eliminated as well:

> Sentiment may be the subject of science, but never the criterion of scientific truth. . . . Sentiments pertaining to social things enjoy no privilege not possessed by other sentiments, for their origin is the same. They, too, have been formed in the course of history; they are a product of human experience, which is, however, confused and unorganized. They are not due to some transcendental insight into reality but result from all sorts of impressions and emotions accumulated according to circumstances, without order and without methodical interpretation [1962: 33].

Again, this is an attempt to dissociate science from common sense—in this case not so much from the content of common-sense beliefs as from typical common-sense attitudes toward society, due to the practical participation of human beings in social life.

Third, the rule requires that science be restricted to categorical statements of *what is,* and eliminate normative directives dealing with *what ought to be.* The normative orientation is treated as a fallacy of several

social-scientific disciplines. Political economy, instead of studying real, concrete economic relations, discusses the normative principles of laissez-
faireism versus state control. Ethics, instead of studying typical human conduct, postulates catalogues of human duties. Sociology, instead of focusing
on social facts, produces political programs. This tendency must be reversed
if a real science of society is to be created.

Here, Durkheim expresses his protest against "utopianism," the third
factor standing in the way of an objective social science. Those three points
together make up his notion of objectivity or value neutrality. They express
his "conviction that only the most abstentious relation to politics and the
marketplace could save the scholar from being swamped by ideological
passions, his role as intellectual arbiter thus weakened." He believed in
"dispassionate study, objective research," and "never for a moment confused his role as a scholar or scientist with the partisanships which are
inescapable in the political sphere [Nisbet, 1974: 11]." Szacki explains it:
"It was a positivistic ideal of a social science free from any prerational and
prescientific ingredients [1964: 88]."

For the sake of completeness, it must be mentioned that Durkheim's
principle "to study social facts as things" has three more components (less
relevant to the present discussion). Thus, fourth, the principle was directed
against all brands of essentialism and expressed the phenomenalist
standpoint requiring science to restrict its analysis to the domain of observable phenomena: "All that is given, all that is subject to observation, has
thereby the character of a thing. To treat phenomena as things is to treat
them as data. and these constitute the point of departure of science [1962:
27]." "There is nothing to be gained by looking behind them to speculate
on their reason for being [1962: xl]."

Fifth, the principle was directed against deductivism, and confirmed the
inductivist creed of Durkheim, requiring one to proceed from the observation of facts to limited generalizations: "Since objects are perceived only
through sense perceptions... science, to be objective, ought to start, not
with concepts formed independent of them, but with these same perceptions. It ought to borrow the materials for its initial definition directly from
perceptual data.... From sensation all general ideas flow [1962: 43–44]."

And finally, sixth, it was directed against introspection, and prescribed
observation of external reality as the only proper method of sociological
research: "A thing differs from an idea in the same way as that which we
know from without differs from that which we know from within. Things
include all objects of knowledge that cannot be conceived by purely mental
activity..., their characteristic properties, like the unknown causes on
which they depend, cannot be discovered by even the most careful introspection [1962: xliii]."

Durkheim presents the most complete and direct formulation of the positivist model for the social sciences. In this model the standpoint of neutralism, or objectivism, acquires central importance.

Max Weber: Values to Be Rigorously Separated from Facts

The most extensive treatment of the problem of objectivity, interpreted explicitly as the problem of valuations, is the contribution of Max Weber. He discusses the problem in two distinct dimensions; first, as the question whether an academic teacher should express his personal value commitments from the chair (this is a problem of academic ethics) and, second, as the question whether value judgments have any legitimate place in the research process or research results of science (this is a problem of methodology). Weber says:

> The problem involved in the "freedom" of a given science from value judgments of this kind—that is, the validity and the meaning of this logical principle—is by no means identical with the question . . . whether in teaching one should or should not declare one's acceptance of practical value judgments, deduced from ethical principles, cultural ideas or a philosophical outlook [1949: 1].

And again he repeats this distinction:

> But in no case . . . should the unresolvable question—unresolvable because it is ultimately a question of evaluation—as to whether one may, must, or should champion certain practical values in teaching, be confused with the purely logical discussion of the relationship of value judgments to empirical disciplines such as sociology or economics [1949: 8].

Only the methodological dimension is relevant to the present discussion of the problem of valuations, but before I focus on it exclusively, let me present briefly Weber's standpoint on the other dimension—the question of academic policy. His main idea is already quite clear from the quoted passages; namely, that values cannot be eliminated but should be "held to a minimum" and strictly separated from statements of fact. In the process of teaching such a separation requires a specific mode of presentation:

> Only when the teacher sets as his unconditional duty, in every single case, even to the point where it involves the danger of making his lecture less lively or attractive, to make relentlessly clear to his audience, and especially to himself, which of his statements are statements of logically de-

duced or empirically observed facts and which are statements of practical evaluations [will the fundamental requirement of intellectual honesty be met] [1949: 2].

As can easily be seen, this directive puts double demands on the academic teacher. First, it requires a high level of critical self-consciousness concerning which are one's fact-based beliefs and which are value-informed ones. Second, it requires full frankness in presenting one's beliefs to the students.

The same separatist doctrine appears in Weber's discussion of the second, methodological dimension of the problem. Here, another dichotomous distinction must be introduced to clarify his position. He seems to be concerned with two aspects of the methodological question; the first may be called the "apragmatic" aspect (see Ajdukiewicz, 1965)—he treats valuations as types of propositions and inquires about their status vis-a-vis factual or categorical propositions in the research results of science. The second may be called the "pragmatic" aspect—he treats valuations as types of activities and inquires about their role vis-a-vis fact-oriented activities in the conduct of scientific research. The two aspects should not be confused or identified with each other. In fact, those who classify, without qualification, Weber as a spokesman for a totally value-free science take into account only the first aspect of his position, neglecting the second. And his solution to the riddle of valuations is radically different in both cases. In the apragmatic aspect, it is the claim of "value freedom"; in the pragmatic aspect, it is the claim of "value relevance."

To be more specific, when the logical characteristics of scientific statements are the focus of attention, Weber formulates two directives. The first comes down to "the insistence on the rigorous distinction between empirical knowledge and value judgments [1949: 49]," or to put it a little differently "the logical distinction between 'existential knowledge,' i.e. knowledge of what *is*, and 'normative knowledge,' i.e., knowledge of what *should be* [1949: 51]." The second directive rejects any attempts to derive value judgments from factual assertions, or to justify value decisions by reference to data, "trends," objective necessities, and so on. As Weber puts it: "In our opinion, it can never be the task of an empirical science to provide binding norms and ideals from which directives for immediate practical activity can be derived [1949: 52]." The same idea is formulated in a different connection: "There is no [rational or empirical] scientific procedure of any kind whatsoever which can provide us with a decision here. The social sciences, which are strictly empirical sciences, are the least fitted to presume to save the individual the difficulty of making a choice, and they should therefore not create an impression that they can do so [1949: 19]." To sum up, Weber's famous statement may be quoted: "An empirical science cannot tell anyone what he should do—but rather what he can do—and under certain circumstances—what he wishes to do [1949: 54]."

The implication of this for a working scientist is the demand for a self-conscious and open separation of facts from values in the body of a theory, and the abstaining from any arguments justifying value commitments by factual, empirical considerations.

> The fundamental imperative of scientific freedom is that in such cases it should be constantly made clear to the readers (and—again we say it—above all to one's self!) exactly at which point the scientific investigator becomes silent and the evaluating and acting person begins to speak. In other words it should be made explicit just where the arguments are addressed to the analytical understanding and where to sentiments [1949: 60].

And in the discussion concerning ideal types and their uses in scientific research, the same idea reappears once more: "The elementary duty of scientific self-control and the only way to avoid serious and foolish blunders requires a sharp, precise distinction between the logically comparative analysis of reality by ideal types in the logical sense and the value judgment of reality on the basis of ideals [1949: 98]."

In regard to the second, pragmatic aspect of Weber's standpoint, the problem is how valuational activities (taking into account some values and utilizing them as the criteria of choice) affect the research-process of science. Weber asserts that such an effect exists, and is unavoidable. His attention turns toward two strategic points where such an effect is most profound: the choice of the research problem, and the choice of the conceptual model applied in the selection and causal interpretation of data. Of the first he says: "The problems of the empirical disciplines are, of course, to be solved 'non-evaluatively.' They are not problems of evaluation. But the problems of the social sciences are selected by the value-relevance of the phenomena treated [1949: 21]." And he adds: "All the analysis of infinite reality which the finite human mind can conduct rests on the tacit assumption that only a finite portion of this reality constitutes the object of scientific investigation, and that only it is 'important' in the sense of being 'worthy of being known' [1949: 72]." Finally, we find further elaboration of this point:

> Only a small portion of existing concrete reality is colored by our value-conditioned interest and it alone is significant to us. It is significant because it reveals relationships which are important to us due to their connection with our values. Only because and to the extent that this is the case is it worthwhile for us to know it in its individual features [1949: 76].

Of the second point, referring to the conceptual model, Weber says: "There is no absolutely 'objective' scientific analysis of culture—or put perhaps more narrowly but certainly not essentially differently for our purposes—of 'social phenomena' independent of special and one-sided viewpoints according to which—expressly or tacitly, consciously or unconsciously—they are selected, analyzed and organized for expository purposes [1949: 72]." Specifying it for the domain of historical studies, he adds: "The values to which the scientific genius relates the object of his inquiry may determine, i.e., decide the 'conception', of the whole epoch, not only concerning what is regarded as 'valuable' but also concerning what is significant or insignificant, 'important' or 'unimportant' in the phenomena [1949: 82]." The same is true of the study of culture: "Inasmuch as the 'points of view' from which they can become significant for us are very diverse, the most varied criteria can be applied to the selection of the traits which are to enter into the construction of an ideal-typical view of a particular culture [1949: 91]."

I have devoted considerable space to the exposition of Weber's views because they are usually considered as the fullest statement in the history of sociology of the problem of valuations, and also because they are often misrepresented. I hope it is obvious by now that Weber was by no means an extreme proponent of neutralism, the simple-minded creator of a "myth of value-free sociology," neglecting the role of values in science. He was much more sophisticated in his treatment of the problem than some contemporary commentators seem to recognize (see, for example, Gouldner, 1969; Kozyr-Kowalski, 1967: 105). And he was certainly quite explicit in his perception of the necessary effect of valuations on the research process, which brings him close to an at least partial endorsement of the axiologistic standpoint.

NEUTRALISM AND AXIOLOGISM IN CONTEMPORARY SOCIOLOGY

Whereas in the history of sociology the neutralist standpoint is clearly dominant, in contemporary sociology there is a significant trend toward a critique of neutralism, and a defense of the opposite, axiologistic position, in some form or other. But neutralism is by no means dead, and my review must start with recent restatements of the old postulate requiring science to be purged of values. In the modern period the neutralist tendency is directly influenced by the philosophical tenets of neopositivism. In their struggle against all metaphysical notions and propositions, lacking in empirical meaning and not subjected to verification, and their struggle for a clear-cut demarcation of science from extrascientific thought, the neopositivists programatically refuse any scientific status to value judgments.

George Lundberg: Neopositivistic Purification of Sociology

The most famous advocate and spokesman for this tendency in the postwar years is George Lundberg. A program of value-free sociology is formulated in his works in extreme form. Lundberg requires both the complete elimination of value judgments from the results of science and the elimination of evaluational activities from the research process: "Too frequently scientists forget this distinction [that is, of facts and values] and put forward absurd scientific claims for what they personally happen to prefer [Lundberg, 1947: 17]." This is seen as basically improper. And the way toward valid social science is precisely through the abandonment of such claims.

> The advancement of the social sciences would probably deprive us in a large measure of the luxury of indignation in which we now indulge ourselves as regards social events.... Such indignation ministers to deep-seated, jungle-fed sentiments of justice, virtue, and general feeling of the fitness of things as compared with what a scientific diagnosis of the situation evokes. In short, one of the principal costs of the advancement of the social sciences would be the abandonment of the personalistic and moralistic interpretation of social events [1947: 15].

Instead, social scientists will have to devote themselves to "a pursuit of knowledge of a kind which is demonstrably true, regardless of the private preferences, hopes and likes of the scientist himself [1947: 16]." The way to this goal will be made easier if the social scientist takes seriously the methodological patterns of the natural sciences—precise experimental techniques, the quantification of concepts, etc.—and imitates them as closely as possible. "My conclusion," Lundberg says, "is that the best hope for the social sciences lies in following broadly in the paths of the other sciences [1947: 17]."

The Followers of Neopositivistic Neutralism

The impact of neopositivistic ideas is still felt. And from time to time a renewed call for the purification of the social sciences from values can be heard. Some years after Lundberg, Philip Hauser extends his program beyond the domain of pure science to the field of applied science. He considers "the formation of value judgments as tasks outside the province of the social scientist," and recommends that

> applied research like pure research should restrict itself to a description of observed relationships between phenomena, to generalization of these relationships, and to predictions of alternative courses of events so far as observed relationships and possible generalizations permit, within frameworks of goals and value judgments set forth by policy makers or action agencies. . . . In both, pure and applied social science, there is no judgment made in favor of X or Y [1949: 213, 211].

The role of a social scientist is restricted accordingly: "Investigator as a social scientist does not assume responsibility for the formation of the values as a product of research [1949: 212]." Values are located exclusively in the extrascientific, political, or practical realm. In science, there is only a place for categorical propositions, claiming that such and such a situation obtains, and, at most, for instrumental propositions, appraising the relative utility of some means for the achievement of certain externally given goals. The total separation of science from values is thereby proclaimed.

The neutralist standpoint is raised to a level of undisputed orthodoxy by Robert Bierstedt, who includes a characteristic formulation in his textbook of sociology. First, we find a prescribed ideal:

> Sociology is a categorical, not a normative, discipline; that is, it confines itself to statements about what it, not what should be or ought to be. As a science, sociology is necessarily silent about questions of value; it cannot decide the directions in which society ought to go, and it makes no recommendations on matters of social policy. . . . Sociology cannot itself deal with problems of good and evil, right and wrong, better or worse, or any others that concern human values. . . . There is no sociological warrant, nor indeed any other kind of scientific warrant, for preferences in values [1963: 12].

Then, some allowance for the realities of the sociologist's cognitive situation is made:

> The spectacles through which he peers at the social process, the categories in which he arranges his manifold and complex data, and the language in which he announces his results are all products of a particular society at a particular time and place. He himself is a product of his society, and conforms—consciously or unconsciously—to its folkways and mores, its institutions and laws, its customs and ideologies, its canons of evidence [1963: 23].

But the remedy for this problem is immediately found in the proper self-consciousness of the scholar:

> For him that extra-dimensionality that is synonymous with objectivity is a goal to be achieved, not a condition given in his scientific situation. . . . The sociologist has to strive, therefore, for an awareness of the biases and prejudices inherent in his own society, lest they interfere with his neutrality and color his conclusions. Without the constant diligence that alone can bring objectivity to his enterprise, the sociologist ceases to be a scientist [1963: 23].

Weber's old idea of the sociologist as *homo duplex*—a scientist in one of his roles, and a citizen in another, with the possibility of a complex dissociation of the two—reappears in the work of Robert Merton. The duty of a scientist is to discover the objective consequences of existing institutions—their functions and dysfunctions, whether consciously perceived and intended by the actors (manifest) or not (latent). By recognizing the latent functions of social arrangements, the sociologist liberates himself from the common-sense perspective; he can

> move beyond prevalent social beliefs, practices and judgment, without entering upon the misplaced career of trying to impose [his] own values upon others. . . . In his capacity as sociologist, emphatically not in his capacity as citizen, the student of social problems neither exhorts nor denounces, advocates nor rejects. It is enough that he discovers to others the great price they sometimes pay for their settled but insufficiently examined convictions and their established but inflexible practices [Merton, 1961b: 710].

A somewhat different rationale for the dissociation of the role of scientist and citizen is provided by Talcott Parsons. He sees the normative components of both roles as fundamentally different, and introduces a distinction between two subsystems of values—intrascientific values and extrascientific values. The intrascientific values comprise those exclusively characteristic of the scientific activity; for example, the criteria for the choice of problems, the criteria for proper concept formation or theory construction, the criteria for acceptance or rejection of scientific hypotheses. The extrascientific values comprise those characteristic of all other domains of human activity: political, ethical, ideological, and so on. "A scientist is never a whole man," Parsons asserts. In his capacity as scientist, he conducts scientific activities and is therefore bound by intrascientific values; in his capacity as citizen he conducts extrascientific activities and is therefore bound by extrascientific values. The two domains are distinct: They do not overlap and should never be merged. Science must not include any values which belong to extrascientific domains. The basic requirement for scientific objectivity is a strict following of intrascientific values and a rigorous rejection of extrascientific values. Any consideration of the latter by a scientist introduces biases and impairs objectivity (see Parsons, 1965b).

The foregoing were some representative examples of contemporary neutralism. But in recent years, several important objections to the neutralist position have been raised, and some authors have moved toward a recognition of valuations as necessary ingredients of scientific research and scientific results. Three examples of this development follow.

Gunnar Myrdal: The Inevitability of Biases in Sociological Study

On the basis of the methodological insights acquired during a monumental research project on racial problems in America, Gunnar Myrdal rejects all the major tenets of the neutralist creed. He claims: "Full objectivity . . . is an ideal toward which we are constantly striving, but which we can never reach [1964: 1035]." And still more explicitly: "A disinterested social science is from this viewpoint, pure nonsense. It never existed, and it never will exist [1964: 1064]."

And the main reason is that "science is nothing but highly sophisticated common-sense [1969: 14]," and in scientific opinions a mixture of beliefs and valuations is as unavoidable as it is in common-sense opinions. More specifically, he considers the directive requiring a complete purification of scientific disciplines from value-judgments as utopian. "No social science or particular branch of social research can pretend to be 'amoral' or 'apolitical.' No social science can ever be 'neutral' or simply 'factual,' indeed not 'objective' in the traditional meanings of these terms. Research is always and by logical necessity based on moral and political valuations, and the researcher should be obliged to account for them explicitly [1969: 74]." Similarly, any attempt to separate the scientific and extrascientific roles of the sociologist is also seen as utopian.

> As social scientists we are deceiving ourselves if we naively believe that we are not as human as the people around us and that we do not tend to aim opportunistically for conclusions that fit prejudices markedly similar to those of other people in our society. . . . We are under the influence of tradition in our sciences, of the cultural and political setting of our environment, and of our own peculiar personal make-ups. . . . The result is systematic biases in our work [1969: 43–44].

The impact of valuations is not restricted to the field of applied science; it is equally strong in the pure sciences. "Biases in research are much deeper seated than in the formulation of avowedly practical conclusions. They are not valuations attached to research but rather they permeate research. They are the unfortunate results of concealed valuations that insinuate themselves into research in all stages, from its planning to its final presentation [1964: 1043]."

There is no way out, but to reveal explicitly and to allow them in the conduct of sociological research and in the body of sociological theories.

> The logical means available for protecting ourselves from biases are broadly these: to raise valuations actually determining our theoretical and practical research to full awareness, to scrutinize them from the point of view of relevance, significance and feasibility in the society under study, to transform them into specific value premises for research, and to determine approach and define concepts in terms of a set of value premises which have been explicitly stated [1969: 5].

C. Wright Mills: Sociology as a Moral and Political Endeavor

In *The Sociological Imagination,* a radical manifesto directed against several orthodox assumptions of American social sciences in the 1950s, C. Wright Mills takes issue with the standpoint of value neutrality. He declares: "By their work all students of man and society assume and imply moral and political decisions [1959: 76]." But this is not only a statement of a tendency; rather, such a notion is supposed to encompass the unavoidable, principal peculiarity of social-scientific research: "There is no way in which any social scientist can avoid assuming choices of values and implying them in his work as a whole [1959: 177]." And moreover: "Whether he wants it or not, or whether he is aware of it or not, anyone who spends his life studying society and publishing the results is acting morally and usually politically as well [1959: 79]."

The reason is that the criterion of truth—crucial for any scientific enterprise—in the social sciences is itself embedded in practical social interests and consequently particularized. Truth is not equally good for everybody. To find out the truth about a robbery is good for the police and for the victims, but bad for the robber. As Mills observed: "Nowadays social research is often of direct service to army generals and social workers, corporation managers and prison wardens [1959: 80]." And as a result, the search for truth becomes a political decision: "The very enterprise of social science, as it determines fact, takes on political meaning. In a world of widely communicated nonsense, any statement of fact is of political and moral significance. . . . In such a world as ours, to practice social science is, first of all, to practice the politics of truth [1959: 178]."

Mills seems to conceive of the necessary link between social science and values as a medium of reciprocal influence. First, "science assumes values"; that is, values influence both the conduct of research and the results of it: "Values are involved in the selection of the problems we study; values are also involved in certain of the key conceptions we use in our formulation of these problems, and values affect the course of their solution [1959: 78]." Second, "science implies values"; that is, the results of science influence value judgments. The influence is not of a strictly logical, but rather of a more loose, psychological sort, but yet telling: "Agreement is now wide enough to make commonplace the notion that one cannot infer judgments of value from statements of fact or from definitions of conceptions. But this does not mean that such statements and definitions are irrelevant to judgment [1959: 77]."

Alvin Gouldner: Dispelling the Myth of Value-free Sociology

In several of his recent works Alvin Gouldner has attempted to formulate a methodological program for sociology that would prevent what he sees as its "coming crisis." His contribution is twofold: He has criticized with searching penetration the orthodox belief in value neutrality, and he has put forth an ideal of "reflexive sociology"—clearly adopting the axiologistic standpoint.

His criticism is mainly directed against Weber, whom he holds responsible for the "myth of neutrality": "Weber formulates an incipient utopia in which an impure world is split into two pure worlds, science and morality [Gouldner, 1973: 63]." The deep-lying sources of the myth are to be found in the social and political conditions in which sociology was striving to achieve autonomy, both intellectual and organizational: "Among the main institutional forces facilitating the survival and spread of the value-free myth was its usefulness in maintaining both the cohesion and the autonomy of the modern university, in general, and the newer social science disciplines, in particular. . . . It was an effort to depoliticize the university and to remove it from the political struggle [1969: 608]." Presently, when autonomy is more or less safeguarded, the functions of the myth are changed:

> The value-free doctrine is useful both to those who want to escape from the world and to those who want to escape into it. It is useful to those . . . who live off sociology rather than for it, and who think of sociology as a way of getting ahead in the world by providing them with neutral techniques that may be sold on the open market to any buyer. . . . In still other cases, the image of a value-free sociology is the armor of the alienated sociologist's self [1969: 610, 611].

Personally useful as it may be, the myth is nevertheless a utopia: It is not to be attained in reality. "The pursuit of 'truth for its own sake' is always a tacit quest for something more than truth, for other values that may have been obscured, denied, and perhaps even forbidden [1973: 65]." Also, it is most detrimental to the conduct of sociology as a science, and its possible social impact, because it implies the abdication of the critical perspective. And "social science can never be fully accepted in a society, or by a part of it, without paying its way; this means it must manifest both its relevance and concern for the contemporary human predicament [1969: 611]."

The positive alternative to value-free sociology is "reflexive sociology." It does not hesitate to allow values and valuations into the scientific realm:

> I do not conceive of the theory of Reflexive Sociology merely as an induction from researches or from "facts." And more important, I do not conceive of these researches or their factual output as being "value-free," for I would hope that their originating motives and terminating consequences would embody and advance certain specific values. A Reflexive Sociology would be a moral sociology [1971: 491].

Also, reflexive sociology does not require of the scientist an impossible feat of dissociating his head and his heart, cognition and commitment: "It is characterized, rather, by the relationship it establishes between being a sociologist and being a person, between the role and the man performing it. A Reflexive Sociology embodies a critique of the conventional conception of segregated scholarly roles and has a vision of an alternative. It aims at transforming the sociologist's relation to his work [1971: 495]."

Having reviewed some representative formulations that the dispute of neutralism and axiologism has taken in past as well as present sociological theory, we shall now analyze it.

WHAT THE DISPUTE IS REALLY ABOUT: AN EXPLICATION

Even a cursory glance at the representative statements of the neutralist or the axiologist position clearly reveals the ambiguity of the dispute itself. What is really at stake? Various dimensions and aspects of the problem are selected and one-sidedly emphasized by the disputants. Some aspects are neglected, some are given insufficient prominence, some are confused with others. The observation Gouldner made almost two decades ago still holds:

> I fear that there are many sociologists today who, in conceiving social science to be value-free, mean widely different things, that many hold

these beliefs dogmatically without having examined seriously the grounds upon which .they are credible, and that some few affirm a value-free sociology ritualistically without having any clear idea what it might mean [1969: 606].

The same can certainly be said of the proponents of the opposite, value-committed position.

Therefore, the primary goal must be to clarify and specify the fundamental meaning of the dispute, and of both opposing positions separately. The strategy here will be to approach this goal by eliminating misunderstandings, and clearing the ground for a positive characterization. Thus, I shall presently attempt to answer the question "What is the dispute of neutralism and axiologism certainly not about?"

What the Dispute Is Not About

At least seven ways in which the dispute is usually carried on must be considered as inappropriate, and as missing the point. First, the dispute is not about teaching policy in academic institutions, but rather about the conduct of scientific research, understood as the pursuit of knowledge. To put it otherwise, it does not concern the ways in which knowledge should be reported, but rather the ways in which knowledge should be gathered. The fact that Weber attached so much attention to the teaching aspect was determined by the particular circumstances of his period; presently the salience of the question posed in this manner is much more limited. And even if in some cases the proper conduct of teaching becomes problematic, it is certainly a distinct and independent issue, both in the sense that it must be solved with different tools and in the sense that the answer to it need not coincide with the answer to the other issue. "How should one teach?" is a problem of academic ethics, or of applied pedagogical theory, and "How should one conduct research?" is a problem of scientific epistemology and methodology. In view of our concerns here, I dismiss the problem of valuations treated as a problem of teaching policy, and shall concern myself exclusively with the place and role of valuations in the creative enterprise of science.

Second, the dispute is not about the general conduct of the people known as scientists, but only about their conduct in the scientific domain (scientists qua scientists). It is a platitude that scientists are also citizens, fathers, lovers, husbands, friends, fans, book readers, movie goers, etc. In all those capacities they profess and express many and diverse value judgments. Even Weber remembered that "an attitude of moral indifference has no connection with scientific objectivity [1949: 60]." And in his biography we find several examples of a most serious, value-determined commitment to some of the political issues of his time. The same is true of the modern social scientists despite the prevalence of the neutralist creed. They are shown, for example, by a recent survey to be "politically more active social animals than most other academic groups [Javetz, 1972: 115]."

The real problem, therefore, is not concerning the right of human beings to evaluate. The real problem is whether while acting in the capacity of a scientist, conducting scientific research, and formulating its results, one should temporarily surrender such a right and self-consciously abstain from valuations; whether it is feasible; and if so, whether it is commendable.

Third, the dispute is not about the elimination of valuations from the scientific domain, but only about the elimination of extrascientific valuations (moral, political, ideological, etc.) as opposed to intrascientific valuations (instrumental, technical, or methodological).

It is almost universally recognized that science employs several criteria for distinguishing facts from appearances, guesses from hypotheses, hypotheses from confirmed laws, theories from random collections of regularities or correlations. And by means of such intrascientific criteria scientists constantly evaluate and reevaluate their procedures and their findings. Popper puts it thus: "Truth is our regulative principle, our decisive scientific value. Relevance, interest and significance (relative to a purely scientific problem situation), are likewise scientific values of the first order; and this is also true of values like those of fruitfulness, explanatory power, simplicity and precision [1976a: 96]." Such valuations are indispensable for any scientific research; there is no science without them. Therefore, the real problem concerns a different type of valuation, the extrascientific type, and its status in the enterprise of science.

Fourth, the dispute is not about the role of valuations in practical or applied subdomains of science, but rather about the role of valuations in theoretical or basic science.

The typical question of applied science is "What means should be employed to reach a given end?" And the practical directive in the form "You should act _____" is always relative to the prescribed end. In applied science, therefore, valuations enter by virtue of simple logic. As Myrdal puts it: "Practical conclusions may thus be reached by rational inferences from the data and the value premises. Only in this way does social engineering, as an advanced branch of social research, become a rational discipline under full scientific control [1964: 1044]." Or, in the words of a leading Polish philosopher: "Value judgments are the fundamental propositions of the practical sciences [Nowak, 1974c: 101]." This is acknowledged more or less commonly, and is usually not debated. The real issue focuses therefore on the pure or theoretical sciences; i.e., on those that strive to answer the questions "How?" and "Why?" of social phenomena and processes. Is there any place for valuations in research of a descriptive or explanatory nature? Here, the answers divide the neutralists and axiologists most noticeably.

Fifth, the dispute is not about the occurrence of valuations as the subject matter of scientific research but rather about their occurrence in research activities or research results achieved by a scientist. As has been emphasized, men are evaluating beings. The values professed by them may become widespread, and then enter the domain of culture or social consciousness. As such, they may become the focus of sociological study, on par with all other aspects of culture or social consciousness. As Martindale observes: "When one deals with human social behavior one is unavoidably concerned with the pursuit of values, or ends, or things people experience as desirable and the various principles or norms—moral, esthetic, ethical, and legal—by which they adjudge behavior in pursuit of values as right [1974: 2]." The fact that the subject matter of sociological research consists of values does not necessitate value judgments on the part of the sociologist. To say that murder is wrong is a valuation. To say that a certain percentage of Americans consider murder wrong is the statement of a fact from the domain of social consciousness. To choose is not the same as to study choice; to decide is not the same as to study decisions; to evaluate is not the same as to study values. Weber made this quite clear: "When the normatively valid is the object of empirical investigation, its normative validity is disregarded. Its 'existence' and not its 'validity' is what concerns the investigator [1949: 39]." And a similar comment may be found in Myrdal: "When valuations are held by an individual or group, they are, like beliefs, a part of reality that can be ascertained by research, though not without difficulty [1969: 16]." The real issue dividing neutralists and axiologists is the presence of valuations in the scientific approach to a subject matter or in a scientific account of a subject matter, rather than in the subject matter itself.

Sixth, the dispute is not about the impact of scientific research or scientific findings on accepted valuations, but rather about the impact of accepted valuations on the conduct of research and the formulation of results. When the link of science and values is discussed, two vectors of this relation can be singled out. I believe that one vector is relatively unproblematic. If the hypothetical impact of science on values is considered in respect of the logical dependency of the latter on the former, it is immediately to be dismissed: No value judgments can be logically derived from a statement of facts—this is an elementary point that admits of no argument. Myrdal's claim may be taken as expressing the consensus of opinion: "The observation of the facts of a given existing situation alone will never permit the conclusion that such a situation is good or desirable or even that this situation is inevitable in the future [1964: 1057]." Or more briefly, in the words of Dahrendorf: "Value judgments cannot be derived from scientific insights [1968: 6]." On the other hand, if the impact of science on values is interpreted in respect of psychological influences, then there is an observed tendency for values to be modified under the influence of changed knowledge. Myrdal gives a good illustration:

> If beliefs are corrected, this exerts pressure on people to change their valuations to such a degree that they can present to themselves and to others what they feel to be consistent opinions, which now must include the corrected beliefs. . . . In the Negro problem the correction of some of the derogatory popular beliefs about Negroes—which, as I pointed out, have become stratified in stereotyped and complex popular theories— should gradually and perceptibly change prejudiced opinions harboring valuations and valuational conflicts [1969: 32–33].

To sum up, all the parties to the dispute of axiologism and neutralism would probably agree that the impact of science on values can be understood not as a matter of logic but as a matter of psychology: Owing to our cognitive makeup, we tend to reduce dissonance and restore balance within the body of accepted opinions as a result of responding to new knowledge. Thus, no meaningful opposition of standpoints can be rooted here.

The real controversy is generated only by the second vector of the relation, and concerns the impact of values on science. This is a dividing issue; the neutralists would deny any influence of valuations on scientific research or results; the axiologists would claim that such influence is unavoidable.

Seventh, the dispute is not about the heuristic impact of valuations, stimulating the choice of fruitful problems, hypotheses, etc., but rather about the role of valuations in the systematic procedures of scientific research, and their place in the context of scientific descriptions and theories. It is rather obvious that some psychological commitment to one's subject matter or research problem is usually conducive to fruitful inquiry. Gouldner emphasizes this point: "Passion and sentimentality serve not only to produce costs and intellectual blindness, but may just as likely serve to enlighten and to sensitize us to certain aspects of the social world [1973: 33]." And Dahrendorf makes a claim that is still stronger: "Perhaps it can even be stated as a general proposition that the quality of scientific research improves to the extent that choice of subject betrays a personal commitment on the part of the researcher [1968: 8]." Thus, the heuristic or inspirational role of valuations in the so-called "context of discovery" is taken for granted by neutralists and axiologists alike.

What they really quarrel about is the role of valuations in the so-called "context of validation": if, how, and at which points, the valuations enter the method of science, and what is the status of value judgments among the descriptive and explanatory propositions of science.

From a review of the main misunderstandings encountered in the dispute of neutralism and axiologism, the real meaning of the controversy begins to appear. Thus, it is established that the dispute is concerned with the following:

1. Science, understood as the creative pursuit of truth
2. Scientists and their conduct in scientific roles
3. Valuations of the extrascientific kind
4. The role of valuations in the pure or theoretical sciences
5. The place of valuations in the scientific approach to any subject matter
6. The impact or influence of valuations on science
7. The impact of valuations on the scientific method and the form of scientific results

To bring those points together, it may be said briefly that the dispute of neutralism and axiologism is concerned with the impact of extrascientific valuations on the procedures and results of the theoretical sciences.

Valuations and Value Judgments

Now, the crucial component of this explication is the term *valuations*. Its meaning is more or less intuitively clear, but must be more extensively discussed and specified. Dahrendorf quotes Weber as complaining that "interminable misunderstandings, and above all terminological (thus wholly sterile) disputes, have arisen over the term 'value . . . judgment' [1968: 5]." Let us see how this crucial notion is understood by some participants in the dispute.

Weber says: "By 'value-judgments' are to be understood, where nothing else is implied or expressly stated, practical evaluations of the unsatisfactory or satisfactory character of phenomena subject to our influence [1949: 1]." Dahrendorf gives the following definition: "Value-judgments are statements about what ought or ought not to happen, what is or is not desired, in the world of human action [1968: 6]." According to Myrdal: "Valuations express our ideas of how [the social reality] ought to be or ought to have been [1969: 15]." And Edel gives a more extended characterization: "Recent social science . . . has tended to retain in the concept of value an element of judgment or discrimination, so that having a value often means in its studies not merely desiring something, but also thinking it or holding it in some way as desirable [1965: 219]."

It is clear that there is a duality of meaning attached to the concept of valuation; it may refer either to a specific human activity or to the results of such an activity. The activity in question is simply comparing a certain object, event, phenomenon, or process with some standard, specifying what is good, proper, just, right, etc. This standard is to be defined within an extrascientific context, taken from the extrascientific domain of social consciousness, or a social-normative system, or an ideology, or common sense. The result of the evaluating activity is simply some statement concerning the relationship of the evaluated object, event, phenomenon, process to the value standard used, and ascribing to it the specific property of being good, proper, just, right, wrong, etc. Thus, valuations may be understood either as certain behavior or as certain propositions. Myrdal perceives this duality: "The term *value* has, in its prevalent usage, a loose meaning. When tightened it is generally taken to refer to the object of valuations, rather than to the valuations themselves [1964: 1031]." Perhaps for the sake of linguistic purity a terminological distinction could be made between valuating as opposed to valuations, or judging in terms of values as opposed to value judgments. But we shall stick to the common usage, insisting only on the meticulous distinction of the relevant meanings.

A parallel duality is attached to the notion of science. It is understood either as a process of research or as a complex result of such a process. Again, the process of research is simply a complex set of activities undertaken by the people called "scientists" in their professional capacity, whereas the results of such a process are certain propositions making up scientific knowledge.

Therefore, the impact of valuations on science may be interpreted in two distinct ways; either as the participation of valuational activities in the conduct of scientific research or as the presence of valuational propositions (value judgments) in the body of scientific knowledge. Obviously, both aspects of the problem are interrelated. If any value judgments appear in scientific knowledge, it is only due to some valuational activities undertaken by the scientists in the process of scientific research. For the same reason, and contrary to popular beliefs, the behavioral aspect of the problem is primary with respect to the linguistic aspect. The value judgments appearing in scientific theories must be considered only as a petrified outcome of valuational activites occurring at some phases of the research process. Thus, the core of the dispute between the neutralists and axiologists seems to revolve around the status of valuational activities in the method of science.

Varieties of Neutralism and Axiologism

The respective claims may be phrased in various ways, with different degrees of strength. Sometimes, they are formulated in a purely descriptive fashion, acknowledging or denying the presence of valuations in the research process. The axiologists would claim that in the actual practice of social-scientific inquiry valuations occur constantly. The neutralists would hold that there are at least some concrete examples of social-scientific inquiry totally free of any valuational elements. This is a relatively weak statement of respective positions, and the dispute at this level is relatively easy to solve. But very often the standpoints are defined in a prescriptive way, considering valuations as necessary or unnecessary, as proper or improper in the domain of science. One may note in passing that in such a case a sort of meta-valuation occurs; the valuation of the fact of valuating itself. But this is not a valuation proper, rather an instrumental valuation of the utility or inutility of some procedure for the attainment of a given end. The axiologists would claim that valuations are an indispensable component of inquiry; the neutralists would hold that they can be eliminated, or at least that their impact can be neutralized by means of specific procedures. Here, the dispute becomes much more complex, and more fundamental considerations in the respective arguments must be treated.

It is interesting to note that in the works of authors engaged in the dispute, descriptive formulations are often combined with prescriptive formulations, and that sometimes the import of their descriptive considerations is different from the import of their prescriptive declarations. Some cross-combined standpoints may be encountered, the most typical one being a mixture of descriptive axiologism with prescriptive neutralism. It may be called a crypto-neutralism and illustrated by all those authors who recognize the actual presence of valuations in all social-scientific research, but at the same time devise various measures and strategies to purify science from valuations, or at least to diminish their impact. Valuations do occur, but they should be avoided as much as possible—such would be the position of crypto-neutralists. An illustration of such a belief is provided by a statement of Popper's: "The purity of pure science is an ideal which is presumably unattainable; but it is an ideal for which we constantly fight—and should fight by means of criticism [Popper, 1976a: 97]."

To simplify what follows, I shall abstract from the mixed cases, and discuss the analytically pure, ideal–typical formulations of both standpoints. Having specified what they mean, we must pass now to a consideration of how they are justified.

THE ARGUMENTS OF THE CONTENDING
PARTIES: AN OVERVIEW

Since at present, the attacking party is certainly that of the axiologists, their arguments will be treated first, and then some counterarguments of the neutralists, defending the traditional, value-free image of sociology.

The Case for Axiologism:
Entry Points for Valuations

Arguments differ depending on the type of thesis being defended. To defend descriptive axiologism, it is sufficient to show that the valuations are in fact appearing both in research process and among scientific propositions. Thus it is not difficult to agree with Andreski that "normally, when we speak about human conduct, we condemn or praise, persuade or promise, threaten or cajole; and to be willing and able to discuss social behavior dispassionately, and without an immediate utilitarian aim in view, remains a hallmark of sophistication uncommon even today [1972: 96]." Also, it is not difficult to agree with Myrdal that as a result of this human tendency "our whole literature is permeated by value judgments despite prefatory statements to the contrary [1964: 1043]." The examples which will support such statements can be found in practically every piece of social-scientific research or social-scientific knowledge.

But it is much more difficult to provide arguments for a prescriptive axiologism, claiming that such a situation is inevitable. Here, it is not enough to quote actual practice; recourse to the grounds of practice must be made.

If the statement of prescriptive axiologism is focused on the behavioral aspect of a research process, then the arguments usually show the points at which some valuational activities must inevitably occur. If the statement of the prescriptive axiologism is focused on the linguistic structure of the research results, then the arguments show the ways in which value judgments inevitably enter the system of scientific propositions. We will consider both types of arguments in turn. Valuational activities are believed to be indispensable in at least eight strategic points of the research process.

First, the decision to start scientific research is already permeated with valuations. It is the option for some specific set of values, characteristic for the ethos of science. Merton defines this notion: "The ethos of science is that affectively toned complex of values and norms which is held to be binding on the man of science. The norms are expressed in the form of prescriptions, proscriptions, preferences, and permissions. They are legitimatized in terms of institutional values [1973: 268–269]." The apex of those values is truth—an adequate knowledge of phenomena, events, or precesses. At first glance, it seems self-evidenct that truth is an unambiguously positive value, that knowledge is always better than ignorance. But some reflection is enough to see that in certain situations truth may be detrimental to human well-being, or at least to the well-being of some people, groups, classes, etc., especially when it gets into conflict with other values. To pursue scientific research, understood as the search for truth, is therefore itself a valuational decision. The book of Genesis provides one illustration: The fate of Adam and Eve may be interpreted as implying that to seek truth is not always advisable. Other examples may be taken from some branches of molecular genetics: Several outstanding scientists have proposed a moratorium on research projects, in view of the dangers inherent in discovering the mechanisms of human heredity. Similar considerations apply to other components of the scientific ethos—criticism, scepticism, universalism, etc. Embarking on any scientific project, a scientist expresses his valuational option in its favor and against its opposite. "The mores of science possess a methodological rationale but they are binding not only because they are procedurally efficient, but because they are believed right and good. They are moral as well as technical prescriptions [Merton, 1973: 270]." A similar observation is made by Mills: "The social scientist at work is not suddenly confronted with the need to choose values. He is already working on the basis of certain values. . . . The values inherent in the traditions of social science are neither transcendent nor imminent. They are simply values proclaimed by many and within limits practiced in small circles [1959: 178]."

The second point where valuations seem to enter inescapably is the choice of a scientific problem: the delimitation of the subject matter or domain of inquiry, the selection of some specific problematic events, phenomena, or processes within this domain, and the posing of questions with respect to the selected object. To be sure, all this can be, and sometimes is, purely accidental. But if real choice is involved, some valuational criteria will of necessity be present. One requirement widely held today is that of a conscious choice of sociological problems in view of their social relevance—their link with issues deemed important and urgent by the members of a society, and their possible implications for society if eventually solved. Lynd (1939) has challenged sociology with the question "Knowledge for what?"—requiring that sociology abandon trivial and insignificant studies and focus instead on fundamental and important problems. And a determination of what is fundamental and important is to be made by reference to prevailing social values. Merton has pointed out that those prevailing values are in fact group-bound and particularistic, which makes the choice of problems even more value-relevant.

> The investigator's social values do influence his choice and definition of problems. The investigator may naively suppose that he is engaged in the value-free activity of research, whereas in fact he may simply have so defined his research problems that the results will be of use to one group in society, and not to others. His very choice and definition of a problem reflects his tacit values [1973: 86].

Several other authors emphasize the necessity of valuations at the initial stage of scientific inquiry. Wirth says: "Without valuations we have no interest, no sense of relevance or of significance, and, consequently, no object [in Myrdal, 1964: 1064]" and Mills calls for "explicit attention to a range of public issues and personal troubles.... In our formulations of problems we must make clear the values that are really threatened in the troubles and issues involved, who accepts them as values, and by whom or by what they are threatened [1959: 130]."

The third point where valuations enter the realm of science is the choice of the conceptual model adopted for the solution of the problem. The view that sociological facts are "given," are somewhere "out there" waiting to be discovered, is appealing in its simplicity, but totally and fundamentally mistaken. Reality itself is infinitely complex, multidimensional, continuous and fluid. And, given human limitations, "if we are to be able to talk about something, we must be able to see it as a limited subject matter. We must be able to say what falls within the subject matter and what without, in order to see what kinds of questions can profitably be asked [Emmet, 1958: 12]." In short, we must slice the cake of experience in a specific way, take some elements, aspects, or dimensions into consideration and disregard or exclude others. What fragment of reality acquires the rank of a fact depends to a large extent on the way the cake is sliced. We do not discover facts that are given; we construct them out of reality with the help of our particular tools. Facts are not merely encountered, they are produced. We filter our experience through the screen of our conceptual apparatus and, as a result, we transform it into scientific constructs, and, of course, scientific facts.

These points were argued very cogently by Ackerman and Parsons:

> Sociology is not a tabula rasa upon which things called "facts" inscribe their determinate and essential paths and shapes.... We approach our data as humans; and as humans, we approach with differential receptivity and intentionality everything toward which we propose cognitive orientation.... Data do not simply impose their structure on our inquiring and open minds; we interact with "facts."... There is a formative input to analysis, the components of which are not born ex nihilo in or of the moment of encounter with "facts"; rather, they are grounded in the orientation and frame of reference of the analyst. Indeed in major part we create, we do not merely encounter, facticity [1966: 24].

I shall attempt to apprehend the essence of this conceptual input inherent in every sociological analysis through the notion of a conceptual model. But several alternative conceptual models are usually available. The selection of a specific one can of course be purely accidental, or guided by intrascientific criteria of simplicity, economy, elegance, coherence. But more often than

not those criteria are valuational; they express some extrascientific commitments of the scholar. "The choice is made from an indefinite number of
possibilities. The same is true when drawing inferences from organized
data. . . . Scientific conventions usually give guidance. But . . . convention
itself is a valuation, usually a biased one [Myrdal, 1964: 1057]."

   The example most often cited is the opposition of the "consensus" or
"integration" model and the "coercion" or "conflict" model. As Cohen
describes these: "One model attributes to social systems the characteristics
of commitment, cohesion, solidarity, consensus, reciprocity, cooperation,
integration, stability and persistence, while the other attributes to it the
characteristics of coercion, division, hostility, dissensus, conflict, mal-
integration and change [1968: 166–167]." Real societies exemplify some
admixture of the traits of both models, so neither can be argued to be true
in their purity. But their choice significantly preconditions the direction of
research and the character of the results. Exclusive emphasis on "consensus"
turns the attention of the sociologist toward the study of stabilizing
mechanisms, self-regulatory processes, compensatory devices, and gives residual status to the phenomena of deviance, social disorder, and change.
And an exclusive emphasis on "conflict" has equally dangerous effects; it
encourages the study of disruption, imbalance, change—to the neglect of
such phenomena as social control, socialization, integration, harmony,
solidarity—an equally important "face" of the social world. Presumably, the
choice of emphasis, the selection of the conceptual model, reflects the value
commitments of the scientist—conservative in the first case, radical in the
second, or some intermediate position on this "master scale of biases in the
social sciences [Myrdal, 1964: 1038]."

   The fourth point where valuations may be relevant is the choice of the
sample for sociological investigation. We are apt to study those populations
closest to our own: those in which we participate or those that we identify
with in the extrascientific context of social life. It is because their problems
and interests are most similar to our own problems and interests as members of society. Perhaps for this reason, "we generalize about the human
group, but we study the adult, middle-class, white, urban male [Mack, 1969:
53]." And the same is true of the more specialized sociological subdiscip-
lines. "Our generalizations about all families are built on knowledge about
middle-class families [Mack, 1969: 53]," and the majority of experimental
studies in social psychology are in fact dealing with the social psychology of
undergraduate students in sociology or psychology departments.

   The fifth strategic point where valuations may play a considerable role is
the choice of the proper technique for research. It is a trivial observation
that each research technique in the social sciences is more or less directly
dealing with and manipulating people. The application of each research

technique may exert some influence on the studied subject matter. And when the subject-matter is living, perceiving, conscious human beings, profound ethical questions immediately arise. Is such an influence permissible, and if so, what are the limits of manipulation? Certainly, the impact of research on the studied subjects varies with each concrete technique, and ranges from the maximum extreme of laboratory experimentation to the minimum extreme of participant observation. But to some extent, it is always present.

In sociological literature valuational dilemmas are most often discussed with reference to experimentation on human beings. The question of the "limits of experiment" is posed. Was Milgram (1963) justified in evoking a high level of emotional stress, dramatic psychological conflicts, and even physiological malfunctions among his subjects, while studying obedience to orders? Was Sherif (1956) acting ethically when instigating hostilities and even hatred between two groups of boy scouts in order to study the origin of group norms in a situation of conflict? Was Asch (1955) above blame for premeditated cheating and misinforming his respondents in his experiments on conformity? (There are many other such examples.)

But valuational choices are by no means absent from other than experimental techniques. May respondents be misinformed of the real purposes of a survey? What sorts of questions should not be raised in interviews? What is the limit on violations of privacy? What is the justification for controlling, cross-examining questions? What pressure can properly be exerted on a respondent to evoke an answer? What is the justification for risking that a questionnaire will arouse latent attitudes, stir up quiescent problems, and eventually undermine the mental balance or emotional stability of a respondent? This is only a sample of the valuational questions that can be raised.

Similar though less often perceived dilemmas face any research worker applying sociometric tests. For there is always a danger that revealing likes and dislikes among group members, spotting cliques and subgroups, identifying leaders, stars, and outcasts may originate serious internal conflicts, and even lead to the total disintegration of the group. Is there a warrant for taking such a risk?

Finally, even the seemingly neutral technique of observation, or participant observation, may easily lead to the infringement of somebody's right to privacy. None of those questions can be answered on purely technical grounds, without recourse to valuations. And the choice of a particular research technique will always reflect the moral, ethical and other extra-scientific convictions of the scholar.

The sixth entrance for valuations to the realm of science is open at the moment when scientific hypotheses have to be accepted or rejected. In a study not limited to descriptive fact finding, this stage is inevitably reached, sooner or later. A theoretical hypothesis, specifying some expected relationship between two states of affairs (two phenomena, events, variables, whatever) is never a simple report about a finite set of observations, but rather refers to an open, unlimited class of cases. Therefore it can never be conclusively and completely confirmed by empirical data. The data give it only some level of plausibility or corroboration. And then, a certain specific degree of plausibility must be settled upon as sufficient for accepting the hypothesis as true, and incorporating it into the body of verified scientific knowledge. This decision is taken by applying particular criteria. Some of them are intrascientific or methodological (e.g., rules of statistical significance). But some are extrascientific or valuational. As Rudner puts it:

> Before we can accept any hypothesis, the value decision must be made in the light of the seriousness of a mistake, that the probability is high enough, or that the evidence is strong enough, to warrant its acceptance.... And clearly how great a risk one is willing to take of being wrong in accepting or rejecting the hypothesis will depend upon how seriously in the typically ethical sense one views the consequences of making a mistake [1969: 755–756].

Since in the social sciences all hypotheses refer more or less directly to human beings, they furnish grounds for practical actions addressed to human beings. If any such action is taken on the basis of a mistaken hypothesis, the consequences may be detrimental or even disastrous to people. This gives a moral, ethical, or, more generally, valuational weight to the seemingly neutral decision of accepting or rejecting a hypothesis. Certainly, in some cases the risk involved will be negligible—for example, a hypothesis concerning the causes of falling attendance at art galleries—and consequently the required degree of confirmation will be relatively low. In other cases the risk can be profound—for example, a hypothesis about the causes of widespread discontent with a political regime—and consequently the required degree of confirmation will be relatively higher. The point is that in both cases no intrascientific, purely methodological rule is sufficient to guide the scholar in making a decision: Extrascientific values must be invoked.

The seventh point when valuations become salient in the process of scientific inquiry is the publication of research results. In all branches of science, a scientist is to some extent responsible for the potential practical consequences of his theoretical findings. He should take such consequences into account, in view of the actual historical and political situation, as well as the predicted goals and motivations of those who control the means of implementing the results of scientific research. This point is cogently argued by Kelman: "Even though the products of pure research are in a sense neutral, the investigator cannot escape responsibility for their probable consequences. . . . In deciding whether or not to proceed with his research, he must try to make some estimate of the probabilities of different uses of his research product, in the light of the existing social forces [1969: 594]."

Such an obligation rests on a scientist in all branches of science. But in the social sciences it is especially pressing, owing to one peculiarity discussed previously; namely, the results of social science may have an immediate impact on social reality, even before they are appropriated by applied scientists, politicians, or administrators and transformed into practical directives. The theoretical, pure results of the social sciences, publicized widely enough to enter the popular mind, may become strong motivating factors for mass activities. And those activities may bring effects that are either beneficial to or disastrous for a society and its members. "Like the nuclear physicist, the social scientist is responsible for knowledge that—in the light of the world situation in which it is being produced—has decided explosive possibilities [Kelman, 1969: 583]." Social knowledge is by itself a powerful social force. Social scientists must weigh carefully all the potential effects of their knowledge and appraise them in terms of their values. Only on such grounds may they make a responsible decision to publish or keep secret their findings.

All the arguments discussed so far focused on the role of valuations, understood as specific activities, in the conduct of scientific research treated as a specific process. But the problem of valuations may also be considered with respect to the outcome of scientific research. Thus, additional arguments must be discussed now—those focusing on the status of value judgments, understood as specific propositions, in the structure of scientific knowledge.

The axiologists emphasize that value judgments may appear in at least three locations in the body of a sociological theory. First, some distinct fragments of sociological theory may have valuational character; that is, articulate explicitly a specific value system. This possibility is mentioned by Wiatr (1971) who conceives the "theory of a socialist society [as a] constructivist theory" including three separate parts: an explanatory theory of the socialist system, a normative model of the socialist system, and the theory of socialist policy and planning—the last derived from the first two. Value judgments enter as main components into the normative model of the socialist system, understood by Wiatr as a "concretization of the general normative theory of socialism (socialist axiology) [1971: 57]." In his view only the constructivist theory can answer all those questions usually addressed to social-scientific results—cognitive, valuational, and practical. Therefore, it is the only form that a proper sociological theory should take.

The second location where value judgments appear within scientific results is the internal structure of the scientific propositions. Some of them have a mixed nature; they inform and appraise at the same time. Such propositions believed to be particularly characteristic of the social sciences are termed "substantive valuations" in contradistinction to "pure valuations" (Kmita, 1964: 119; Nowak 1974c: 82–87). Substantive valuations give a description or explanation of an object and at the same time express a valuational attitude toward it. "Their emotional overtones are coupled with a report on those characteristics of the object which evoke our praise or condemnation. . . . They communicate both my attitude and the properties with respect to which the attitude is taken [Ossowska, 1967: 469]." Several examples from sociological literature may be quoted: Weber's law of growing rationalization of social life, Tönnies's principle describing the movement from the *Gemeinschaft*-type to the *Gesellschaft*-type of society as basically regressive, Marx's law of social progress or his theory of alienation. In this way, value judgments also enter those fragments of a theory that have a seemingly neutral character ("explanatory theory," in the conception of Wiatr, and not only "normative theory").

The third resort of valuations is the connotation of sociological concepts. Most often they are not purely descriptive, but include valuational overtones. This is a peculiarity of concepts that refer directly to human problems. As Kula puts it: "The words describing human affairs are always linked with innumerable valuational associations [1958: 145]." Consider such terms as *fascism, totalitarianism, democracy, progress, development, harmony, integration, solidarity, deviation, innovation, conformity, discrimination, exploitation, unemployment, alienation, ideology, socialization, proletariat, bourgeois* and almost all others included in sociological dictionaries. Some could argue that this valuational character of sociological terms is due only to the juvenility of sociology and its too-close alliance with common sense and the everyday experiences of men. They would suggest that the development of a strict, technical vocabulary for sociology would purify sociological terms of their emotive and normative burden. But some other scholars claim that it is a fundamental, principal peculiarity, not to be eradicated by any measures. For example, Andreski declares:

> Personally, I do not believe this will ever be achieved, because (apart from other obstacles to progress in this field) of the impediment (irremediable to my mind) that, no matter how aseptic and odorless when first coined, psychological and sociological terms very quickly acquire undertones of praise or blame in accordance with whether the reality to which they refer is liked or not [1972: 100].

The Case for Neutralism:
Guarding against Valuations

The foregoing closes the list of arguments typically put forward by the axiologists. What is the response of the neutralists? How do they argue their case that social research can and should be free of valuations, and social knowledge free of value judgments. The evidence that valuations and value judgments do occur in the social sciences is so strong that neutralists rarely attempt to discuss the descriptive aspect of the problem. Rather, they concentrate their attack on the prescriptive thesis, and argue that valuations are not in principle unavoidable. A characteristic statement by Nagel may be quoted: "The difficulties are not necessarily insuperable, for since by hypothesis it is not impossible to distinguish between fact and value, steps can be taken to identify a value bias when it occurs, and to minimize if not to eliminate completely its perturbing effects [1961: 489]." Several strategies are suggested to overcome valuations and to eliminate them from the scientific process, as well as from scientific results.

Some strategies are individualistically oriented; they require that the corrective measures be taken by a single social scientist. One of them is personal training in critical, skeptical, objectivistic attitudes, with the help of psychoanalysis and familiarity with the sociology of knowledge (see Rumney and Maier, 1953). Another is the development of proper motivations on the part of scientists—a purely cognitive interest, an unbiased desire to understand. McEwen has asked what requirements social scientists must meet in order to achieve objective knowledge despite the valuational characteristics of data. And his answer is: "Scientific objectivity should be identified by reference to the reflective attitude of the investigator himself who is dominantly motivated by the desire to know. . . . It is the Faustian quest for the satisfaction of never completely satisfying his intellectual curiosity for increasingly more reliable knowledge [1963: 31–33, 215]."

Some other strategies are collectivistically oriented; they put faith in the corrective measures undertaken by the community of social scientists. A typical statement of such a position is found in Nagel's work:

> The difficulties generated for scientific inquiry by unconscious bias and tacit value orientations are rarely overcome by devout resolutions to eliminate bias. They are usually overcome, often only gradually, through the self-corrective mechanisms of science as a social enterprise. For modern science encourages the invention, the mutual exchange, and the free but responsible criticisms of ideas; it welcomes competition in the quest for knowledge between independent investigators, even when their intellectual orientations are different; and it progressively diminishes the

effects of bias by retaining only those proposed conclusions of its inquiries that survive critical examination by an indefinitely large community of students, whatever be their value-preferences or doctrinal commitments [1961: 490].

A similar solution to the riddle of valuations is suggested by Dahrendorf:

Science is always a concert of many. The progress of science rests at least as much on the cooperation of scholars as it does on the inspiration of the individual. This cooperation must not be confined to the all too popular "teamwork"; rather, its most indispensable task is mutual criticism. . . . In the long run, this procedure alone can protect sociology—though not the individual sociologist—against the danger of ideological distortion [1968: 14].

Two more arguments of a similar sort are worth quoting. Popper says: "The objectivity of natural and social science is not based on an impartial state of mind in the scientists, but merely on the fact of the public and competitive character of the scientific enterprise and thus on certain social aspects of it. . . . Objectivity is based, in brief, upon mutual rational criticism, upon the critical approach, the critical tradition [1976b: 293]." And Blau prescribes the same approach: "The best chance to develop a valid theory (strictly speaking, one whose probable validity is high) is to give the diverse viewpoints of different social scientists free play to permit them to correct one another's biases [1969: 129]."

Finally, the strategies of the third type most directly inspired by the positivistic and neopositivistic tradition see escape from valuations in an imitation of natural-scientific methodology and the slow coming of age of sociology as a scientific discipline. Particular attention is attached to the fundamental reform of sociological language, away from the vernacular and toward a precise technical, unambiguous vocabulary. Also, the formalization or symbolization of sociological propositions, connected with the application of mathematical calculi, is believed to eliminate valuations. Last but not least, some improved techniques of empirical research, as well as the theoretical interpretation of data—the development of scaling techniques and measurement procedures, the application of computers and sophisticated statistical measures—all those are supposed to lead to a totally detached, value-free, objective study of social life. Its coming is seen as only a matter of time.

Several interesting insights attach to both the axiological and the neutralist points of view. But the dispute remains unresolved, and the time has come to show that the dilemma of axiologism and neutralism is spurious, and can be overcome by presenting an alternative solution, indebted to some ideas of both traditional standpoints, but also basically different from either of them.

COMMITMENT AS
A DIALECTICAL SOLUTION

The point of departure for my dialectical strategy of dealing with the seemingly unresolvable dilemma is the search for some meta-assumptions that both share. Is there anything in common between the axiologists and the neutralists?

The Common Meta-assumptions: The Traditional
Notion of Objectivity

At first glance, in the ideal–typical formulations outlined earlier both standpoints appear as completely opposite and mutually exclusive. But if one looks under the surface, and uncovers the hidden presuppositions of neutralism and axiologism, an important area of commonality, an important similarity of approach to the problem of valuations, will be discovered.

Both standpoints accept the same notion of scientific objectivity, which shall be labeled as traditional notion of objectivity, or Objectivity$_1$. This notion can be explicated by means of four assumptions: First, objectivity is an absolute property of scientific research and scientific results; that is, it can be predicated of research or of results by critically examining their internal form or structure. Second, the property in question determining objectivity is lack of bias; or, to put it in other words, objectivity is the converse of bias. Third, bias is always the result of valuations, and valuations always produce bias. Fourth, valuations are therefore contradictory to objectivity; valuational activities preclude objectivity of scientific method, and value judgments preclude the objectivity of scientific results. If any valuational activities are spotted in scientific research, its method can for this very reason be seen as nonobjective. And if any value judgments are spotted in scientific knowledge, such knowledge can be regarded as nonobjective.

Such a notion of objectivity is close to the extrascientific, common-sense meaning attached to this term. Wirth describes it in the following way: "In the language of the Anglo-Saxon world to be objective has meant to be impartial, to have no preferences, predilections or prejudices, no biases, no preconceived values or judgments in the presence of the facts [in Krimerman, 1969: 691]." Similar definitions have also been explicitly formulated in sociology. For Merton *objective* means not distorted by the predilections of the scientist (1973: 75). Gouldner considers as the significant component of objectivity

> the capacity to acknowledge "hostile information"—information that is discrepant with our purposes, hopes, wishes, or values. . . . Here, then, objectivity consists in the capacity to know and to use—to seek out, or at least to accept it when it is otherwise provided—information inimical to our own desires and values, and to overcome our own fear of such information [1973: 59].

The traditional notion of objectivity (Objectivity$_1$) is accepted by neutralists and axiologists alike. The neutralists hold that Objectivity$_1$ is attainable in the social sciences, and should be striven for. The axiologists hold that Objectivity$_1$ is not attainable in the social sciences and should be rejected as an unrealistic and improper goal. Their position is expressed succinctly by Rudner:

> It concedes, or at least does not question, the objectivity of the scientific method, but holds instead that the social sciences cannot use such an objective method; the social sciences must either eschew or supplement the use of the scientific method in such a fashion that the resulting methodology falls short of the degree of objectivity characteristic of the scientific method [1966: 78].

The Rejection of Common Meta-assumptions: A New Notion of Objectivity

If the common meta-assumptions of the neutralistic and axiologistic standpoints have been found to be linked by a common notion of objectivity, the dialectical way to overcome the dilemma must lead through the rejection of such a notion and its replacement with an alternative. I shall term it the new notion of objectivity, or Objectivity$_2$. This notion can be explicated by means of four composite assumptions, the converse of the previous ones.

First, objectivity is now conceived as a relative property of scientific research and scientific results; that is, it cannot be predicated of research or of results by critically examining their internal form or structure. Second, this relativization has a two-fold nature. First, objectivity of results is relative to the real state of affairs in the given domain of reality. It is tantamount to a semantic relationship of adequacy or correspondence between the content of a scientific proposition and the phenomena, events, or processes as they really occur. In brief, scientific results are objective if and only if they are true. Objectivity of scientific results is synonymous with their truth. Second, Objectivity of research is relative to the truth of the results achieved by research. It is tantamount to the pragmatic relationship of instrumentality between the scientific method and scientific knowledge. Scientific method is objective if and only if it is instrumental in attaining true scientific knowledge. Objectivity of a method is synonymous with its reliability or fruitfulness in the search for knowledge. Such a relative notion of objectivity with respect to the method of science is put forward by Rudner: "The sense of 'reliability' involved would appear to be satisfied by the following criterion: Method A is more reliable than Method B if, and only if, its continued employment is less liable to error (i.e., is less likely to result in our continuing to believe, or coming to believe false sentences) [1966: 76]." To repeat, objectivity here means the truth of results and the usefulness of a method for the achievement of true results.

Third, value judgments do not impair the truth of research results, and valuations in the research process do not prevent the attainment of true results. They do not produce bias, or at least do not have to produce bias. Rather, value-judgments are the necessary, indispensable ingredients of true knowledge, and valuations are the necessary and indispensable components of the method or procedure rendering true knowledge.

Fourth, therefore value judgments and valuations are not obstacles to but rather prerequisites for scientific objectivity.

The insights suggesting a new notion of objectivity have occurred to several authors, particularly those who have taken the natural-scientific methodological patterns to be improper for the social sciences, and have struggled for the creation of a new, antinaturalistic and antipositivistic methodology, more suitable for the study of man and society. Mannheim says: "A new type of objectivity in the social sciences is attainable not through the exclusion of valuations but through the critical awareness and control of them [1936: 706]." Rejecting the traditional version of objectivity, understood as the elimination of biases, Krimerman argues: "Here if the inquirer casts aside his values, if he attempts, say, an ethically neutral investigation, he will fail to understand—he will distort or oversimplify—the phenomena he is studying. In brief, coming to know certain propositions about human conduct or institutional life requires principles of value, but at no point is this the case in the physical sciences [1969: 694]." This idea is developed by Glass: "Objectivity is to be sought, not through studied indifference to meanings, but through heightened awareness of the assumptions used and values involved, making them clear and open to examination." He proposes "enlarging the conception of objectivity to include not only 'spectator-knowledge' (laissez-faire, uninvolved knowledge, knowledge about, knowledge from the outside), but also experiential knowledge [Glass and Staude, 1972: 6]." Similarly, Gouldner finds fault with the views of Becker in his neglect of the positive functions of valuations: "One reason why Becker's analysis founders on the problem of objectivity is precisely because it regards the sociologist's value commitment merely as an inescapable fact of nature rather than viewing it as a necessary condition of his objectivity [1973: 58]." More generally, the intellectual tendency to move from the traditional to the new notion of objectivity is believed to be the characteristic trait of contemporary social science: "The positive and constructive significance of the evaluative elements in thought had to be recognized. If the earlier discussions of objectivity laid stress upon the elimination of personal and collective bias, the more modern approach calls attention to the positive, cognitive importance of this bias [Wirth, in Krimerman, 1969: 691]."

Toward a Dialectical Alternative

Of the implications of the new notion of objectivity, the most obvious one is the breaking of the one-to-one correspondence between the concept of value involvement and the concept of bias. In the traditional notion there existed a definitional link between the two. Now, each may be treated as an independent dimension.

If the aspect of valuations is the focus, the two opposite standpoints will be these:

Axiologism$_1$ = Sociology cannot and should not avoid valuations.

Neutralism$_1$ = Sociology can and should avoid valuations.

On the other hand, if the focus is on the aspect of bias, a different pair of standpoints appears:

Axiologism$_2$ = Sociology cannot attain unbiased knowledge and utilize unbiased methods.

Neutralism$_2$ = Sociology can attain unbiased knowledge and utilize unbiased methods.

As both dimensions are independent, those two dichotomies can be cross-combined, without danger of logical inconsistency (see Figure 5.1).

Four possible solutions to the problem of valuations are produced. Three of them are particularly interesting; the fourth is a purely analytical possibility, with no recognized referent in sociological literature. The combination of Neutralism$_1$ and Neutralism$_2$ yields extreme neutralism, in which we recognize simply the traditional standpoint of neutralism informed by the traditional notion of objectivity. It claims that sociology can be purifed of valuations, and therefore can attain unbiased knowledge, by pursuing the unbiased method. The combination of Axiologism$_1$ and Axiologism$_2$ yields extreme axiologism, in which we easily recognize the traditional standpoint

The Aspect of Valuations

	Axiologism$_1$	Neutralism$_1$
Neutralism$_2$	Committment	Objectivism
Axiologism$_2$	Subjectivism	

The Aspect of Bias

Figures 5.1

of axiologism informed by the traditional notion of subjectivity. It claims that sociology cannot be purified of valuations and therefore it can only attain biased knowledge, by virtue of employing a biased method. All this is already well known from the history of the dispute.

But the combination of Axiologism$_1$ and Neutralism$_2$ yields a new standpoint, not encountered in the traditional debate. I shall call it a standpoint of commitment. It is clearly informed by the new notion of objectivity, and it claims that sociology should employ valuations as the necessary ingredient of an unbiased method leading to unbiased knowledge of social reality.

The standpoint of commitment satisfies my criteria for a viable dialectical alternative, overcoming the traditional dilemma of valuations. First, because it rejects, at least in part, both traditional positions: Against extreme neutralism it holds that sociology cannot and should not be value free; against extreme axiologism it argues that sociology need not abandon its claims for true knowledge and an unbiased method. Second, because at the same time it provides continuity, at least in part, with both traditional positions: With extreme neutralism it holds that sociology can be unbiased; with extreme axiologism it argues the sociology cannot escape valuations. Third (what is clearly entailed by the foregoing), it is essentially a new standpoint, not identical with any of the traditional ones.

The Riddle of Commitment

To be sure, the standpoint of commitment may raise several doubts. And the most important one is phrased thus by Gouldner: "Granted, all standpoints are partisan; and granted, no one escapes a partisan position.

But aren't some forms of partisanship more liberating than others? [1973: 56–57]?" In language more related to our discussion, the same question is posed by Pomian: "Is there such a system of valuations, such a world view, as allows one to perceive and to understand most of the phenomena available in a given historical epoch, and to achieve in their description, confirmation and explanation the greatest possible objectivity? [1961: 7]?"

The four-part crux of the problem is clearly that (a) there are certainly numerous systems of values which may be applied by the sociologist in his research, and reflected in his findings; (b) each of those systems, when applied by the sociologist, will contribute to the production of different images of social reality; (c) at most, one of those images may be true, or objective; (d) therefore, there must be some criterion for choosing the value system most instrumental in the attainment of objective knowledge, from among all available value systems. Otherwise, a complete relativism of sociological knowledge, some form of extreme sociological solipsism, will have to be admitted.

The cognitive worth of different commitments is unequal. Some are more fruitful than others. As Lange puts it: "Contrary to the ideological systems obscuring reality, those ideological systems that unmask reality present a strong stimulus encouraging scientific cognition [1961: 267]." Well, but which is which? How shall one distinguish obfuscating values from illuminating ones?

There are two arguments that allow one to approach the solution to this riddle. The first argument is based on the insights provided by the sociology of knowledge. The fundamental idea of the sociology of knowledge may be summarized in the formulation of Merton as "the problem of patterned differentials among social groups and strata in access to knowledge [1973: 102]." He proceeds to characterize this problem in the following way:

> In its strong form, the claim is put forward as a matter of epistemological principle that particular groups in each moment of history have monopolistic access to certain kinds of knowledge. In the weaker, more empirical form, the claim holds that some groups have privileged access, with other groups also being able to acquire that knowledge for themselves but at greater risk and cost [1973: 102].

Thus, the cognitive situations and cognitive opportunities of social groups or even of individuals located differentially in the social structure are different. There are some locations more conducive to the attainment of an objective perspective on society, its phenomena and processes, and some locations from which any perspective on society is distorted. The study of society from the perspective (or on behalf) of one social group will therefore be more objective—instrumental for the attainment of objective knowledge—than the study from the perspective (or on behalf) of another group.

The second argument attempts to interpret more precisely what is really meant by the metaphorical injunction to study from the perspective (or on behalf) of a certain group. The sense of this statement is rendered in the following way: First, participation in a specific group, or location at a certain point of a social structure, implies particular vested interests of the group members or the occupants of given positions. Those interests are objectively, structurally determined. They specify what state of affairs would be conducive—under given structural or situational conditions—to the fullest satisfaction of the maximum scope of needs for the maximum number of individuals. For example, to spot land would be a vested interest for a group of survivors sailing in a lifeboat. Second, vested interests in turn imply particular values, which provide justification of those interests and help to realize them. Group solidarity, courage, optimism, prolonged effort, and deferred gratification would be some of the relevant values in my example of the lifeboat. Third, therefore, it may be said that participation in a certain group or the occupancy of a certain social position is tantamount to the acknowledgment of a particular value system relevant to that group or that position. And to study from the perspective (or on behalf) of a certain group means simply to apply a value system of that particular group in the course of sociological research, and to affirm those values in the body of a sociological theory.

Both arguments can now be brought together. They imply that the value system most conducive to the attainment of true (objective) sociological knowledge will be that one which reflects the interests of the group whose location in the social structure provides it with the most unbiased perspective. The question which value system to choose as the guideline for sociological, scientific commitment is now transformed into the question: Which group has the largest cognitive opportunities thanks to its most cognitively privileged position in the social structure?

Some Solutions to the Riddle of Commitment

Several answers are provided to the question as it has been rephrased. Three of them, perhaps most typical of non-Marxist social science, will be singled out. I shall label them—after Merton—*the theory of insiderism, the theory of outsiderism,* and *the theory of avant-gardism.*

The common-sense rationale for the doctrine of insiderism is quite simple: The best view is gained from the inside; the most extensive knowledge is that of a participant. To put it figuratively, one must be Caesar to understand Caesar. Therefore, the problems characteristic of a given social category, group, or class can be best studied and explained only by the members of the collectivity. "The Insider doctrine holds that one has monopolistic or privileged access to knowledge or is excluded from it by virtue of group membership or social position [Merton, 1973: 105]." Merton is certainly right that a general and uncritical adoption of this principle would result in an extreme segmentation and particularization of sociological studies. Besides, if this principle is understood literally, then its validity is undermined by the fact that several most thorough and successful studies of human collectivities have been produced not by their members but rather by scholars—outsiders. Three names come to mind immediately: Gunnar Myrdal, a Swede who achieved an unsurpassed understanding of the racial problem in America; Alexis de Tocqueville, a Frenchman who produced the most penetrating analysis of the American political system; and Bronislaw Malinowski, a Pole who has given the most extensive account of the social and cultural institutions of the Polynesians. And many other names could be cited. Moreover, equally numerous examples can be provided to show that the scientists living in a given society are often blind to its most crucial problems. Thus actual membership in a group is clearly no guarantee of scientific perspicacity.

But the doctrine of insiderism may also be interpreted in a more sophisticated manner. It may be taken to refer not to actual membership but rather to intentional membership—the subjective identification of the scholar with the group he is studying. This form of the principle requires that the scholar adopt the cognitive perspective of the group being studied, or—what amounts to the same thing—that he accept its characteristic value orientations. Perhaps the most famous discussion of such a principle is provided by Thomas and Znaniecki in the methodological note to their fundamental study of Polish emigrants to the United States (1927, vol.I: 1–86), and codified later by Znaniecki as the doctrine of the "humanistic coefficient":

> The primary empirical evidence about any cultural human action is the experience of the agent himself, supplemented by the experience of those who react to his action, reproduce it or participate in it. . . . The scientist who wants to study these actions inductively must take them as they are in the human experience of those agents and re-agents; they are his empirical data inasmuch and because they are theirs [Znaniecki, 1969: 221].

The doctrine of insiderism, if pushed to the limit, has some quite dangerous implications. A new variety of social monadology is proclaimed. There are as many closed-group worlds as there are groups in human society. Those group worlds are mutually impenetrable. Their reality can be understood only by the participating actors. No comparative knowledge is possible, no generalizations over and beyond the particular group microcosms, no laws of human behavior or social processes. A particularistic and seg-mented image of the social world is produced, leading to abdication of any efforts to reach universal, general knowledge.

The second proposal in the search for a cognitively privileged perspective is the doctrine of outsiderism. Its common-sense rationale is quite opposite to that of insiderism. It claims that a most extensive view is gained from the outside, the best perspective is that of an outsider. To put it figuratively, one must be other than Caesar to understand Caesar. Therefore, the prob-lems characteristic of a given social category, group, or class can best be studied and explained only by those who stand apart, and do not participate in the group life.

Two implementations of this doctrine are usually considered the most significant in contemporary sociology. The first is indebted to Karl Mann-heim's sociology of knowledge. Mannheim's attempt is to build a general theory of the social or "existential" determinants of cognition. All ideas are seen as the products of the particular social situation or structural position of the thinker; they are bound to a location within the society. The social factors "are relevant not only to the genesis of ideas, but they penetrate into their forms and content and they decisively determine the scope and inten-sity of our experience and observation, [that is,] the 'perspective' of the subject [Mannheim, 1936: 240]." But are all the "perspectives" equally one-sided and therefore unscientific? In Mannheim's view there is one exception to this rule, one social stratum that is recruited from all social classes, but not participating in any, one social category whose members stand "above" the rest of society, whose cognitive perspective arises as a synthesis of the plural particularistic perspectives of all classes, and there-fore achieves universalistic properties. This privileged stratum, able to master an undistorted, adequate image of social reality and acquire the necessary detachment, is the socially unattached intelligentsia.

A belief in the exceptional position of the intelligentsia is also expressed in the political writings of Mannheim on the planning and purposeful recon-struction of the post-war social order. Here the leading role is assigned again to those social groups that are able to transcend particularistic perspectives, and that, owing to rigorous training have developed their intellectual and moral abilities to such an extent that they can eschew their private, narrow interests and act on behalf of the whole society (Mannheim, 1974: 112).

The main weakness of Mannheim's conception is a lack of sufficient theoretical grounds for ascribing exceptional cognitive status to in-tellectuals, or the intelligentsia. As Coser (1971) remarks, this group is introduced ad hoc, as a "kind of Deus ex Machina." The warrant for their cognitive dominance is found in the psychological abilities, skills, attitudes of the individual members, rather than in the structural location of the whole group.

> Even if it be granted that men of ideas often manage to divest themselves from certain biases and prejudices that infect the multitude . . . the intellectuals are by no means immune from the passions, the temptations, and the corruptions of their time. Individual intellectuals may indeed at times manage to be *au dessus de la mêlée;* intellectuals as a category are not. Education and intellectual endeavors may indeed lead to a measure of critical detachment, but they do not suffice to make intellectuals into pristine custodians of pure reason [Coser, 1971: 436].

A second version of the doctrine of outsiderism is represented by Howard Becker, and some other students of deviance and social pathology. The reasoning in this version is almost the antithesis of Mannheim's doctrine, even though the rationale is similar. The group which is really outside society, and therefore possesses a detached, undistorted perspective, is not there of its own choice and effort, as the intelligentsia certainly are. Rather, it is pushed to a marginal status, and stigmatized as "outsiders" by the respectable social establishment. This is the group of "underdogs," outcasts, and "deviants" of all sorts. From their perspective, the most unbiased picture of the social world is possible, because they have no stakes in any of the existing institutions, rules, or norms. As Gouldner comments on Becker: "This school of thought represents a metaphysics of the underdog and of the underworld; a metaphysics in which conventional society is viewed from the standpoint of a group outside of its own respectable social structures [1973: 30]."

It is not claimed that membership in the group of social deviants is a guarantee of sociological knowledge. Rather, the call is for the identification of the scholar with that group, which is "more sinned against than sinning," for studying society on its behalf, for applying its value systems in the research process. Even with this caveat Becker's answer to the question "Whose side are we on?" as social scientists is not sufficiently grounded in theoretical considerations, and must rather be taken as a moral creed. This is convincingly argued by Gouldner:

> Clearly, Becker presents no logical solution to this quandary. . . . I share Becker's underdog sympathies. Yet I also believe that sociological study from an underdog standpoint will be intellectually impaired without clarifying the grounds for the commitment. A commitment made on the basis of unexamined ideology may allow us to feel a manly righteousness, but it leaves us blind [1973: 34].

The third and the relatively most recent proposal in the search for the cognitively superior group may be labeled the *doctrine of avant-gardism.* Its rationale includes the metaphor of a theater or the infantry: Those who are up front see the most. The core of the doctrine is that the most objective truth about society can be obtained only by those who constitute the front lines of society, who march in front of it, who lead in the succession of generations—the young. Several proclamations of the creed have been formulated by the leaders of student rebellions in the late sixties in Europe and the United States: Mario Savio, Rudi Dutschke, Daniel Cohn-Bendit. The idea recurs in some of the programatic statements of the "radical sociologists." One of them, Freiberg, argues for the particular cognitive opportunities of students, especially students of sociology:

> In the process of having ideology crammed down their throats as if it were science, they have reacted not only to the practice of sociology as ideological, but also to the social role it plays on grander scales. They have seen through the ideology of modern technological society, and have become aware of the power relations that in fact structure society, to which sociology never refers [Freiberg, 1973: 11].

Marcuse (1968) provides a refined formulation of similar ideas, finding the warrant for objectivity not in being young or youthful, but in an ideological identification with the subculture of the young and its characteristic system of values. But even here, no coherent theoretical argument, nothing stronger than common-sense convictions or personal sympathies, is put forward. The doctrine of avant-gardism fails rather as the two other, previously discussed epistemological principles do. The riddle of commitment is not solved in a satisfactory manner by any of the non-Marxist sociological theories.

COMMITMENT IN MARXIAN SOCIOLOGICAL THEORY

The following argument is now to be advanced: The standpoint of commitment that has been constructed as the dialectical solution to the dilemma of valuations was adumbrated in the sociological writings of Karl Marx. What is more, Marx pointed out coherently and with theoretical underpinnings which commitment is most conducive to the attainment of an objective and adequate knowledge of society.

Commitment and Objectivity in Marx

The first point is almost self-evident: It is a widely recognized peculiarity of Marxian theory, which in fact has prevented some positivistically oriented thinkers from considering it as a theory at all, that it is permeated with valuations. Marx does not make the slightest attempt to avoid or to eliminate valuations; he couches some aspects of his theory in explicitly normative terms—for example, his image of a communist society; he introduces propositions of a double character, informative and valuational at the same time (for example, the law of progress, the law of impoverishment); he uses concepts of a double nature—factual and valuational (for example, alienation, exploitation, the bourgeoisie). As Kolakowski observes, "Marx refuses to dissect his thought into 'factual,' 'prescriptive,' or 'technological' components; . . . he refuses to consider separately what the world is like, what it should be like to fulfill certain valuational criteria, and which means must be taken to realize those values [1976: 329]." According to Swingewood, "Marx argues that values and facts are not separated into two mutually exclusive domains, but are bound together in an indissoluble dialectical union [1975: 52]." A similar comment is made by Andreyeva:

> The specific features of . . . Marxism lie in the fact that the investigation concerns itself with the conditions under which the contradiction between science and values is removed. This removal of the contradiction is effected through the acceptance by the investigator of such values of society whose right to exist can be scientifically substantiated, rather than through exclusion of values from science [1974: 8].

Marx's own theoretical practice proves therefore most conclusively that he fully concurred in the assumption of Axiologism$_1$—that sociology cannot escape valuations and must accept them as a legitimate part of a scientific enterprise.

But at the same time Marx was most explicit about his ambition to create a real science of society, uncovering its "natural" laws of motion, different in content from the laws of psychology or biology, but equally external, regular, objective, and necessary. This ambition is most persistently declared in *Capital* but can be discovered in all other works of his as well. Meyer gives an apt appraisal of this scientific aspect of Marxism: "Marxism is one might effort to make valid generalizations concerning the way in which the multiple forces at play in human society are interrelated, and how they affect each other. It is an attempt to draw a vast and complex blueprint of our entire social structure, in its social, economic, political, historical, and psychological dimensions [1969: 11]." There can be no doubt that Marx fully endorses the assumption of Neutralism$_2$—that sociology can attain objective (i.e., true) knowledge of human society.

The recognition of those two, apparently opposite, claims in the Marxian heritage has led some commentators to ascribe an internal contradiction, strain, duality, or cleavage to the Marxian system. Quite often, the critical, or valuating, Marx is opposed to the scientific, or fact-oriented, Marx; Marx the politician and ideologist to Marx the academic thinker. Kolakowski (1976) has even distinguished three separate intellectual tendencies in the Marxian heritage: the romantic tendency, expressed best in Marx's criticism of capitalist society; the Promethean and Faustian tendency, most pronounced in the program for the classless, unalienated society of the future; and the rationalistic and deterministic tendency, which issues in the theory of historical materialism (418–426). In all such appraisals there looms the idea of some incongruence, ambiguity, or even contradiction between the valuational and factual (or theoretical) aspects of Marxism.

But the real Marxian position seems to be best interpreted as the new objectivity—Objectivity$_2$—the belief that valuations are no obstacle to but rather a prerequisite of truth, and that only within a valuational perspective can a complete and adequate knowledge of society be achieved. It is a notion of a complete dialectic unity of facts and valuations, coupled with the notion of a functional usefulness of valuations with respect to facts. This is intuitively acknowledged by all those who utilize seemingly contradictory terms in referring to Marxian thought: "scientific ideology," "ideological science," "scientific socialism," "scientific communism," etc. But it is also quite explicitly recognized by several contemporary commentators. Andreyeva describes the Marxist conception of sociology as

> a science which must be built up on the foundation of exact, objective facts collected by strictly scientific methods, and at the same time, as a science organically including an evaluation not only of its own cognitive means but also of reality itself.... From the standpoint of Marxism, sociology is above all a science, i.e., it includes a precise, objective knowledge of social reality. At the same time it is specific in that the measure of its objectivity directly depends on how fully the viewpoint dictated by the progressive social ideal is realized in its scientific stock [1974: 16].

Lange reads Marx as affirming that "the possibility of a scientific understanding of reality in the realm of the social sciences ... is dependent on the application of ideology [i.e., a value system] unmasking and illuminating reality [1961: 268]." Wiatr explains: "In the view of the founders of Marxism, science is ideological, which means that it is instrumental in the realization of the class interest of the proletariat, but at the same time it is objective and unbiased, because the realization of this interest is best served by knowledge which is true, and free of any distortions and limitations [1973a: 57]."

Thus, all the composite assumptions of the standpoint labeled *commitment* are found to underlie Marx's sociological writings, whereas neither the neutralist position nor the axiologist position seems to offer a correct representation of his views or his theoretical practice.

Accepting the standpoint of commitment, Marx obviously had to solve the problem posed earlier in my analytic reconstruction; namely, whether all sorts of commitment are equally useful for the attainment of true knowledge, and, if not, which is the most instrumental one. He apparently followed the same steps as were outlined earlier, attempting to reduce the problem to the level of systematic structural differentials between human groups in their access to knowledge.

Marx is widely acknowledged as the forefather of the sociology of knowledge, calling attention to the fact that human mental products, including scientific ideas, are deeply rooted in the conditions of group life and to some extent reflect their peculiar conditions. Criticizing preceding philosophical trends, Marx says: "It has not occurred to any of these philosophers to inquire into the connection of German philosophy with German reality, the relation of their criticism to their own material surroundings [Marx and Engels, 1975: 59]." And in *The Communist Manifesto* he develops this observation into part of the cornerstone of his materialistic philosophy: "Does it require deep intuition to comprehend that man's ideas, views and conceptions, in one word, man's consciousness, changes with every change in the conditions of his material existence, in his social relations and in his social life? What else does the history of ideas prove, than that intellectual production changes its character in proportion as material production is changed? The ruling ideas of each age have ever been the ideas of its ruling class [Marx and Engels, 1968: 51]." Because only some ideas can be true, only some conditions of existence, or some structurally determined locations in a society, will be conducive to the attainment of true knowledge. Knowledge is relative, but not hopelessly relativistic. The problem is to find which groups of people sharing particular life-conditions or similarly situated in a society will represent the strongest cognitive potential. Here Marx is true to his structuralist approach. He is not concerned with the psychological, individual differences in cognitive potential. He is concerned only with the differences contingent upon the placement of individuals within the social structure. Individuals interest him only as representatives of structural categories: occupants of positions, players of structurally determined roles (e.g., in the division of labor), members of particular groups (e.g., social classes).

The correlative argument, that "studying social reality from the position of a particular group" means simply to identify with the vested interests of this group, and to apply the value system reflecting those interests in the conduct of inquiry as well as to embody it in the content of research results, is also quite in line with Marxian procedure. A leading authority on Marxian methodology clearly concurs in such an interpretation: "The propositions that the sociology of knowledge attempts to establish do not link the position of a group directly with specific theories, but rather the position of a group with the value systems functioning in it, and those finally with the kind or types of theories [Nowak, 1974b: 95]."

In effect, Marx apparently reformulates the riddle of commitment as the question "Is there a group in society whose value system would be most instrumental, or even absolutely instrumental, in the attainment of complete, unbiased, and objective understanding of social life?" This closes the first part of my argument. Marx was found to endorse the standpoint of commitment and the new notion of objectivity. Now, the second part of the argument must trace the reasoning that led him to ascribe unique cognitive opportunities to the social class of the propertyless proletariat and its particular system of values.

Marxian Solution to the Riddle of Commitment

Marx's argument seems to involve three consecutive steps. First, he attempts to determine which type of group allegiances (membership in which social groups) plays the strategic, decisive role in conditioning human cognitive opportunities. Or, to look at the same problem from another angle, he wants to specify which aspects or dimensions of a social structure are most significant in constraining or stimulating social cognition. Second, he attempts to establish which kinds of group allegiances, among those of the strategic type, are conducive, and which are detrimental, to the attainment of objective social knowledge. Or, to look at the matter from the opposite side, he wants to find out which locations in that dimension of the social structure that was earlier selected as strategic retard and which stimulate social cognition. And, third, he attempts to identify a single concrete group allegiance most conducive to the attainment of objective social knowledge. Or, to look at the matter from the opposite side, he wants to spot a particular location in the social structure most privileged in its potential opportunities for social cognition. Let me trace those three steps in rough outline.

Marx was conscious of the multiple group memberships of every individual in modern society. But, he seemed to reason, some of those memberships must be more strategic than others in their impact on cognitive opportunities. He treated this impact not as a direct but rather as a mediated one. Membership in a group does not ipso facto determine knowledge of society. Rather, it determines the vested interests of the group members; those vested interests become reflected in the value systems, applied in the cognitive process, and finally circumscribe the kind of social knowledge attainable. This is a premise of the Marxian theory of interests. Now according to Marx's sociology of knowledge, the ideas held by people are ultimately determined by the material conditions of their life.

The same conclusion follows from both premises. From the first premise, the following logical chain begins. *Question:* Which values will determine the content of social ideas in the strongest way? *Answer:* Those which are the dominant or master values in the axiological system of the group. *Question:* Which values have the status of dominant or master values in the axiological system of the group? *Answer:* Those which reflect the most vital interests of the group members. *Question:* Which type of vested interests of the group members must be considered as strategic or vital? *Answer:* Those which are generated by fundamental human needs and arise in the process of satisfying those needs; that is, in the process of production and reproduction of material life (economic interests). *Question:* Which group allegiances are based on common economic interests, or, to put it another way, which groups bring people together because of their shared economic interests? *Answer:* Social classes. *Conclusion:* Membership in a social class is the most significant factor conditioning human cognitive opportunities. Class structure is the strategic dimension of the social structure in retarding or stimulating the social cognition.

From the second premise another argument leads to the same conclusion. *Question:* If the material conditions of life are the ultimate determinants of human ideas, which type of group allegiances will be strategic for the attainment of social knowledge? *Answer:* Those which are based on shared material conditions. *Question:* Which factor is most significant in determining the totality of material conditions? *Answer:* Property, and particularly property that comprises the means of prediction. *Question:* Which factor can therefore be considered as the primary social bond among people sharing similar material conditions? *Answer:* Similarity of property situation. *Question:* Which groups are integrated on the basis of such a bond? *Answer:* Social classes. *Conclusion:* Membership in a social class is the most significant factor conditioning human cognitive opportunities. Class structure is the strategic dimension of the social structure in retarding or stimulating social cognition.

It is easy to see that the crucial theoretical claim is introduced at the phase involving fundamental needs (in the first sequence) or material conditions (in the second). In the totality of Marxian theory it is by no means an a priori axiom; rather, it is derived from more fundamental propositions—those inferred from observation of the history of human society as well as social life in Marx's day. It led him to believe that "the history of all hitherto existing society is the history of class struggles [Marx and Engels, 1968: 35]," or the constant clash of groups united by common economic interests or property situation. The theoretical claim is also arrived at deductively—from a paradigm of human nature, adumbrated in Marxian philosophical anthropology, as well as from an analysis of the economic mechanisms of capitalism, carried out in Marxian political economy. The inductive and deductive justification for considering class structure as the most strategic type of social differentiation will be discussed in more detail in Chapters 6 and 7. It will become evident then that the focus on class structure as the crucial determinant of cognitive opportunities was by no means an ad-hoc solution, but rather a logical implication of the whole Marxian theory of man and society.

Let me proceed to the second step in Marxian reasoning. If classes are crucial, which kind of class membership helps and which hinders cognitive opportunities? Which classes have the better vision and wider perspective, and which the more impaired vision and more limited perspective? Marx answers: The crucial factor is the progressiveness of the class. But this answer immediately generates three further querries: What does it mean to be progressive? Which classes are progressive? What has the factor of progressiveness to do with access to social knowledge?

To be progressive seems to involve three things in Marxian thinking: in the objective structural dimension, to have vested interests in the social change or transformation of a society; in the behavioral dimension, to act in the direction of social change or social transformation (to be engaged in revolutionary activities); in the psychological dimension, to manifest change-oriented attitudes.

The simplest Marxian model of class divisions is drawn in dichotomous terms—owners and nonowners: those who have the means of production, and those who have not (the latter having labor as their only marketable possession). But it would be an oversimplification to believe that the have-nots are always and without exception progressive, and that the owners are always and without exception regressive. Marx introduces a historical dimension to the analysis and treats the progressiveness of a class as relative to concrete historical circumstances, and especially to the particular phase of development of each socioeconomic formation. Generally speaking, the classes that are progressive in the early phases of their socioeconomic formation become regressive in the late phases, when their economic hegemony is safely established. Feudal landlords have played a significant progressive role in the elimination of slavery and the establishment of feudal society. Similarly, "the bourgeoisie, historically, has played a most revolutionary part. . . . It has put an end to all feudal, patriarchal, idyllic relations. It has pitilessly torn asunder the motley feudal ties that bound man to his 'natural superiors,' and has left no other nexus between man and man than naked self-interest [Marx and Engels, 1968: 37–38]." The progressiveness or regressiveness of a given class must always be determined by concrete, historical analysis. This point was emphasized by Lenin: "We can never know with what speed and how successfully a particular historical movement will develop in a given epoch. But we can know, and we do know, which class stands at the center of this or that period, holding sway over the essential characteristics of the historical situation, and determining the major direction of social development [1951, vol.21: 151]." The progressive classes, understood in this way, are believed to command larger cognitive possibilities than the regressive classes, at least with respect to objective and adequate knowledge of the social world.

But why? What is the mechanism linking the progressiveness of a class with its cognitive potential? Marxian reasoning seems to be thus: The progressive historical situation of a class entails its peculiar cognitive interest; namely, to reveal, clarify, unmask all the social mechanisms and principles that safeguard the dominance of the opposite class, and that by implication can be utilized in undermining this dominance. Also, it has a cognitive interest in all those dynamic principles that show how human society can be transformed, restructured, rebuilt. Therefore, the body of social knowledge accessible to its perspective is wider than the body of social knowledge accessible to the perspective of the regressive class; it includes some knowledge that was excluded, obscured, distorted, or pushed under the carpet by the previously dominant class. But such cognitive opportunities are restricted in some fashion, for the progressive class has a vested interest in obscuring, distorting, or falsifying those social mechanisms and principles that provide the objective basis for its own future dominance. Lange called it the mechanism of social aperception: "Aperception determines the scope of the potential social consciousness of a given class or social group, its intellectual horizon, and by the same token limits the scope of scientific propositions that can be reached in a given social condition by a given class or social group [1961: 265]." Hochfeld, in a similar vein, has called attention to the "restrictions of the mental horizons of the classes producing particular ideologies. Those restrictions, in the case of the possessing classes, even those interested in the development of productive forces, were enforced either by conscious defense or, more often, by un-self-conscious rationalization of social privileges [1963: 109]."

To sum up this point: The notion of progressiveness introduced here, and considered as the main determinant of the cognitive perspective of a class, may be referred to as *relative progressiveness*. It is relative in a double sense. First, it is historically relative; that is, it depends on the circumstances in which the class finds itself. Second, it is epistemologically relative; that is, it safeguards a wider, more extensive, more adequate social knowledge, that is yet a knowledge that is partial and limited, and selected by means of specific criteria. Briefly, it generates particularized knowledge. Therefore, the search for a structural warrant for a full, undistorted, absolute social knowledge cannot be considered as successfully completed. The progressive classes are clearly predisposed to the attainment of social truth, but to break all intellectual barriers, to dispose of all limitations and biases, something more must be involved than progressiveness understood in relative terms.

This leads to the third and final step in Marx's argument. There is one class in the whole of history, Marx claims, radically different from all other classes. Itself a product of all earlier history, it is born with the rise of the capitalist socioeconomic order. Its central peculiarity is the fact that to realize its own individual interests, it must bring about the total destruction of the class structure. The complete abolition of class distinctions, as distinguished from the replacement of the old class divisions with new ones, is its vested interest. In this way, its special interest becomes coextensive with the common interest of mankind—to free itself from the inhuman, alienating social situation generated by the existence of class structure, to attain universal human emancipation. Merton summarizes the idea thus: "Marx . . . advanced the claim that after capitalistic society had reached its ultimate phase of development, the strategic location of one social class would enable it to achieve an understanding of society that was exempt from false consciousness [1973: 102]."

This class is the proletariat. Marx's remarks on it clearly indicate the uniqueness of it as a social category. In the early texts, in a characteristic poetic style he describes the proletariat as "a class with radical chains, a class *in* civil society that is not a class *of* civil society [italics added]," "a social group that is the dissolution of all social groups," "a sphere that has a universal character because of its universal sufferings and lays claim to no particular right, because it is the object of no particular injustice but of injustice in general," "a sphere that cannot emancipate itself without emancipating itself from all other spheres of society and thereby emancipating these other spheres themselves [Marx and Engels, 1975: 39–40]." In the later works, the same idea recurs in a more analytic formulation: "If the proletariat during its contest with the bourgeoisie is compelled, by force of circumstances, to organise itself as a class, if by means of revolution it makes itself the ruling class, and, as such, sweeps away by force the old conditions of production, then it will, along with these conditions, have swept away the conditions for the existence of class antagonisms and of classes generally, and will thereby have abolished its own supremacy as a class [1968: 53]." Thus, the progressiveness of the proletariat is not derivative of concrete historical circumstances, and thereby historically changing—as in the case of all other classes— but rather it is inherent in the fundamental nature of that class. By definition proletariat is always progressive, and cannot become regressive, because the next phase of its own history is not the establishment of its own class dominance but its own dissolution in a universal classless society.

Thanks to its unique structural position, the proletariat, for the first time in history, has a cognitive interest in attaining complete and unlimited social knowledge, the full truth about the mechanisms and principles of all possible class dominations, the total understanding of the "laws of motion" of human society. It is a class not interested in any obfuscations of, distortions of, or restrictions on social knowledge. It is a class whose perspective is the most liberating and the least constraining. As Engels put it: "The more impartially and rigorously the science is conducted, the more closely it represents the interests of the proletariat [1947, vol.I: 476]." Thus the proletariat is a unique social class, which may be said to embody absolute progressiveness. Again, this concept, counterpoised to the notion of relative progressiveness, must be understood in a double way: First, the proletariat is absolutely progressive because its progressiveness is an immanent, essential, and constant characteristic necessitated by the class's very nature, not by historical circumstances. Second, it is absolutely progressive because its cognitive perspective is free of any conceivable structural limitations, and opens the way toward a total, objective understanding of social life.

Thus the Marxian solution to the riddle of commitment was finally reached: in order to attain objective knowledge of society, the scientist should adopt the perspective of the proletariat, and hence represent the interests of this particular class by applying its system of valuations in the course of research, and affirm it in the body of research results.

The Marxian notion of commitment could easily lead to some misunderstandings. Two of them are particularly notorious in simplistic interpretations of Marxism, and therefore must be clearly identified and guarded against. The first fallacy is to confuse the epistemological category of "the perspective of the proletariat" with the sociological category of "actual membership in the working class." Sometimes, Marx is incorrectly believed to claim that only the workers are able to utilize "the perspective of the proletariat," and thereby attain objective truth about society and its regularities. This of course is patent nonsense, easily refutable just by recalling that Marx, Engels, Lenin, Lukacs, and Gramsci could by no stretch of the imagination be considered workers, and that they yet represented "the perspective of the proletariat" at its most perspicacious. But even stronger counterarguments against such a misinterpretation can be found in the writings of Marx himself. In *The Communist Manifesto* he mentions the possibility that some members of the bourgeoisie may reach a high level of objective social knowledge: "A small section of the ruling class cuts itself adrift and joins the revolutionary class, the class that holds the future in its hands. Just as, therefore, at an earlier period a section of the nobility went over to the bourgeoisie, so now a portion of the bourgeoisie goes over to the proletariat, and in particular a portion of the bourgeoisie ideologists, who have raised themselves to the level of comprehending theoretically historical movement as a whole [Marx and Engels, 1968: 44]." In "The Eighteenth Brumaire" a similar idea occurs to Marx, when he opposes identifying group-membership with ideological position:

> One must not imagine that the democratic representatives are indeed all shopkeepers or enthusiastic champions of shopkeepers. According to their education and their individual position they may be as far apart as heaven from earth. What makes them representatives of the petty bourgeoisie is the fact that in their minds they do not get beyond the limits that the latter do not get beyond in life, that they are consequently driven, theoretically, to the same problems and solutions to which material interest and social position drive the latter practically. This is, in general, the relationship between the political and literary representatives of a class and the class they represent [Marx and Engels, 1968: 121].

The message seems clear. By the adoption of the perspective of the proletariat Marx does not mean actual membership in this particular class, but rather a sort of intentional membership—the identification of the thinker with the interests of this class and with the related system of values.

The second fallacy is to mix up the subjective or psychological with the objective or structural meaning attached to the category of class interest. Sometimes Marx is believed to claim that the guideline for sociological study is to be discovered in the subjective opinions widespread among the members of the working classes, and referring to their perceived or felt interests. The class interest of the proletariat is understood here as the actual, empirically recognizable state of the consciousness common among or prevailing within the working class. Marx himself explicitly rejected such a crass simplification. In "The Holy Family" he stressed. "It is not a question of what this or that proletarian or even the whole proletariat momentarily imagines to be the aim. It is a question of what the proletariat is, and what it consequently is historically compelled to do. Its aim and historical action is prescribed, irrevocably and obviously, in its own situation in life, as well as in the entire organization of contemporary civil society [Marx and Engels, 1960, vol.II: 43]."

Again, the message seems quite clear. The "interest of the proletariat" is neither an empirical descriptive category nor a subjective psychological category. Rather it is a theoretical model that represents the objectively feasible but at the same time maximally ambitious aspirations and goals of the working class, derived from the objective structural situation of that class in the society as a whole. The actual, empirical, subjective consciousness of the workers may approach this theoretical model to some extent and in some situations. The tendency for the empirical consciousness of the workers to move toward the objective class interest is parallel to the process of the crystalization of a class, from the stage of the class in itself to the stage of the class for itself. When a class is transformed from an aggregate of individuals to an organized social entity, a class consciousness reflecting the objective class interest is slowly developed. But even then it does not develop spontaneously, but rather requires the organizational and theoretical efforts of the leaders, who instill and promote the "correct," historically adequate perception of the class interest among the class members.

Such an interpretation of the category of class interest, clearly in line with Marx's own interpretations, was developed extensively by George Lukacs (1971). A recent explication of this category, following Lukacs's lead is given by Schaff:

> What a given class (that is, the human individuals of which that class consists...) actually think under given conditions, and what the real interests of a class are, and hence what it should think, and how it should act, which is formulated as a theory and an ideology (the realization of class interests) are two different things. . . . The identification of "empirical psychological consciousness" and "attributed consciousness"—i.e., the consciousness of a given class and the theoretical and ideological form of the realization of the interests of that class—is the limit of the interaction of the two. This is the ideal condition, which may be postulated but which is never attained in practice [1972: 342, 351].

The Marxian solution to the riddle of commitment is neither final nor complete. It opens the way for its own further clarification and refinement, and, ultimately, for the explicit specification of a value system related to the objective class interest of the proletariat, and prescribed as the guideline for objective sociological research. This is a complex endeavor, which requires separate considerations.

For now, it is sufficient to point out the one indisputable merit of the Marxian standpoint of commitment that makes it far superior to all alternative proposals: It is not opportunistic or ad hoc, but rather very strongly grounded in Marx's ideas about the nature of man and society—in his total sociological theory. One can reject it only at the cost of rejecting the rest of Marx's theory as well. The epistemological and methodological principle appears as the other side of the ontological and substantive assertions. Marx's intellectual system demonstrates once again its coherence and unity.

PART IV

THE DILEMMAS OF
SOCIAL REALITY—
ONTOLOGICAL

Having posed, and solved in some manner, the main problems dealing with the nature of sociology as a science and as a social science, sociologists had to approach the most fundamental set of dilemmas: those dealing with the substantive charac- teristics of their proper subject matter. Two points were obvious; first, that human societies consist of people, and, second, that human societies are something else besides individual people. But here consensus ended. More specific inquiry into the nature of the individual and the character of human society led to a far-reaching differentiation and polarization of standpoints.

It might seem only the second of those problems, the nature of society, was of immediate relevance to sociology; whereas the first was properly the focus of atten- tion for psychologists. But this would be a misleading simplification. None of the social-scientific disciplines could ignore either of the two closely interlinked ques- tions. No adequate psychology could totally disregard the fact that a human individual—its proper subject of concern—was always a member of some wider society, placed in some location within the social structure. And no adequate sociology could forget about the components of society—human individuals, whose activities and attitudes significantly influence the shape of social wholes.

To be sure, each of the social-scientific disciplines approached those questions in a different manner, with different emphases, but each had to face both of them.

Thus sociology encountered two major ontological questions: What is the nature of man? What is the essence of society? Those questions resulted in two major theoretical dilemmas.

The first dilemma, as posed in the context of sociological inquiry, focused on the properties of human action. It may be called the dilemma of subject or object. *Some sociologists treated men as totally autonomous subjects, initiating, regulating, and controlling their activities toward goals they had selected, along whatever course they believed to be most conducive to reaching those goals, guided by values and following norms of their own choosing. Man as an active subject, rather than a passive object, a producer rather than a product, an agent rather than a pawn, an actor rather than a reacting puppet—such is the image conveyed by the proponents of the position that shall be here called* autonomism. *Some other sociologists took the opposite standpoint. They treated men as totally dependent objects, devoid of any initiative or control with respect to their own activities, striving toward goals set for them, along strictly predetermined paths, guided by values and following norms imposed on them. Man as a passive object rather than an active subject, a product rather than a producer, a pawn rather than an agent, a reacting organism rather than an actor—such is the image conveyed by the proponents of the position that shall be here called* passivism.

The second dilemma crucial for sociology focused on the properties of the entities typically studied by sociologists—groups, collectivities, civilizations, cultures, societies, etc. It may be called the dilemma of aggregates or wholes. *Some sociologists treated such entities simply as pluralities of individuals, larger or smaller sets of aggregates—nothing else and nothing more. Their standpoint is most often referred to as* individualistic. *Some others considered social wholes to be separate, supra-individual forms of reality with specific properties and regularities of their own—something other and something more than an aggregate of individuals. I shall refer to their position as* collectivistic.

It is obvious that both dilemmas deal with fundamental properties of social reality. For this reason I have grouped them together as ontological dilemmas—dilemmas of theoretical substance. Following our established pattern, I shall attempt to show that both dilemmas are spurious and misleading, and that they should be rejected. In their place I shall propose alternative solutions to the problems that generated them.

CHAPTER 6

Man as Object or Subject: Passivism, Autonomism, Creativism

In the history of sociology one shall not encounter many statements dealing directly and explicitly with the nature of man. Traditionally, within the social sciences all questions concerning individual human beings were believed to belong to the province of psychology. And one of the main intellectual justifications for creating sociology as a new scientific discipline was the presumed existence of some class of phenomena or processes totally distinct from psychological ones, some social facts of a supra-individual character. The realm of human reality was seen as wider in scope than purely individual phenomena and as not exhaustively covered by psychological cognition. The attempt to emancipate sociology as an independent scientific discipline was responsible for the tendency to avoid any psychological—that is, individually focused—considerations.

But it was not easy to get rid of man the individual from sociological thinking. Whatever social entities were discussed, however social facts were conceptualized, man always reappeared as a basic component. When sociologists focused on social actions, man the individual was there as "actor." If they focused on social interaction, he was involved as "partner." If they focused on more established social relationships, he appeared as "party" or "side." If they focused on social groups or collectivities, he was seen as "member." If they focused on social structure or social system, he was there as "occupant" (of positions) or "performer" (of roles).

Thus, even though sociologists were reluctant to provide explicit accounts of the nature of man, some implicit assumptions of this sort were inescapable in any and every sociological theory. Herzberg says that "no society can exist without an explicit conception of what people are like [1966: 13]." One may paraphrase this statement and claim that no sociology can exist without an implicit model of man. I am in agreement with Skidmore: "The models of man . . . have often been forgotten or ignored in sociological work. It is emphasized here . . . that the models of man, far from being only minor or unimportant aspects of sociological theory, constitute sets of premises foundational to sociological accounts [1975a: 4]."

What follows is a brief review of some typical standpoints in past and present sociological theory. It attempts to disclose their implicit assumptions on the nature of man.

THE PASSIVISTIC TRADITION

Herbert Spencer: Man in the Social Organism

Herbert Spencer is usually held responsible for the introduction to sociology of an idea which proved particularly long-lived and influential—that of the organic analogy. In his view, society could be considered as an entity similar in important respects to an organism. He did not believe it to be literally an organism; he simply claimed that it can be treated as one for heuristic purposes. And the rationale for the application of the organic analogy was found in the fact that both an organism and a society represented examples of organized, integrated, functioning wholes. He said: "Though in foregoing chapters sundry comparisons of social structures and functions to structures and functions in the human body have been made, they have been made only because structures and functions in the human body furnish familiar illustrations of structures and functions in general [1893, vol.I: 580]."

The image of society as an organized system of mutually interdependent elements fulfilling specified functions has clear implications with respect to the image of an individual. As Martindale reads Spencer: "With the advance of organization . . . every part comes to have a very special function which it performs in a relatively inelastic and irreplaceable manner [1960: 67]." The basic elements of society—human individuals—pursue their courses of life within rigidly predetermined locations in a social organism, and assume roles important to the organism as a whole.

Spencer's implicit image of man and its passivistic implications are summarized by Meltzer, Petras, and Reynolds: "Individuals were considered to be engulfed by the organism of society in such a way as to preclude the individual injection of creativity into the social order. . . . Individuals were conceived to be caught in the network of forces over which they had no control [1975: 46–47]."

Emile Durkheim: Man as Socially Molded

For Durkheim, society is a specific domain of facts, social facts, and one of the crucial properties of social facts is their external, constraining power over individual human beings. "A social fact is to be recognized by the power of external coercion which it exercises or is capable of exercising over individuals, and the presence of this power may be recognized in its turn either by the existence of some specific sanction or by the resistance offered against every individual effort that tends to violate it. . . . The individual finds himself in the presence of a force which is superior to him and before which he bows [Durkheim, 1962: 10, 123]." The social facts "impose themselves upon him, independent of his individual will"; they are the "ways of acting, fixed or not, capable of exercising on the individual an external constraint [1962: 2, 11]."

In more substantive terms Durkheim described social facts as states of collective consciousness, "collective representations," or to put it in modern parlance, as various components of the social normative system: "legal and moral rules, popular aphorisms and proverbs, articles of faith wherein religious or political groups condense their beliefs, standards of taste established by literary schools, etc. [1962: 7]." Those norms and values are given for individuals; individuals encounter them, acquire them by means of socialization, are forced to follow them by the mechanisms of social control, and only insofar as they incorporate them in their personalities and their conduct do they become full-fledged, truly human beings. As Durkheim put it: "The individual gets from society the best part of himself, all that gives him a distinct character and a special place among other beings, his intellectual and moral culture. If we should withdraw from men their language, sciences, arts and moral beliefs, they would drop to the ranks of animals. So the characteristic attributes of human nature come from society [1915: 347]."

Men, in all that was human and not merely animal in their nature, were seen as products of society, thinking and doing what was ordained in it. Durkheim's emphasis on social facts led to "making the human personality an aspect of, a representation of, an extension of society, and arising from the structures and authorities of society through the process of socialization

[Nisbet, 1974: 109]." He was vigorously opposed to the idea that society was produced by men and men were creators of society as active, determining forces. As Fletcher summarizes his views:

> It was perhaps the greatest intellectual illusion of all to think that—because the minds of individuals were equipped with the perceptions, conceptions, expectations, motives which were operative in their society—the nature of society could be simply explained in terms of their conscious intentions as individuals. On the contrary, Durkheim insisted, man would only truly and realistically come to know himself, and to have such control over his society and his conditions of life as he desired, if he overcame this illusion and saw plainly that it was the collective life of society, the interconnected complex of many associations, which had been creative of the nature of his own experience [1971, vol.II: 272].

William G. Sumner: Man as the Slave of Folkways

A similar emphasis on extra-individual, normative phenomena as molding the beliefs and activities of individuals is clearly displayed in the works of William G. Sumner. The association of human individuals generates a pervasive, relatively rigid and petrified network of folkways and mores as well as laws and institutions.

> The folkways are unconscious, spontaneous, uncoordinated. . . . Folkways come into existence now all the time. The folkways are habits of the individual and customs of the society which arise from efforts to satisfy needs. In time, the folkways become the "right" way to do all things. They extend over the whole of life. . . . There is a right way to catch game, to win a wife, to make one's self appear, to cure disease, to honour ghosts, to treat comrades or strangers, to behave when a child is born, on the warpath, in council, and so on in all cases which can arise [Sumner, 1906: 46, 41].

The justification of folkways is found in the tradition, which is its own warrant. When the justification is more complex, invoking more abstract notions of justice, welfare, etc., the folkways are transformed into mores. "They are the ways of doing things which are current in a society to satisfy human needs and desires, together with the faiths, notions, codes and standards of well living which inhere in those ways, having a genetic connection with them [1906: 66]." Out of the mores, the institutions and laws are slowly crystalized. They are specific clusters of structures and functions based on mores, but deliberately established. Property, marriage, and religion are examples of them.

Such a complex normative order provides a regulatory framework within which individuals think and act. "The body of the folkways constitutes a societal environment. Every one born into it must enter into relations of give and take with it. He is subjected to influences from it, and it is one of the life conditions under which he must work out his career of self-realization [1906: 73]." The individual appears a passive being, embedded in the network of folkways, mores, and laws, which constrain him and regulate his conduct almost completely.

Vilfredo Pareto: Man as Determined by "Residues"

All the authors discussed so far have treated man as determined, molded, constrained, pushed by external forces, by society's normative, cultural, or structural influences. But the passivistic image of man can also be based on a different rationale. Man can be seen as determined internally—from the inside—by instincts, drives, or dispositions of a specific kind. Vilfredo Pareto exemplifies this point of view.

An analysis of the nonlogical actions that, he believes, predominate in social life and are most typical of human actors led Pareto to the discovery of common, constant, repeatable motivational elements, basic mental dispositions moving people to action. He gave them the name residues: "The residues are the manifestations of sentiments and instincts just as the rising of the mercury in a thermometer is a manifestation of the rise in temperature [1971: 47]." It must be noted that the term *instinct* is used here in a special sense. The only claims Pareto made about residues were that they forcefully influenced human conduct, and that they influenced it from the "inside" of the psyche. He did not treat them as necessarily inborn or biologically inherited, as the term *instinct* might suggest that he did. This is emphasized by Lopreato:

> Some of the sentiments might properly be called "primary drives" today. This is the case, for instance, with the basic sex residue, which provides the sixth category in Pareto's classification of residues. Others may be more properly termed basic values, or mores, deeply learned and entrenched. Such is the case with the "residues of sociality." . . . Pareto is so impressed by the power of social forces that transcend human reason or motivation that he treats those forces as if they were biological instincts. . . . At close scrutiny there is very little doubt that many "instincts" are treated by Pareto as deeply entrenched norms [In Pareto, 1971: 8–9].

But whatever their origin, purely biological or at least partly social, the residues constitute the main determining forces of human conduct, and every adequate sociological explanation must ultimately refer to them. As

Martindale summarizes Pareto's views: "Pareto maintains that residues are not, like tastes, merely the source of conduct. They function throughout the whole course of conduct developing from the source. . . . Society is a pre-logical phenomenon. Individuals, the molecules of the social system, are possessed of certain sentiments manifested in residues. These sentiments, and not the rationalizations of them, determine the forms of social life [1960: 467]." What men think and do is the outcome of residues, rather than of their conscious rational or intentional control.

Spencer, Durkheim, Sumner, and Pareto may be considered the representatives of the trend in the history of sociology that emphasized the passive aspects of human nature. In their writings some of the main elements of the passivistic image of man were introduced, destined to reappear time and again in the further development of sociological theory. But before I attempt to trace such continuities, we shall briefly consider the classic formulations of the autonomistic image of man.

THE AUTONOMISTIC TRADITION

Max Weber: Man as a Rational Actor

Weber switched the focus of sociological study to the level of individual human action. He refused to consider society as an independent, specific, superindividual reality, but rather attempted to analyze it as a complex end result of the multitudinous activities of societal members. As Freund aptly points out: "The originality of Weber's contribution lies in the fact that he did not sever social structures and institutions from the multifarious activities of man, who both builds them up and endows them with significance. Central to his sociology, therefore, is the concept of social action. . . . He was concerned . . . with achieving the most objective understanding possible of how men evaluate and appraise, use, create and destroy their various social relationships [1969: 88]."

Now, the way in which he conceived action obviously provides the key to his image of the actor—a human individual. Three observations must be made in this respect. First, Weber conceived action as endowed with meaning by the acting individuals. "Behavior will be called 'human behavior' only insofar as the person or persons involved engage in some subjectively meaningful action. . . . The term 'social behavior' will be reserved for activities whose intent is related by the individuals involved to the conduct of others and is oriented accordingly [1964: 29]." In the case of human action, meaning enters as the crucial determinant, and must be revealed by the operation of understanding if an adequate account of the action is to be given. As Martindale observes: "Throughout his analyses Weber assumes that subjectively intended meaning is a causal component in conduct. This is his most general hypothesis [1960: 387]." The element of meaning gives the action some flavor of indeterminacy; the human actor has some freedom in attaching meaning to the action, and in this way intervenes actively in its course. As Giddens puts it: "To affirm an element of contingency in human conduct, in Weber's view, is not to deny its regularity and predictability; but it is to emphasize once again the contrast between meaningful conduct and the invariant response characteristic of, for example, a subconsciously mediated withdrawal reaction to the painful stimulus [1971: 153]."

Human autonomy is still more obvious when the second property of action is considered; namely, its purposeful character. Action is conceived in terms of a means–ends scheme, as an instrument for reaching specified goals. This aspect of Weber's approach is stressed by Fletcher: "For Weber the distinguishing features of sociology lay crucially in what earlier writers had referred to as the 'teleological' dimension of its subject-matter; the fact that men in society were, at least in part, purposive in their activities [1971, vol.II: 418]."

Purposeful action can take various forms. But among the types of action there is the one that is most significant for two reasons: first, because it is most amenable to scientific understanding; and, second, because it is becoming more and more typical in modern society. This is action "rationally oriented to goals"—the basic type in Weber's fourfold typology. Freund is certainly right that "interpretative sociology gives priority to goal-oriented conduct. . . . It may be defined as conduct in which, once the goal has been chosen, due consideration is given to the appropriate means and full account is taken of the foreseeable consequences which may conflict with the line of action decided upon [1969: 106]," And the historical tendency for this type of action to predominate is stressed by Coser: "In modern society, Weber argued, whether in the sphere of politics or economics, in the realm of the law and even in interpersonal relationships, the efficient application of means to ends has become predominant and has replaced other springs of social action [1971: 218]." This is the third characteristic ascribed by Weber to human conduct. Obviously it implies the largest scope for human autonomy; an individual appears as an efficiently calculating agent, endowed with rational control over his action.

The three properties of human action as conceptualized by Weber—its meaningfulness, purposefulness, and rationality—entail the image of an individual as an autonomous actor, rather than a dependent product of some influences. This image, quite opposite to the passivistic one reviewed earlier, may be summarized, in the words of Fletcher, thus:

> Men oriented their actions to each other in terms of meaning. They
> actively sought to achieve certain ends of which they were (often) con-

sciously aware. They employed certain means (and discarded others) in striving to attain these ends. They exercised choice, they deliberated, they calculated, they took decisions, and they then acted in relation to other men to accomplish their purposes. They exercised will in disciplining their thought and emotions, in channeling their energies and resources, in the conscious pursuit of clearly foreseen objectives [1971, vol. II: 383–384].

George H. Mead: Man as Constructing Acts

The acts of individual human beings are also in the focus of attention of George H. Mead. But he goes much further than Weber in studying the internal anatomy of an act and developing a paradigm of a human actor.

His main line of attack is directed against the behavioristic image of the human action, according to which "people of such and such a make up, placed in such and such circumstances and played upon by such and such determining factors, will uniformly behave in such and such a way [Blumer, 1972]." Three main assumptions of such an approach are found inadequate. First, the relationship between stimuli and resulting action is not direct, but rather mediated through the complex process of working out a line of action by an individual. As a result, "because the act mediates between organism and environment, the future is always to some extent uncertain. The very nature of the act makes life partially unpredictable and indeterminate [Strauss, 1962: xi–xii]." Second, the individual does not merely respond to environmental determinants, pressures, or circumstances, but actively attempt to handle a situation; he approaches it selectively, picks up or indicates to himself some elements or aspects as relevant, and neglects the others, transforming the amorphous field of stimuli into a meaningful world of objects. To quote Blumer again: "One does not simply react to an object, but puts himself in the position to do something about an object [1972]." Third, the acts are not to be considered in the atomistic fashion, as single stimulus–response units, but rather as complex developing processes, having specific "careers" through time. As Mead has remarked: "The social act is not explained by building it up out of stimulus plus response; it must be taken as a dynamic whole—as something going on—no part of which can be considered or understood by itself—a complex organic process implied by each individual stimulus and response involved in it [1964: 120–121]."

An act is seen as constructed rather than released, as involving an active orientation to an environment rather than a passive reaction, and as a process rather than a singular event. These characteristics of an act are outlined most clearly in a summary of Mead's views given by Blumer:

Action is built up in coping with the world instead of merely being released from a preexisting psychological structure by factors playing on that structure. By making indications to himself and by interpreting what he indicates, a human being has to forge or piece together a line of action. In order to act the individual has to identify what he wants, establish an objective or goal, map out a prospective line of behavior, note and interpret the actions of others, size up his situation, check himself at this or that point, figure out what to do at other points, and frequently spur himself on in the face of dragging dispositions or discouraging settings. . . . A human act is self-directed or built up. . . . [A person's] acts are still constructed by him out of what he takes into account. What he takes into account are the things that he indicates to himself. . . . He is not in the mere recipient position of responding to such matters; he stands over against them and has to handle them [Blumer, 1966: 236].

Such a character of a human action is made possible by the fact that a human actor is not a mere organism, but rather an organism furnished with a self. By a self Mead meant the ability to look at oneself as an object. "A human being may perceive himself, have conceptions of himself, and act toward himself. [As a result, he] can designate things to himself. . . . Through further interaction with himself, he may judge, analyze, and evaluate the things he has indicated to himself. And by continuing to interact with himself he may plan and organize his action with regard to what he has designated and evaluated [Blumer, 1966: 234–235]." This ability of self-conscious reflection, which makes a man an active agent facing the world and coping with it, is itself originated in society. As Mead puts it: "The self is something which has a development; it is not initially there, at birth, but arises in the process of social experience and activity; that is, develops in the given individual as a result of his relations to that process as a whole and to other individuals within that process [1962: 212]." And he adds: "The self, as that which can be an object to itself, is essentially a social structure, and it arises in social experience [1962: 217]." It is to be emphasized as one of the most significant insights of Mead that the self, which is a warrant of human autonomy vis-a-vis the world and society is not inborn, but rather created in the process of participation in society.

Florian Znaniecki: Man as Creating Cultural Reality

For Florian Znaniecki social actions constitute the primary subject matter of sociological research, "the stuff out of which all the more complex and elaborate social realities are made [1969: 212]." The study of social actions is a prerequisite for understanding society and culture. "Without knowing what the various ways are in which men tend to deal actively with other men and how these ways have evolved, we cannot understand their efforts to regulate normatively their mutual activities by customs, mores, and laws, or the social positions they individually occupy and the functions they perform in their communities, or the organized groups they create, maintain, and destroy [Znaniecki, 1969: 24]." Consequently, the core of his writings is a discussion and analysis of social action. In the judgment of Bierstedt: "Certainly no one in the history of the discipline concentrated so steadfastly upon action as the basic category of sociological inquiry, and no one before or since analyzed actions in such comprehensive detail [1969: 21]."

Man enters the field of sociological interest only as a participant in social actions—their originator or recipient. Znaniecki says: "The sociologist has nothing to do with human beings as natural entities, as they 'really' are, individually or collectively, in their psycho–biological characters; he leaves their study to the psychologist, anthropologist, human geographer. But in observing the cultural world he finds that in this world men play a double role. First, they are conscious agents or active subjects.... Secondly, men are also empirical objects of activity [1969: 203–204]." Therefore the key to an understanding of human nature, insofar as it is relevant to the sociologist, is to analyze social actions.

The image of social action is entailed by Znaniecki's general theoretical approach—the so-called culturological standpoint, which holds that the human world is made of values, not of things. Values are objects endowed with meaning by acting individuals. A special class of objects comprises other human beings. Every distinctively human action is undertaken with respect to some meaningful value; social actions are addressed to other people considered as values—they are "actions bearing upon men as their objects and intending to provoke definite reactions on their part [Znaniecki, 1969: 185]." The essence of human action is therefore the application of meanings to objects, and, in effect, their transformation into values.

This feature of an action, as seen from the point of view of an individual, is grasped by the concept of an attitude. Boskoff clarifies the sense of this concept: "Znaniecki defines attitudes as definitions of a situation by the agent, by which two important types of decisions are reached: (1) the selection of significant facts from the empirical complex and relevant values bearing on these facts, and (2) whether or not the situation thus defined can be adequately expressed in active behavior [1969: 72–73]." There is no value without somebody's corresponding attitude. Hence, there is no cultural reality outside human attitudes and actions. The cultural world is constructed by acting people. In the words of Znaniecki: "Every cultural system is found by the investigator to exist for certain conscious and active historical subjects; that is, within the sphere of experience and activity of some particular people, individuals and collectivities.... This essential character of cultural data we call the humanistic coefficient, because such data, as objects of the student's theoretic reflection already belong to somebody else's active experience and are such as this active experience makes them [1969: 137]." And further:

> No object as experienced by an active human individual can be defined merely by its sensory content, for on its meaning rather than on its sensory content depends its practical significance for human activity. Not because of what it "is" as a natural datum, but because of what it "means" as a humanistic, cultural datum, does an object of activity appear to the agent as "useful" or "harmful," "good" or "bad," "beautiful" or "ugly," "pleasant" or "unpleasant" [1969: 223].

The human actor appears here as the conscious creator of cultural reality; interpreting the world, defining it, ascribing meaning to its components, orienting his conduct toward it. This creative potential is present in various degrees in several types of actions. It is lowest in habitual or repetitive (ritualistic or routine) actions, higher in imitative or reproductive actions, and highest in creative or innovative actions. As Boskoff comments: "For Znaniecki, the type of social action most distinctly human is the creative action, in which new values are produced by the action. . . . The completed action presents consequences that are not derivable either from the objective conditions of the situation or from previous reactions to a similar configuration of objective conditions [1969: 75]." In creative actions the human actor achieves the highest degree of autonomy, liberating himself both from the constraints of tradition and from the actual situation.

PASSIVISM AND AUTONOMISM IN CONTEMPORARY SOCIOLOGY

The opposition of two images of man—the passivistic and the autonomistic—is still encountered in modern sociological theory. To illustrate this continuity of sociological tradition I shall cite some examples of important theoretical schools. Since each of these schools is, internally, extremely complex and heterogenous, I shall only sketch those general assumptions that the representatives of them seem to share, and that entail a specific view of the nature of man. We shall start with those standpoints having clearly passivistic implications.

Structural Functionalism: Man as a Normatively Determined Component of a System

Structural functionalism inherits two ideas from the passivistically inclined authors discussed earlier. From Spencer it takes the model of society as an organic system. From Durkheim it takes the idea that superindividual reality is basically normative. Man is seen as a component of a system with a specified place and functions, whose conduct is regulated by specified norms and values. His location in the system is apprehended by the concept of a role, and his subjugation to normative regulation by conceiving of a role in normative terms, as a set of prescribed patterns of action, and by defining action as necessarily involving some normative orientation. The link between the normative system of a society and the individuals as actors and performers of roles is provided by the mechanisms of socialization and social control, which result in the internalization of normative prescriptions or at least in overt conformity. This basic image may be illustrated now by some typical statements of structural functionalists.

The systemic assumptions of structural functionalism are well-known and have been extensively discussed (see Sztompka, 1974). Parsons claims that the approach typical of structural functionalism is

> to see acting units as parts of organized systems, which have properties other than those attributable to isolated units and the most general conditions of interaction between "men as men." They have languages, cultural values, legal systems, various kinds of institutional norms, and generalized media. Concrete behavior is not a function simply of elementary properties, but of the kinds of systems, their various structures and the processes taking place within them [1971: 35].

The obvious implications of such approach are revealed by Eisenstadt and Curelaru: "Given the strong systemic emphasis of the structural–functional school, the very autonomy of the individual—in his orientation to the social situation—has been neglected. He was reduced thereby to a 'socialized' role performer acting according to the presumed needs of the social system [1976: 197]." The same point is made by Skidmore: "When Parsons deals at the social system level, he is almost forced by the mode of analysis to abandon concern with the individual (the model of man) in favor of treating 'roles' as the system-constituting units at the social system level [1975a: 111]."

The normative bias of structural functionalists is also evident, and equally often emphasized. Parsons considers the normative regulation to be a constitutive, definitional ingredient of the notion of action. For him, action always involves some considerations of a normative type. "All behavior is normatively regulated [1968, vol.I: 45]." Levy includes in his list of the functional requisites of any social system (which is in fact tantamount to a definition of society) the normative regulation of goals as well as the choice of means by the members. He says: "The goals ... must be sufficiently articulated to insure the performance of socially necessary activities if the society is to persist. . . . There must be regulation of the choice of means to tell how these goals may be won [1952: 177, 182]." In order to be effectual in actual conduct those normative prescriptions must be internalized, or at least conformed to by actors.

> For the society to persist, there must be transmitted specifically to each individual . . . so much of the modes of dealing with the total situation, of the modes of communication, of the shared cognitive orientations, goal systems, attitudes involved in the regulation of means, modes of affective expression, and the like, as will render him capable of adequate performance in his several roles throughout life, both as concerns skills and attitudes [Levy, 1952: 189].

A consensus on norms and values in a society, a common normative framework fully internalized by societal members, is the main factor responsible for social order. As Scott comments: "Parsons holds norms, especially internalized norms, to account for social order. . . . The equilibrium of social systems appears to be increasingly explained on the basis of internalized commitment to common systems of norms [1969: 261]." The "overintegrated view of society" based on consensus is matched by the "oversocialized image of man" completely determined by social requirements: "Decisions for action are really 'made' at the social system level and carried out by men playing roles [Skidmore, 1975a: 117]."

What traits of human nature become crucial when man is seen as the diligent performer of socially prescribed roles? First, he must be *willing* to learn a lesson; he must possess a certain "sensitivity to the demands the system places upon him," he must be ready to receive "the message regarding each of the social system demands [Skidmore, 1975a: 116]." This attitude may be called *conformity proneness*. And second, a man must be *able* to learn a lesson; he must possess a capability to perceive, internalize, and implement societal requirements in his actions. This trait is often referred to as *plasticity*. It is by no means accidental that Parsons conceives as a fundamental property of human nature "the plasticity of the human organism, its capacity to learn any one of a large number of alternative patterns of behavior instead of being bound by its genetic constitution to a very limited range of alternatives [Parsons, in Skidmore 1975a: 116]."

The image of human nature that appears in structural–functional theory is fundamentally passivistic. Its main outline is summed up by Skidmore:

> The picture of man that emerges from the consideration of Parsons's structural model focused on the system level is thus one of man playing roles according to the specifications laid down by the system of action itself.'. . . The individual has no choice concerning the type of social act in which he will engage in each of the roles he plays. The acts have been "typed" according to the needs of the system itself. . . . The actor is seen as a functionary for the system, acting in ways that are determined by it [1975a: 117].

Social Behaviorism: Man as a Passive Receiver of
Stimuli and an Emitter of Responses

Another influential trend in sociological theory that entails the passivistic image of man is informed by the perspective of psychological behaviorism. From the behavioristic point of view, an organism appears as a sort of black box receiving certain stimuli from the environment in which it is placed, and emitting certain activities as responses to those stimuli. It is assumed that a one-to-one correspondence exists between a type of stimulus received and a type of response emitted. Therefore, whatever the organism does is seen as completely determined by the field of environmental stimuli in which the organism actually operates. To quote a relevant characterization: "Mechanomorphic psychology (behaviorism) views man as an object acted upon from the outside by various forces or driven from within by other forces which are to be characterized chiefly by their relation to the outside (e.g., thirst, hunger, sexual appetite) [Bugental, 1967: 8]."

Now, the crucial problem for behaviorism is to specify the nature of the link between a stimulus and a response—to provide some concrete interpretation of the mechanism determining the character of the activity emitted as a response to a specific type of stimulation. In the most influential branch of behaviorism, this mechanism is described as operant conditioning, or instrumental learning; an organism emits such activities as have brought him some gratification before (they are reinforced), and refrains from such activities as have brought him some displeasure (they are extinguished). In brief, an organism seeks pleasure and avoids pain; it pursues rewards and shuns punishments.

The assumptions of the behavioristic perspective have been applied by Homans to the elementary social behavior of people. His conception, regarded sometimes as an early form of exchange theory is founded on two heuristic models: As far as the activities of a single individual are concerned, the model of a pecking pigeon, or a rat in a maze, taken from the experimental studies of behaviorists, is applied; and only when the focus moves to the interactions of a plurality of individuals, is the model of a market, taken from the studies of economic exchange, employed. The market situation complicates the picture, but does not change the principles guiding the elementary social behavior of each participant. Those principles are clearly informed by instrumental-learning theory. For example, the "success proposition" says: "For all actions taken by persons, the more often a particular action of a person is rewarded, the more likely a person is to perform that action [Homans, 1974: 16]." Another principle, called the "value proposition," claims: "The more valuable to a person is the result of his action, the more likely he is to perform the action [Homans, 1974: 25]." And the "deprivation–satiation" proposition stipulates: "The more often in the recent past a person has received a particular reward, the less valuable any further unit of that reward becomes for him [1974: 29]." As Skidmore observes, "It is obvious that Homan assumes man is an animal who follows the laws of reinforcement. . . . The property of man, as man, is his response to positive reinforcement [1975a: 36, 37]."

The set of reinforcement principles, or laws of instrumental learning, defines for Homans human nature. He says: "At the level of the elementary forms of social behavior there is neither Jew nor Gentile, Greek nor barbarian, but only man [1974: 5]." Human nature is seen as a uniform pattern or mechanism of reactions to changing and varied environmental contingencies, and under those varied conditions producing all diversities of behavior. In the words of Homans: "A particular kind of reward may be valuable to one man or to the members of one group, a different kind valuable to another; and since the pursuit of different rewards often requires different actions, what the two men or groups do may differ concretely. Yet, the proposition: the more valuable the reward, the more frequent or probable the action that gets the reward, holds good for both [1967: 41]." This common mechanism is nothing else but human nature.

At the heart of it, it is a passivistic picture, a picture of man reacting to an environment, responding to stimuli, motivated solely by payoffs, pushed and pulled by circumstances—a manipulable automaton. Two voices of caution raised against such an image of man are worth quoting. Staats observes: "A primary objection to behaviorism and learning theory is that it makes of man a 'reactive,' not a creative creature. It is said, and rightly so, that the simple conception that human behavior is learned does not provide for originality and creativity [1975: 473]." And Maslow: "The various behaviorisms all seem to generate inexorably such a passive image of a helpless man, one who (or should I say 'which'?) has little to say about his (its?) own fate, who doesn't decide anything. . . . My crucially important experience of being an active subject is . . . either denied altogether . . . or is simply pushed aside as 'unscientific,' i.e., beyond respectable scientific treatment [1966: 15]."

For such reasons several sociologists have rejected passivistic assumptions and opted for an image of man safeguarding his autonomy and creativity. Some examples of the schools holding to autonomism shall now be discussed.

Symbolic Interactionism: Man as a Conscious Master of Circumstances

One of the schools addressing itself most openly to the dilemma discussed in this chapter is certainly that of symbolic interactionism. Skidmore has noted that "since the focus of symbolic interactionism is the individual and his relationships with others, it will be found to contain a fairly explicit model of man [1975a: 141]."

In modern sociology symbolic interactionism is developed as a self-conscious continuity of the early works of Cooley and Mead. But it departs from, develops, and enriches that theoretical tradition in several directions. Some authors attempt to develop distinct, general theoretical approaches, identifying the essence of human society in terms of some selected aspect of the traditional symbolic-interactionist image. Examples may be provided by the dramaturgical school of Goffman, the ethnomethodological school of Garfinkel, and the ethogenetic school of Harre and Secord. Other authors focus attention on some substantive problems or concepts of traditional symbolic interactionist framework attempting to develop more limited "middle-range" theories dealing in depth with each of them. Examples may be found in the theory of the self concept, role theory, and reference group theory.

The already immense but still growing popularity of symbolic interactionism and its offspring may be traced to a widespread dissatisfaction with both structural functionalism and behavioristic exchange models. Symbolic interactionism happens to reject one major point that those otherwise disparate approaches have in common; namely, the image of man as simply a responding, reacting creature. In structural functionalism man is seen as responding to normative expectations or functional requirements dictated by a system with an assumed consensus on norms and values; in behavioral-exchange theories man is seen as responding to stimuli present in the environment. As against structural functionalism, symbolic interactionsm "conceives of the human being as creating or remaking his environment, as 'carving out' his world of objects, in the course of action, rather than simply responding to normative expectations [Meltzer, Petras, and Reynolds, 1975: 64]." And it "sees cultural norms, status positions, and role relationships as only the framework within which social action takes place, and not the crucial and coercive determinant of that action [1975: 64]." As against behavioral exchange theory, symbolic interactionism claims that "man's perception is more then the receiving of stimuli by the senses. It is the interpretation of that stimuli in terms of symbols as it relates to the individual in his special way [Skidmore, 1975a: 152]." And to quote Meltzer *et al.* again: In the symbolic-interactionist framework "the behavior of men and women is 'caused' not so much by forces within themselves (instincts, drives, needs, etc.) or by external forces impinging upon them (social forces, etc.), but by what lies in between a reflective and socially derived interpretation of the internal and external stimuli that are present [1975: 2]."

It can already be seen from those critical charges leveled by symbolic interactionism against competing approaches that the positive message of this school consists mainly of a specific image of human action, and consequently of a specific image of man as actor. The key to the view of man is to be found in the picture of human activity. As Skidmore observes: "It is the interpretation of action that is all-important to the symbolic interactionist [1975b: 227]." And the interpretation of action is founded on three basic premises: "(1) human beings act toward things on the basis of the meanings that the things have for them, (2) these meanings are a product of social interaction in human society, (3) these meanings are modified and handled through an interpretive process that is used by each individual in dealing with the signs he encounters [Meltzer et al., 1975: 1]." Those premises lead to the following consequence: "Since much of the environment's influence is experienced in the form of social meanings, and meanings are learned by individuals in social interaction, behavior is constructed and circular, not predetermined and released [Meltzer et al., 1975: 3]." The same conclusion is reached by Skidmore: "Conduct is built up toward objects which have significance for a person [1975b: 210]."

If action is interpreted in this way, human actors must of necessity be treated as "active, creative beings who could play a conscious role in the control of their own destinies [Meltzer et al. 1975: 7]." Or, to be more specific, "In the interactionist image, human beings are defined as self-reflective beings. Human beings are organisms with selves, and behavior in society is often directed by a self [Meltzer et al., 1975: 2]." In short, "the individual is a minded organism with a self [Skidmore, 1975a: 142]."

The Dramaturgical School: Man on a Social Stage

There are obviously many distinct aspects in such an image of action and of a human actor. Some current schools seem to have picked up some single one and, pushing it to an extreme, produced one-sided, simplistic reconstructions of social reality. The aspect of conscious manipulation of symbols in interaction with fellow human beings was selected as the most crucial focus by the dramaturgical school associated with Erving Goffman.

In one of the first works in an extended series of monographs, he stated his approach as follows: "I shall consider the way in which the individual . . . presents himself and his activity to others, the ways in which he guides and controls the impression they form of him, and the kinds of things he may and may not do while sustaining his performance before them [Goffman, 1959: xi]." And in a later work he says, "The individual does not go about merely going about his business. He goes about constrained to sustain a viable image of himself in the eyes of others [Goffman, 1963: 185]." The assumption underlying all of Goffman's work is explained thus by Petras and Meltzer: "Goffman's dramaturgical metaphor has as its point of departure the premise that when human beings interact each desires to 'manage' the impressions the other receive of him. Each, in effect, must put on a 'show' for the others [1973: 3]."

This image of man as a detached, rational impression manager (Meltzer *et al.*, 1975: 71), "as a role player and manipulator of props, costumes, gestures and words" in the course of interpersonal encounters (Cuzzort, 1969: 192) is only one of the modern manifestations of the symbolic interactionist perspective.

Ethogenetics: Man as a Planning Agent

Another perspective, known as ethogenetics, focuses on a different aspect of the symbolic interactionist tradition, and again pushes it to an extreme, providing a new, one-sided version of the theory. This aspect is man's ability to predict and plan his activities in advance.

The crucial notion of symbolic interactionism was that of a symbol. It was conceived in the tradition of the school as an outline of a possible course of action, together with its possible end. A symbol was always seen as referring to

> a possible completed act or series of possible acts. Each of these possible acts are epitomized or telescoped into a symbol. It is these possible outcomes that constitute the meaning of the symbol. . . . Since the symbol epitomizes an act, that is, since it telescopes the representation of a future state of affairs into itself, its meaning includes the image of that future state of affairs. . . . This allows persons to adjust their activities to impending states of affairs, which in turn may result in the alteration of each person's intended activites [Skidmore, 1975a: 143–145].

One may say briefly that a symbol was conceived as a sort of a microplan for action conceived by the acting individual.

Now, Harre and Secord take this idea and extend it into a central property of human "self-directed and self-monitored behavior [1972: 9]." They say:

> People, alone among animals, possess the power to monitor their monitorings, to be aware of being aware, etc. . . . This is exercised in giving monitoring commentaries upon monitored performances, and in the special case of acting by following a rule or plan, which is to act to make an anticipatory commentary come true. . . . The most characteristic form of human behavior is the conscious following of rules and the intentional carrying out of plans [Harre and Secord, 1972: 85, 91].

The anthropomorphic model of man, which they suggest as the only adequate representation of real human experiences and performances, is clearly informed by the autonomistic assumption and counterpoised to all passivistically inclined conceptions. "Much of human behavior does not have the character of things happening to a person. Instead it consists of things that people have made happen for various reasons. A person is an active agent in much of his social life. [Harre and Secord, 1972: 39]." More explicitly, they describe man thus: "A man then is a mechanism, but one which monitors and controls the way he performs. We have seen how such a being will most economically control the manner of his actions by following rules, and by forming and attempting to realize plans [1972: 97]."

Ethnomethodology: Man in a Network of Shared Understandings

The third modern trend indebted to symbolic interactionism is ethnomethodology, associated with Harold Garfinkel. The link between this school and symbolic interactionism is explained thus by Wallace: "Insofar as ethnomethodology embraces a theoretic (rather than methodological) viewpoint, it is clearly symbolic interactionist [1969: 35]." The crucial focus of ethnomethodology may be seen to rest on a network of interpersonal, symbolic communication and the necessity to decode that network in order to make human actions "accountable." In a traditional symbolic-interactionist approach, the aspect of interpersonal communication was always emphasized. But ethnomethodology abstracts this aspect, removes it from the other, and takes it to provide a key to an understanding of social reality. As Garfinkel puts it: "I use the term 'ethnomethodology' to refer to the investigation of the rational properties of indexical expressions and other practical actions as contingent ongoing accomplishments or organized artful practices of everyday life [1967: 11]." The term *indexical expressions* is used to signify shared meanings taken for granted in a given community and implemented in the interactions of its members. In the interpretation of Timasheff and Theodorson, "Ethnomethodology means the study of 'folk' or commonsense methods of constructing and maintaining social reality. . . . The ethnomethodologist avoids the whole question of reality and emphasizes instead the study of the ways an image of social reality is created [1976: 301–302]."

It is self-evident that man appears here as an active being, endowed with the potential to create the social reality in which he participates together with his fellow human beings.

Social Action Theory: Man as a "Cognizer" and "Cathecter" Exercising Choice

The autonomistically oriented schools discussed so far have been more or less closely following the theoretical tradition of Cooley and Mead. But some impact on contemporary sociology was also exercised by the tradition of social-action theory as initiated and developed by Weber and Znaniecki.

This may be illustrated by the so-called general theory of action proposed by Talcott Parsons in the early period of his work, and developed by several followers. The main components of the traditional action scheme are retained. First, action is seen in terms of a means–ends nexus; second, it is seen as having subjective, meaningful reference for the actors participating; and third, it is seen as involving some choice on the part of the actors. Each of these points in the conceptualization of human action is at the same time considerably enriched and developed.

The means–ends framework is emphasized very strongly in the interpretation given to the Parsonian concept of action by Swanson: "Any behavior that involves some awareness of a goal, and that is organized to choose means for reaching such a goal which have previously been learned to be more effective rather than less effective, will be action [Swanson 1953: 126]." As Parsons puts it: "It is impossible even to talk about action in terms that do not involve a means–end relationship with all the implications just discussed. This is the common conceptual framework in which all change and process in the action field is grasped [1968, vol.II: 733]."

Also, the subjective reference of an action, considered always from the point of view of an actor, is heavily stressed. The scheme of action, Parsons says, "deals with phenomena, with things and events, as they appear from the point of view of the actor whose action is being analyzed and considered [1968, vol.I: 46]." And in this connection a more specific analytic distinction is introduced. Subjective reference takes two modes: "The cognitive mode involves the various processes by which an actor sees an object in relation to his system of need-dispositions. . . . The cathectic mode involves the various processes by which an actor invests an object with affective significance [Parsons and Shils, 1962: 59]." The traditional concept of the definition of a situation is thereby extended, and made to include not only intellectual interpretation but also emotionally fraught attitudes.

But the crucial point is introduced when Parsons acknowledges the existence of "an independent determinate selective factor," the factor of "volition or will," or else "freedom" or "autonomy" of the will (Parsons, 1968, vol.I: 45). He points out explicitly that action is "a process in which the concrete human being plays an active, not merely an adaptive role [1968, vol.I: 439]." And "the creative, voluntaristic element which we have found to be involved in the factor of ends precludes action ever being completely determined [Parsons, 1934: 287]."

The significance of those statements for the Parsonian image of human action is clearly perceived by several commentators. Scott points out that "Parsons . . . argued that a primordially creative element, independent of the natural world of 'heredity and environment,' was active in valuation and the choice of goals [1969: 246]." And Skidmore makes the same observation: "In Parsons's voluntaristic emphasis . . . there is considerable room for choice on the part of the individual and self-determination of action. The model of man is definitely constructed in terms of alternatives and modes of choosing between alternatives [1975a: 180]."

The image of human action outlined above has clear implications for the image of a human actor, and his essential nature. Man appears as intelligent, a rational "cognizer," an emotional "cathecter," and a relatively free decision maker, possessing a large degree of autonomy in his choices. Those three interlinked traits of human nature are summed up very skillfully in Skidmore's appraisal of Parsons.

> Two major assumptions about the nature of man arise from Parsons' use of utilitarian thought. Man is a cognizer, having the ability to relate specific objects to categories according to the attributes of the objects. He is basically emotional, since before he can act, he must establish a cathexis with the object of action. . . . However Parsons also sees man as the volunteer for his own actions. That is, Parsons's man is not a naive robot, performing those functions set for him by society. . . . While society has a hand in forming the individual's dispositions to act, it is always the individual who formulates and carries through the action [1975a: 105, 186].

In those three ways "actors are the authors of their own actions [Skidmore, 1975a: 84]."

WHAT THE DISPUTE IS REALLY ABOUT: AN EXPLICATION

Now that the main standpoints in the dispute of autonomism and passivism have been presented, the meaning of the dispute is to be clarified. Perhaps no other sociological dilemma has caused so many misunderstandings. And it is necessary to get rid of them before the core meaning of the dilemma will be disclosed. I shall begin the explication from the negative side, disposing of those issues that in my interpretation are irrelevant to the main problem. Therefore, I shall first explain what the dispute of autonomisms and passivism is not about.

What the Dispute Is Not About

First, it is not a dispute about the psychological constitution of man, but rather about the sociological image of man. To be sure, the focus of attention rests on the individual, but an individual can be seen from various points of view. For a psychologist, the individual per se is the crucial subject matter, and his concern is focused on the functioning of the mind or personality in its cognitive, emotional, volitional, motivational and other aspects. For a sociologist, the crucial subject matter is composed of specific objects of a superindividual nature—collectivities, groups, societies, social relationships, interpersonal links, interactions, etc. The sociological perspective applied to any phenomenon comes down to perceiving that phenomenon in the context of such specific sociological objects—as an element of such objects, or at least in relation to them. Therefore, the individual is a subject matter relevant to sociology only insofar as he is implicated in some wider social reality. Seen from a sociological perspective, he will appear as a component of social wholes, or at least as regularly related to such wholes. A sociologist will always look at an individual from an external perspective of wider, superindividual or interindividual entities, and his participation in them, rather than from the point of view of his internal, psychological make up.

To be specific: There are several entities of a superindividual, or interindividual sort. One might present them in the following list—from the simplest to the most complex: (*a*) social actions (insofar as they are social they involve some other persons, at least as referents or recipients of an individual activity; therefore they can be treated as the superindividual phenomena); (*b*) interactions; (*c*) social relations; (*d*) social groups; (*e*) social structures. From the sociological perspective an individual shall therefore be seen not as a full-fledged, multidimensional person, but rather as an abstract, one-dimensional: (*a*) actor in a social action; (*b*) partner in the interaction; (*c*) participant in the social relationship; (*d*) member of a social group; or (*e*) occupant of a social position and performer of a social role attached to this position in a social structure. Therefore, for sociology the issue of human nature concerns the characteristics of man in his capacities as actor, partner, participant, member, occupant, or performer—and in those capacities only.

The key to this particular aspect of human nature is to be found in the characteristics of human activity. Activity is the means by which an individual participates in larger social entities. Some specifically directed or oriented actitivites make up an interaction; persistent, repeatable, and normatively regulated activities vis-a-vis one another involve two individuals in a social relationship; activities creating a bond with some people and separating them from other people make an individual a member of a social group; and a specific set of activities defines the social role that an individual is expected to perform by virtue of his structural position, and which most often he actually performs.

To sum up this important point: The sociological image of man is arrived at by considering the characteristic properties of a human activity, and then deriving the necessary, indispensable properties of an agent. The following logic is employed: *If the nature of human activity is such* [however defined], *what are the necessary qualities that anybody participating in such activity must possess?* What is reached as a result of that argument is an image of man as agent: This is precisely what the sociological image of man amounts to.

Second, the dispute of autonomism and passivism does not directly address the question of the universal or historical character of human nature—this is a separate problem with a long philosophical tradition. The dilemma is concerned with the specification of the characteristic traits of human activity, and consequently of the human actor, and not so much with the status of those traits in the dimension of time—whether they are immutable and universal or not. Both those who construe human action and the image of the human actor in autonomistic terms and those who construe them in passivistic terms can equally well treat their reconstructions as either universally valid or valid only within a historical context. In fact, the autonomists and passivists alike seem to adopt a compromise standpoint asserting that some dimensions of human nature are universal, and some not. Three versions of such a compromise standpoint are encountered. According to the first, and probably the oldest one, man has certain constant, universal needs, drives, dispositions, that can be satisfied in varied and historically changing ways (example: Malinowski's theory of needs). According to the second, relatively later version, the basic mechanisms of human activity (e.g., the laws of learning, reinforcement, instrumental conditioning) are constant and universal, but the uses these mechanisms are put to, the goals they help to reach, the dangers they help avoid, the needs they satisfy, are varied and changing. For example, in one of the most influential formulations this approach leads to the claim that the ways in which individuals learn are common to the whole of humanity, but that the content of the lesson is infinitely differentiated and historically as well as culturally specific (e.g., Homan's theory of elementary social behavior). And according to the third—and perhaps the least-popular version—it is the milieu, the setting in which a human infant becomes fully human, that is constant and universal for humankind (e.g., the family, the primary groups, etc.), whereas both how it learns to be human and what it learns from social tradition is varied historically and culturally (e.g., Cooley's theory of the primary groups).

To sum up: To ask meaningfully what human nature is, one must assume beforehand that there is human nature—a range of traits, properties, characteristics, common to men as men. All participants in the dispute of autonomism and passivism accept such an assumption. The concrete ways in which they delimit the scope of universal traits, and counterpoise it to the class of historically changing traits (if any) make up a separate issue, which is not directly relevant to the problem here discussed.

The third misunderstanding has to do with the distinction between some factors that determine human action from the inside, or internally, and some that determine it from the outside, or externally. This is a common-sense distinction. In everyday thinking an individual is often perceived as either instigated to action by some internal pressures or pushed and pulled around by some external forces. In the light of this distinction, the autonomistic assumption is often identified with an emphasis on internal determinants, the passivistic assumption with an emphasis on external ones.

But the essence of the dispute is certainly not here. An individual may be a slave of instincts or a slave of social norms; in either case he is a slave, and hence passive, even though his slavery originates "inside" in the first case and "outside" in the second. On the other hand, an individual can be a master of his drives or a master of social situations; in either case he is a master, hence autonomous, even though his mastery is exercised over internal factors in the first case, and external ones in the second. It follows that passivism has something to do with a subjugation to pressures, whether internal or external, and autonomism has something to do with a control over them. The question of internality or externality of pressures is irrelevant to the main issue. This criterion does not differentiate between autonomistic and passivistic points of view.

Almost the same argument may be repeated with respect to the fourth misunderstanding. This one postulates a distinction between subjective determining factors (perceptions, feelings, emotions, attitudes, etc.) and objective environmental or bodily parameters (the external situation, the biological, hereditary constitution of the human organism, etc.). Those who emphasize the subjective factors are identified, and wrongly, with the autonomists, and those who emphasize the objective factors with the passivists. And again the core of the issue is misplaced. Subjective states can keep a man in an equally powerful grip—make him passive—as the objective factors. And conversely, autonomy can be exercised equally well with respect to the subjective as to the objective circumstances. The criterion of subjectivity or objectivity does not differentiate between the autonomistic and passivistic positions.

The fifth misunderstanding is based on the distinction of the conscious as opposed to the unconscious (or subconscious) determination of human conduct. An equivalence is seen between an emphasis on unconscious determinants and a passivistic standpoint, as well as between an emphasis on conscious determinants and an autonomistic standpoint. But it is enough to point out that one may be fully conscious of psychological (internal) or environmental (external) constraints limiting or excluding one's free choice, and still be perfectly unable to do anything about them. Consciousness of one's impotence is not tantamount to autonomy. Half the equation is then patently untrue. And even though consciousness of a situation and of one's own potentialities seems to be a prerequisite for autonomous control, and thus the second half of the equation appears correct, the factor of consciousness does not of itself differentiate between autonomistic and passivistic assumptions.

The sixth misunderstanding stems from the distinction of spontaneous (chaotic, random, impulsive) activity and deliberate (systematic, orderly, rational) activity. Those who ascribe spontaneous characteristics to human action are sometimes believed to profess passivistic assumptions concerning human nature, and those who see human action as deliberate are thought to profess the opposite, autonomistic assumptions. But there is no necessary correspondence, not to speak of identity, between those issues. Autonomy may be expressed in deliberate activity, and equally well in spontaneous activity. And the same is true of passivism, which may result in deliberateness as well as spontaneity. It all depends on the nature of the determinants (influences, pressures impinging on the individual, from without or from within, from the objective, given environment or from his subjective internal environment). If those pressures are themselves systematically ordered, the activity that appears systematic or deliberate will be the outcome of passivistic adaptation, and the apparently chaotic or random activity will be indicative of autonomy. On the other hand, if the pressures are themselves random and chaotic, a passivistic adaptation will result in spontaneous, chaotic, and random reactions, whereas autonomous control will be revealed by deliberate, consistent, rational conduct—all the surrounding chaos notwithstanding. The factor of spontaneity or deliberation does not differentiate between the two standpoints we are presently concerned with.

The seventh misunderstanding involves an identification of autonomy with isolation (solitude, marginality), and passivism with social engagement. As shall be shown later, true autonomy is not reached by a withdrawal from society or a rejection of it, but rather by active participation in society. Autonomy—not necessarily against, but for and through society—is also a possibility encountered in the human world. And conversely isolation may be equally well a mark of subjugation and passivism as a mark of autonomy and independence. No necessary correspondence exists between these separate dichotomies.

The remaining three issues mistakenly mixed up with the problem of autonomism and passivism are so clearly irrelevant to the core substance of the dilemma that I shall mention them only for the sake of completeness. Misunderstanding Number Eight treats autonomy and passivism as specific personality traits and identifies them with innovative tendencies, as opposed to conformity proneness or submissiveness, respectively. The same psychological bias is evident in Misunderstanding Number Nine, in which autonomy is equated with egocentric attitudes and passivism with altruistic or sociocentric ones. And the tenth misunderstanding leads to the identification of autonomy with active, dynamic, temperamental dispositions, whereas passivism is interpreted as something like laziness, inertia, or lack of initiative. In view of our ealier discussion of the peculiarities of the sociological perspective and its clear-cut distinction from the psychological point of view, no more arguments are necessary to show the irrelevance of these latter three dichotomies to the issue of the sociological image of man.

The Focus of the Dispute:
Control over Human Activities

The major misunderstandings eliminated, we shall approach the issue from the positive side and attempt to explicate the essential content of each of the two standpoints. In spite of numerous misunderstandings, there exists a considerable degree of consensus—which can be discovered in the literature—concerning the core difference between the autonomistic and passivistic positions. Perhaps the clearest statement is given by Harre and Secord: "Regularities in human behavior may be explained according to several different schemata. Two extremes are: (1) the person acting as an agent directing his own behavior, (2) the person as an object responding to the push and pull of forces exerted by the environment. The former emphasizes self-direction, the latter environmental contingencies. [1972: 8]." In their view, the differentiating criterion concerns "the extent to which the person is regarded as an agent directing his own behavior. At one extreme he may be seen simply as an object responding to the push and pull of forces exerted by the environment. At the other, he may be seen as an agent guiding his behavior toward some explicit goal by some means of which he is thoroughly aware [Harre and Secord, 1972: 136]." In brief, this is a difference between things done *to* a person and things done *by* a person.

The line demarcating the two opposite images of man and his action is drawn in a similar manner by Blumer: "Action is built up in coping with the world instead of merely being released from a pre-existing psychological structure by factors playing on that structure. . . . The human being ceases to be a responding organism whose behavior is a product of what plays upon him from the outside, from the inside, or both [1966: 235–236]." Another statement of the same sort was given by Miller in his 1969 presidential address to the American Psychological Association, in which he distinguished two opposite types of beliefs about human nature—one treating human beings as machines and focusing on the impact of external reinforcements, the other regarding people as endowed with imagination, ingenuity, and creativity, as exercising self-control over their actions, and as striving consciously for goals selected by themselves (see also Wrightsman,

1972: 94). In a similar vein Bell and Mau claim that "critical differences in human behavior are hypothesized to result from . . . images which put man in the image as a causal factor compared to those which do not [1970: 222]." Meltzer, Petras, and Reynolds counterpoise "images of behavior as constructed rather than released" and "images of role performance as role-making rather than role-playing [1975: 63]." Skidmore suggests considering the extent to which "action is constructed, or built up, rather than being the release of certain activities as responses to forces or pressures inherent in situations [1975a: 155]." And Staats sees the crucial distinction between images of man focusing on the issue of "self-direction versus passive responding [1975: 468]."

Thus, the core difference is perceived to be that between an image of man as an active subject and an image of man as a passive object. And the factor that distinguishes an active subject from a passive object is clearly the degree of control one exercises over one's activities. Thus, autonomism will be interpreted as a position ascribing such control to a human being, and passivism as a position denying such control to him. Or focusing on the action rather than the agent, autonomism will be interpreted as a position treating human action as controlled by a human agent, passivism as a position claiming that action is not under control of a human agent. In our explication, the central notion is that of control.

Two questions seem crucial: What is the control exercised over? What is the substance of control? If we ascribe (or refuse to ascribe) the ability of control to a human individual, there are several objects of control that we can have in mind. First, we may think of control over a singular act, or episode; for example, I am switching on the ignition in my car. Second, we may think of control over a sequence of acts; for example, I am driving the car through the streets to a university. Third, we may think of control over the multiplicity of acts extending over a whole life; for example, I persistently strive to become a world-renowned artist. It is important to be clear as to what object of control is considered, for quite diverse capabilities of an agent will have to be assumed in each case. The standpoint of autonomism may consequently be seen as allowing of different formulations. The strongest formulation will claim that a man is master of his life; the weaker that he can control his conduct; the weakest, that he can control isolated episodes. Conversely, the standpoint of passivism can also be posited in three ways. The strongest will deny man even the ability to control episodes; the weaker will concede some control over them, but at the same time reject the possibility of controlling the longer sequences of conduct; and the weakest will concede control over episodes as well as conduct, but deny mastery over one's life in its totality.

In all those various forms of control, distinguished on the basis of the object over which the control is exercised, the content of control is the same, and seems to involve the following: first, some level of reflection on the actual situation in which an individual finds himself, as well as on the knowledge, skills, abilities, facilities, that he commands, and that are necessary for action in that situation—call it self-consciousness. The second aspect is some foresight as to the possible courses of action that can be taken in the recognized situational circumstances by an individual with his recognized abilities and capacities—this may be referred to as planning. The third aspect of control is choice among the foreseen, alternative courses of action—decision making. The last aspect is the undertaking of the course of action chosen—or simply, action.

Again, the autonomistic and passivistic standpoints can take various forms depending on the strength of the claim they make ascribing or denying to a human activity some or all aspects of control. Thus, the strongest formulation of autonomism will require all aspects to be present and define control as self-consciousness plus planning plus decision making plus action; whereas the weakest formulation will focus only on self-consciousness and treat it as a sufficient definitional criterion of control. Two intermediate formulations are possible. Conversely, the strongest formulation of passivism will claim all aspects of control to be absent and deny even the faculty of self-consciousness to the human agent, whereas the weakest formulation will only deny the ability of purposeful, persistent action. Again, two intermediate formulations can be posited between these extremes.

The Sociological Image of Man

Let me repeat now the main steps in the explication. The sociological image of man was identified by a focus on the characteristics of a human action, and the capacity of man as agent. The justification for such a view was that it is by and through his actions that an individual enters into those wider, superindividual or interindividual wholes that are the proper subject matter of sociology—the proper referents of the sociological perspective. The crucial aspect of an action was conceived as its susceptibility or unsusceptibility to control by a human agent, and the crucial faculty of an agent was conceived as his ability or inability to control his actions. Is action controlled or not controlled by a human agent? Has a human agent control or is he devoid of control over his actions? These questions were the crucial issues apparently dividing the autonomists and the passivists. If man was conceived in autonomistic terms, as an active subject, as the independent locus of control, then a specific set of properties could be ascribed to him as an immediate derivation.

If my reconstruction of the meaning of control is correct, such properties, necessary for exercising control include, first, some degree of reflectiveness or self-consciousness (interpretative relation to the environment); second, some ability to anticipate and project future courses of action; third, some ability to make decisions; and fourth, some persistence in carrying out the decisions made.

On the other hand, if man was conceived in passivistic terms, as a passive sufferer of influences, then an opposite set of properties was immediately entailed. Again, if my reconstruction of the notion of control is correct, then the properties characteristic of an agent devoid of any control over his deeds will include, first, complete unreflectivity, a purely receptive relation to the environment; second, an immersion in immediate circumstances; third, automatic responsiveness to stimuli, however conceived; and fourth, a spontaneous following of the influences of the moment.

Such properties, and such properties only, can be validly included in a sociological discussion of human nature. They make up the sociological images of man in their two main varieties, analyzed in the present chapter. The autonomistic image and the passivistic image seem to be mutually exclusive; they apparently leave no room for any other conception of man. I shall attempt to show that their mutual exclusiveness is a seeming one, and that in fact the dilemma of autonomism and passivism is as spurious as the other dilemmas considered so far. Both standpoints will be rejected, and the alternative, dialectical solution to the riddle of human nature will be offered.

CREATIVISM AS A DIALECTICAL SOLUTION

The logic employed in the construction of an alternative, dialectic solution will be similar as in the case of previous dilemmas. If both traditional assumptions are to be rejected, the first step is to discover such beliefs as both of them share. They may be interpreted as higher-order assumptions common to both standpoints. Such higher-order assumptions will have to be rejected and replaced with their opposites. Then all the implications of this new set of higher-order meta-assumptions will have to be made explicit, leading to the formation of a new dialectical standpoint on the issue of the nature of man.

Common Meta-assumptions:
The Absolute Perspective

But are there any common points between two apparently opposite and mutually exclusive theoretical positions? Let me refer to their substantive content again. As a result of the explication carried out in the previous chapters, the core of the autonomistic standpoint was found to be an image of man as an active subject, a controller of his own actions. But no action is carried out in a vacuum; rather, it occurs in some environment composed, on the one hand, of natural factors (including man's biological nature), and, on the other hand, of social factors (including other people, established social patterns, cultural norms and values, etc.). Control over one's own actions comes down therefore to control over the environment. The autonomistic position can now be read as the claim of the autonomy or independence of man vis-a-vis his environment.

Conversely, the image of man as a passive object, characterized by a complete lack of control over his own actions, will entail the claim of the total dependence of man on environmental factors.

But the differences notwithstanding, both standpoints take it for granted that environment is something separate from the acting man. Autonomism neglects the influence of the environment and places the locus of control in man. Passivism neglects the influence of man, and places the locus of control in the environment. But both treat man and the environment as separate entities. The dissociation of man and environment is therefore the first higher-order meta-assumption that both standpoints certainly share.

The second higher-order assumption common to both standpoints will easily be discovered if one looks closer at those properties taken as definitional characteristics of human nature. Those are the properties that have man as their referent and are couched in absolute rather than relational terms. In the case of autonomism, they are conceived as the prerequisite traits for a man to exercise control over his actions. In the case of passivism they are conceived as the prerequisite traits mandating a total abdication of control over one's actions. In both cases, the focus is on man and his characteristic traits.

The Rejection of the Common Meta-assumptions: The Relational Perspective

Now let me show that in spite of their apparent plausibility, those higher-order assumptions are untenable and can be replaced by their opposites. First, instead of treating man and environment as separate entities, one can perceive both as a fully integrated unity. Man can be seen as inseparable from the environment, bound by necessary relationships to both his natural environment (including his biological endowment) and his social environment (other people, civilization, norms of conduct, etc.). By no stretch of the imagination can a man be dissociated from those environmental factors; he can acquire, affirm, and express his humanity only in and through the environment, by virtue of those necessary links that bind him to "nature" as well as to other people. The image of man as standing over or prostrating himself beneath the environment, as ruling or ruled by it—in brief, as placed against the environment—must be rejected.

And then, the second higher-order assumption will also lose its footing. If man is seen as closely interlinked with the environment by necessary relationships, then one is to search for the key to human nature in the characteristics of those relationships. The focus shifts from the absolute properties of man to the relational properties of his typical association with the environment. It is a specific relation of man to environment that is now perceived as the property distinguishing human kind from the inanimate as well as the animal world. Such a specific relation is found to exist between man and both components of his environment, the natural and the social. Man is human not because he is such and such (possesses certain absolute characteristics) but because he enters into specific relationships with nature as well as with other people.

Toward a Dialectical Alternative

The adoption of a unitary and relational point of view, in place of a separatist and absolute one allows a sociologist to reformulate the traditional assumptions in a new way. The standpoint that shall be called the *new autonomism* will define the relationship between man and his environment in some specific way, and the standpoint that shall be named the *new passivism* will define this relation in the other, directly opposite way. For example, in some typical version of the new autonomism, this relationship will be conceived as inventive creation, and in equally typical version of the new passivism as receptive imitation.

Now, if we remind ourselves of the basic object of this discussion, it can easily be seen that, so far, our success is only partial; we have rephrased both traditional standpoints, but we have not solved their opposition. The dilemma is still present, and the crucial next step must be taken in order to overcome it.

Let us approach this end by suggesting that two separate aspects in the relationship between man and his environment be distinguished—the actual and the genetic aspect. Seen in its actual aspect the relationship appears in a timeless void, as it actually occurs in a given moment. The question one must address here is "What is the typical relationship of any particular man to the particular environment in which he finds himself?" One of the answers, which shall be labeled New Autonomism$_1$, claims that man will typically enter into some sort of creative, productive relationship with nature, as well as into some type of creative association with society—both components of his environment. Another answer shall be labeled New Passivism$_1$, and found to claim that man will typically enter into some sort of imitative or adaptive relationship with nature and society. But those solutions refer only to the first aspect of the issue, the actual.

Seen in the second, genetic aspect, the relationship of man and environment appears in a temporal, diachronic dimension, from the point of view of its origin. The question one has to face becomes a little different. "Whatever the typical nature of the relationship between man and his environment, how did such a relationship originate?" One of the answers, which shall be labeled New Autonomism$_2$, claims that the relationship in all its aspects—both the form it takes and the content it has—is generated by the inborn, immanent characteristics of man. Man enters into a creative relationship, because in this way he expresses his basically creative nature; man creates artistic objects, because he has aesthetic dispositions and this is the way to express them. The opposite answer, which shall be labeled New Passivism$_2$, considers the specifically human relationship to the environment (at least with respect to its content, but also sometimes with respect to its form) as shaped under the impact of environmental contingencies, owing to the specific and historically varied characteristics of natural circumstances, biological endowment, the social situation, and one's life experiences. According to this point of view, both what I can do vis-a-vis the environment (i.e., what my abilities, skills, faculties are) and what can be done in that environment (i.e., what opportunities for and limitations on my actions are present) is not autonomously or immanently decided by myself, but rather individually or collectively inherited and, from my point of view, encountered and given.

Now, it can easily be seen that both aspects—actual and genetic—are mutually independent. Therefore, without the risk of contradiction, the solutions given to each of them can be cross-tabulated, with four logically possible standpoints appearing as the result (see Figure 6.1).

The standpoint identified by the combination of New Autonomism$_1$ and New Passivism$_2$ will be considered as a dialectic solution to the dilemma, and referred to as Creativism. It is a dialectic solution because it is not tantamount to either of the original positions, but includes the crucial components of both. It is their negation and continuation simultaneously. Let me describe this dialectical standpoint a little more extensively.

In the actual dimension, creativism strongly emphasizes human autonomy. This factor is revealed in the relationship to the natural environment, where man shows creativity, ingenuity, originality—constantly transforming nature to suit his needs. He constructs objects, produces goods, creates civilizations. In this process he also creatively shapes his own biological endowment (a significant part of the natural environment), by developing his skills, abilities, powers, by creating new needs and aspirations, etc.

The Actual Aspect

	New Autonomism$_1$	New Passivism$_1$
New Passivism$_2$	Creativism	Absolute Passivism
New Autonomism$_2$	Absolute Autonomism	

The Genetic Aspect

Figure 6.1

Human autonomy is equally revealed in his relationship to the social environment. He constantly produces new associations, groups, and collectivities; establishes new institutions; introduces new patterns of social organization; initiates new ways of life, new social norms, and new values; creates political and cultural systems, religious doctrines and artistic creeds, science and ideology.

At the same time, in the genetic dimension the dialectical position stresses that creation is never ex nihilo, but always occurs in a given, received network of opportunities and limitations, predetermining to a large extent what can be done. Those opportunities and limitations are primarily inherited in the given natural environment that provides certain raw materials, resources, facilities, abilities, powers, and is deficient with respect to others. The special case of those natural opportunities and limitations is of course the individual genetic endowment or biological constitution, which can encourage certain activities and hamper others. Opportunities and limitations are also inherent in the social environment, where the established patterns of social structure may act as constraints on as well as stimulants for action. Such patterns of social structure are socially (or else, culturally) inherited from previous generations, and for any generation must be considered as a field of givens within which any attempts at creative change have to fit themselves. The special case of such opportunities and limitations is provided by the differential scope of human life experiences with respect to various structural patterns (norms, values, institutions, etc.). Some experiences may provide encouragement, and some discouragement.

To sum up: In Creativism man is seen as actually autonomous, but genetically restricted; possessing control over his actions, but only within limits

determined by the encountered natural environment, by his biological constitution, by the social structures within which he operates, and by his
experiences with respect to all earlier factors. An additional virtue of this
standpoint is the new solution it provides to the old dispute concerning the
universal or historical character of human nature. To the three solutions I
have mentioned earlier, it adds a fourth. Like some other compromise
standpoints it asserts that human nature is both universal and historical. But
it defines the universal and historical dimensions in a new and original way:
Human nature is universal in the type of relationship that exists between
man and nature; namely, a creative link within environmental restrictions,
as well as between man and society; an associational bond within structural constraints. It is historical in the concrete content and scope of activity,
determined by a varied and changeable field of opportunities and limitations. To illustrate: Man produces goods by subjecting nature to purposeful
transformations—it is a universal trait of his to do so—but what he produces, what materials and tools he utilizes, are historically changing. And
similarly, man enters into associations with others—it is a universal trait of
his to do so—but what types of associations predominate (of cooperation or
exploitation, solidarity or hostility, love or hatred) are historically determined. The universal dimension is entailed by the claim of New Au-
tonomism$_1$; the historical dimension is entailed by the claim of New
Passivism$_2$, which together, as we have seen, combine to produce the dialectical standpoint of Creativism.

This standpoint will be further illustrated by considering in more detail
the theory in which it is expressed most fully; namely, the Marxian theory of
man.

CREATIVISM IN MARXIAN
SOCIOLOGICAL THEORY

The Concept of Man in
the Focus of Marxian Thought

There is a prolonged and involved debate concerning the role and place
of the image of man in Marxian sociological theory. Some commentators
seem to read Marxism as an exclusively macrosociological doctrine, focused
on large-scale social wholes—classes, nations, economies, polities,
socioeconomic formations, etc.—and on large-scale historical transformations: revolution, development, progress, etc. Such interpretations are typical of a dogmatic, mechanistic, or vulgar approach to Marxism, such as
reigned at the end of the nineteenth and the beginning of the twentieth

century and turned into an official creed during the Stalinist period. But in recent decades this approach has been on the defensive, and the prevailing tendency in the West, as well as in the East, is to read Marxism as a multidimensional theoretical system in which a theory of man not only has a distinct place but is located at the center. Two representative opinions can be quoted. According to a contemporary American commentator, "Marx's theory of alienation places the acting and acted-upon individual in the center of his account. . . . Man continues, of necessity, to occupy a central position in Marx's theories [Ollman, 1975: ix, xii]." And in a recent book by a Soviet philosopher we find the following comment:

> Sociological and philosophical understanding of the essence of man and the historical development of his nature is a component of Marxism which is not accidentally attached, but rather constitutes the core of the Marxian system. . . . From the very beginning, the Marxist interpretation of history comprised not only a theory of social development but also a view on the essence of man. The standpoint, according to which historical materialism is exclusively concerned with the general laws of social development and treats an individual with "annihilating contempt and cold cruelty," is totally and fundamentally mistaken [Keshelava, 1977: 12–13].

I fully subscribe to these views. The central position of the image of man in Marxian theory is safeguarded by two emphases typical of the Marxian approach. First, it is generated by Marx's humanistic axiological standpoint, in which man is the highest value and his well-being the ultimate criterion of historical progress. Second, it results from the theoretical attempt to uncover the real laws of motion of human history, and the belief that "history is nothing but the activity of men in pursuit of their ends."

The definite set of assumptions concerning the nature of man is presupposed by all Marxian theories, and also by those dealing mainly with large-scale social wholes and historical processes. But there are some places where Marx addresses the issue of man directly—in at least two ways: first, in a positive way, specifying the characteristic, essential traits of man as a "natural being," and a "species being," and discussing in detail the most typical human faculty, namely labor, and the most typical human activity, namely work; second, in a negative way, constructing a complex theory of pathological conditions in which man abdicates his specifically human traits, and becomes alienated and reduced to a subhuman status. The theory of normal, healthy human nature and the theory of pathological, alienated human nature will serve as the source for my reconstruction, in which I shall attempt to demonstrate that Marx accepted all the basic tenets of the theoretical position here termed *creativism,* and rejected the extreme, one-sided versions of both autonomism and passivism.

The Positive Image: A Theory of Human Nature

Marx approached the issue of man from the sociological perspective, and he produced a view of man that is preeminently sociological. Whereas several other thinkers dealing with the problem of man were giving mixed accounts, in which the sociological perspective was coupled with psychological considerations, Marx was almost exclusively concerned with the sociological dimension; he was interested in man only as an agent carrying out some activity linking him with the external—natural and social—world. The characteristics of human nature were deduced as the necessary prerequisites for carrying out specifically human activities and participating in a specifically human way in the world.

This almost purely sociological focus of Marx coupled with some commentators' mistaken belief that a valid discussion of man can be carried out only in psychological terms resulted in a false interpretation of Marxian theory as concerned exclusively with social wholes, and neglectful of the individualistic dimension. What Marx did in fact neglect was merely the specific consideration of individual psychology; he certainly had little to say about mental processes, cognition, emotions, and all the rest of the individual's internal constitution. Instead, he looked at man from the outside, and produced a complex sociological image of man as an actor, a member of collectivities, participant in social relations, a component in social structures, etc.

In keeping with his sociological perspective, Marx and Engels conceived the properties of human action to be the key to an understanding of human nature. They claimed explicitly, "The whole character of a species . . . is contained in the character of its life activity, and free, conscious activity is man's species character [1960 vol.I: 553]." And also: "As individuals express their lives, so they are [1975: 61]." As Ollman aptly observes: "For Marx man manifests himself as a species being through activity of a kind, quality, and pace that could only be done by human beings [1975: 84]."

The characterization of human action encountered in Marx has two distinct dimensions. One is the analytic dimension, according to which the internal components of action and the main traits of the actor are discussed. The other is the contextual dimension, according to which action is seen from an external perspective, as itself a component of some wider wholes.

The analytic account of action is basically similar to the view presented by the autonomistically inclined authors discussed earlier. First, action is conceived as conscious and purposeful, in terms of a means–ends scheme. As Engels develops this point, "in the history of society . . . actors are all endowed with consciousness, are men acting with deliberation or passion, working towards definite goals; nothing happens without a conscious purpose, without an intended aim [Marx and Engels, 1968: 622]."

Second, action is seen as involving some degree of self-consciousness or critical self-awareness, on the part of the actors. As Marx puts it, "Man is a being for himself." And he expands on this point thus: "The animal is immediately identifiable with his life activity. It does not distinguish itself from it. Man makes his life activity itself the object of his will and conscious ness. He has conscious life activity. . . . Conscious life activity directly distinguishes man from animal life activity [Marx and Engels, 1960: vol.I: 553]."

Third, the action is conceived as normally preceded by some anticipation or planning. "At the end of every labor process, we get a result that already existed in the imagination of the laborer at its commencement" [Marx, 1954, vol.I: 174]." And also: "What distinguishes the worst architect from the best of bees is this, that the architect raises his structure in the imagination of the laborer at its commencement [1954, vol.I: 174]."

Fourth, the action is believed to involve some degree of persistence in its execution. According to Marx man as opposed to the animal "not only effects a change of form in the material on which he works, but he also realizes a purpose of his own that gives a law to his modus operandi, and to which he must subordinate his will [1954, vol.I: 174]."

All the principal ingredients of the notion of control exercised by man over his actions are present in Marx. If the analytic perspective were the only one utilized by Marx in his discussion of human action, he could easily be classified as an autonomist. But Marx supplements his analytic treatment with another view of human action—this time from the contextual perspective. This allows him to avoid the pitfalls of traditional autonomism and reject the assumption of a dissociation between an acting man and his environment as well as the assumption of absolute, immanent human properties independent of the context of relationships in which an individual is involved.

Man can fulfill himself and realize his potential only by activity directed toward the world. Thus, human action is seen as externally oriented; it is a mediating link between man and his environment. By virtue of human activity, epitomized in the process of labor, the gap between man and environment is bridged, and thus disappears. Work brings about an objectification of man in his products and a humanization of nature by subjecting it to human needs. Consequently, the unity of man and his environment is affirmed. This two-way process is summarized thus by Keshelava: "In order for a man to become a 'human natural being' and for nature to become 'humanized,' nature must be filtered through the transforming activity of work, where on the one hand natural objects obtain a shape suitable to human needs and on the other hand man himself is historically created [1977: 106]." A similar interpretation of Marx is found in Ollman: "What all men have in common, according to Marx, is the ability to appropriate nature at the same time that they objectify themselves in it, developing themselves and altering nature simultaneously. The chief means for making the world a part of oneself and oneself a part of the world is the individual's productive activity [1975: 127]."

If man is seen in unity with his environment, both natural and social, his properties cannot be grasped by immanent analysis, in abstraction from the links binding him to the natural world and to other people. Human nature is made up of relational, not absolute properties; it is a derivative of the network of those relationships to nature and to society in which a man is enmeshed. Marx himself has said, "The human essence is no abstraction inherent in each single individual. In its reality it is the ensemble of social relations [Marx and Engels, 1968: 29]." Swingewood reads this thesis thus: "Marx's point, of course, was that human nature is not a property which simply inhabits man, such as the egoism of the 'economic man,' but rather is a relation between men [1975: 95]"—and also, one may add, between men and nature. "Man without any relations to nature is a relationless void; without any specifically human relations to nature, he is an animal; and without his animal relations to nature, he is a dead human being... [Ollman, 1975: 85]."

There are two types of relations that are specifically human and that may be conceived as defining the nature of man. One can be called *creation,* and the other *participation.* In creative activity man externalizes his powers, abilities, talents, by producing objects. In those objects he confirms himself; they become the objectified expression of his individual potential: "He duplicates himself not only intellectually, in his mind, but also actively, in reality, and thus can look at his image in a world he has created [Marx and Engels, 1960 vol.I: 554]." Two types of objects may be distinguished. One consists of natural objects transformed, shaped, infused with form and meaning, by the acting individual. The process in which they are created is mainly human work: "Labour is, in the first place, a process in which both man and nature participate, and in which man of his own accord starts, regulates, and controls material reactions between himself and nature [Marx, 1954: I:173]." Another category of objects consists of social patterns, institutions, organizations, etc. Swingewood notes that "perhaps the most important point is Marx's emphasis on man as the creator of the social world, who is then trapped by ideology, alienation, and reification, processes against which he nevertheless maintains a stubborn and persistent struggle as part of a social class [1975: 213]."

Creating a world of human impress out of a natural environment, and creating patterns of social organization out of fluid and random human encounters, a man is also re-creating, enriching, and perfecting his own self—his knowledge, abilities, skills, etc. Creation becomes self-creation. Marx says, "By thus acting on the external world and changing it, [man] at the same time changes his own nature. He develops his slumbering powers and compels them to act in obedience to his sway [1954, vol.I: 173]." This creative relationship to the world, typical of human kind, allows us to refer to man as *homo creator,* although this name gives only a partial account of human nature.

There is a second relationship equally characteristic of man—that of participation. It links him with his fellow human beings. As Ollman puts it: "Man's activity (work, creativity) must be done with and for others.... Consequently [man] is a social being [1975: 106]." And Kolakowski quotes Marx as saying, "Thanks only to his relationship with the individual Paul is the individual Peter able to relate to himself as a human being [1976: 322]." Marx, it should be noted, often emphasizes the equivalence of humanness and social existence. There is no man outside society; each man is bound to others by innumerable relationships of interdependence; and the social bond is constitutive of the human condition and human nature.

> Man is in the most literal sense of the word a *zōon politikon,* not only a social animal but an animal that can develop into an individual only in society. Production by isolated individuals outside society—something that might happen as an exception to a civilized man who by accident got into the wilderness and already dynamically possessed within himself the forces of society—is as great an absurdity as the idea of the development of language without individuals living together and talking to one another [Marx, 1955: 226–227].

Thus, another equally important side of man is expressed by the words *homo socius.*

The activity in which both aspects of human nature are revealed most completely, and which therefore may be conceived as a human "species activity" distinguishing a man from other animals is—as has already been emphasized—work, production, labor. "As individuals express their lives so they are. What they are, therefore, coincides with their production, both with what they produce and with how they produce [Marx and Engels, 1975: 61]." And in a different connection Marx says even more explicitly, "Man differs from the animal in that he produces [Marx and Engels, 1960, vol.I: 553]." In the productive process man appears as *homo creator:* "Labor is a positive, creative activity [1953: 507]." But he also appears as *homo socius:* "All production is the appropriation of nature by the individual within and through a certain form of society [1955: 230]." In productive activity Marx locates the universal aspects of human nature, since it epitomizes two fundamental relational properties of man: his creativity vis-a-vis the natural world, and his participation vis-a-vis the social world. As Marx emphasizes this universal character of human nature, "The work process ... is the everlasting nature-imposed condition of human existence, and therefore is independent of every social phase of that existence, or rather common to every such phase [1954, vol.I: 179]."

The Negative Image: A Theory of Alienation

There is no space here for a systematic account of Marx's theory of alienation (there is an ample literature on the subject [see, for instance, Schacht, 1970; Ollman, 1975; Schaff, 1965; Keshelava, 1977]), but some remarks are necessary to corroborate the positive image of man presented by Marx, and as outlined before, with his ideas on the pathology of human nature—the negative image of man he depicts in his studies of capitalism and, more generally, of class societies. Man is seen here as the antithesis of his "species nature," because of the inhuman structural conditions in which he finds himself, and as able to regain his humanity only by means of a total and radical transformation of social structure.

The condition of man in a capitalist or class-divided society is first of all characterized by a total loss of autonomy, a total lack of control over one's own actions. It is most typical in man's most important activity—work.

> His labor is not voluntary but compulsory, forced labor. . . . How alien it really is is quite evident from the fact that when there is no physical or other compulsion, labor is avoided like the plague. . . . The external character of labor for the worker shows itself in the fact that it is not his own but someone else's, that he does not belong to himself in his labor but to someone else. . . . It is an activity that is directed against himself, that is independent of him and does not belong to him [Marx and Engels, 1960, vol.I: 551].

Man abdicates control over the process of work as well as over the products of work: "The object he produces does not belong to him, it dominates him. . . . Alienation appears not only in the result but also in the process of production and the productive activity itself [1960, vol.I: 550]."

The second dimension of alienation is the dissociation of man and environment, with the growing subjugation of man to external environmental pressures. As Swingewood puts it, "Man becomes dominated by the world of things, by processes which his own activity has created [1975: 100]"—or, in the words of Marx, "Objects begin to rule the producers instead of being ruled by them [1960, vol.I: 548]."

The third aspect of alienation is the substantial reversal of the relationships binding men with the natural as well as the social milieu. Man is no longer creative. "Species life, productive life, procreative life, turns into a mere means of sustaining the worker's individual existence [Marx and

Engels, 1960, vol.I: 553]." And again: "The worker . . . does not confirm himself in his work; he denies himself, feels miserable instead of happy, expends no liberal physical and intellectual energy, but mortifies his body and ruins his mind [1960, vol.I: 550]." And he no longer participates in free cooperative associations; he becomes isolated, estranged from other people, and hostile to them—alienated from his fellow man. And so the human condition becomes inhuman. By reading Marx's powerful criticism of the fate of man in a class society, the same image of man and his nature as that encountered directly in his early philosophical writings reappears implicitly.

The Genetic Dimension:
The Origins of Human Faculties

So far, I have been concerned only with the actual aspect of human nature—the ways in which it is manifested vis-a-vis the environment in a single moment of time, in a timeless perspective. The rephrasing of the traditional autonomistic position in relational terms allowed us to reach a formulation that has been referred to as *new autonomism*. But Marx does not stop here. He introduces the second, genetic dimension to his considerations and asks not only how human nature manifests itself, but how it originated in the first place. This question has two distinct components. First, it inquires about the origins of the human propensity or faculty to be creative and to participate in a society. Second, it inquires about the origin of particular forms in which these properties or faculties are expressed. How is it that man is creative and socially oriented? How is it that he creates this and not that, and participates in these and not those social arrangements?

Marx's answer is rooted in the belief that human beings do not act in a vacuum. The field of their activities is doubly conditioned, or, to put it figuratively, closed in two directions—first, in the historical direction, by the whole past tradition, and, second, in the contemporary direction, by the whole actual situation.

The level of development reached by the faculties of creativeness and participation is conditioned by the historical process. All the properties of man prerequisite for exercising these faculties are historically shaped. This is true even of basic perceptive abilities: "The forming of the five senses is a labor of the entire history of the world down to the present [Marx and Engels, 1960, vol.I: 584]." Moreover, historical origins can be traced with respect to self-consciousness, foresight, decision-making ability, persistence, and other specifically human traits. This is true in both the philogenetic perspective, where the level reached by humanity is seen as historically conditioned, and in the ontogenetic perspective, where the level reached by an individual is experientially conditioned. Anyway, genetic factors determine what man is and what he can do.

But it is not only the level of human potential that is historically conditioned. The environment in which human action takes place is also to be treated as the outcome of a long historical process. It is true of the social environment, where a certain type of social organization (patterns, institutions, norms, values) is reached, and of the natural environment, which is mastered by man to a certain, specified degree. Man acts in the environment which he inherited. Thus not only what he can do but what can be done is historically conditioned.

At any moment man finds himself in a complex situation, in which both the level of his own potential for creating and participating and the natural and social circumstances in which he creates and participates are historically given. Man creates with his existing powers out of existing materials and within existing conditions, which he inherited. Man participates to the extent allowable by his existing abilities in the existing network of social relations, social organizations, social institutions. This historically inherited situation constitutes the immediate milieu of his action, opening a set of opportunities, and enforcing a set of limitations. As Ollman interprets Marx's position on this issue, "Man is always surrounded by factories, currency, implements, clothing, types of shelter, gods, prayers, moral codes, rules, laws, statutes, art, literature, philosophical ideas, scientific hypotheses, and forms of family life suited to what he has become, and he is constantly trying to fit them better to what he is becoming [1975: 97]." And in the words of Marx himself: "The productive forces are . . . the result of practical human energy; but this energy is itself conditioned by the circumstances in which men find themselves, by the productive forces already acquired, by the social form which exists before they do, which they do not create, which is the product of preceding generation [1949: 26]."

Placed in such a field of opportunities and limitations man loses his absolute, abstract autonomy. Within a genetic perspective he shows his passive aspect; he appears as a product rather than a producer. And from this perspective human nature cannot be treated as universal, but rather as historical. The universal dimension of human nature—man's creative and participating relationship with the environment—is supplemented by the historical dimension: the changing and developing modes of creation and participation. To the thesis of a *new autonomism,* formulated in the actual dimension, the thesis of a *new passivism,* formulated in the genetic dimension, is added.

Thus, all the components of the dialectical standpoint, which was analytically defined as *creativism,* are clearly illustrated by Marxian theory. Marx presents a coherent and complex image in which man is seen neither as absolutely autonomous nor as absolutely passive, but rather as a subject and an object simultaneously, and his nature is seen as neither absolutely universal nor absolutely historical, but universal and historical at the same time. This aspect of dialectics, which signifies "the active interplay between subject and object ... whereby an individual acts upon the world at the same time as the world acts upon him [Giddens, 1971: 210]," is clearly perceived by Marx himself, as well as by Marxists. Emphasizing the autonomous dimension as against the abolutization of passivism, Marx says: "The materialist doctrine that men are products of circumstances and upbringing, and that, therefore, changed men are products of other circumstances and changed upbringing, forgets that it is men that change circumstances and that the educator himself needs educating [Marx and Engels, 1968: 28]." Emphasizing the passive dimension, as against the absolutization of autonomism, Lenin says: "The goal is to reject the infantile and naive, purely mechanistic views of historical subjectivists, who satisfy themselves with the empty claim that history is made by living individuals, and forget to analyze which social situations, and in which ways, condition the conduct of those individuals [1951, vol.I: 445]." Combining these two emphases Topolski claims, "The most characteristic feature and the basic norm of Marxian Dialectics is such an interpretation of external (objective) determinants of human activity as does not eliminate the activistic dimension . . . i.e., makes man a real creator [1974: 319]."

In Marxian theory, the one-sidedness of both traditional approaches to man was overcome. The dilemma of autonomism and passivism was shown to be spurious and misleading, and in its place an alternative, dialectical standpoint was suggested, which gave a more adequate, more realistic, multidimensional picture of man, as a member of society.

CHAPTER 7

Society as a Whole
or as an Aggregate:
Collectivism, Individualism,
Structuralism

Society was born as a science when a new domain of reality began to be consciously perceived—a new domain of facts that had not been studied by any existing scientific discipline. This domain consisted of human collectivities, from the smallest groups to the most inclusive societies. And immediately a crucial question had to be posed: What is the nature of such collectivities, and particularly what is their ontological status vis-a-vis human individuals, who constitute their ultimate parts?

This question has been raised time and again in the history of sociology and is still one of the most vital concerns for theoretically oriented sociologists. Abel is correct that "the mode of existence of collectivities, groups, societies, organizations and so forth is a major concern for sociological theory. The issue is still unresolved [1970: 29]." And some authors do not hesitate to define this problem as the most fundamental one for scientific sociology. Nadel identifies "the focus of sociology and its perpetual problem" as "the relation of the social order and the individual being, the relation of the unit and the whole [1957: 401]." Martindale claims that "there are no more basic problems to men attempting to account for themselves and for their social world than the comparative significance to be assigned to the individual and to the collective [1964: 461]."

Naturally enough, the question "Do the collectivities really exist or not?" gave birth to opposite answers. The affirmative answer, ascribing some specific mode of existence to social entities, and treating them as some reality sui generis, was opposed to the negative answer, refusing any distinct mode of existence to social entities, and resolving them completely into the participating individuals. Those were the typical, extreme solutions organizing the field of the dispute. "No orientations to the problems of existence are more fundamental than those which take the individual as primary (individualism) and those which take the collective as primary (collectivism) [Martindale, 1964: 453]."

In this discussion I shall retain the designations introduced by Martindale, *collectivism* and *individualism*. But one must be aware that the dispute is often labeled differently: For example, Ginsberg speaks of "holistic" versus "compositive" standpoints (1968: 56–70); Sorokin (1966) as well as Cohen (1968) of "holistic" versus "atomistic" assumptions; Gellner (1969) counterpoises "holism" and "individualism"; some other authors speak of "collectivistic" as opposed to "elementaristic approaches"—and so on. Despite the terminological variety, the meanings assigned to the competing assumptions are more or less similar. Before I give systematic explication of those meanings, let me present a brief overview of representative statements made in the dispute by the sociological classics. I shall start with the spokesmen for collectivism.

THE COLLECTIVISTIC TRADITION

It is not accidental that the collectivistic standpoint should prevail among the founders of sociology. Struggling for the establishment of the new discipline, they could not afford any misgivings about its specific subject matter and its independent existence. They had to affirm the domain of social phenomena and processes as real, separate, and worthy of painstaking study.

Auguste Comte: The Societal Consensus

Auguste Comte considered sociology a necessary extension of the order of sciences. The main justification for that necessity was seen in the objective existence of a distinctive level of facts not studied in any adequate fashion by any other discipline. Social facts were defined by reference to specific social wholes, or social organisms. Studying the elements of such organisms (which is the province of biology or psychology, or more generally, the "analytic" disciplines) is not sufficient.

> There can be no scientific study of society, either in its conditions or its movements, if it is separated into portions and its divisions are studied apart. The methodical division of studies which takes place in the simple inorganic sciences is thoroughly irrational in the recent and complex science of society. . . . It is no easy matter to study social phenomena in the only right way—viewing each element in the light of the whole system [1966: 158].

And this methodological prescription is rooted in an ontological claim: "Society is no more decomposable into individuals than a geometric surface is into lines, or a line into points [quoted in Lukes, 1968: 119]." To cite an appraisal of this aspect of Comte's sociology given by a contemporary commentator: "For Comte a society was a system of interconnected parts. This system was something more than, something other than, the individuals within it, and therefore it required special study [Fletcher, 1971, vol.I: 177]."

The assertion of a distinct existence of social wholes was coupled with the assertion of the causal priority of a whole over its parts. One of the fundamental assumptions of Comte's social "statics" is the belief that the components of society are bound together by some form of a "universal consensus"; they fit together in some regular, nonrandom fashion. Each component derives some of its fundamental properties from the position it has within the consensus of a whole, from the function it plays within it. As a contemporary authority on Comte puts it: "If we transpose the idea of the primacy of entity over element into sociology, we find that it is impossible to understand the state of a particular social phenomena unless we restore it to its social context. We do not understand the state of religion, or the exact form assumed by the state in a particular society, unless we consider that society as a whole [Aron, 1968, vol.I: 77]."

Both ideas together—the belief in the specific nature of the social systems, and the belief in the significance of placement within the system for the properties of the components—make up the earliest formulation of the collectivist standpoint. For this reason, some commentators consider Comte as the founder of organicism (e.g., Martindale, 1960; Timasheff, 1967), or even functionalism (e.g., Fletcher, 1971; Aron, 1968)—two later theoretical developments that pushed the collectivistic position to an extreme.

Herbert Spencer: The Social Organism

Herbert Spencer expands the systemic view of society by an application of his organic analogy. He meticulously discusses the respects in which society is similar, and the respects in which it is dissimilar, to a biological organism. The main points of the analogy address those properties of society that define it as specific whole, such as the internal differentiation of structures, the corresponding differentiation of functions among the components, and the persistence of the totalities despite the turnover of elements. "We consistently regard a society as an entity, because, though formed of discrete units, a certain concreteness in the aggregate of them is implied by the general persistence of the arrangements among them throughout the area occupied. And it is this trait which yields our idea of a society [Spencer, 1893, vol.I: 436]." A methodological directive follows as a corollary: "We have to consider the inter-dependence of structures, and functions, and products, taken in their totality. . . . The highest achievement in sociology is so to grasp the vast heterogenous aggregate, as to see how the character of each group at each stage is determined partly by its own antecedents, and partly by the past and present actions of the rest upon it [quoted in Fletcher, 1971, vol.I: 274]."

Thus, acknowledging the existence of social systems as a specific type of reality with determinate attributes, and in this respect closely following Comte, Spencer nonetheless rejected any claims as to the primacy of social wholes over individuals. Quite the reverse; both in the genetic dimension and in the ethical dimension, he professed an individualistic orientation. Forms of social organization evolve out of the union of individual human beings guided by utilitarian considerations, and reflecting the inherent properties of human nature. "Living together arose because, on the average, it proved more advantageous to each than living apart [Spencer, 1893, vol.I: 134]." Owing to such an origin, societal forms must be treated as instrumental for the needs and requirements of the members of a society, serving the interests of the participating individuals. As Fletcher reads this claim: "Societies did not exist independently of individuals; they did not obliterate individuals; they did not compound individuals into some new metaphysical 'collective entity'; but they were systems of institutions which were something more than, and other than individuals, possessing clearly discernible attributes [1971, vol I.: 335]."

Emile Durkheim: Collective Representations

The collectivistic standpoint is most clearly, forcefully, and consistently defended in the sociological works of Emile Durkheim. He claims: "A whole is not identical with the sum of its parts. It is something new, and all its properties differ from those displayed by the parts of which it is composed [in Aron, 1968, vol. II: 78]." And also: "Whenever certain elements combine, and thereby produce, by the fact of their combination, new phenomena, it is plain that these new phenomena reside not in the original elements but in the totality formed by their union [Durkheim, 1962: xlvii]." This general idea is translated into the field of sociology:

> Society has for its substratum the mass of associated individuals. The system which they form by uniting together, and which varies according to their geographical disposition and the nature and number of their channels of communication, is the base from which social life is raised. The representations which form the network of social life arise from the relations between the individuals thus combined.... Collective representations, produced by the action and reaction between individual minds that form a society, do not derive directly from the latter, and consequently surpass them [1953: 24-25].

Social facts, which are best illustrated by such phenomena as customs, laws, mores, traditions, and religious beliefs, are characterized by their externality with respect to the individual who encounters them, by their constraining power as experienced by individuals in all spheres of life, and by their wide dispersion among populations. The locus of social facts, which are superindividual, distinct from any beliefs or actions of individual people, is for Durkheim in the sphere of social consciousness.

The extremeness of his position may be seen in the fact that he endows the level of collective, superindividual social facts with independent causal potential, and postulates the existence of cause-and-effect relations directly among the social facts, at their specific level, without the mediation of acting individuals. Some commentators perceive here a grave danger of reification, or "misplaced concreteness":

> He went to the extreme of maintaining that "social facts" existed as "things" in their own right; that they were interlinked by cause and effect relations in the "social system" as an entirety; and that they, and changes in them, could only be explained in terms of other "social facts"—and not in terms of the conscious action of the individual members of society" [Fletcher, 1971, vol.II: 258-259].

Also, an extremeness of form is to be seen in the doctrine of the social determination of individual actions and beliefs. The "social mold" theory is presented without qualification: Man is seen as the product of society, totally shaped by the impact of social facts or social, superindividual, and external forces.

Thus with Durkheim collectivism reaches its apogee. To summarize Durkheim's collectivistic position in the words of a contemporary commentator: "Durkheim saw society as the fundamental reality, with individuals sociologically discoverable largely as personifications of society's roles, statuses, and norms. . . . He was radical in his unrelenting opposition to the whole view of the individual and society that was in Durkheim's time so largely current. Durkheim rejected individualism on every possible ground [Nisbet, 1974: 15]."

THE INDIVIDUALISTIC TRADITION

But the collectivist standpoint was by no means the only one, even in the nineteenth century. What follows are examples of its opposite—the individualistic position.

John S. Mill: Society as a Cluster of Acting Individuals

The idea of society suggested by John S. Mill may be considered as a complete negation of collectivism and of all the major elements of the collectivist image. First, at the most general level, Mill rejects any notion of emergent, qualitatively new results of complex interhuman associations: "The effect produced in social phenomena by any complex set of circumstances amounts precisely to the sum of the effects of the circumstances taken singly [Mill, 1884: 583]." Second, Mill claims quite explicitly that there is nothing in society but individuals and their activities:

> All phenomena of society are phenomena of human nature generated by the action of outward circumstances upon masses of human beings. . . . Men in a state of society are still men. Their actions and passions are obedient to the laws of individual human nature. Men are not, when brought together, converted into another kind of substance with different properties, as hydrogen and oxygen are different from water [Mill, 1884: 572–573].

Third, Mill rejects any suggestion as to a reciprocal causal influence between one social phenomenon and another. As Fletcher observes:

> What he was particularly concerned to make clear beyond doubt . . . is that these elements of social organization cannot, by any stretch of imagination or any stretch of scientific methodology, be conceived as having cause-and-effect relationships between each other as self-existent entities. If a change in one of these institutions is followed by changes in other institutions, it is not that it has caused them. . . . It can only be because the first change has been mediated through the experience and action of people in such a way as to bring about the subsequent changes [1971, vol.I: 214].

Max Weber: The Focus on Social Actions

Max Weber's individualistic orientation is quite obvious both in his negative, critical comments directed against the collectivistic approach and in his own positive program of scientific sociology.

> It is the method of the so-called "organic" school of sociology to attempt to understand social interaction by using as a point of departure the "whole" within which the individual acts. . . . This functional frame of reference is convenient for the purposes of practical illustration and for provisional orientation. . . . But at the same time if its cognitive value is overestimated and its concepts illegitimately "reified," it can be highly dangerous [Weber, 1947: 102].

And in another connection he is still more straightforward in his criticism: "If I am now a sociologist . . . I am so essentially in order to put an end to the use of collective concepts, a use which still haunts us. In other words, even sociology can only start from the action of one or a few, or many individuals; i.e., pursue a strictly 'individualistic' method [quoted in Frisby, 1976: xiii]."

This critical attitude toward all forms of collectivism is consistent with Weber's own image of sociology as "a science which attempts the interpretive understanding of social action in order thereby to arrive at a causal explanation of its course and effects [1947: 88]." All social phenomena, including wide social wholes—social relationships, associations, institutions, and groups—are seen as completely resolvable into complex networks of social actions. These collectivities are "solely the resultants and modes of organization of the specific acts of individual men, since these alone are for us the agents who carry out subjectively understandable action [Weber, 1968, vol.I: 13]." And the focus of sociology is precisely the interpretative understanding of such actions, revealing their subjective (motivational) and cultural (normative) meaning.

MacRae gives a good summary of Weber's standpoint on this issue: "Social action is the basic unit of the social, the atom, ultimately irreducible, a tiny impenetrable essence. The atomic unit of the social is the single deliberate action of an individual directed to affecting the behavior of one or more other persons. . . . Society is the sum of unit social acts [1974: 68]."

Georg Simmel: Society as the Web of Interactions

Simmel rejected the collectivistic view of society as an organism or a system. In his own perspective "society is merely the name for a number of individuals, connected by interaction [Simmel, 1950: 10]." And further: "Society exists where a number of individuals enter into interaction [1971:

23]." There is nothing more and nothing else in society than human individuals. But the crucial aspect distinguishing the sum of individuals from a society is the set of interpersonal relationships. "The energy effects of atoms upon each other bring matter into innumerable forms which we see as 'things.' Just so the impulses and interests which a man experiences in himself and which push him out toward other men bring about all the forms of association by which a mere sum of separate individuals are made into a 'society' [1971: 127–128]." This point is developed more extensively in a different connection, or from a different perspective. Man, Simmel believes, has an inherent tendency "to live with other men, to act for them, with them, against them, and thus to correlate his condition with theirs. . . . The significance of these interactions among men lies in the fact that it is because of them that the individuals, in whom these driving impulses and purposes are lodged, form a unity, that is a society [1971: 23–24]." This image of society as a network of interpersonal relationships entails a specific model of sociology as the study of those typical forms in which the relationships usually appear: "If, therefore, there is to be a science whose subject matter is society and nothing else, it must exclusively investigate these interactions, these kinds and forms of sociation [1971: 25]." And still more explicitly: "If society is conceived as interation among individuals, the description of the forms of this interaction is the task of the science of society in its strictest and most essential sense [1950: 21–22]."

Abel gives this summary of Simmel's perspective: "Society is not a substance but an event. It consists of processes, and it is the sum of these processes. . . . Society is the sum of those forms of relationships by virtue of which individuals are transformed into a society [1970: 79]." It must be emphasized that Simmel's solution to the problem of the nature of society is far from the extremes of traditional individualism. His moderate position comes closest to contemporary theoretical attempts to overcome the ontological problem by the introduction of the notion of a social structure.

COLLECTIVISM AND INDIVIDUALISM IN CONTEMPORARY SOCIOLOGY

The dispute of collectivism and individualism is by no means outdated. It is still a significant controversy, providing a touchstone for the classification of contemporary sociological theories.

Systemic Models in Structural Functionalism

The school of modern sociology most clearly associated with the collectivist view of society is the structural–functional school. The subject matter of sociological study is here conceived as a specific system, or a whole. Let us review some typical statements of representative structural functionalists. Radcliffe-Brown has written: "If functionalism means anything at all, it does mean the attempt to see the social life of a people as a whole, as a functional unity [1935: 634]." For Bronislav Malinowski, the proper subject of anthropological study is culture. And defining culture he remarks: "Culture is a reality sui generis and must be studied as such. . . . Culture is a well-organized unity [1934, vol.III: 623]." In a later work Malinowski emphasizes the same point: "Culture is an integral whole. . . . It is a system of objects, actions, and attitudes in which all parts are means for a goal [1969: 36, 150]." Merton, a notable adherent of the structural–functional perspective, has described the central orientation of functionalism as "the practice of interpreting data by establishing their consequences for the larger structures in which they are implicated [1957: 46–47]." And Parsons is equally explicit on this point: "The most essential condition of successful dynamic analysis is continual and systematic reference of every problem to the state of the system as a whole [1964: 216]."

Many adherents of the functionalist tradition share the same fundamental orientation—a view of social life as incorporated in systems. Their concrete definitions of a social system differ to a large extent. In fact, at least five varieties of system models can be distinguished within the functionalist school: the model of a simple system, the model of a teleological system, the model of a functional system, the model of a purposeful system, and the model of a multiple system (see Sztompka, 1974). But in spite of all the differences, society is always conceived as an entity that is not decomposable into elements (human individuals, social actions, roles, etc.). It has some specific properties as a whole—"functional requirements," "functional imperatives," or "functional prerequisites" that must be fulfilled. And it is characterized by specific processes, or mechanisms, of a compensatory or regulatory nature that safeguard the fulfillment of those requirements and the preservation of internal order or equilibrium. Thus, the most characteristic, essential feature of functionalism is its focus on social wholes.

The Implicit Systemic Image in Conflict Theory

It is well known that modern conflict theory arose from conscious opposition to functionalism. It was destined to provide an alternative view of society in which a focus on stability, harmony, and consensus is replaced by a focus on change, conflict, and constraint (Dahrendorf, 1968: 128). But the fundamental image of a social system as a specific whole is retained. It is a systemic whole which undergoes changes, it is a systemic whole which is ridden by internal conflicts, and it is within a systemic whole that some constraints are exercised over some of the elements or subsystems by other elements or subsystems.

In a comprehensive study of contemporary conflict theory Mucha claims that both the functionalist and conflict models of society share the same perspective: "Both consider the society in systemic terms [1978: 71]." This is true even if some of them explicitly reject the term *system,* substituting other terms; for example, *"imperatively coordinated associations"* (Dahrendorf, 1959). But according to Mucha, it is obviously even more true of those proponents of conflict models of society who apply directly both the systemic analysis and the theoretical category of the system. He considers the representatives of this tendency to include Coser, Dahl, Gluckman, Rex (Mucha, 1978: 72).

Modern Systems Theory

A collectivistic, systemic image of society is also characteristic of those theories that attempt to apply notions developed within the so-called General Systems Theory (GST), cybernetics, information theory, etc., to the field of sociology. The main ambition of those working in this direction is to extend the notion of a social system beyond the limitations of traditional functionalism. Buckley is a well-known spokesman for this tendency: "I have been concerned about the possibility that the now standard use of the notion of 'social system'—derived principally from equilibrium and organismic models—is deluding us into believing that we have been using modern systems theory for some time [1967: vii]."[1] He expresses "a feeling of the inadequacies of the mechanical-equilibrium and organismic models, as well as a belief that modern systems research can provide the basis of a framework more capable of doing justice to the complexities and dynamic properties of the sociocultural systems [Buckley, 1967: vii]." The traditional mechanical and organic system models are rejected, and the so-called complex-adaptive or morphogenetic model introduced in their place. It describes systems which "rather than minimize organization, or preserve a given fixed structure..., typically create, elaborate, or change structure as a prerequisite to remain viable, as ongoing systems [Buckley, 1967: 5]."

Thus, we encounter a situation similar to the opposition of functionalism and conflict theory. The concrete content of the system—its properties, typical processes, etc.—are viewed in a different fashion, but at the same

---

[1]This and all subsequent quotes cited to Buckley, 1967, are from W. Buckley, *Sociology and Modern Systems Theory,* © 1967. Reprinted by permission of Prentice-Hall, Inc., Englewood Cliffs, New Jersey.

time, the generalized image of a system is retained and society is viewed as an organized, complex entity sui generis, "a kind of whole with some degree of continuity and boundary [Buckley, 1967: 41]."

These are some selected illustrations of modern approaches assuming a collectivistic standpoint. We shall now consider some schools radically departing from collectivism, and assuming the individualistic position.

The Individualistic Focus in Early Exchange Theory

The most persuasive spokesman for individualistically oriented sociology is the founder of the so-called "exchange school"—Geoge C. Homans. For him "the ultimate units of social behavior are men and their actions [1967: 62]." Everything else is resolvable into human actions and their more or less complex configurations. To reiterate from Chapter 2, "The characteristics of social groups and societies are the resultants, no doubt the complicated resultants but still the resultants, of the interaction between individuals over time—and they are no more than that [Homans, 1974: 12]." The wholes, systems, etc., are just short-hand denominations devised by common sense to deal with the complexity and multiplicity of elementary phenomena. "Human institutions and human societies often appear so well established and so powerful that they dominate individual men and escape human control altogether. . . . It is not true that these monsters consist of the actions of men and something more. They are the actions of men; they can be analyzed into individual actions with nothing left over [1973: 551]."

Consequently, sociological theory must focus on elementary social behavior and the networks of interpersonal exchanges, because here all the fundamental laws and principles of society are to be discovered. This program is persistently realized in Homan's works. In the appraisal of Mulkay, "Homans' theoretical strategy has entailed a withdrawal from sociology's long-standing interest in the institutional structure of societies, in favour of a consideration of relatively minor behavioral variations within small groups [1971: 177]."

An Act as a Component of Society
in Symbolic Interactionism

In the view of symbolic interactionists, society is nothing more than a complex network of human acts, adjusted or fitted together in multiple ways. It has no independent or separate existence of its own. As Blumer puts it, "The essence of society lies in an ongoing process of action, not in a posited structure of relations [1966: 240]." The simplest molecule out of which society is built is known as a "social act" or a "joint action." As

Blumer defines it: "It refers to the larger collective form of action that is constituted by the fitting together of the lines of behavior of the separate participants. . . . Everywhere we look in a human society we see people engaging in forms of joint action. Indeed the totality of such instances—in all of their multitudinous variety, their variable connections, and their complex networks—constitutes the life of a society [1966: 239]." The individualistic image of society is still more explicit in this remark: "A society is seen as people meeting the varieties of situations that are thrust on them by their conditions of life. These situations are met by working out joint actions in which participants have to align their acts to one another [1966: 241]."

Skidmore gives an apt summary of Blumer's ideas, seeing them as derived directly from the tradition of George H. Mead: "Society is best conceived of as a vast series of individual selves fitting together their individual lines of action. This means that the symbolic interactionist does not imagine persons as being caught up in social structures at all. They are not participating in something they do not make for themselves, even though the resultant actions may become habitual and what other sociologists could call structured [Skidmore, 1975b: 226]." The study of an internal structure of a single act—its anatomy and its dynamics ("career")—becomes the main preoccupation of the symbolic interactionists.

Having reviewed representative statements of the collectivistic and individualistic positions, as they are encountered in past as well as contemporary sociological theory, we shall now attempt to clarify the dispute.

WHAT THE DISPUTE IS REALLY ABOUT: AN EXPLICATION

We begin the discussion from the negative side, and shall attempt to eliminate the misunderstandings and misleading formulations in respect of the relevant issues, and so attempt to answer the question "What is the dispute of collectivism and individualism not about?"

What the Dispute Is Not About

The most pervasive ambiguity in philosophical appraisals of the dispute has to do with the distinction between its methodological and ontological aspects. Sometimes the problem is discussed as a methodological one, dealing with the proper procedures of concept formation and theory construction in the social sciences. In such a discussion the issue of the character of social concepts and social laws is raised. Some claim that social concepts can be defined by means of nonsocial ones (those referring to individuals, their activities, motivations, intentions, dispositions, etc.). Others reject such a possibility and ascribe independent methodological status to both social concepts and social laws. (These positions were discussed in Chapter 3, in connection with reductionisim and antireductionism.) It is certainly a significant issue, but it should be discussed separately and not confused with the ontological problem of the inherent characteristics of the objects and processes studied by the social sciences. And this is precisely what is referred to here as the dilemma of individualism and collectivism.

Thus the dispute as construed in this chapter is neither about the definability or indefinability of social concepts in terms of individual ones, nor about the reducibility or irreducibility of social laws to individual ones. Looked at from a different perspective, it is not concerned with the proper strategy of explanation in social science, the ultimate character of explanatory principles adduced in the explanations, whether they are social or "psychological."

By the same token, the dispute as defined here does not refer to the problem of verification. It is true that the present techniques of social-scientific research are mainly attuned to the observation of individuals and their activities, and not to the direct study of social wholes. But, first of all, it is not in principle impossible to conceive of some new techniques in the future as would allow immediate observation of social entities, and not merely of their constitutive components. And even now, it is a matter of degree: "Many features of social phenomena are observable (procedure of the court), while many features of individuals are not (e.g., intentions) [Lukes, 1968: 122]." But second, and most significantly, the factual limitations of research techniques have nothing to do with the question of the existence or nonexistence of certain phenomena, processes, or objects.

So far, three misunderstandings have been eliminated—those that have originated in improper slips from the methodological to the ontological domain: The first identified the issue of individualism versus collectivism with the problem of the definitional reduction of concepts; the second with the problem of the explanatory reduction of laws; and the third with the problem of verificational procedures typical of the social sciences.

The next two misunderstandings stem from defining the issue of individualism and collectivism in axiological terms. The ontological problem is here mistakenly identified with the ethical or political problem. Thus, the fourth misunderstanding is encountered when both ontological positions are treated as ethical or ideological creeds. This mistake is well illustrated by Martindale, who defines the one possible meaning of the relevant terms thus:

> Individualism is an ideology which maintains that the person is the highest of all values and the vindication of a society is to be found in its assistance in the maximum unfolding of the individual's potential. Collectivism is an

ideology which maintains that the highest of all values is the society (and the peace and harmony it guarantees). While individuals are important, they are second to the community, for without the community the individual is insignificant [1964: 461].

The immediate corollary constitutes the fifth misunderstanding: the identification of the dispute of individualism and collectivism with the battle of political doctrines, liberal and totalitarian. A characterization of this position can be found in Martindale: "Individualism leads naturally to the assumption that society and institutions are instrumental—institutions are made for people, not people for institutions. Collectivism leads naturally to the position that internal peace is the highest of all values, without which chaos only ensues.... People must order their behavior to the priority of the community [1964: 461]."

The significance of ideological or political questions is not to be discounted, but they must not be treated as synonymous with ontological questions. If they are not rigorously distinguished, the arguments from one domain can easily be mustered to defend the claims referring to the other domain. For example, liberal policies may be justified by some individualistic ontology (or a collectivistic ontology rejected on the basis of its possible totalitarian implications). This is a dangerous and certainly an unscientific practice.

Three other misleading characterizations of the dispute to be eliminated from further discussion may be grouped under the heading *psychological*.

Some authors treat the terms *individualism* and *collectivism* as referring to prevailing attitudes or motivational tendencies of a population. For example, this usage is sometimes ascribed to de Tocqueville, for whom *individualism* designated the tendency of the typical American "to draw apart from his fellow-creatures and to leave society at large to itself." Ginsberg clarifies this usage: "Under this term, and under the parallel terms 'particularism' or 'subjectivism,' are included a number of traits or qualities such as a tendency to turn inwards, a desire for independence or for freedom from external constraint, distinctiveness in self-expression, passing into self-will and self-absorption [1968: 57]." *Collectivism,* then, would signify opposite personality traits. The irrelevance of this usage to our concerns here is evident.

For other authors, the issue of individualism and collectivism revolves around the characteristics of common-sense perception. They discuss the occurrence of so-called "collectivistic" or "holistic" concepts in social consciousness. The fact that people commonly think and speak of nations, classes, armies, civilizations, is taken as supportive of the claim that such entities exist in some independent ontological fashion. Of course, it may be argued that social consciousness and language reflect some real, objective traits of social reality. But the argument is weak; one notes the multiplicity of concepts referring to supernatural entities, deities, mythological beings, etc., in the languages of all known human cultures. Moreover, even if the argument is seriously considered, it is still only an argument and should not be confounded with the matter it is supposed to substantiate. The dispute of collectivism versus individualism is not about the nature of social consciousness or linguistic habits, but about the nature of objective social reality.

And finally, some authors focus attention on the objects or goals toward which individuals or collectivities strive, and raise the problem of so-called "group goals" or "group interests." For example, according to Agassi: "The major question to which holism gives rise concerns the relation between the distinct interests of the group and those of the individuals belonging to it [1973: 190]." But the question is not whether some group interest can be computed by votes or polls. The question is whether groups per se possess some interests not derivable from or reducible to the interests of individuals. Collectivists would ascribe such independent goals or interests to groups or institutions, or societies; individualists would claim that "institutions do not have aims—only individuals have aims, interests, needs, intentions, or make decisions [Wisdom, 1970: 272]." Agassi considers it "the central thesis of individualism" that "only individuals have aims and responsibilities [1973: 189]." Again, this may be an important problem, but it has no connection with the ontological problem considered here.

The Focus of the Dispute: The Status of Superindividual Entities

What is the meaning of the dispute if it is interpreted exclusively in ontological terms? What sort of fundamental properties of social objects is at stake? The following remarks of Sorokin express the essential difference between the two standpoints:

> The proponents of singularistic–atomistic theories often do not see the forest for the trees. More exactly, their attention is given mainly to the trees, that is, to individuals, and much less, if at all, to the forest, or the total society, and to its ecological formations.... The systemic theories see the forest as a unified ecosystem and study its trees as interdependent parts or components of the forest as a whole. In their opinion, the forest has a reality, properties and functions quite different from those of the sum of its singularistic trees [1966: 37, 133].

And now, some more serious definitions of the respective positions, phrased in ontological parlance. Ginsberg defines sociological individualism as "the theory that society is to be conceived as an aggregate of individuals whose relations to each other are purely external [1968: 58]." Danto construes the typical standpoint of individualism as "insisting that, in the social world, only human individuals are real, and superhuman or social individuals, are not. . . . Individuals are the only members of the social world [1973: 315]." A similar claim is put forward by Lukes: "In the social world only individuals are real. . . . Social phenomena are constructions of the mind and do not exist in reality [1968: 122]." Sorokin gives a somewhat more extensive description of individualist positions: "They claim also that, ontologically, any social group is the mere sum of its interacting members and apart from them does not have any reality of its own. . . . Society is an aggregate of singularistic or separate individuals and their social actions, behind and beyond which there is no ontological entity called society [1966: 37]." A somewhat different emphasis is apparent in Wisdom who points out that "in the extreme form of individualism, society is a mode of individual operations and partakes of no independent power [1970: 272]." This aspect seems also to be crucial for Watkins, who believes that "no social tendency is somehow imposed on human beings from above (or from below)—social tendencies are the product (usually undesigned) of human characteristics and activities and situations, of people's ignorance and laziness as well as of their knowledge and ambition [1957: 271–272]."

And now some of the characteristic formulations of the collectivist standpoint. Referring to social wholes by the term *superhuman individuals* Danto claims that "though they may be said to contain human beings amongst their parts, nonetheless they are not wholly to be identified with these parts, and enjoy, so to speak, a life of their own [1973: 313]." Such a claim for the existence of superhuman individuals is here conceived as the essence of collectivism. Almost the same characterization is given by Brodbeck, who uses the term *holism* instead of *collectivism*. "It is called 'holism' because its proponents generally maintain that there are so-called wholes, group entities which have undefinable properties of their own [1969a: 283]." In a more elaborate characterization of Sorokin:

> In the sociocultural world, these thories stress a profound difference between unified sociocultural wholes, and a mere assemblage of individuals and of a singularistic conglomeration of sociocultural facts and events. . . . The organized social groups (social systems) or cultural systems have a reality sui generis, and in their structures, properties and behavior display most significant differences from those of a mere sum of their unassembled and unintegrated components [1966: 133]."

Another aspect is touched on by Addis: "The sociological variables form a closed system, i.e., there is a process among the sociological variables alone, . . . psychological variables, e.g., individual choices and items of behavior are irrelevant to the social process. . . . The social process is causally independent of human direction [1969: 322]." And a similar point is again emphasized by Wisdom: "In the extreme form of what, following Gellner, we may best call holism, societal power overrides individuals who have no share of it [1970: 272]."

Now, let me clarify and single out the main dimensions of the dispute. Obviously the issue is about the ontological status of those entities appearing in the domain of social studies that are different from the individual human beings, or, in brief, about the status of superindividual entities like groups, classes, collectivities, crowds, nations, cultures, civilizations, societies, etc. The existence of such entities is problematic, mainly because they are not directly observable. The situation is in some respects the obverse of that of physics; there the objects of the macroscale are directly perceived, and the components at the microlevel are not. The second becomes therefore problematic and the issue of the ontological status of atoms, molecules, etc., is raised. In sociology, the objects at the macrolevel are not directly perceived, whereas the microscale components—human individuals, their activities—certainly are. This time, the first becomes problematic, and the issue of the ontological status of groups, collectivities, social wholes is raised. So the question is addressed to the social wholes. But what is the content of the question?

Ideal–Typical Formulations of the Respective Positions

Two components of the question may be distinguished. The first is the aspect of existence. Do the social wholes really exist, or, more precisely, do they constitute a separate ontological category from the category of human individuals and their actions? The second is the aspect of causality. Are the social wholes causally effective agents? Note that a positive answer to the question dealing with causality presupposes a positive answer to the question of existence. Something that does not exist cannot partake in the causal sequence, or exert independent influence on something else. But the reverse relationship does not hold. Causal effectiveness is only one possible index of objective existence.

The distinction of the existential and causal aspects of the problem is only the first approximation. Let us probe a little deeper. The claim of existence entails several more specific assertions: first, that a social whole possesses a certain uniqueness with respect to other social wholes; it is externally distinguishable from them by means of a specified boundary ("it is a social individual"); second, that a social whole possesses a certain unity; it is a real entity internally integrated to the extent that it operates as a going concern, and undergoes changes as a totality ("has a life of its own," "changes in togetherness"); third, that a social whole possesses a certain autonomy with respect to its parts; it has properties, functions, characteristic processes that cannot be meaningfully predicated of the parts ("is a reality sui generis"); fourth, that a social whole possesses a certain continuity despite the turnover of parts; it is perceived as a whole even though all the elements have undergone changes ("sameness in spite of a change of its parts," "independent fate as a whole").

In a similar vein, the claim of causality can also be dissected into at least two more specific assertions: first, that a social whole is causally effective with respect to the other social wholes (i.e., that there exists a causal process among social wholes not mediated by the level of individual actions); second, that a social whole is causally effective with respect to its parts (it exerts some independent power, influence, or determining impact on the individuals who are its members).

Now, the collectivistic standpoint may be defined as the acceptance of all those claims, and the individualistic standpoint by their rejection, coupled with a defense of the opposite claims, Thus, the model formulation of collectivism will read thus: Social wholes (groups, collectivities, societies, cultures, civilizations, etc.) do really exist and act as causal agents; that is, they are distinguishable from other social wholes, are internally integrated or unified, are at least partly autonomous with respect to their elements, preserve some continuity independently of the fate of these elements, and exert causal influence on other social wholes and on their own components. And the model formulation of individualism will read thus: So-called social wholes do not have independent existence or causal potential; that is, they are just fluid aggregates (or congeries or clusters) of human individuals (or their activities), overlapping with other similar aggregates, additive in nature, lacking any separate properties other than those statistically computed of the properties of individuals, devoid of any continuity over and above the fates of individuals, causally connected only via the activities of individuals, and possessing no independent power over those individuals.

These are the ideal-typical, extreme, analytically pure formulations of the respective theoretical standpoints. In theoretical practice they are never phrased in such a pure fashion. Some authors emphasize existential aspects, some causal aspects, some even more specific fragmentary dimensions. Also, they formulate their claims in stronger or weaker ways. And almost all combine ontological considerations with some of the methodological points (treated in my discussion of reductionism). At the price of a certain abstractness, the analytic explication provided here has one significant asset: It allows one to approach the dialectic solution to the dispute—namely, the alternative standpoint—combining some insights of collectivism and individualism, but being identical with neither. This solution is our next concern.

STRUCTURALISM AS
A DIALECTICAL SOLUTION

From the Substantial to the Structural Emphasis

The question of the ontological status of social wholes was most often put thus: "Is a society a distinct substance—a specific substratum, a new type of reality, a particular sort of being?" The collectivists answered in the affirmative, the individualists in the negative. But with opposite answers both joined together in a common search—a search for some specific social substance, a social reality sui generis. But the same question can be put in a different way: "Is a society a distinct structure—a new type of organization, a new network of relationships?"

The switch from a substantive to a structural focus is generally characteristic of modern science. In several domains of knowledge the properties and regularities of the objects studied are found to originate not so much in the inherent character of the materials or substratum out of which those objects are built, but rather in the arrangement or organization of components. And conversely, the properties and regularities of components are derived from their position within wider, more comprehensive networks of relationships—the external structure. Some authors believe that such an approach issues in a most significant transformation in scientific thinking, and label it the *structuralist revolution.* It probably started with Wittgenstein's (1953) claim that the scientist should pay attention to the network, the geometry of arrangement, and not to the characteristics of the things the network encompasses. The idea was advanced by von Bertalanffy: "We may state as characteristic of modern science that the scheme of isolated units acting in one-way causality has proved to be insufficient. Hence, the appearance in all fields of science of notions like wholeness, holistic, organismic, Gestalt, etc., which signify that in the last resort we must think in terms of elements in mutual interaction [1968: 45]." Some authors believe that the general historical tendency works toward "the gradual inclusion of all science into a systemic-structural framework [Sadovsky and Yudin, 1967: 191]."

This trend has also asserted itself in the domain of the social sciences. "Reflecting that interest in growing systemness which is evident in any sphere of life, the social sciences have also begun to change their orientation. Earlier, they were concerned with individuals or groups at the most, with man in relation to other individuals and groups. . . . Now one can also note a growing interest in the systems in which men are involved, in the whole, in the interdependencies between parts and the whole [Chodak, 1973: 124]." In the fifties Mills already treated the structural approach as the essential ingredient of the sociological imagination: "To be aware of the idea of social structure and to use it with sensibility is to be capable of tracing linkages among a great variety of milieux. To be able to do this is to possess the sociological imagination [1959: 10–11]." In current sociological literature the structural point of view is very heavily stressed. In the program for the meeting of the American Sociological Association in 1974, Blau makes the following claim: "The idea of social structure is at the very core of sociology. . . . The structural approach is designed to explain, not the behavior of individuals, but the structure of relations among groups and individuals that finds expression in this behavior [1974: 1]." Nisbet shares this emphasis: "Of all contributions that sociology has made to contemporary thought none is greater than, if indeed as great as, its envisagement of human behavior in terms of social structure [1974: 73]." Goode claims that "larger structural problems are central to sociology [1973: 20]." And Coser has added his voice: "Let me reiterate that I consider the study of social structures to lie at the very center of the sociological enterprise [1975: 218]."

The Notion of a Social Structure

The notion of social structure is by no means self-evident, and some clarification of this concept is necessary, in view of its notorious elusiveness. The best way to begin is to list those concepts which are believed to be opposite to structure. They are *chaos, formlessness, amorphousness, the ceaseless flux of events, idiosyncratic human behavior that exhibits no regularities, unpatterned behavior,* and there are others. And conversely the typical characterizations of a structure encountered in sociological literature would include *social order, social system, patterned modes of behavior, the arrangement of the units, the organization of relationships, the configuration of relationships within which man acts, relations among groups and individuals, the patterns discernible in social life, consistent, more or less persisting regularities, the interdependence of parts, the geometry of arrangement, the network of relationships, the ordered arrangement of parts, definable articulation, the interconnectedness of diverse elements, constancies of interpersonal behavior, invariant relations, ascertainable pattern, the observable uniformity of action or operation, the relational complex,* and the like.

It is easy to see that a set of common intuitions is present in all those concepts:

1. There is a plurality of elements—parts or units, components, or "atoms."
2. Those elements are linked by a plurality of relationships—relations, interconnections, or interdependencies.
3. The relationships are integrated in a pattern, cluster, arrangement, network, or configuration of a specific nature, distinguishable from other patterns and making up a definable unity, to some extent invariant with respect to the components.

A comprehensive definition bringing these points together may be taken from the work of Nadel: "Structure indicates an ordered arrangement of parts, which can be treated as transposable, being relatively invariant, while the parts themselves are variable [1957: 8]."

Numerous typologies of social structures may be developed in terms of two criteria: first, the character of elements claimed to be linked by the pattern of relationships; second, the character of relationships linking those elements together. For the present discussion two distinctions are most relevant. First, the structures may be conceived either in concrete or in abstract terms. When the concrete approach is taken, both elements and the relationships are interpreted as observable, or immediately perceivable. The model example is provided by the notion of a social group, understood as a plurality of persons connected by direct interactions. Social structure is interpreted in such terms by Radcliffe-Brown, who maintains that "the components of social structure are persons [1935: 4]," understood as full-fledged individuals. When the abstract approach is taken, both the elements and the relationships are interpreted as theoretical constructs, not observable or perceivable in any immediate way. The model example is provided by the notion a social system, understood as a plurality of roles (or actions, positions, or statuses of the "actors"); i.e., segmented, abstracted images of individuals, linked by patterned social relations—normatively prescribed, repeatable forms of organization or coordination. Social structure is perceived in such terms by Ackerman and Parsons: "Social systems are comprised of interactive roles with a collectivity referent, the interaction being ordered in its specificity by norms grounded in and oriented by values. The structure of the social system consists of the patterning of symbolic references among those four categories of units [1966: 36]."

The second distinction relevant in the present context allows one to differentiate structures composed of elementary units (conceived of as internally unstructured) from structures of structures (i.e., those which connect complex, internally structured objects). In the first case one may speak of structures of the first order, or primary structures; in the second case, of structure of the second, third, . . . nth order, or secondary structures. As Kmita puts it: "The elements of the respective structure (the components of its universum) need not be conceived as individual objects. In particular cases they may be treated as structures themselves; then we encounter structures of the higher order [1970: 66]." This insight allows one to see in a new light the traditional distinction of microstructures and macrostructures — the first being an example of a primary (first-order) structure, the second of a secondary (higher-order) structure of structures. Of course one must remember that all this is relative to the perspective taken by the investigator. The ultimate components for the sociological perspective—human individuals—may be treated as complex structures themselves from some other (for example, psychological) perspective. An interesting type of secondary structure is the one composed of the links between structures of different orders. For example, the relationships between the microstructure and the macrostructure may be seen as a specific structure consisting of the relationships described in the literature as "bridging principles," "cross-sectional connections," "coordinating principles," etc. Finally, the set of relationships between structures of different types— for example, between concrete and abstract structures—may also be conceived as a specific structure itself, which may be labeled *cross structure*. The potentialities of such a mode of analysis are very rich, and will be illustrated in the next part of our discussion, dealing with the Marxian theory of society.

Toward a Dialectical Alternative

If the dispute of collectivism and individualism is rephrased in terms of the structuralist approach, the crucial question becomes whether the so-called social wholes represent a distinctively new, emergent organization of human individuals and their activities. The traditional formulations of the dispute, in terms of a specific substance, may be signified by the subscript "1," and the formulation in terms of a specific structure by the subscript "2." Four standpoints in the dispute can be distinguished:

Individualism$_1$ = No specific social substance exists; only individual human beings are the real substratum, or the basic components of society.
Collectivism$_1$ = There exists a specific social substance, a social reality sui generis, a particular ontological mode of being.
Individualism$_2$ = No specific structure can be discerned in society; society is only an amorphous, random aggregate or cluster of human individuals.

Collectivism$_2$ = Social wholes have distinct structure; they represent a more complex level of organization of human individuals, an intricate network of relationships of various orders.

Note, that the aspect of substance and the aspect of structure are mutually independent. There is no danger of internal contradiction if both dichotomies are cross-tabulated as shown in Figure 7.1.

The combination of Individualism$_1$ and Individualism$_2$ renders an extreme version of individualism: The only real components of society are human individuals who are not regularly interrelated, but rather constitute a totally amorphous, unorganized aggregate. I label it (amorphic) Atomism. The combination of Collectivism$_1$ and Collectivism$_2$ renders an extreme version of collectivism: Social wholes are real objects of a specific substantive nature, organized internally in a specific fashion. I label this standpoint Reified Holism. The combination of Collectivism$_1$ and Individualism$_2$ renders a position according to which society represents a new emergent domain of reality, a new substance; but the newness is not due to the specific structural organization of elements. I call it Nonstructural Emergentism.

Finally, the combination of Individualism$_1$ and Collectivism$_2$ renders a standpoint which seems most interesting and fruitful. It claims that the only really existing objects in a society are human individuals (their actions, the products of their actions). But a plurality of human individuals, interlinked in a complex fashion by a network of social interactions and social relations, constitutes a specific structure, which has new properties and new regularities. There is nothing else in a society but people. At the same time, society is something more than a plurality of people. "Something more" is

		The Aspect of Substratum	
		Individualism$_1$	Collectivism$_1$
The Aspect of Organization	Collectivism$_2$	Structuralism	Reified Holism
	Individualism$_2$	Atomism	

Figure 7.1

precisely the structure of their mutual relationships. To put it another way, sociology is certainly about people, but it does not follow that it must be written in terms of people. Such a position will be called (sociological) Structuralism, and will be treated as the dialectical alternative to the dilemma of individualism and collectivism.

This position preserves some significant insights of both traditional positions, but at the same time avoids some of their unwelcome implications. From traditional collectivism it takes the belief that social objects are "something else" or "something more" than a simple sum of individuals. But unlike traditional collectivism, it avoids the danger of reification. From traditional individualism it takes the claim that the basic components of society are individuals. But unlike traditional individualism it avoids the danger of treating individuals as singularistic, unconnected atoms. More specifically, the standpoint of sociological structuralism allows us to conceptualize (a) the uniqueness of social wholes, by referring to the unique structural organization of elements; (b) the unity or integration of social wholes, by emphasizing the particular intensity (network, configuration) of structural relationships within such wholes as opposed to outside relationships; (c) the autonomy of a social whole with respect to its parts, by specifying properties or regularities of structures and their transformation, which cannot be predicated of the elements; (d) the idea of the continuity of social wholes in spite of the changes in their human elements, by invoking the notion of invariant structures, independent of the concrete components; (e) the causal impact of one structure on the other, by referring to the mediating activities of the individuals, across the boundaries of structures within which each of them is implicated, or the even more immediate links of two structures by virtue of one and the same individual participating in both of them; (f) the independent power of the whole over its parts, by invoking the notion of external structure and structural constraints, determining the properties of elements in dependence on the position they take within the wider whole.

Therefore, sociological structuralism provides a comprehensive solution to all those riddles that gave birth to the dispute of collectivism and individualism. Some participants in the dispute come close to an explicit stipulation of this solution. One may quote Mandelbaum: "Societal facts are concerning the forms of organization present in a society [1969a: 633]." A similar note is struck by Ginsberg: "In the sociological investigations we are not concerned with the intentions of individuals, but rather with structural relations and their bearing on individuals [1968: 61]." Several ideas involved in the position of sociological structuralism can be spotted in a comment by Wisdom: "The group-structure . . . is an example of such an emergent phenomenon. . . . It is a different order of eventuality. And not only is it unforeseeable, but it may even be unrecognized after it has arisen. (And it may exercise some control over our behavior without our being aware of it) [1970: 292]."

But perhaps nowhere else have the implications of this position been traced so extensively, and the concrete applications of it so widely made, as in the sociological theories of Marx. We shall proceed now to a consideration of them.

STRUCTURALISM IN MARXIAN SOCIOLOGICAL THEORY

Among the commentators and followers of Marxian doctrine there is hardly any consensus on the fundamental ontological properties of his image of society. Strikingly opposite characterizations are encountered. To quote just two recent examples: Israel writes, "In order to base sociology (and knowledge) on Marxian epistemology one has to accept on the ontological level the position of methodological individualism [1972: 145]," whereas Swingewood argues, "Marx's approach is the opposite of methodological individualism and sociological phenomenology [1975: 37]."

In my opinion, the diversity of interpretations is due precisely to the complex, dialectical nature of Marx's actual standpoint. Without a recognition of such complexity, a reader's selective attention can easily focus on one aspect of his position, and a one-sided reconstruction will certainly result. I shall argue that Marx adheres to a position that can be labeled *sociological structuralism,* and rejects both amorphic atomism and reified holism. To prove this point I must show, on the negative side, that Marx was explicitly critical of the atomistic view of society, as well as the reified, holistic image and, on the positive side, that he explicitly accepted both constitutive assumptions of the structuralist position—namely, the assumptions of Individualism$_1$ and Collectivism$_2$. Then a demonstration of these points by means of the substantive Marxian theories of social structure must be provided.

Marx Against Atomism and Reification

The atomistic, individualistic view of society as a random aggregate of acting individuals, without any specific properties or regularities of its own, is totally alien to Marx's thought. He is never directly concerned with an analysis of intentions, purposes, motivations, dispositions, etc., of individual human beings, but rather with the "natural laws" of human society produced partly as intended and partly as unintended results by the activities of human masses. This point is aptly emphasized by Kolakowski: "Historical materialsm is by no means a theory of motivation; and therefore it does not purport to predict the actions of particular individuals. . . . It refers exclusively to the mass-phenomena which are born without conscious intentions, by force of certain regularities specific for the social life, and equally unintended as the laws of nature [1976, vol.I: 347]."

But Marx is even more critical of attempts to see society as a reified, superindividual whole. He says: "It is above all necessary to avoid restoring society as a fixed abstraction opposed to the individual [Marx and Engels, 1960, vol.I: 580]." And in a different connection, taking issue with the views of Proudhon, he argues "Mr. Proudhon the economist understands very well that men make cloth, linen or silk materials in definite relations of production. But what he has not understood is that these definite social relations are just as much produced by men as linen, flax, etc. [1949: 33]." Swingewood is undoubtedly right that "the concept of society as a system dominating its members is anathema to Marx's social theory [1975: 192]."

To sum up, neither the extreme form of individualism nor the extreme form of collectivism appears as an adequate representation of Marxian ontological commitments.

Marx for Some Aspects of Individualism

Now let me turn to the positive side of the Marxian standpoint. According to my explication, the position of sociological structuralism, treated as the dialectical solution to the dilemma of individualism and collectivism combined two constitutive assumptions, labeled Individualism$_2$ and Collectivism$_2$. The assumption of Individualism$_1$ referred to the substantive aspect of social wholes, and claimed that the only substratum of society, its only real ontological components, are human individuals (their actions, results of their actions). There is no specific substance that could be called social, no separate type of being, no social reality sui generis.

In his *German Ideology* Marx says:

> The premises from which we begin are not arbitrary ones, not dogmas, but real premises from which abstraction can only be made in the imagination. They are the real individuals, their activities and the material conditions under which they live, both those which they find already existing and those produced by their activity. . . . The first premise of all human history is, of course, the existence of living human individuals [Marx and Engels, 1975: 59–60].

And in another connection two famous statements are made: "History does nothing; it does not possess immense riches, it does not fight battles. It is men, real men, who do all this, who possess things and fight battles. It is not 'history' which uses men as a means of achieving—as if it were an individual person—its own ends. History is nothing but the activity of men in pursuit of their ends [1960, vol.II: 114]." And again: "Men make their own history, but they do not make it just as they please: they do not make it under circumstances chosen by themselves, but under circumstances directly encountered, given and transmitted from the past. [1968: 97]."

This aspect of Marx's position is convincingly summed up by Kolakowski:

> The only reality of historical process consists of people and their interactions. The ultimate components of history are individual conscious activities. The composite image of these activities produces historical regularities, diachronic laws, which describe the transformations of one society into another, as well as functional laws which describe the general connections between several aspects of social life [1976: 347].

Marx for Some Aspects of Collectivism

The crucial point now is to establish Marx's adherence to the assumption of Collectivism$_2$ (which referred to the organizational aspect of social wholes, and claimed that they possessed a distinct structure of relationships, represented a new complex level of organization with emergent properties and regularities of its own). According to the logic of this assumption it would of necessity entail (*a*) the image of a social whole as a relational structure; a network of social relationships that generate some properties and regularities pertaining exclusively to the social whole, and unable to be predicated meaningfully of the elements; (*b*) the image of each component of a social whole as significantly determined in its properties by a position within the relational structure; influenced by its placement within the network of social relationships.

In the view of several contemporary commentators the focus on social relations, as against the focus on the autonomous properties of social substances, is a most characteristic trait of Marxian ontology. For example Ollman says: "Every factor which enters into Marx's study of capitalism is a 'definite social relationship.' The relation is the irreducible minimum for all units in Marx's conception of social reality. This is really the nub of our difficulty in understanding Marxism, whose subject matter is not simply society, but society conceived of 'relationally' [1975: 14–15]." Swingewood makes a similar observation: "The stress is on society as a definite structure within which human intentions and actions occur [1975: 37]." And Meyer puts the same point somewhat differently: "Marxism views society as a social universe, an all-embracing system in which everything is related to everything else [1969: 28]."

If we look closely at the statements of Marx himself, a full corroboration of the relational view of social reality will easily be found. Marx asks: "What is society, whatever its form may be?" and answers "the product of men's reciprocal action [1949: 137]." More specifically, he claims

> The relations of production in their totality constitute what is called the social relations, society, and, specifically, a society at a definite stage of historical development, a society with a peculiar, distinctive character. Ancient society, feudal society, bourgeois society are such totalities of production relations, each of which at the same time denotes a special stage of development in the history of mankind [Marx and Engels, 1968: 81].

In the *Grundrisse* we find a still more explicit statement: "Society is not a sum of individuals, but it expresses the totality of those relations and situations, in which the individuals mutually confront each other [1953: 176]." Commenting on this aspect of Marxian thought Lenin says: "Society is not a simple, mechanical aggregate of these or those institutions, the simple, mechanical accumulation of these or those phenomena. . . . It is rather a social organism, a holistic system of social relations, a social formation [1951: 191–192]." The main goal that Marx sets himself is to discover the laws of motion of social formations; both the internal mechanisms of their functioning and the dynamic principles of their historical development. Those mechanisms and principles are predicated of social wholes, and seen as a complex outcome of their internal structure.

If society is seen as a complex relational structure, then, correlatively, each component of society is perceived in a structural context, as determined by its position within the social whole. In the preface to *Capital* Marx says: "Here individuals are dealt with only in so far as they are the personifications of economic categories, embodiments of particular class-relations and class-interests [1954]." In another connection his structural orientation is clearly illustrated:

> What is a Negro slave? A man of the black race. The one explanation is as good as the other. A Negro is a Negro. He only becomes a slave in certain relations. A cotton-spinning jenny is a machine for spinning cotton. It becomes capital only in certain relations. Torn from those relationships it is no more capital than gold in itself is money or sugar—the price of sugar [Marx and Engels, 1968: 81].

In *The Grundrisse* we find almost the same idea: "To be a slave or to be a citizen are social determinations, the relationships of Man A and Man B. Man A is not a slave as such. He is a slave within society and because of it [1971: 77]."

A particularly strong influence on the beliefs, attitudes and activities of an individual is exerted by his position within the class structure, the role played in the production of goods. In some sense, individuals become the embodiments of class relations. "Capital shows itself more and more as a social power, whose agent the capitalist is. . . . The capitalist fulfills his function only as personified capital; he is capital turned into a person. Similarly, the worker is only the personification of labour [in McLellan, 1971: 117–118]." Even though some exceptions are allowed, in the majority of cases what the individuals think and do is determined by their class situation. "It is very possible that particular individuals are not always influenced in their attitudes by the class to which they belong, but this has as little effect upon the class struggle as the secession of a few nobles to the *tiers etat* had on the French Revolution [in McLellan, 1971: 161]."

In the words of Kolakowski: "By participation in social relationships, individuals become something other than they are in themselves [1976: 323]." And similarly, Swingewood points out that in Marx's perspective "the individual is part of a pre-existing whole; he acquires significance only in terms of his relations with other parts and with the whole [1975: 34]." Thus the second implication of the assumption of Collectivism$_2$ may plausibly be ascribed to Marxian thinking.

In the course of our discussion all the components, both negative and positive, of the standpoint defined here as the sociological structuralism were shown to be present in the works of Marx. To close this part of my argument, a more synthetic description of Marx's position, closely corresponding with my explication of sociological structuralism, may be given in the words of two distinguished commentators: Kolakowski reads Marx as holding that

> The social life generates new qualities, which are not reducible to natural qualities and cannot be immediately perceived. . . . Those are the interpersonal relationships producing autonomous laws. . . . They constitute the wholes subjected to specific laws, and therefore they endow the participant of those wholes—human subjects—with the peculiarities not discoverable in the extra-human world. In this sense the human individual is not understandable—to himself nor to the theoretical analyst as a simple "natural being"—but only as a participant in the social process [1976: 323].

Meyer is even more explicit:

> Marxism is one mighty effort to make valid generalizations concerning the way in which the multiple forces at play in human society are interrelated, and how they affect each other. It is an attempt to draw a vast and complex blueprint of our entire social structure, in its social, economic, political,

historical and psychological dimensions. In order to accomplish this task of making a systematic study of human society, it has developed a conceptual scheme concerning the integration of these multiple forces and the manner in which they react on each other [1969: 11].

The conclusions reached so far by means of a general, analytical argument will be presently corroborated by a closer scrutiny of the substantive Marxian theories, in which the structural point of view is explicitly and self-consciously applied.

Two Images of Social Structure in Marx's Theory: Formations and Classes

In my opinion, there are two distinct models of society in Marx's theory. Both represent society as a particular, internally structured whole. But the types of structure they ascribe to society are in both cases different; in one case it is an abstract structure (i.e., the elements and the relationships are conceived in abstract, theoretical terms); in another case it is a concrete structure. (i.e., the elements and the relationships are conceived in concrete, empirical terms). The first model appears in the theory of socioeconomic formation, the second in the theory of social classes. I shall give an outline of both models, limited to those points relevant to the immediate purpose of these considerations; namely, the illustration of some uses that an assumption of sociological structuralism has in Marx's works.

The foundations of Marx's theory of socioeconomic formation, developed most extensively in *Capital*, are laid down in this famous passage from "The Preface to a Contribution to the Critique of Political Economy":

> In the social production of their life, men enter into definite relations that are indispensable and independent of their will, relations of production which correspond to a definite stage of development of their material productive forces. The sum total of these relations of production constitutes the economic structure of society, the real foundation on which rises a legal and political superstructure and to which correspond definite forms of social consciousness. . . . At a certain stage of their development, the material productive forces of society come into conflict with the existing relations of production. . . . From forms of development of productive forces these relations turn into their fetters. Then begins the epoch of social revolution. With a change of economic foundation the whole immense superstructure is more or less rapidly transformed [Marx and Engels, 1968: 182–183].

The abstract model of society implicit in the preceding remarks, as well as in several others by Marx, may be illustrated by means of the scheme shown in Figure 7.2. What is the nature of elements and relationships included in this model? It is easy to note that there is no direct reference to men, their activities, the results of these activities, etc.; but rather the components of a social structure are conceived as abstract, theoretical constructs. The forces of production are understood as the technological equipment necessary for the human control of nature, and comprise such diverse empirical items as tools, machines, and raw materials, but also the level of human skills, knowledge, abilities. The relations of production are conceived as the economic organization of a society including the sum total of those interpersonal relationships into which people enter by virtue of common participation in the production of goods—the relations of cooperation, competition, division of labor, exploitation, differential ownership of the means of production, differential participation in the distribution and consumption of economic goods, etc. The political and legal superstructure is defined as all those institutions—law, a political system, administration, social control, propaganda, ideology—that are subservient to the given mode of production, or economic substructure (i.e., subsystem including the forces and the relations of production in some more or less balanced unity). Finally, the so-called forms of social consciousness—literature, art, music, science, religion and perhaps also common sense—constitute a residual category of those intellectual and spiritual creations that have some level of autonomy with respect to the economic substructure, as well as the political and legal superstructure.

Now, all those constructs are kept together by a set of determinate relations. And those relations are also to be conceived in abstract terms. The most significant relations, responsible for the autodynamic tendencies of the whole structure (i.e., the constant tendencies to generate changes from internal, endogenous sources) are defined as the dialectical contradictions, or strains. They occur at three points in the structure of socioeconomic formation (marked by solid-line arrows in Figure 7.2). First, at the border of society and nature, as a constantly reappearing contradiction between any

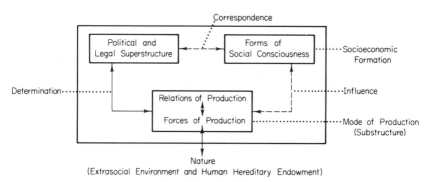

Figure 7.2

existing level of technology and the challenges posed by the extrasocial environment as well as human biological limitations. Such a contradiction provides the impetus for the permanent development of productive forces. The second contradiction appears between the achieved level of technology and the existing social organization of productive processes, unfit for the most effective application of available productive forces. Such a contradiction provides the impetus for the progressive changes of productive relations. The third contradiction affirms itself between the newly established type of productive relations and the traditional system of political, legal and ideological institutions, no longer instrumental for the economic substructure. This contradiction leads to the transformation of the political regime and the legal organization of society.

Besides relationships of the contradictory type, the model includes relationships described as dialectical correspondences (marked by broken-line arrows), by which a mutual influence, or correlations of respective factors, are meant. Such relations link the forms of social consciousness with both the economic mode of production and the political superstructure.

The model of a social structure outlined here has a somewhat metaphysical flavor, precisely because it is couched exclusively in abstract-theoretical terms. "Forces" are said to contradict some "relations"; "substructures" contradict some "superstructures." But it must be realized that behind these abstract categories stand the real activities of human masses. One could say, with Marx: "Economy does nothing, does not contradict anything. It is people, real people who do all those things."

The second model of a social structure drawn by Marx supplements the model of a socioeconomic formation with a more realistic, down-to-earth, concrete picture in which people, their interests, their consciousness, and their activities are brought back into the analytic focus. This model underlies the Marxian theory of classes.

The constitutive components of the class structure are human groups of a specific type, known as social classes. Even though Marx was never completely specific on the definition of a class, the context of his considerations seems to imply that the crucial factor integrating a plurality of individuals into a class is the differential ownership of a particularly significant type of commodity; namely, the means of production (tools, machines, raw materials, land, capital, etc.). Giddens articulates the almost universal consensus reigning today on this issue: "Classes are constituted by the relationship of groupings of individuals to the ownership of private property in the means of production [1971: 37]." Such a criterion logically entails the image of society as divided into two opposing, polar classes—those who have the ownership of the means of production, and those who have to sell their labor in order to survive. An eminent Polish Marxist labels it a "polar model of a social structure": "At the one pole, there are monopolistic privileges, associated with a sovereign and particularly qualified control over the act of labor and the distribution of its product; at another pole, there is submission and dependence, associated with the execution of labor, the conditions of which and the distribution of whose product are beyond any control of the laborers [Hochfeld, 1963: 165]." Another Polish sociologist calls it a "dichotomous scheme of one-sided dependence: Two classes are the terms of the asymmetrical relation, I mean the relation of one-sided dependence. These classes are characterized by attributes mutually opposed: dominating–dominated, exploiting–exploited, propertied–nonpropertied, working–idle [Ossowski, 1957: 175]."

In *The Communist Manifesto* this image is claimed to be characteristic of "the history of all hitherto existing society": "Freeman and slave, patrician and plebeian, lord and serf, guildmaster and journeyman, in a word oppressor and oppressed, stood in constant opposition to one another, carried on an uninterrupted, now hidden, now open fight, a fight that each time ended either in a revolutionary reconstitution of society at large or in the common ruin of the contending classes [Marx and Engels, 1968: 35–36]." Of course it is a simplified, or idealized, image; and in reality there have always been several groups or collectivities of an intermediate nature, appearing together or cutting across polar class divisions. "In the earlier epochs of history, we find almost everywhere a complicated arrangement of society into various orders, a manifold gradation of social rank [1968: 36]." But there exists a peculiar historical tendency to simplify social distinctions, and to eliminate all groupings—or at least to eliminate the strategic importance of all groupings—except those based on the differentials of ownership. This tendency is ultimately affirmed in capitalist society: "The epoch of the bourgeoisie possesses however this distinctive feature: It has simplified the class antagonisms. Society as a whole is more and more splitting up into two great hostile camps, into two great classes directly facing each other: Bourgeoisie and Proletariat [1968: 36]." Thus, by virtue of a historical trend, the analytic, simplified model can be treated as the ever more adequate approximation of reality—no longer just a model, but rather an approximate description of actual phenomena.

Alongside the trend toward polarization, there is another one—toward a growing internal crystalization of classes. This is grasped by Marx's distinction of "class in itself" and "class for itself." Commonality of the ownership position among a plurality of individuals is not sufficient for their real operation as a full-fledged class. They are still only an atomistic aggregate of people—a class in itself. Only when they acquire some consciousness of the commonality, and a corresponding opposition to other classes—only when they initiate mutual communication and interaction, only when some more persistent internal organization of social relationships appears within the class (e.g., organized leadership, political representation)—may it be said to constitute a class for itself: a real social entity. For example, in the early phases of the formation of capitalism, a proletariat is only a class in itself: "This mass is already a class in opposition to capital, but not yet a class for itself [Marx, 1949: 178]." To change into a class for itself, several additional qualities must appear. As Aron defines them: "For there to be a class, there must be a consciousness of unity, a feeling of separation from other social classes, and even a feeling of hositility toward other social classes [1968, vol.I: 205]."

Now, those components of a social structure are linked by means of specific relationships. Marx describes the typical relationships between classes in dialectic terms—as mutual opposition. But at least three types of such relationships are singled out, depending on the level of crystalization reached by the respective classes. First, there is the objective contradiction of interests between those who have and those who have not; the larger the scope and extent to which the interests of the owners are realized, or their needs satisfied, the more difficult it becomes for the nonowners to realize their interests or to satisfy their needs. This may be labeled *class contradiction,* due primarily to the factor of scarcity. Second, the objective *contradiction* may become subjectively perceived by the members of the respective classes. Then it produces feelings of hostility, distrust, enmity on both sides. This type of relationship may be called *class antagonism.* And finally, the antagonism may acquire external manifestations in the economic, political, or ideological arena—it is transformed into more or less organized mass behavior of the members of the respective classes, directed against the members of the opposite class. The name *class conflict* or *class struggle* seems most appropriate here.

Note that three types of interclass relationships singled out above form a sort of cumulative hierarchy, parallel to the levels of internal crystalization of a class. The class in the full, complete sense appears only at the top of this hierarchy. In Marx's words: "Separate individuals form a class only to the extent that they must carry on a common struggle against another class [Marx and Engels, 1968: 172]."

Obviously, the contradictions, antagonisms, or conflicts are only the most significant, strategic links in the class structure, which do not exhaust all the possibilities of interclass relationships. Sometimes, cooperation, integration, solidarity, alliances of all sorts, may also, at least temporarily, be encountered. But again, the historical tendency is to eliminate such secondary forms of relationships and to radicalize class contradictions toward a naked, "shameless, direct, brutal exploitation" on the part of the owners, coupled with an uncompromising, revolutionary struggle on the part of the nonowners. This process reaches its height in capitalist society, in the opposition of the bourgeoisie and the proletariat. The analytic process of crystalization affirms itself historically, owing to objective developmental tendencies inherent in the class structure.

From such considerations it seems obvious that the model of a class structure differs in important respects from the model of a socioeconomic formation. But it is by no means an alternative model, dissociated from the previous one. Quite the reverse; it must be treated as complementary, as providing the abstract categories of socioeconomic formation with the flesh of concrete, empirically and historically perceivable phenomena.

The Cross Structure: A Unified Social System

The links or correspondencies between the two structures may be interpreted as a structure of structures, or a structure of the second degree. And to close my discussion, some suggestions as to its fundamental characteristics will now be adduced.

It may be said that the model of a socioeconomic formation presents a theoretical rationale for the self-destruction of capitalism, whereas the model of a class structure describes the empirical mechanism of this process. As Aron puts it: "There are . . . two possible representations of the capitalist dialectic of self-destruction; an economic dialectic, which is a new version of the contradiction between the constantly increasing forces of production and the relations of production that determine the income distributed to the masses, and a sociological dialectic functioning via the growing dissatisfaction and revolt of the proletarianized workers [1968, vol.I: 175]. A similar idea occurs to McLellan: "For Marx, classes were the basic social groups by means of whose conflict society developed in accordance with changes in its economic substructure [1971: 151]."

A certain isomorphism is here claimed between the two images of a social structure. Classes may be seen as representations of abstract socioeconomic categories, class conflict as the implementation of the contradictions between socioeconomic categories. Conversely, the abstract categories of socioeconomic formation may be interpreted as generalized, short-hand concepts to cover the essential components of social classes, and the abstract contradictions between socioeconomic categories (the productive forces and productive relations, the substructure and superstructure) as a generalized, short-hand description of the essential dimensions of class conflict.

There are two fundamental relationships that seem to connect both structures; those relationships constitute the structure of the second degree, or more precisely the cross structure. The first is the relationship claimed by

Marx to exist between the position occupied by man within society and his objective interest, understood as an imaginable state of affairs, or social situation under which the maximum satisfaction of his needs would be guaranteed. Let us call it *the principle of relativization of interest* with respect to social position. The second is the relationship between a man's objective interest and his subjective, conscious perception of the world. Let us call it the *principle of existential determination of consciousness.*

Those two principles allow us to reconstruct the logic of Marx's argument, linking two analytically distinguished structures in a coherent, complex image of the social world and its functioning.

First, in the productive process people enter particular social relations, relations of production, the most important of which are property relations. The position they take vis-a-vis each other in the context of such relations— as owners of property or as nonowners of property—is the most essential aspect of their total social status (the model of a socioeconomic formation).

Second, the positions objectively occupied in the economic substructure determine the objective interests of the occupants; for the owners their vested interests come down to the preservation of the status quo, which safeguards their privileges and allows them to satisfy their needs to the maximum degree, whereas for the nonowners an inability to satisfy their needs requires the abolition of the status quo, and the consequent redistribution of privileges (linking principle I).

Third, the shared objective interests bring some people together, and disassociate them from some other people, who have opposite objective interests. The process of crystalization of social classes is initiated; two aggregates of people appear with opposite objective interests, or as Marx would have it "two classes in themselves" (the model of a class structure).

Fourth, as a reflection of objective interest class consciousness is born—a set of beliefs, values, norms, expectations referring to the actual situation of a class, and justifying the efforts to preserve or to change that situation. At the same time, the objective contradiction of class interests is raised to the level of emotional hostility, hatred, enmity; i.e., a class antagonism spreads out (linking principle II).

Fifth, the members of a class initiate mutual communication and various forms of organization to promote their consciously entertained interests, and to prevent the interests of another class from being realized. Ideological programs, political creeds, and political doctrines are formulated. The "class in itself" changes into a "class for itself," and class antagonism into class struggle (the model of a class structure).

Sixth, as a result of a successful revolution (possibly but not necessarily violent), one of the classes acquires political power, and transforms the political superstructure, introducing new legal institutions, proclaiming its particular interests as binding universal principles (the model of a socioeconomic formation).

Seventh, the economic substructure is changed by means of reforms instituted by the new political authorities; a new network of productive relations appears that safeguard the interests of the ascendent class (the model of a socioeconomic formation).

Eighth, the productive forces as already developed acquire the opportunity to be utilized to the greatest extent, and new incentives for their further development are born (the model of a socioeconomic formation).

When the theory of socioeconomic formation is rewritten in such a form, and enriched by the propositions of the theory of classes, there is no longer any basis for the allegation that it has a metaphysical or mystical flavor. It becomes clear how abstract social or economic laws affirm themselves by means of concrete human activities, and how concrete human activities serve as the implementation of abstract social and economic laws. The multilevel, complex model of a social structure typical of the Marxist orientation comes closer to a full understanding and explanation of social reality and its ontological peculiarities than any of the alternative, one-sided, and simplistic images of the collectivists and individualists.

PART V

OUT OF THE THEORETICAL CRISIS

CHAPTER 8

Recapitulation

The goal of a book like this is attained if it provokes discussion and controversies, and its success can be measured by the intensity of rejection and criticism it encounters: After all, this is the dialectical way by which real science develops. The truth spelled out by Whitehead, that "the clash of doctrines is not a disaster but an opportunity" is relevant not only to sociological doctrines but to doctrines about sociology as well. There are several suggestions as to how to get out of the theoretical crisis in which sociology presently finds itself; the program of dialectical sociology is certainly only one of them.

To help those who should choose to overcome the crisis dialectically, the model of dialectical sociology is presented here. I wish to restate now my initial premises, the logic of my argument, and the main conclusions reached. The worst possible fate of an author is to be misunderstood, or to be accused of something he does not hold to—hence the following restatement of my beliefs, for the record.

THE PREMISES OF THE ARGUMENT

First, I believe that sociology is in fact in a state of crisis in respect of theory, and the symptom of this is the widespread feeling of disappointment, discontent, fruitlessness, or irrelevance experienced by the members of sociological community.

Second, I believe that the real locus of the crisis is to be discovered at the level of the fundamental assumptions—ontological, epistemological and methodological—that underlie current empirical research as well as theory construction.

Third, I believe that the essence of the crisis is the statement of those assumptions in dichotomous, mutually contradictory terms, with a tendency to a growing polarization of standpoints on almost every conceivable issue, and the transformation of the theoretical disputes into seemingly unsolvable dilemmas.

Fourth, I believe that the theoretical crisis so defined has not only a destructive but also a constructive potential. I reject the nihilistic approach of those who refuse any scientific status to sociology, as well as the opportunistic approach of those who suggest some form of eclecticism as a solution to our present perplexities. On the contrary, I suggest that the polarization of the theoretical field has reached a level extreme enough to allow for the overcoming of traditional solutions and the formulating of a new, unified paradigm for sociology.

Fifth, I believe that the new paradigm cannot be built ex nihilo, by the total rejection of the sociological tradition. Quite the reverse: It must be shown to appear as a logical outcome of this tradition; it must safeguard all the valuable components of earlier theoretical attempts, eliminating their misleading or mistaken claims.

THE STRATEGY OF THE ARGUMENT

The method I propose for reaching a new paradigm may be called a method of dialectical critique. It is in some sense patterned on the approach utilized by Karl Marx in his criticism of the classical political economy, or the German idealistic philosophy. The essence of the method is to continue and reject at the same time, or more precisely to dissect analytically the existing formulations of the opposite theoretical positions to the extent that several aspects or dimensions are revealed, and some of them synthetically cross-combined while others are dismissed. By the force of such logic the resulting alternative is opposite to both traditional standpoints, but at the same time preserves their significant elements. It may be said to overcome not only each of the traditional standpoints taken singly but the whole theoretical dilemma in its entirety, proving it to be spurious.

The method is applied in the course of this book to six selected dilemmas. It must be emphatically stressed that they are not thought of as composing

Table 8.1

Problem	Dilemma	Dialectic solution
1. Science or humanities?	Naturalism versus antinaturalism	Integralism
2. Science of man or science of society?	Reductionism versus antireductionism	Separatism
3. Knowledge or action?	Cognitivism versus activism	Constructivism
4. Detachment or bias?	Neutralism versus axiologism	Commitment
5. Object or subject?	Passivism versus autonomism	Creativism
6. Wholes or aggregates?	Collectivism versus individualsm	Structuralism

329

an exhaustive or complete list. Rather, they are singled out because of the focal role they have played in current debates, at least as they appear from the perspective of a Polish sociologist. This personal fact may be adduced for justifying several omissions. For example, I do not consider the dispute about the dynamic, developmental, or historical nature of social reality to be significant any longer, because in the tradition of Polish sociology (Marxist, but also non-Marxist), this is taken for granted and almost universally accepted. Similarly, I believe that the dispute of extreme inductive and extreme deductive strategy of theory construction is already outdated, having given way to some form of mixed hypothetical (or idealizational) approach, combining both logical procedures. Finally, the battles of the so-called "grand theory" and narrow empiricism seem luckily to be over, and a general agreement on the necessity of empirical theory and theoretically informed research clearly prevails. Therefore I have dismissed such dilemmas from consideration here. Perhaps there are other similar omissions. But it should not invalidate the argument concerning those dilemmas which are selected and included.

Two of them are methodological. The first addresses the place of natural-scientific methods in sociological research; the second focuses on the issue of the reduction of sociological knowledge to psychological knowledge.

The next two dilemmas refer to epistemological problems: The third is concerned with the proper goal of sociological study; the fourth is concerned with the place of values in the sociological enterprise.

Finally, the last two dilemmas touch ontological questions: The fifth inquires about the nature of human agents, the sixth about the nature of societal wholes.

In each case, the possible solutions are constructed as extreme, simplified ideal types, and then the dialectical alternatives are reached, by their analytic cross combination. This may be summed up in tabular form (see Table 8.1).

THE OUTCOME OF THE ARGUMENT

The dialectic solutions to each of the six dilemmas can be combined together. As a result, a coherent system of assumptions dealing with the status of sociology, its goals, its scope, and its subject matter appears. It may be considered as the core of a dialectical paradigm for sociology.

In the dialectical paradigm constructed here, sociology is conceived as a distinct science of society, following the general rules of scientific logic, but within those rules developing a specific methodology suitable to the study of its peculiar subject matter (integralism). Sociology is further conceived as a science linked with the other sciences of man by mutual reductive relationships, with a provision for a significant residuum of irreducible concepts and laws to be included in specific sociological explanations (separatism). Sociology is seen as directly relevant to social practice, and social practice as providing an ultimate corroboration of sociological knowledge (constructivism). Sociology is seen as approximating objectively adequate knowledge, owing to its self-conscious adherence to the interests and values of the most progressive segments of society (commitment). Men, the ultimate components of society, are seen as collectively creative and productive, within the scope of opportunities and limitations set by the social and nonsocial environment, as well as by historical heritage (creativism). And finally, society—the proper subject matter of sociology—is conceived as a plurality of individuals bound together by a specific structure of interindividual relationships, and consequently displaying some emergent properties and regularities of its own (structuralism).

This is a specific view of sociology, and one basically at odds with both traditional alternatives—positivistic sociology, and subjectivistic sociology.

A CAVEAT ON MARXISM

Now, the crucial point is that, while analytically different from prevailing orientations, the new paradigm is not chronologically new—for it is already present, to be sure in a rudimentary and undeveloped form, in Marx's theory of society, formed more than a century ago. And in no other theory since that time has it appeared in an equally coherent fashion. A careful scrutiny of Marxian theory seems to corroborate this claim with respect to each of the six assumptions.

Marxism appears here as an analytic point of arrival, rather than as a taken-for-granted, dogmatic point of departure. Or, to put it differently, the dialectical paradigm is a logical outcome of the critical reinterpretation and reappraisal of the main nondialectic (and non-Marxist) trends in the history of sociology, as well as in contemporary sociological theory. And only later, a close actual approximation to the dialectical model is discovered in the Marxian theoretical tradition.

In a sense, this could have been expected. If a method of dialectical criticism as applied here is in fact informed by or borrowed from Marx, then it must have led to substantive results, at least partly convergent with those of Marx. But dogmatism here is dogmatism only of an analytic method, and not of the results. The dialectical paradigm outlined here is not conceived as a final, closed, dogmatic solution, but rather as an orientation, which may provide a stimulus for further development of Marxism itself, as well as other sociological theories. As Thomas Kuhn says,

> The success of a paradigm . . . is at the start largely a promise of success discoverable in selected and still incomplete examples. Normal science consists in the actualization of that promise, an actualization achieved by extending the knowledge of those facts that the paradigm displays as particularly revealing, by increasing the extent of the match between those facts and the paradigm's predictions, and by further articulation of the paradigm itself [1970: 23–24].

This job remains to be done. In my view it must be done along the lines suggested by a dialectical paradigm if sociology is to realize its calling—to become a science of society, but also a practical force for changing society.

References

Abel, T.
  1952 The present status of social theory. *American Sociological Review* 17: 156–164.
  1970 *The Foundation of Sociological Theory.* New York: Random House.
Ackerman, C., and T. Parsons
  1966 The concept of social system as a theoretical device. In *Concepts, Theory and Explanation in the Behavioral Sciences,* ed. G. J. DiRenzo, pp 24–42. New York: Random House.
Addis, L.
  1969 Freedom and the Marxist philosophy of history. In *Readings in the Philosophy of the Social Sciences,* ed. M. Brodbeck, pp. 317–335. New York: Macmillan.
Adorno, T. W.
  1976 On the logic of the social sciences. In *The Positivist Dispute in German Sociology,* eds. T. W. Adorno *et al.,* pp. 105–122. London: Heinemann.
Adorno, T. W. *et al.*
  1950 *The Authoritarian Personality.* New York: Harper and Row.
Agassi, J.
  1973 Methodological individualism. In *Modes of Individualism and Collectivism,* ed. J. O'Neill, pp. 185–212. London: Heinemann.
Ajdukiewicz, K.
  1965 *Logika pragmatyczna [Pragmatic Logic].* Warsaw: Polish Scientific Publishers.
Allen, V. L.
  1975 *Social Analysis: A Marxist Critique and Alternative.* London: Longman.

Andreski, S.
  1972   *Social Sciences as Sorcery.* New York: St. Martin's.
Andreyeva, G. M.
  1974   Modern aspects of the problem of values in social cognition. Moscow: Soviet Sociological Association (mimeographed).
Aron, R.
  1968   *Main Currents in Sociological Thought,* vols. I and II. Garden City: Doubleday-Anchor.
Asch, S. E.
  1955   Opinions and social pressure. Reprinted from *Scientific American;* San Francisco: W. H. Freeman and Company.
Barton, A
  1971   Empirical methods and radical sociology: A liberal critique. In *Radical Sociology,* eds. J. D. Colfax and J. L. Roach, pp. 460–477. New York: Basic Books.
Baumgartner, T., *et al.*
  1975   A systems model of conflict and change in planning systems. *General Systems* 20: 167–183.
Beattie, J. H. M.
  1959   Understanding and explanation in social anthropology. *British Journal of Sociology* 10: 45–60.
Beck, L. W.
  1968   The natural science ideal in the social sciences. In *Theory in Anthropology,* eds. R. A. Manners and D. Kaplan, pp. 80–89. Chicago: Aldine.
Becker, H.
  1945   Interpretive sociology and constructive typology. In *Twentieth Century Sociology,* eds. G. Gurvitch and W. E. Moore, pp. 70–95. New York: The Philosophical Library.
Bell, D.
  1977   Review essay: the once and future Marx. *American Journal of Sociology* 1: 187–197.
Bell, W., and J. A. Mau
  1970   Images of the future: theory and research strategies. In *Theoretical Sociology,* eds. J. C. McKinney and E. A. Tiryakian, pp. 205–234. New York: Appleton-Century-Crofts.
Bendix, R., and B. Berger
  1959   Images of society and problems of concept formation in sociology. *In Symposium on Sociological Theory,* ed. L. Gross, pp. 92–118. Evanston: Row Peterson.
Berger, P., and T. Luckmann
  1967   *The Social Construction of Reality.* New York: Doubleday-Anchor.
Berghe, van den, P.
  1963   Dialectic and functionalism: toward a theoretical synthesis. *American Sociological Review* 28: 695–705.
Bierstedt, R.
  1960   Sociology and humane learning. *American Sociological Review* 25: 3–9.
  1963   *The Social Order.* New York: McGraw-Hill.
  1965   Social science and public service. In *Applied Sociology: Opportunities and Problems,* eds. A. W. Gouldner and S. M. Miller, pp. 412–420. New York: Free Press.
  1969   Introduction. In *Florian Znaniecki on Humanistic Sociology,* ed. R. Bierstedt, pp. 1–36. Chicago: The University of Chicago Press.
  1975   Comment on Lenski's evolutionary perspective. In *Approaches to the Study of Social Structure,* ed. P. Blau, pp. 154–158. New York: Free Press.
Bierstedt, R., *et al.*
  1964   *Modern Social Science.* New York: McGraw-Hill.

Birnbaum, N.
    1971   The crisis in Marxist sociology. In *Radical Sociology,* eds. J. D. Colfax and J. L. Roach, pp. 108–131. New York: Basic Books.
Blain, R. R.
    1971   On Homans' psychological reductionism. *Sociological Inquiry* 41:3–25.
Blalock, H.
    1970   The formalization of sociological theory. In *Theoretical Sociology,* ed. J. C. McKinney and E. A. Tiryakian, pp. 271–300. New York: Appleton-Century-Crofts.
Blau, P.
    1964   *Exchange and Power in Social Life.* New York: John Wiley.
    1969   Sociological analysis: Current trends and personal practice. *Sociological Inquiry* 2: 119–130.
    1970   Comment. In *Explanation in the Behavioral Sciences,* eds. R. Borger and F. Cioffi, pp. 329–339. Cambridge: University Press.
    1974   Focus on social structure. In the ASA Annual Meeting Program. Montreal.
    1975   Parallels and contrasts in structural inquiries. In *Approaches to the Study of Social Structure,* ed. P. Blau. New York: Free Press.
Blumer, H.
    1966   Sociological implications of the thought of George Herbert Mead. *American Journal of Sociology* 1: 535–548. (Reprinted in *Sociological Theory,* ed. W. L. Wallace, pp. 234–244. London: Heinemann, 1969.)
    1969   *Symbolic Interactionism.* Englewood Cliffs, New Jersey: Prentice-Hall.
    1972   The analysis of the act. Lectures at the University of California at Berkeley, September–December—author's personal notes.
Boskoff, A.
    1969   *Theory in American Sociology.* New York: Thomas Y. Crowell.
    1971   Process-orientation in sociological theory and research: Untasted old wine in slightly used bottles. *Social Forces* 50: 1–12.
    1972   *The Mosaic of Sociological Theory.* New York: Thomas Y. Crowell.
Bottomore, T.
    1973   Introduction. In *Karl Marx,* ed. T. Bottomore. Englewood Cliffs, New Jersey: Prentice-Hall.
    1975   Structure and history. In *Approaches to the Study of Social Structure,* ed. P. Blau, pp. 159–171. New York: Free Press.
Boulding, K.
    1966   *The Impact of the Social Sciences.* New Brunswick, New Jersey: Rutgers University Press.
Brodbeck, M.
    1962   Explanation, prediction and "imperfect" knowledge. In *Minnesota Studies in the Philosophy of Science,* vol. III, eds. H. Feigl and G. Maxwell, pp. 231–272. Minneapolis: The University of Minnesota Press.
    1969a   Methodological individualisms: Definition and reduction. In *Readings in the Philosophy of the Social Sciences,* ed. M. Brodbeck, pp. 280–303. New York: Macmillan.
    1969b   Ed. *Readings in the Philosophy of the Social Sciences.* New York: Macmillan.
    1973   On the philosophy of the social sciences. In *Modes of Individualism and Collectivism,* ed. J. O'Neill, pp. 91–110. London: Heinemann.
Bronowski, J.
    1965   *Science and Human Values.* New York: Harper and Row.
Brown, R.
    1963   *Explanation in Social Science.* London: Routledge Kegan Paul.

1970   Comment. In *Explanation in the Behavioral Sciences,* eds. R. Borger and F. Cioffi, pp. 297–305. Cambridge: Cambridge University Press.

Buck, R. C.
1963   Reflexive predictions. *Philosophy of Science* 4: 359–374.

Buckley, W.
1967   *Sociology and Modern Systems Theory.* Englewood Cliffs, New Jersey: Prentice-Hall.

Bugental, J. F. T.
1967   The challenge that is man. In *Challenges of Humanistic Psychology,* ed. J. F. T. Bugental. New York: McGraw-Hill.

Bunge, M.
1967   *Scientific Research,* vols. I and II. Berlin: Springer.

Burns, T.
1973   A structural theory of social exchange. *Acta Sociologica* 16: 188–208.
1976   The dialectics of social systems. Oslo: University of Oslo Working Papers (mimeographed).

Burns, T., and W. Buckley
1976   *Power and Control: Social Structures and Their Transformations.* London: Sage Publications.

Catton, W.
1966   *From Animistic to Naturalistic Sociology.* New York: McGraw-Hill.

Chodak, S.
1973   *Societal Development.* New York: Oxford University Press.

Cohen, P. S.
1968   *Modern Social Theory.* London: Heinemann.

Coleman, J.
1975   Social structure and a theory of action. In *Approaches to the Study of Social Structure,* ed. P. Blau, pp. 76–93. New York: Free Press.

Colfax, J. D., and J. L. Roach (eds.)
1971   *Radical Sociology.* New York: Basic Books.

Collins, R.
1975   *Conflict Sociology.* New York: Academic Press.

Comte, A.
1896   *The Positive Philosophy of Auguste Comte,* ed. H. Martineau. London: Bell
1912   *Systeme de Politique Positive,* vols. I–IV. Paris: Crês.
1966   *Comte,* ed. B. Skarga. Warsaw: Wiedza Powszechna.

Coser, L. A.
1956   *The Functions of Social Conflict.* New York: Free Press.
1967   *Continuities in the Study of Social Conflict.* New York: Free Press.
1969   Letter to a young sociologist. *Sociological Inquiry* 2: 131–137.
1971   *Masters of Sociological Thought.* New York: Harcourt Brace Jovanovich.
1975   Structure and conflict. In *Approaches to the Study of Social Structure,* ed. P. Blau, pp. 210–219. New York: Free Press.

Cuzzort, R. P.
1969   *Humanity and Modern Sociological Thought.* New York: Holt Rinehart Winston.

Cuzzort, R. P., and E. W. King
1976   *Humanity and Modern Social Thought.* Hinsdale, Illinois: The Dryden Press.

Dahrendorf, R.
1958   Out of utopia: Toward a reorientation of sociological analysis. *American Journal of Sociology* 64: 115–127.
1959   *Class and Class Conflict in Industrial Society.* Stanford: Stanford University Press.

1968 *Essays in the Theory of Society*. Stanford: Stanford University Press.
1976 Remarks on the discussion of the papers by K. R. Popper and T. W. Adorno. In *The Positivist Dispute in German Sociology*, eds. T. W. Adorno *et al.*, pp. 123–130. London: Heinemann.

Danto, A. C.
1973 Methodological individualism and methodological socialism. In *Modes of Individualism and Collectivism*, ed. J. O'Neill, pp. 312–337. London: Heinemann.

DeMaree, W. R.
1973 Operant sociology: A behavioral model of man and social organization. Paper presented at the Midwest Sociological Society Annual Meetings in Milwaukee (mimeographed).

Denisoff, R. S.
1972 *Sociology: Theories in Conflict*. Belmont: Wadsworth.

DiRenzo G. J.
1966 Toward explanation in the behavioral sciences. In *Concepts, Theory and Explanation in the Behavioral Sciences*, ed. G. J. DiRenzo, pp. 231–291. New York: Random House.

Dodd, S. C.
1952 All-or-none elements and mathematical models for sociologists. *American Sociological Review* 17: 167–177.
1974 Intercohort feedback and the evolution of global society. In *The ASA Annual Proceedings*, pp. 74–75. Montreal: ASA.

Dray, W. H.
1969 Explaining-what in history. In *Readings in the Philosophy of the Social Sciences*, ed. M. Brodbeck, pp. 343–348. New York: Macmillan.

Durkheim, E.
1915 *Elementary Forms of Religious Life*. New York: Macmillan
1953 *Sociology and Philosophy*. New York: Free Press.
1962 *The Rules of Sociological Method*. New York: Free Press.

Easton, D.
1953 *The Political System*. New York: Alfred Knopf.

Edel, A.
1965 Social science and value: A study in interrelations. In *The New Sociology*, ed. I. L. Horowitz, pp. 218–238. New York: Oxford University Press.

Eilstein, H.
1961 *Jedność Materialna Świata* [*The Material Unity of the World*]. Warszawa: Ksiazka i Wiedza.

Eisenstadt, S. N.
1968 The development of sociological thought. In *International Encyclopedia of the Social Sciences*, vol 15: 23–35. New York: Macmillan.
1973 Some reflections on the "crisis" of sociology (mimeographed).

Eisenstadt, S. N., and M. Curelaru
1976 *The Form of Sociology: Paradigms and Crises*. New York: John Wiley.
1977 Sociological theory and an analysis of the dynamics of civilization and revolutions. *Daedalus* 2: 59–78.

Emmet, D.
1958 *Function, Purpose and Powers*. London: Routledge Kegan Paul.

Eulau, H.
1958 H. D. Lasswell's developmental analysis. *Western Political Quarterly* 11: 229–242.

Fayerabend, P.
  1977   Marxist fairy-tales from Australia: a reply. *Inquiry* 20: 370–380.
Fletcher, R.
  1971   *The Making of Sociology,* vols. I–II. New York: Charles Scribner's Sons.
Freiberg, J. W.
  1973   Sociology and the ruling class. Boston University (mimeographed).
Freund, J.
  1969   *The Sociology of Max Weber.* New York: Vintage Books.
Friedrichs, R. W.
  1970   *A Sociology of Sociology.* New York: Free Press.
  1972   Dialectic sociology: Toward a resolution of the current "crisis" in Western sociology.
          The British Journal of Sociology 23: 263–274.
Frisby, D.
  1976   Introduction. In *The Positivist Dispute in German Sociology,* eds. T. W. Adorno *et al,*
          pp. ix–xliv. London: Heinemann.
Galtung, J.
  1967   *Theory and Methods of Social Research.* London: Allen and Unwin.
Garfinkel, H.
  1967   *Studies in Ethnomethodology.* Englewood Cliffs, New Jersey: Prentice-Hall.
Geblewicz, E.
  1967   O pewnych charakterystycznych róznicach w problematyce i metodach nauk w
          poczatkowym stadium rozwoju i nauk zaawansowanych [On some characteristic dif-
          ferences in the problems and methods of the sciences in the early and advanced
          stages of development]. In *Fragmenty filozoficzne,* vol. III. Warszawa: Polish Scien-
          tific Publishers.
Gellner, E.
  1969   Explanations in history. In *Readings in the Philosophy of the Social Sciences,* ed. M.
          Brodbeck, pp. 254–268. New York: Macmillan.
Gewirth, A.
  1969   Can men change laws of social science. In *The Nature and Scope of Social Science: A
          Critical Anthology,* ed. L. I. Krimerman, pp. 217–227. New York: Appleton-
          Century-Crofts.
Gibson, Q.
  1960   *The Logic of Social Enquiry.* London: Routledge Kegan Paul.
Giddens, A.
  1971   *Capitalism and Modern Social Theory.* Cambridge: Cambridge University Press.
Giddings, F.
  1898   *The Elements of Sociology.* New York: Columbia University Press.
Ginsberg, M.
  1968   *Essays in Sociology and Social Philosophy.* Baltimore: Penguin Books.
Glass, J. F., and J. R. Staude
  1972   *Humanistic Society: Today's Challenge to Sociology.* Santa Monica: Goodyear.
Goffman, E.
  1959   *The Presentation of Self in Everyday Life.* Garden City: Doubleday.
  1963   *Behavior in Public Places.* New York: Free Press.
  1967   *Interaction Ritual.* Garden City: Doubleday-Anchor.
  1969   *Strategic Interaction.* Philadelphia: University of Pennsylvania Press.
Goldstein, L.
  1968   The phenomenological and naturalistic approaches to the social. In *Theory in An-
          thropology,* eds. R. A. Manners and D. Kaplan, pp. 97–104. Chicago: Aldine.

1969a The two theses of methodological individualism. In *The Nature and Scope of Social Science: A Critical Anthology*, ed. L. I. Krimerman, pp. 625–631. New York: Appleton-Century-Crofts.

1969b The inadequacy of the principle of methodological individualism. In *The Nature and Scope of Social Science: A Critical Anthology*, ed. L. I. Krimerman, pp. 612–620. New York: Appleton-Century-Crofts.

Goode, W. I.

1973 *Explorations in Social Theory*. New York: Oxford University Press.

1975 Homans' and Merton's Structural Approach. In *Approaches to the Study of Social Structure*, ed. P. Blau, pp. 66–75. New York: Free Press.

Gouldner, A

1956 Explorations in applied social science. *Social Problems* 3: 169–181.

1959 Reciprocity and autonomy in functional theory. In *Symposium on Sociological Theory*, ed. L. Gross, pp. 241–270. Evanston, Illinois: Row Peterson.

1969 Anti-minotaur: The myth of a value-free sociology. In *The Planning of Change*, eds. W. G. Bennis *et al.*, pp. 604–618. New York: Holt Rinehart & Winston.

1971 *The Coming Crisis of Western Sociology*. London: Heinemann.

1972 Two Marxisms. Paper presented at the International Congress of Sociology at Caracas, Venezuela.

1973 *For Sociology*. New York: Free Press.

1974 Marxism and social theory. *Theory and Society* 1: 17–35.

Gross, L. (ed.)

1959 *Symposium on Sociological Theory*. Evanston: Row Peterson.

Harre, R., and P. F. Secord

1972 *The Explanation of Social Behavior*. Oxford: Basil Blackwell.

Hauser, P. M.

1949 Social science and social engineering. *Philosophy of Science* 16: 209–218.

1971 On actionism in the craft of sociology. In *Radical Sociology*, eds. J. D. Colfax and J. F. Roach, pp. 425–436. New York: Basic Books.

Helmer, O., and N. Rescher

1969 On the epistemology of the inexact sciences. In *The Nature and Scope of Social Science*, ed. L. I. Krimerman, pp. 181–203. New York: Appleton-Century-Crofts.

Hempel, C. G.

1965 Science and human values. In *Aspects of Scientific Explanation*, ed. C. G. Hempel, pp. 81–98. New York: Free Press.

1966 *Philosophy of Natural Science*. Englewood Cliffs, New Jersey: Prentice-Hall.

Herzberg, F.

1966 *Work and the Nature of Man*. New York: T. Y. Crowell.

Hochfeld, J.

1963 *Studia o marksowskiej teorii spoleczeństwa* [*Studies on the Marxian Theory of Society*]. Warszawa: Polish Scientific Publishers.

Homans, G. C.

1950 *The Human Group*. New York: Harcourt Brace Jovanovich.

1962 *Sentiments and Activities: Essays in Social Science*. Glencoe: Free Press.

1964a Bringing men back in. *American Sociological Review* 29: 809–818.

1964b Contemporary theory in sociology. In *Handbook of Modern Sociology*, ed. R. E. L. Faris, pp. 251–277. Chicago: Rand McNally

1967 *The Nature of Social Science*. New York: Harcourt Brace Jovanovich.

1968 A life of synthesis. *The American Behavioral Scientist* 5: 2–7.

1969 Comment on Blau's paper. In *A Design for Sociology: Scope, Objectives and Methods*, ed.

R. Bierstedt, pp. 80–85. Philadelphia: The American Academy of Political and Social Sciences.

1970   The relevance of psychology to the explanation of social phenomena. In *Explanation in the Behavioral Sciences,* eds. R. Borger and F. Cioffi, pp. 313–328. Cambridge: Cambridge University Press.

1973   Fundamental social processes. In *Sociology: An Introduction,* ed. N. J. Smelser, pp. 549–594. New York: John Wiley.

1974   *Social Behavior: Its Elementary Forms.* New York: Harcourt Brace Jovanovich.

1975   What do we mean by social structure. In *Approaches to the Study of Social Structure,* ed. P. Blau, pp. 53–65. New York: Free Press.

Horowitz I. L.

1967   The Rise and Fall of the Project Camelot. Boston: MIT Press.

Hovard, R. B.

1971   Theoretical reduction: The limits and alternatives to reductive methods in scientific explanation. *Philosophy of the Social Sciences,* 1:83–100.

Hummell, H. J., and K. D. Opp

1968   Sociology without sociology. *Inquiry* 11: 205–226.

Inkeles, A.

1966   *What is Sociology?* Englewood Cliffs, New Jersey: Prentice-Hall.

Israel, J.

1972   The principle of methodological individualism and Marxian epistemology. *Acta Sociologica* 14: 145–150.

Jaroszewski, T. M.

1974   *Rozwazania o praktyce: wokól interpretacji filozofii Karola Marksa* [*The Essays on Social Practice: An Interpretation of Karl Marx's Philosophy*]. Warszawa: Polish Scientific Publishers.

Jarvie, I. C.

1970   Understanding and explanation in sociology and social anthropology. In *Explanation in the Behavioral Sciences,* eds. R. Borger and F. Cioffi, pp. 231–247. Cambridge: Cambridge University Press.

Javetz, R.

1972   "American sociologists: A study in the sociology of sociology." Ph.D. dissertation, Harvard University.

Jones, R. A.

1977   On understanding a sociological classic. *American Journal of Sociology* 83: 279–319.

Kantor, J.

1953   *The Logic of Modern Science.* Bloomington: Principia Press.

Kedrov, B. M.

1968   Karl Marx and the unity of the natural sciences and the humanities. In *Karl Marx and Modern Philosophy,* pp. 79–105. Moscow: Progress Publishers.

Kelman H. C.

1969   Manipulation of human behavior: An ethical dilemma for the social scientist. In *The Planning of Change,* eds. W. G. Bennis *et al.,* pp. 582–594. New York: Holt Rinehart & Winston.

Kemeny, J. G.

1959   *A Philosopher Looks at Science.* Princeton, New Jersey: Van Nostrand.

Keshelava, V. V.

1977   *Humanizm rzeczywisty i pozorny* [*Humanism: Real and Illusory*]. Warszawa: Ksiazka i Wiedza.

Kirk, R.

1961   Is social science scientific? *The New York Times Magazine,* June 25: 11–18.

Kmita, J.
1964 Problem wartości logicznej ocen [The problem of logical value of judgments]. *Studia Filozoficzne* 1: 111–127.
1968 Strukuralizm jako koncepcja metodologiczna [Structuralism as a methodological standpoint]. *Kultura i Spoleczeństwo* 2: 45–62.
1970 Uwagi o holizmie marksowskim jako koncepcji metodologicznej [Remarks on Marxian holism as a methodological position]. In *Zalozenia metodologiczne "Kapitalu" Marksa [The Methodological Assumptions of Marx's Capital]*, ed. J. Topolski, pp. 59–122. Warszawa: Ksiazka i Wiedza.
1971 *Z metodologicznych problemów interpretacji humanistycznej [On Methodological Aspects of Humanistic Interpretation]*. Warszawa: Polish Scientific Publishers.
Kmita, J., and L. Nowak
1968 *Studia nad teoretycznymi podstawami humanistyki [Studies on Theoretical Foundations of Human Sciences]*. Poznan: Wydawnictwo Poznanskie.
Kolakowski, L.
1976 *Główne nurty marksizmu [The Main Trends of Marxism]*, vol. 1. Paris: Instytut Literacki.
Kotarbinski, T.
1970 Przeglad problemow nauk o nauce [The review of the problems of metascience]. In *Studia z zakresu filozofii, etyki i nauk spolecznych [Studies on Philosophy, Ethics, and the Social Sciences]*, pp. 85–115. Wroclaw: Ossolineum Publishers.
Kozielecki, J.
1976 *Koncepcje psychologiczne czlowieka [The Psychological Images of Man]*. Warszawa: Polish Editorial Institute.
Kozyr-Kowalski, S.
1967 *Max Weber a Karol Marks [Max Weber and Karl Marx]*. Warszawa: Ksiazka i Wiedza.
1976 O ortodoksyjnym marksizmie [On orthodox Marxism]. *Studia Filozoficzne* 12: 17–23.
Krech, D. *et al.*
1962 *Individual in Society: A Textbook of Social Psychology*. New York: McGraw-Hill.
Krimerman, L. I. (ed.)
1969 *The Nature and Scope of Social Science: A Critical Anthology*. New York: Appleton.
Krzeminski, I.
1974 *Stanowisko redukcjonistyczne w naukach spolecznych* [The reductionist standpoint in the social sciences], *Studia Socjologiczne* 3: 87–115.
Kuczynski, J.
1976 *Homo creator; wstep do dialektyki czlowieka [Homo Creator: An Introduction to the Dialectics of Man]*. Warszawa: Ksiazka i Wiedza.
Kuhn, T. S.
1970 *The Structure of Scientific Revolutions*. 2nd ed. Chicago: University of Chicago Press.
Kula, W.
1958 *Rozwazania o historii [Reflections on History]*. Warszawa: Polish Scientific Publishers.
Kurtz, P.
1965 *Decision and the Condition of Man*. Seattle: University of Washington Press.
Lachenmeyer, C. W.
1971 *The Language of Sociology*. New York: Columbia University Press.
Lange, O.
1961 *Ekonomia polityczna [Political Economy]*, vol. 1. Warszawa: Polish Scientific Publishers.
Lasswell, H. D.
1948 *The Analysis of Political Behavior: An Empirical Approach*. London: Routledge Kegan Paul.

342 References

Lenin, V. I.
  1951 *Dziela* [*Collected Works*]. Warszawa: Ksiazka i Wiedza.
Lenski, G.
  1966 *Power and Privilege: A Theory of Social Stratification.* New York: McGraw-Hill.
  1975 Social structure in evolutionary perspective. In *Approaches to the Study of Social Structure,* ed. P. Blau, pp. 135–153. New York: Free Press.
Levy, M.
  1952 *The Structure of Society.* Princeton, New Jersey: Princeton University Press.
Lipiec, J.
  1974 Uwagi o metodologii historiozofii [Remarks on the methodology of history]. In *Metodologiczne implikacje metodologii marksowskiej,* ed. J. Kmita, pp. 348–356. Warszawa: Polish Scientific Publishers.
Lipset, S. M. *et al.*
  1956 *Union Democracy.* New York: Free Press.
Lockwood, D.
  1956 Some remarks on the "social system." *British Journal of Sociology* 7:134–146.
  1964 Social integration and system integration. In *Explorations in Social Change,* eds. G. K. Zollschan and W. Hirsch, pp. 244–257. Boston: Houghton Mifflin.
Lundberg, G. A.
  1947 *Can Science Save Us?* New York: David McKay. [Portions reprinted in *Readings in General Sociology,* eds. R. W. O'Brien *et al.*, pp. 11–18. Boston: Houghton Mifflin], 1961.
Lukacs, G.
  1971 *History and Class Consciousness.* Cambridge: The MIT Press.
Lukes, S.
  1968 Methodological individualism reconsidered. *The British Journal of Sociology* 19: 119–129.
  1970 Some problems about rationality. In *Rationality,* ed. B. R. Wilson, pp. 194–213. Evanston: Harper and Row.
Luria, A. R.
  1975 O redukcjonizmie w psychologii [On reductionism in psychology]. *Studia Filozoficzne* 8: 81–88.
Lynd, R.
  1939 *Knowledge for What?* Princeton, New Jersey: Princeton University Press.
Machlup, F.
  1961 Are the social sciences really inferior? *The Southern Economic Journal* 27: 173–184.
MacIver, R. M.
  1937 *Society: A Textbook of Sociology.* New York: Farrar and Rinehart.
Mack, R. W.
  1969 Theoretical and substantive biases in sociological research. In *Interdisciplinary Relationships in the Social Sciences,* eds. M. Sherif and C. W. Sherif, pp. 52–63. Chicago: Aldine.
Malewski, A.
  1956 Postulaty praktycznej uzyteczności a rozwój nauk spolecznych [The postulates of practical utility and the development of the social sciences]. *Zeszyty naukowe UAM w Poznaniu* 1: 2–13.
  1961 Dwa modele socjologii [Two models of sociology]. *Studia Socjologiczne* 3: 42–54.
  1964 *O zastosowaniach teorii zachowania* [*On the Applications of the Theory of Behavior*]. Warszawa: Polish Scientific Publishers.
Malewski, A., and J. Topolski.

1960   *Studia z metodologii historii [Studies on the Methodology of History]*. Warszawa: Polish
        Scientific Publishers.
Malinowski, B.
    1934   Culture. In *Encyclopaedia of the Social Sciences,* vol.4, ed. E. R. A. Seligman. New
            York: Macmillan.
    1969   *A Scientific Theory of Culture and Other Essays.* New York: Oxford University Press.
Mandelbaum, M.
    1969a   Societal facts. In *The Nature and Scope of Social Science: A Critical Anthology,* ed. L. I.
            Krimerman, pp. 632–641. New York: Appleton. (Reprinted from *The British Jour-
            nal of Sociology* 6, 1955: 305–317.)
    1969b   Societal laws. In *The Nature and Scope of Social Science: A Critical Anthology,* ed. L. I.
            Krimerman, pp. 642–650. New York: Appleton. (Reprinted from *The British Jour-
            nal for the Philosophy of Science* 8, 1957: 211–224.)
Manners, R. A., and Kaplan, D. (Eds.)
    1968   *Theory in Anthropology.* Chicago: Aldine.
Mannheim, K.
    1936   *Ideology and Utopia.* New York: Harcourt Brace Jovanovich.
    1957   *Systematic Sociology.* London: Routledge Kegan Paul.
    1974   *Czlowiek i spoleczeństwo w dobie przebudowy [Man and Society in an Age of Reconstruc-
            tion]*. Warszawa: Polish Scientific Publishers.
Marcuse, H.
    1968   *Reason and Revolution: Hegel and the Rise of Social Theory.* Atlantic Highlands, N. J.:
            Humanities Press.
Martindale, D.
    1959   Sociological theory and the ideal type. In *Symposium on Sociological Theory,* ed. L.
            Gross, pp. 57–91. Evanston: Row Peterson.
    1960   *The Nature and Types of Sociological Theory.* Boston: Houghton Mifflin.
    1964   The roles of humanism and scientism in the evolution of sociology. In *Explorations in
            Social Change,* eds. G. K. Zollschan and W. Hirsch, pp. 452–490. Boston: Houghton
            Mifflin.
    1974   *Sociological Theory and the Problem of Values.* Columbus: Charles Merrill.
Marx, K.
    1949   *Nedza filozofii [The Poverty of Philosophy]*. Warszawa: Ksiazka i Wiedza.
    1953   *Grundrisse der Kritik der politischen Ekonomie.* Berlin.
    1954   *Capital,* vols. 1–3. Moscow: Progress Publishers.
    1955   *Przyczynek do krytyki ekonomii politycznej [Introduction to the Critique of Political Econ-
            omy]*. Warszawa: Ksiazka i Wiedza.
    1971   *The Grundrisse,* ed. and trans. D. McLellan. New York: Harper and Row.
Marx, K., and F. Engels
    1947   *Dziela wybrane [Selected Works]*. Warszawa: Ksiazka i Wiedza.
    1960   *Dziela [Collected Works]*. Warszawa: Ksiazka i Wiedza.
    1968   *Selected Works.* Moscow: Progress Publishers.
    1975   *O materializmie historycznym [On Historical Materialism]*. Warszawa: Ksiazka i
            Wiedza.
Marx, K., F. Engels, and V. I. Lenin
    1977   *On Dialectical Materialism.* Moscow: Progress Publishers.
Maslow, A. H.
    1936   Problem-centering versus means-centering science. *Philosophy of Science* 13: 326–
            331.
    1966   *The Psychology of Language.* Chicago: Regnery.

Mayrl, W. W.
    1973   Ethnomethodology: Sociology without society. *Catalyst* 7: 15–28.
McClung Lee, A.
    1976   Sociology for whom? In *ASA Annual Meeting Program*, pp. 2–3. New York.
McDougall, W.
    1948   *An Introduction to Social Psychology*. London Methuen.
McEwen, W. P.
    1963   *The Problem of Social-Scientific Knowledge*. Totowa, New Jersey: Bedminster Press.
McKinney, J. C.
    1950   The role of constructive typology in scientific sociological analysis. *Social Forces* 28: 235–240.
    1957   The polar variables of type construction. *Social Forces* 35: 300–306.
McLellan, D.
    1971   *The Thought of Karl Marx*. New York: Harper and Row.
    1975   *Karl Marx*. New York: Viking Press.
McRae, D. G.
    1957   Social theory: Retrospect and prospect. *The British Journal of Sociology* 8: 97–105.
    1974   *Max Weber*. New York: Viking Press.
Mead, G. H.
    1962   The Social Psychology of George Herbert Mead, ed. A. Strauss. Chicago: University of Chicago Press.
    1964   *George Herbert Mead on Social Psychology*. Chicago: University of Chicago Press.
Meltzer, B. N. *et al.*
    1975   *Symbolic Interactionism: Genesis, Varieties and Criticism*. London: Routledge Kegan Paul.
Merton, R. K.
    1949   The role of applied social science in the formation of policy. *Philosophy of Science* 16: 161–181.
    1957   *Social Theory and Social Structure*, 2nd ed. Glencoe: Free Press.
    1961a Now the case for sociology. *The New York Times Magazine,* June 25: 18–22.
    1961b Social problems and sociological theory. In *Contemporary Social Problems*, eds. R. K. Merton and R. A. Nisbet, pp. 697–737. New York: Harcourt Brace Jovanovich.
    1965   Notes on problem-finding in sociology. In *Sociology Today*, vol. I, eds. R. K. Merton, L. Broom, and L. S. Cottrell, pp. ix–xxxiv. New York: Harper and Row.
    1967   *On Theoretical Sociology*. New York: Free Press.
    1973   *The Sociology of Science*. Chicago: University of Chicago Press.
    1975   Structural analysis in sociology. In *Approaches to the Study of Social Structure*, ed. P. Blau, pp. 21–52. New York: Free Press.
Meyer, A. G.
    1969   *Marxism: The Unity of Theory and Practice*. Ann Arbor: University of Michigan Press.
Milgram, S.
    1963   Behavioral study of obedience. *The Journal of Abnormal and Social Psychology* 4: 371–378.
Mill, J. S.
    1884   *A System of Logic Ratiocinative and Inductive*. London: People's Editions.
Mills, C. W.
    1959   *The Sociological Imagination*. London: Oxford University Press.
    1963   *The Marxists*. London: Penguin Books.
    1967   *Philosophy of Science Today*. New York: Basic Books.
    1970   Is it a science? In *Sociological Theory and Philosophical Analysis*, eds. D. Emmet and A. MacInntyre, pp. 20–35. New York: Macmillan.

Morganbesser, S.
   1967   *Philosophy of Science Today*. New York: Basic Books.
   1970   Is it a science? In *Sociological Theory and Philosophical Analysis*, eds. D. Emmet and
          A. MacInntyre, pp. 20–35. New York: Macmillan.
Mucha, J.
   1978   *Konflikt i spoleczeństwo [Conflict and Society]*. Warszawa: Polish Scientific Publishers.
Mulkay, M. J.
   1971   *Functionalism, Exchange and Theoretical Strategy*. London: Routledge Kegan Paul.
Myrdal, G.
   1953   The relation between social theory and social policy. *The British Journal of Sociology*
          4: 210–242.
   1964   *The American Dilemma*. New York: Harper and Row.
   1969   *Objectivity in Social Research*. New York: Pantheon Books.
Nadel, S. F.
   1957   *The Theory of Social Structure*. Glencoe: Free Press.
Nagel, E.
   1961   *The Structure of Science*. New York: Harcourt Brace Jovanovich.
Nikitin, E. P.
   1975   *Wyjaśnienie jako funkcja nauki [Explanation as a Function of Science]*. Warszawa:
          Polish Scientific Publishers.
Nisbet, R. A.
   1970   Developmentalism: A critical analysis. In *Theoretical Sociology*, eds. J. C. McKinney
          and E. A. Tiryakian, pp. 167–204. New York: Appleton-Century-Crofts.
   1974   *The Sociology of Emile Durkheim*. New York: Oxford University Press.
Nowak, L.
   1971   *U podstaw marksowskiej metodologii nauk [The Foundations of Marxian Methodology]*.
          Warszawa: Polish Scientific Publishers.
   1974a *U podstaw marksistowskiej aksjologii [The Foundations of Marxist Axiology]*. Warszawa:
          Polish Scientific Publishers.
   1974b Model nauk empirycznych w koncepcji twórców marksizmu [The model of empirical
          science in the works of the founders of Marxism]. In *Metodologiczne implikacje
          metodologii marksistowskiej*, ed. J. Kmita, pp. 109–142. Warszawa: Polish Scientific
          Publishers.
   1974c *Zasady marksistowskiej filozofii nauki [The Principles of the Marxist Philosophy of
          Science]*. Warszawa: Polish Scientific Publishers.
Nowak, S.
   1965   *Studia z metodologii nauk spolecznych [Studies in the Methodology of the Social Sciences]*.
          Warszawa: Polish Scientific Publishers.
   1970   *Metodologia badań socjologicznych [Methodology of Sociological Research]*. Warszawa:
          Polish Scientific Publishers.
Ollman, B.
   1975   *Alienation: Marx's Conception of Man in Capitalist Society*. Cambridge: Cambridge
          University Press.
Ossowska, M.
   1967   Rola ocen w kształtowaniu pojęć [The role of valuations in concept-formation]. In
          Fragmenty filozoficzne [Philosophical Essays], vol. III, pp. 459–470. Warszawa: Polish
          Scientific Publishers.
Ossowski, S.
   1957   *Striktura klasowa w spolecznej świadomości [The Class Structure in the Social Conscious-
          ness]*. Lódź: Ossolineum Publishers.

1962 *O osobliwościach nauk spolecznych.* [*On the Peculiarities of the Social Sciences*]. Warszawa: Polish Scientific Publishers.

1967 *Dziela* [*Works*]. vol. 4. Warszawa: Polish Scientific Publishers.

Pareto, V.

1963 *The Mind and Society,* vols. 1 and 2, ed. A. Livingston. New York: Dover Publications.

1966 *Vilfredo Pareto: Sociological Writings,* ed. S. E. Finer. London: Pall Mall Press.

1971 *Vilfredo Pareto: Selections from his Treatise,* ed. J. Lopreato. New York: Thomas Y. Crowell.

Parsons, T.

1934 The place of ultimate values in sociological theory. *International Journal of Ethics* 45: 282–316.

1948 The position of sociological theory. *American Sociological Review* 13: 156–164.

1964 *Essays in Sociological Theory.* Glencoe: Free Press.

1965a An outline of the social system. In *Theories of Society,* eds. by T. Parsons *et al.,* pp. 30–79. New York: Free Press.

1965b Max Weber und die Soziologie heute [Max Weber and contemporary sociology]. In *Verhandlungen des 15 Deutschess Soziologentages* [*Proceedings of the XV German Sociological Convention*]. Tubingen: Springer Verlag.

1968 *The Structure of Social Action,* vols. 1 and 2. New York: Free Press.

1971 Levels of organization and the mediation of social interaction. In *Institutions and Social Exchange,* eds. H. Turk and R. L. Simpson, pp. 23–35. Indianapolis: Bobbs Merrill.

Parsons, T., and E. A. Shils

1962 *Toward a General Theory of Action.* New York: Harper & Row.

Petras, J. W., and B. N. Meltzer

1973 Theoretical and ideological variations in contemporary interactionism. *Catalyst* 7: 1–8.

Piaget, J.

1970 The place of the sciences of man in the system of sciences. In *Main Trends of Research in the Social and Human Sciences,* pp. 1–57. The Hague: Mouton.

Poggi, G.

1965 A main theme of contemporary sociological analysis: Its achievements and limitations. *The British Journal of Sociology* 16: 283–294.

Polak, F. L.

1961 *The Image of the Future,* vols. 1 and 2. New York: Oceana Publications.

Pomian, K.

1961 Wstep [Introduction]. In L. Goldman, *Nauki Humanistyczne a Filozofia* [*The Human Sciences and Philosophy*]. Warszawa: Ksiazka i Wiedza.

Popow, S. I.

1970 *Kritika sovremennoy burzuaznoy socjologii* [*A Critique of Contemporary Bourgeois Sociology*]. Moscow: Izdatielstvo Nauka.

Popper, K. R.

1960 *The Poverty of Historicism.* New York: Basic Books.

1976a The logic of the social sciences. In *The Positivist Dispute in German Sociology,* eds. T. Adorno *et al.,* pp. 87–104. London: Heinemann.

1976b Reason or revolution? In *The Positivist Dispute in German Sociology,* eds. T. Adorno *et al.,* pp. 288–300. London: Heinemann.

Radcliffe-Brown, A. R.

1935 On the concept of function in the social science. *American Anthropoligist* 37: 3–21.

Rex, J.

1961 *Key Problems of Sociological Theory.* London: Routledge Kegan Paul.

Robson, R. A. H.
1968   The present state of theory in sociology. In *Problems in the Philosophy of Science,* eds. I.
       Lakatos and A. Musgrave, pp. 349–70. Amsterdam: Martinus Nijhoff.
Rose, A. M.
1954   *Theory and Method in Social Sciences.* Minneapolis: University of Minnesota Press.
1962   *Human Behavior and Social Process.* Boston: Houghton Mifflin.
1967   The relation of theory and method. In *Sociological Theories: Inquiries and Paradigms,*
       ed. L. Gross, pp. 207–219. New York: Harper and Row.
Rudner, R.
1954   Philosophy and social science. *Philosophy of Science* 21: 164–241.
1966   *Philosophy of Social Science.* Englewood Cliffs, New Jersey: Prentice-Hall.
1969   No science can be value-free. In *The Nature and Scope of Social Science,* ed. L.
       Krimerman, pp. 748–754. New York: Appleton-Century-Crofts.
Runciman, W. G.
1973   What is structuralism? In *The Philosophy of Social Explanation,* ed. by A. Ryan, pp.
       188–202. New York: Oxford University Press.
Ryan, A.
1971   *The Philosophy of the Social Sciences.* London: Macmillan.
Rybicki, P.
1965   Problemy ontologiczne w socjologii [Ontological problems of sociology]. *Studia
       Socjologiczne* 2: 7–46.
1970   The approaches in sociological classics and the current phrasing of issues in relating
       microsociology and macrosociology. Paper presented to the Seventh World Con-
       gress of Sociology. Varna: International Sociological Association (mimeographed).
Sadovsky, V. N., and E. T. Yudin
1967   O spiecifikie mietodologiczieskogo podchoda k issliedowaniu sistiem i struktur [On
       the specificity of methodological approach to systems and structures]. In *Logika i
       Metodologia Nuki [Logic and Methodology of Science],* pp. 191–200. Moscow: Iz-
       datielstwo Nauka.
Schacht, R.
1970   *Alienation.* Garden City, New York: Doubleday-Anchor.
Schaff, A.
1965   *Marksizm a jednostka ludzka [Marxism on the Human Individual].* Warszawa: Polish
       Scientific Publishers.
1972   The consciousness of a class and class consciousness. *The Philosophical Forum* 3–4:
       340–359.
Schaffner, K.
1967   Approaches to reduction. *Philosophy of Science* 34: 139–150.
Schrag, C.
1967   Philosophical issues in the science of sociology. *Sociology and Social Research* 51:
       361–372.
Schutz, A.
1967   *The Phenomenology of the Social World.* Evanston: Harper & Row.
1970a *On Phenomenology and Social Relations,* ed. H. R. Wagner. Chicago: University of
       Chicago Press.
1970b Concept and theory formation in the social sciences. In *Sociological Theory and
       Philosophical Analysis,* eds. D. Emmet and A. MacIntyre, pp. 1–19. New York:
       Macmillan.
Scott, J. F.
1969   The changing foundations of the Parsonian action scheme. In *Sociological Theory,* ed.
       W. L. Wallace, pp. 246–267. London: Heinemann. (Reprinted from *American
       Sociological Review,* October 1963: 716–735.)

Scott, K. J.
  1973   Methodological and epistemological individualism. In *Modes of Individualism and Collectivism*, ed. J. O'Neill, pp. 215–220. London: Heinemann.
Shanin, T.
  1972   Units of sociological analysis. *Sociology* 6: 351–367.
Sherif, M.
  1956   Experiments in group conflict. Reprinted from *Scientific American*. San Francisco: W. H. Freeman.
  1966   Theoretical analysis of the individual-group relationship in a social situation. In *Concepts, Theory and Explanation in the Behavioral Sciences*, ed. G. J. DiRenzo, pp. 47–74. New York: Random House.
Shils, E.
  1965   The calling of sociology. In *Theories of Society*, eds. T. Parsons *et al.*, pp. 1405–1448. New York: Free Press.
Simmel, G.
  1950   *The Sociology of Georg Simmel*, ed. K.H. ·Wolff. New York: Free Press.
  1971   *Georg Simmel On Individuality and Social Forms*, ed. D. N. Levine. Chicago: University of Chicago Press.
Skidmore, W. L.
  1975a *Sociology's Models of Man*. New York: Gordon and Breach.
  1975b *Theoretical Thinking in Sociology*. Cambridge: Cambridge University Press.
Smelser, N. J.
  1968   *Studies in Sociological Explanation*. Englewood Cliffs, New Jersey: Prentice Hall.
  1969   Some personal thoughts on the pursuit of sociological problems. In *Sociological Inquiry* 39: 155–167.
Soares, G. A. D.
  1968   Marxism as a general sociological orientation. *The British Journal of Sociology* 19: 365–374.
Sorokin, P. A.
  1956   *Fads and Foibles in Modern Sociology and Related Sciences*. Chicago: Greenwood.
  1966   *Sociological Theories of Today*. New York: Harper & Row.
Spencer, H.
  1893   *Principles of Sociology*, vols. 1–3. London: Willimans and Norgate.
  1894   *The Study of Sociology*. London: Kegan Paul, Trench, Trubner.
Sprikin, A. G.
  1968   *Zarys filozofii marksistowskiej* [*An Outline of Marxist Philosophy*]. Warszawa: Ksiazka i Wiedza.
Staats, A. W.
  1975   *Social Behaviorism*. Homewood: Dorsey Press.
Stinchombe, A.
  1968   *Constructing Social Theories*. New York: Harcourt Brace Jovanovich.
Stouffer, S. *et al.*
  1950   *The American Soldier*. Princeton: Princeton University Press.
Strasser, H.
  1975   Social technologists and social emancipists: Factors in the development of sociology. In *Determinants and Controls of Scientific Development*, eds. K. Knorr *et al.*, pp. 431–447. Dordrecht: Reidel.
  1976   *The Normative Structure of Sociology*. London: Routledge Kegan Paul.
Strauss, A. (ed.)
  1962   *The Social Psychology of George Herbert Mead*. Chicago: University of Chicago Press.

Such, J.
1970 Prawa przyrody a prawa spoleczeństwa w ujeciu K. Marksa i F. Engelsa [The laws of nature and of society in the view of Marx and Engels]. In *Zalozenia metodologiczne Kapitalu Marksa*, ed. J. Topolski, pp. 219–322. Warszawa: Ksiazka i Wiedza.
Sumner, W. G.
1906 *Folkways: A Study of the Sociological Importance of Usages, Manners, Customs, and Morals*. Boston: Ginn and Company.
Swanson, G. E.
1953 The approach to a general theory of action by Parsons and Shils. *American Sociological Review* 18: 125–134.
Swingewood, A.
1975 *Marx and Modern Social Theory*. London: Macmillan.
Szacki, J.
1964 *Durkheim*. Warszawa: Wiedza Powszechna.
Szczepański, J.
1969 *Socjologia: rozwój problematyki i metod* [*Sociology: The Development of Problems and Methods*]. Warszawa: Polish Scientific Publishers.
Szmatka, J.
1975 Zagadnienie redukcji teoretycznej w filozofii nauki i socjologii [The problem of theoretical reduction in the philosophy of science and sociology]. *Studia Filozoficzne* 3: 87–103.
1976 O holizmie i indywidualizmie w naukach spolecznych [On holism and individualism in the social sciences]. *Studia Filozoficzne* 7: 17–39.
Sztompka, P.
1971 Some conditions of applicability of sociological knowledge. *Polish Sociological Bulletin* 1: 5–16.
1973 *Teoria i wyjaśnienie* [*Theory and Explanation*]. Warszawa: Polish Scientific Publishers.
1974 *System and Function: Toward a Theory of Society*. New York: Academic Press.
1976a Strategy of theory-construction in sociology. *Polish Sociological Bulletin* 4: 5–16.
1976b On the peculiarities of social sciences once again. In *Studies in Methodology*, pp. 33–56. Wroclaw: Ossolineum Publishers.
1977 O marksistowskiej koncepcji rozwoju spolecznego - nieco inaczej. [On the Marxist notion of social development - a little differently]. *Studia Filozoficzne* 12: 81–93.
1978 The dialectics of spontaneity and planning in sociological theory. Paper presented to the World Congress of Sociology. Uppsala: International Sociolo gical Association (mimeographed).
1979a Marxism, functionalism and systems-approach. In *Polish Essays in the Methodology of the Social Sciences*, ed. J. J. Wiatr, pp. 133–136. Dordrecht, Holland: Reidel.
1979b Strategy of theory construction in sociology. In *Polish Essays in the Methodology of the Social Sciences*, ed. J. J. Wiatr, pp. 133–156. Dordrecht, Holland: Reidel.
Szymanski, A.
1971 Toward a radical sociology. In *Radical Sociology*, eds. J. D. Colfax and J. L. Roach. pp. 93–107. New York: Basic Books.
Thomas, W. I., and F. Znaniecki
1927 *The Polish Peasant in Europe and America*. New York: Alfred Knopf.
Timasheff, N. S.
1967 *Sociological Theory*. New York: Random House.
Timasheff, N. S., and G. A. Theodorson
1976 *Sociological Theory: Its Nature and Growth*. New York: Random House.

Topolski, J.
1968   *Metodologia historii* [*Methodology of History*]. Warszawa: Polish Scientific Publishers.
1970   Zalozenia metodologiczne *Kapitalu* Marksa [Methodological assumptions of Marx's *Capital*]. *Studia Filozoficzne* 3–4: 3–33.
1974   Aktywistyczna koncepcja procesu dziejowego [The activist notion of the historical process]. In *Metodologiczne implikacje epistemologii marksistowskiej* [*Methodological Implications of Marxist Epistemology*], ed J. Kmita, pp. 309–324. Warszawa: Polish Scientific Publishers.
1977   *Marksizm i historia* [*Marxism and History*]. Warszawa: Polish Editorial Institute.
1978   *Rozumienie historii* [*Understanding of History*]. Warszawa: Polish Editorial Institute.
Turner, J. H.
1974   *The Structure of Sociological Theory*. Homewood, Illinois: Dorsey Press.
von Bertalanffy, L.
1968   *General System Theory*. New York: George Braziller.
Wagner, H. R.
1963   Types of sociological theory: Toward a system of classification. *American Sociological Review* 28: 735–742.
Wallace, W. L.
1969   *Sociological Theory: An Introduction*. London: Heinemann.
Ward, L. F.
1902   *Dynamic Sociology*, vols. 1 and 2. New York: Appleton.
Warshay, L. H.
1971   The current state of sociological theory: Diversity, polarity, empiricism, and small theories. *The Sociological Quarterly* 12: 23–45.
Watkins, J. W. N.
1953   Ideal types and historical explanation. In *Readings in the Philosophy of Science*, eds. H. Feigl and M. Brodbeck, pp. 723–743. New York: Appleton.
1957   Historical explanation in the social sciences. *The British Journal for the Philosophy of Science* 8: 104–117. (Reprinted in *Readings in the Philosophy of the Social Sciences*, ed. M. Brodbeck, pp. 269–280. New York: Macmillan.)
Weber, M.
1947   *The Theory of Social and Economic Organization*. Glencoe: Free Press.
1949   *The Methodology of the Social Sciences*. Glencoe: Free Press.
1964   *Basic Concepts in Sociology*. New York: The Citadel Press.
1968   *Economy and Society*, eds. and trans. G. Roth and C. Wittich. Totowa, New Jersey: Bedminster Press.
Wiatr, J. J.
1971   Teoria spoleczenstwa socjalistycznego: problemy i perspektywy [A theory of socialist society: problems and perspectives]. *Studia Socjologiczne* 3: 53–79.
1973a *Marksistowska teoria rozwoju spolecznego* [*The Marxist Theory of Social Development*]. Warszawa: Polish Scientific Publishers.
1973b Alienation, disalienation and the structure of Marxist social theory. Boston University (mimeographed).
1974   Zalozenia budowania teorii spoleczenstwa socjalistycznego [The assumptions of the theory of socialist society]. *Studia Socjologiczne* 2: 55–78.
Willer, D. E.
1967   *Scientific Sociology: Theory and Method*. Englewood Cliffs, New Jersey: Prentice-Hall.
Willer, D. E. and M. Webster
1970   Theoretical concepts and observables. *American Sociological Review* 35: 748–756.
Winch, P.
1958   *The Idea of the Social Science*. London: Routledge Kegan Paul.

Winch, R. F.

1947 Heuristic and empirical typologies. *American Sociological Review* 12: 68–75.

Wisdom, J. O.

1970 Situational individualism and the emergent group-properties. In *Explanation in the Behavioral Sciences,* eds. R. Borger and F. Cioffi, pp. 271–296. Cambridge: Cambridge University Press.

1971 Science versus the scientific revolution. *Philosophy of the Social Sciences* 1: 123–144.

Wittgenstein, L.

1953 *Philosophical Investigations.* London: Oxford University Press.

Wrightsman, L. S.

1972 *Social Psychology in the Seventies.* Monterey: Brooks and Cole.

Wrong, D.

1961 The oversocialized conception of man in modern sociology. *American Sociological Review* 2: 183–193.

Zeitlin, I. M.

1967 *Marxism: A Reexamination.* New York: Van Nostrand.

Zetterberg, H. L.

1954 *On Theory and Verification in Sociology.* Stockholm: Almquist.

1962 *Social Theory and Social Practice.* New York: The Bedminster Press.

Znaniecki, F.

1919 *Cultural Reality.* Chicago: University of Chicago Press.

1934 *The Method of Sociology.* New York: Farrar and Rinehart.

1936 *Social Actions.* New York: Farrar and Rinehart.

1969 *Florian Znaniecki on Humanistic Sociology,* ed. R. Bierstedt. Chicago: University of Chicago Press.

Author Index

Subject Index